T0304206

SOCIALIST ECONOMIC INTEGRATION

SOVIET AND EAST EUROPEAN STUDIES

Books in the series

A. Boltho *Foreign Trade Criteria in Socialist Economies*
Sheila Fitzpatrick *The Commissariat of Enlightenment*
Donald Male *Russian Peasant Organisation before Collectivisation*
P. Wiles, ed. *The Prediction of Communist Economic Performance*
Vladimir V. Kusin *The Intellectual Origins of the Prague Spring*
Galia Golan *The Czechoslovak Reform Movement*
Naum Jasny *Soviet Economists of the Twenties*
Asha L. Data *India's Economic Relations with the USSR and Eastern Europe, 1953–1969*
T. M. Podolski *Socialist Banking and Monetary Control*
Rudolf Bićanić *Economic Policy in Socialist Yugoslavia*
S. Galai *Liberation in Russia*
Richard B. Day *Leon Trotsky and the Politics of Economic Isolation*
G. Hosking *The Russian Constitutional Experiment: Government and Duma 1907–14*
A. Teichova *An Economic Background to Munich*
J. Ciechanowski *The Warsaw Rising of 1944*
Edward A. Hewett *Foreign Trade Prices in the Council for Mutual Economic Assistance*
Daniel F. Calhoun *The United Front: the TUC and the Russians 1923–28*
Galia Golan *Yom Kippur and After: the Soviet Union and the Middle East Crisis*
Maureen Perrie *The Agrarian Policy of the Russian Socialist-Revolutionary Party from its Origins through the Revolution of 1905–1907*
Gabriel Gorodetsky *The Precarious Truce: Anglo-Soviet Relations 1924–27*
Paul Vyšný *Neo-Slavism and the Czechs 1898–1914*
James Riordan *Sport in Soviet Society: Development of Sport and Physical Education in Russia and the USSR*
Gregory Walker *Soviet Book Publishing Policy*
Felicity Ann O'Dell *Socialisation through Children's Literature: the Soviet Example*
Stella Alexander *Church and State in Yugoslavia since 1945*
Sheila Fitzpatrick *Education and Social Mobility in the Soviet Union 1921–1934*
T. H. Rigby *Lenin's Government: Sovnarkom 1917–1922*

SOCIALIST ECONOMIC INTEGRATION

ASPECTS OF CONTEMPORARY ECONOMIC PROBLEMS IN EASTERN EUROPE

JOZEF M. VAN BRABANT

CAMBRIDGE UNIVERSITY PRESS

CAMBRIDGE

LONDON   NEW YORK   NEW ROCHELLE

MELBOURNE   SYDNEY

CAMBRIDGE UNIVERSITY PRESS
Cambridge, New York, Melbourne, Madrid, Cape Town, Singapore,
São Paulo, Delhi, Dubai, Tokyo

Cambridge University Press
The Edinburgh Building, Cambridge CB2 8RU, UK

Published in the United States of America by Cambridge University Press, New York

www.cambridge.org
Information on this title: www.cambridge.org/9780521153041

First published 1980
This digitally printed version 2010

A catalogue record for this publication is available from the British Library

Library of Congress Cataloguing in Publication data
Brabant, Jozef M. van.
Socialist economic integration.
(Soviet and East European studies)
Bibliography: p.
Includes index.
1. Europe, Eastern – Economic integration.
2. Sovet ėkonomicheskoĭ vzaimopomoshchi.
I. Title. II. Series.
HC244.B7275 338.947 79–23766

ISBN 978-0-521-23046-9 Hardback
ISBN 978-0-521-15304-1 Paperback

To Miyuki, Katja, and Anja
With humility and gratitude

Contents

vii

Chapter 3. The role and organization of trade   99

Chapter 4. The evolution of the Council   172

Figures and tables

Figures

Tables

Acknowledgments

The present monograph is the result of several years of research, which has been generously supported by a number of persons and institutions. For providing financial and other logistical aid during the earlier stages of this product, I wish to acknowledge the assistance of the Belgian National Foundation for Scientific Research, the Belgian Ministry of Education and Culture, the Center for Economic Research at the Catholic University of Louvain, and the East Europe Institute at the Free University of Berlin. Secretaries and library personnel at the institutes in Louvain and Berlin, as well as in other places where I have had the good fortune to take advantage of such services, have been most helpful and very patient indeed.

Most of the ideas presented here were first developed in lectures, discussions, seminars, or a friendly chat with students and colleagues. Some of them were published earlier in a different format, especially in *Documentation sur l'Europe Centrale, Jahrbuch der Wirtschaft Osteuropas – Yearbook of East-European Economics, Kyklos, Osteuropa Wirtschaft, The ACES Bulletin,* and *Tijdschrift voor Economie.* Detailed advice, comments, and queries from two anonymous referees and excellent editorial assistance on the part of Cambridge University Press are gratefully acknowledged. Many other people share in what is good in this book, but responsibility for not always heeding their advice or admonitions, for misrepresenting information gleaned from them, or for factual errors in reporting East European events is, of course, solely mine. Finally, a warm word of thanks to my wife, who as always has been supportive beyond the call of matrimonial duty. Filial devotion and tacit cooperation from my daughters Anja and Katja also contributed immeasurably to completing this project.

I am presently associated with the Department of International Economic and Social Affairs of the United Nations Secretariat in New York. Although this working environment has been invaluable in rounding off important portions of the monograph, it bears stressing most emphatically that the views expressed in this study are my own and do not imply expression of any opinion whatsoever on the part of the United Nations Secretariat.

Jozef M. van Brabant

June 1979

Note on transliteration and referencing

For brevity's sake, bibliographical references in the text are identified by (first) author and date of publication. In the absence of a name, the reference consists of a simple acronym of the organization sponsoring the publication or one key word from the title. Because these are meant to be codes to the bibliography, where full details are listed, diacritical signs, name prefixes, and the second part of double names are deleted from the code in the text. References to works by more than one author consist of only the first author's name.

Cyrillic-language publications or names of persons from cyrillic-script countries or regions are transliterated according to the so-called scientific transliteration system advocated by the USSR Academy of Sciences. A distinction is made between the three Russian e's and, in the case of Bulgarian sources, the Russian šč sign is replaced by št. Whenever possible, names of writers, personalities, or places are spelled according to the convention of the home country, possibly followed by transliteration as indicated. The affiliated organs of the CMEA are normally referred to by their Russian name, because in most cases the official or working language of these organizations is Russian.

Abbreviations

BLEU	Belgian-Luxembourg Economic Union
BTPA	Bilateral Trade and Payments Agreement
CMEA	Council for Mutual Economic Assistance
COCOM	Coordinating Committee for East–West Trade Policy
Cominform	Communist Information Bureau
CPE	Centrally Planned Economy
ERP	European Recovery Program
FTE	Foreign Trade Enterprise
GTC	Gross Trade Creation
IBEC	International Bank for Economic Cooperation
IEO	International Economic Organization
IIB	International Investment Bank
IO	Input-Output
ISDL	International Socialist Division of Labor
MFT	Monopoly of Foreign Trade and Payments
MTE	Market-type Economy
NTC	Net Trade Creation
OEEC	Organisation for European Economic Co-operation
ROW	Rest of the World
SEI	Socialist Economic Integration
SMP	Social Marginal Productivity
TD	Trade Diversion
WMP	World Market Price

Introduction

At the moment of writing, the centrally planned economies of Eastern Europe (CPEs) are celebrating the thirtieth anniversary of their common economic organization – the Council for Mutual Economic Assistance (CMEA). As on earlier occasions, a variety of survey articles and numerous other commemorative contributions complement an intensive publicity campaign to inform the general public about one aspect or another of socialist cooperation and the Council's role therein. In spite of the substantial surge in volume, the overall tone and informative level of the new publications do not differ markedly from earlier work. In particular, disproportionate attention is devoted to past successes and to how further strengthening of cooperation in the years ahead will improve economic conditions in the region. Comprehensive critical analyses of integration achievements and failures incurred in the past, on the other hand, are much scarcer. A cursory glance at this, by now, vast literature is bound to leave the reader with the impression that during the past three decades the policy makers of Eastern Europe have been most anxious to foster an intricate network of economic relationships across national frontiers.

The recent East European literature on integration suggests that by now the entire region is in effect the real market of supply and demand upon which economic and other policy decisions of the members are predicated. Cursory acquaintance with East European events might also generate this impression not only, and perhaps not even mainly, because of the geographical proximity and economic necessity of the CPEs; political and organizational similarities among these countries could be considered the crucial cornerstone in the building up of regional in-

tegration out of economic and political forces that have been
extremely disparate throughout much of East European history,
most recently and perhaps most vividly during the period between the two world wars. In spite of the current efforts to
promote such an optimistic and sweeping interpretation of the
evolution of regional cooperation in Eastern Europe, the truth
about the present stage of socialist economic integration (SEI),
which has become the catchall phrase of recent years, is far from
being that simple and logical.

An in-depth analysis of the features and achievements of SEI
will lead to a more tempered, sober evaluation: Despite the
CMEA's long existence, the process of gradually reducing differences in relative economic scarcities in the various member
countries is still in its initial stages. This paradoxical situation
stems not so much from the fact that integration became the official goal of East European cooperation endeavors only in the
late 1960s (Faddeev 1974a, p. 16), but rather because of a
number of quasi-permanent obstacles to harmonizing these
economies more closely. It should be stressed too that the absence of more comprehensive integration results cannot be attributed to a lack of official blueprints, bilateral and multilateral
agreements, and sub rosa controversies on the ways and means
of drawing these economies together. A thorough examination
of selected aspects of why previous efforts directed at fostering
SEI have not so far produced the expected results will constitute
the central nexus of the substantive issues discussed in this book.

1. Objectives and methods of analysis

The principal aim of this study is to build up an economic interpretation and clarification of the problems currently faced by
the East European leaders, assuming that economic integration
in the region is indeed politically feasible and desired. At the
same time, one cannot really address economic features of SEI
without mentioning politics and history, however briefly, and it
will therefore be instructive to poach from time to time on the
territory of other disciplines. Although the objective here is not
primarily of a historical and political nature, a step-by-step elaboration of a perspective on the legacies of the past will be pro-

vided insofar as the factors bunch into major determinants of contemporary and future events pertaining to SEI. This economic discourse will be developed without becoming too economistic. That is to say, a serious effort will be made to avoid creating the impression that the frequently profound shifts in economic cooperation among the CPEs are occurring autonomously and spontaneously, instead of being part and parcel of the general process of sociopolitical change or modernization in which a variety of political, economic, social, and other factors intersect. Integration is in any case a multidimensional process in which economics plays a major role but in which at various stages a number of other considerations intervene with varying intensity. This is all the more so in Eastern Europe, where because of the nature of the social systems the "primacy of politics" stands and exerts profound influence on SEI. Although the fundamental nature of the constraints on drawing the CPEs more closely together would indeed seem to arise from basic political incompatibilities, a genuine political treatise on SEI endeavors must, however, be deferred to those more competent in such matters. In view of the nature and planning system of the CPEs, it is important to clarify why SEI has been – and will continue to be in the future – an uncommonly tedious and difficult enterprise even if and when this goal is unconditionally accepted by the competent policy makers. It is with this in mind that the present study will by and large address itself directly to the economic issues of the integration process, without completely ignoring the institutional and political realities of the area.

One of the very crucial features of SEI is the potential dominance of Soviet predilections in molding regional policies. This stems to a significant extent from the sheer weight of Soviet economic power: Roughly, 90 percent of land and energy resources, 70 percent of population, 65 percent of national income, 60 percent of industrial and 75 percent of agricultural output, and 40 percent of foreign trade fall to the USSR's account. In short, because the Soviet industrial and military capacities are second only to those of the United States, the extent of Soviet power should be beyond dispute. As a result, both the conception and realization of SEI are bound to be strongly influenced by, if not fully subjected to, Soviet preferences and initiatives. Although this is one weighty political factor to be reckoned with in an economic discourse, it bears noting that despite the overwhelming preponderance of Soviet power, situations do arise that the smaller partners can and, at times, do exploit to their own advantages.

Certainly, it is rather implausible for political, economic, and strategic reasons to envision East European integration developing without the USSR's participation, and this undoubtedly complicates the assessment of the benefits and costs of SEI for the other participants. The disparity between the political and economic power of the USSR and the other members may possibly engender rivalry and suspicion instead of the necessary mutual trust. Integration may thus become a contest, where each side attempts to extract the maximum advantage at the minimum price. In the context of the asymmetrical distribution of power in Eastern Europe, this contest will inevitably entail an unequal division of advantages and disadvantages of SEI.

It would be fundamentally misleading, however, to attribute the political factors of SEI and its ramifications only to the presence of a superpower as one participant in a union of otherwise relatively small-to-medium-sized nations. Although the USSR has obviously had the political power to impose its precepts in the last resort, there has been a marked reluctance to exercise that power in the face of determined opposition from other members. One very important, yet frequently neglected, causal factor is the nature of "sovereignty," an important political factor that will often crop up as a key obstacle to SEI, although its real role in molding regional cohesion should not be overrated. The parallel between developments in intra-CMEA affairs and political aspirations toward national independence is all too easily drawn. It is important to realize that autonomy in the conduct of economic affairs is virtually the only "political sovereignty" the leaders of the smaller CPEs enjoy, and this was not won immediately after the states started their "socialist independence." These countries had very little genuine choice in the conduct of their domestic and foreign economic affairs until at least the mid-1950s, and it was only after Stalin's death that one could detect weighty, albeit hesitant, policy innovations in economic matters. To give up part of this hard-won limited autonomy would be a very painful process under any circumstances, even if assertion of sovereignty implies a considerable cost in terms of economic efficiency through holding down the chances of regional specialization.

A third important component related to economic affairs is the nature of the world socialist system as it has evolved since the Second World War. The basic reason why these economies did not aggressively seek an intensive international socialist division of labor (ISDL), and failed to embrace from the start proper measures to implement it, is principally a matter of the political system under Stalin. The choice of relative national autarky over fostering regional specialization "was not despite, but rather because of the Soviet tutelage" (Kaser 1967, p. 17), because these Soviet directives were believed to be ideologically correct as well as quite consistent with the USSR's own industrialization experience. Socialist ideology continues to be a potent force indeed in matters related to economic cooperation (for example, in the now in-vogue rationalizations of the "advanced socialist society"), and occasionally this factor will have to be heeded.

A related point is the general nature of international economic relations of CPEs. In J. Viner's felicitous phrasing, "private enterprise, as such, is normally nonpatriotic, while government is automatically patriotic" (Viner 1944, p. 316). In economies where everything is in principle controlled by the state, because the state as society's caretaker performs economic functions in its capacity as proprietor of the means of production in addition to the traditional functions ensuing from its political sovereignty, the conduct of economic affairs, internal as well as external, will by its very nature be codetermined by noneconomic motives. A recent contribution entitled "integration is the realization of the unity of politics and economics" (Brauer 1974) underlines this proposition rather well.

2. Integration and its forms in Eastern Europe

In the light of the above observations, it seems appropriate to justify the term "integration." Economic integration is understood here as a process aimed at the leveling up of differences in relative scarcities of goods and services by the conscious elimination of barriers to trade and other forms of interaction between at least two different states. Because neither the CMEA nor any other East European organization has ever been explicitly entrusted with this task and the individual CPEs have done precious little to seek actively the reduction of relative scarcities in the region, it is highly questionable whether the term "integration" is appropriate in the context of East European economic cooperation until at least the late 1960s. The reason for using this general definition here is that the gradual reduction of differences in relative scarcities in the various members of the region has most certainly been aimed at, or hoped for, since the late 1940s, though admittedly such considerations have not played a pivotal role in the formulation and implementation of actual economic policies. Where there is no chance of confusion, "integration" will be used interchangeably for "cooperation," "coordination," "division of labor," and similar terms.

The above alternative use of terms has been deliberately selected, in full awareness of the fact that a score of East European leaders and writers have attempted to distinguish rigorously between the phase of "economic cooperation" and that of "economic integration," the dividing line being sometime in the late 1960s, coinciding in fact with the elaboration and approval of the official integration program[1] as the blueprint for further policy actions. As far as substantive issues are concerned, however, this distinction is purely semantic. It is certainly not an inevitable sequence of events that the acceptance of a political document on integration with that name will almost automatically entail the emergence of the relevant economic processes or will inevitably generate them.

Recent discussions about SEI can be divided into two classes, depending upon the stereotype of economic policies and institutions that receives preponderant attention: strict central planning on the regional level and market-based decision making in the national economies as a prerequisite for efficient regional integration along the lines indicated by real economic scarcities. Needless to add, there has been a great proliferation of variants in the form of one mixture or another of these two types of policies and institutions. Also, the officially accepted concept – as formally endorsed in 1971 in the Complex Program – is a combination of these, at first sight, mutually exclusive alternatives. But the official guidelines seem to put greater trust in the role of central planning in the process of promoting SEI than in gradually transforming the CPEs into full-fledged market-type economies (MTEs), not necessarily patterned after any of the existing capitalist paradigms. Reaching the official objective of the first integration phase, extending into the late 1980s, has been predicated on the reinforcement of plan coordination without, however, curtailing the ability of any member to pursue its own goals. Although the exact meaning of plan coordination has so far been left deliberately vague, the essence of SEI must apparently be cast in the following terms: (1) the joining of forces in the ex ante forecasting of economic events, (2) the control over actual developments by means of traditional planning tools but also with the aid of monetary and financial instruments typical of MTEs, and (3) the greater influence of monetary and financial tools in the elaboration and implementation of national and regional plans.

Monetary and financial tools for promoting integration through the indirect coordination of national economic policies should receive preponderant attention in discussions about the future of SEI, for a variety of reasons. First, the current interest in formulating ways and means of enhancing integration also through the extensive utilization of these coordination instruments is very topical and apparently quite sincere. Second, past efforts aimed at accelerating SEI by means of selected forms of monetary cooperation have remained unfruitful. The reason for this foundering will yield valuable information, especially as inputs to a dispassionate examination of the most likely evolvement of SEI and its ramifications for the members. Third, neither supranational planning along the lines of traditional central planning in the CPEs (de jure by means of a regional planning bureau or de facto as a result of coordinating national plans) nor the conversion of the CPEs into MTEs will be feasible in view of the more general objectives set by the CPEs. Fourth, during the past decade the attention of the policy makers of several CPEs has gradually been deflected from relying exclusively on a highly centralized administration of their economies, so typical of the 1950s, to the search for a more technical and flexible, less doctrinaire interpretation of socialist planning. In that vein, "plan" and "market" are evidently not mutually exclusive instruments of reaching some goals with limited means. Neither does the dichotomy hold on the regional level, for the successful coordination of national plans and their implementation critically depend on parametric criteria of efficient choice. An optimal use of planning presupposes therefore the use of market-type indicators to reach acceptable, realistic decisions and, as a result, SEI will have to be pursued by suitably combining plan and market elements.

The gradual shift in the CPEs leading, on the one hand, to the concentration of macroeconomic decision-making authority in their respective coordination centers and, on the other, to the delegation of the day-to-day, more microeconomic problems to planning bodies on the lower rungs of the plan hierarchy (and sometimes to individual enterprises) is likely to be further extended rather than curtailed. Certainly, recentralization might crop up, which could temporarily reverse the devolution process. Yet, in view of the intricate problems of a modern industrial society, the leaders of the CPEs can only hope to cope with the attendant multifarious issues by broadening, rather than restricting, the devolution of decision-making authority and responsibilities. This is surely so if the CPEs at the same time still wish to honor their basic commitment to various other objectives of socialism. The combination of centralized planning for growth, technical progress, and stability on the one hand, and decentralized decision making at the actual production and consumption level on the other, must be better adapted to changing realities and exigencies so that contemporary problems can be dealt with efficaciously. This shift in emphasis becomes all the more compelling if the effective market horizon of those charting economic policy in the CPEs is in fact to be gradually widened so that it will eventually encompass Eastern Europe as a whole. If this is indeed an important objective of SEI, then a more effective use of the instruments of monetary and financial cooperation will be indispensable.

However, before indirect coordination instruments will be allowed to supplement and, in some instances, to replace coordination through central planning and the dovetailing of traditional national plans at the CMEA level, several rather drastic changes in the economic administration of the individual members will have to be implemented. East European leaders are not oblivious of the need for greater differentiation in policy instruments. They are also keenly aware of the advantages and disadvantages of enlarging the variety, scope, and application sphere of policy instruments. During the past thirty years or so, individual CPEs and the CMEA as a whole have intermittently approved plans to this end. In several instances – in fact, in all important, complicated, cases – the original intentions were quickly frustrated by actual developments, in some instances largely political, that forestalled the implementation of official agreements. An attempt to explain this failure and to draw useful inferences for future actions, mainly in economic terms, will cover the second group of problems under discussion here. However, the more specific analyses of the evolving role and scope of indirect instruments of guiding and coordinating SEI have been presented in detail in a separate volume (Brabant 1977); although extensively relying on that analysis, the emphasis here will be on the comprehensive analysis of the overall environment for deepening SEI.

3. Scope and content

When the members of an economic union are sovereign states, their specific, separate interests will make for explicit or hidden conflicts about the advantages of the union that decision makers within any one centralist organization may try to transcend. An inquiry into the historical angle of the economic relations among the CMEA members and their separate interests is appropriate because contemporary cooperation in the area continues to be surrounded by circumstances that derive largely from three broad types of legacies from the past with repercussions and implications for the present and future of SEI.

First, the organizational structure and the responsibilities of the CMEA are not necessarily compatible with the promotion of an efficient ISDL in Eastern Europe. Although its founding may have been inspired by a sincere desire to achieve effective economic relations among CPEs, the CMEA has never matured into a large-scale, well-disciplined enterprise designed to oversee and foster SEI. The regional organization has, in fact, never been endowed with the power to promote desirable or expedient dependences among the members, nor has this crucial issue been of focal interest to the CMEA or the separate CPEs, for that matter.

Second, the development policies pursued by the CPEs since the Second World War have not been conceived and implemented with widespread economic cooperation as the effective horizon. In fact, the first wave of socialist economic policies was aimed at making the members as self-sufficient as possible by introducing import-replacing industries and gradually building up a relatively self-contained economic profile. Furthermore, these policies were not implemented by means of economic instruments, nor were the economic growth targets derived from a gleaning of real scarcity indicators. The institutional and economic organization of the contemporary CPEs, although no longer as autarkic and inward-looking as in the early 1950s, continues to be governed largely by national economic and social aspirations, rather than by a desire to dovetail their rather small economies effectively with the regional or world economy. This means that SEI can only take root and mature as a result of a gradual, but nonetheless drastic, restructuring of the member economies.

Third, the national and regional institutions and decision-making instruments used to promote integration leave very much to be desired. When socialist observers maintain that integration signals, in fact, a "qualitatively new level of cooperation among [CPEs]" (Ladygin 1974, p. 24), they apparently mean that this process must be implemented and stimulated by different means than those hitherto used. SEI will therefore require not only intricate transformations in the field of international economic relations, but also a very different type of internal economic organization to underpin efforts on the regional level.

The need for a relatively comprehensive survey, analysis, and evaluation of the past and present forms of economic relations within the CMEA has become particularly acute as a result of recent efforts to decentralize internal decision making and to embrace more far-reaching forms of integration transcending the traditional reliance on simple commodity relations. The emergence, for instance, of common enterprises, jointly funded research, labor and capital mobility, and the like has necessitated a thorough reappraisal of the conditions for integrating CPEs, especially in view of the fact that these instruments and institutions are expected to prop up SEI without, however, resorting to the automatism of the market mechanism.

MTEs have institutionalized the choice of alternatives mainly on the basis of indirect coordination instruments. The many imperfections of the market mechanism are not, of course, the subject proper of the present study. Market-led integration has nonetheless interesting features, and occasional reference to the functioning of some well-established means of coordinating decisions in MTEs will prove appropriate. It is, of course, true that "under the conditions of the planned administration of the economy, commodity–money[2] relations are radically different from capitalist free market relations" (Larionov 1973, p. 71), but the experience of MTEs is not altogether irrelevant for other social systems. To facilitate a better grasp of the "characteristics of the functioning of prices, credit, and money under the conditions of a planned economy of the socialist countries" (Nazarkin 1973, p. 83), it will prove useful to work out a number of ideas concerning the basic features of the CPEs and their development since the war in order to clarify how one could tackle the more intricate problems of economic coordination, which is so important in integrating independent states.

An examination of past and present events is essential if one is to understand the contemporary functioning of foreign trade and other external economic relations of the CPEs. East European legal specialists often point out that, as a result of the special relations existing between friendly economies trading through a network of state monopolies, legally binding agreements have to be applied primarily in their dealings with nonsocialist countries (Meznerics 1968, p. 365). Although true to some extent, the statement should by no means be interpreted as if a greater degree of firm commitment in intra-CMEA relations with corresponding sanctions were completely superfluous. As the past has amply demonstrated, the absence of binding coordination agreements specified in all relevant[3] details has made implementation of these contracts and fulfillment of reciprocal obligations rather haphazard.

An attempt will be made here to pinpoint the economic arguments for and against agreements that lack either sufficient details or that are not well supported by economic instruments, as distinct from the political merits of such protocols. The "mutual confidence and the will to cooperate, characteristic of socialist organizations, irrespective of their relationship to the state" (Meznerics 1968, p. 367) may well be a plus, provided this trust is in no way restricted and the expressed will to cooperate embedded in official agreements will indeed motivate policy makers to translate it into concrete plan targets. However, in a world of sovereign states it is hard to imagine that all partners will be altruistically inclined, and no unity of interest seems to have prevailed so far.[4] Conflicting interests must therefore interfere with what might be the good of the socialist commonwealth, however defined. In fact, disunity and divergent motives have been stumbling blocks considerably complicating the realization of even the most elementary steps of the integration process. This will be attributed here to: (1) the origins of the Council and the way in which the organization gradually evolved, (2) the economic policies and preferences in the separate members, and (3) the hindrances encountered when integrating very inward-looking economic organisms.

The background to the CMEA's creation is explored in Chapter 1 in an effort to clarify the original aims of the Council. Was integration seen as an important element of the policies implemented with the aid of the CMEA? Which preferences, if any, ruled at that time? And what types of instruments were instituted to follow up these preferences to maximum effect? The gradual elaboration of the economic policies and institutions of the CPEs will be investigated in Chapter 2. The inward-looking aspects of the strategy for economic growth and the antitrade biases of the model adopted in the early 1950s delimit the scope of international commitment of the separate CPEs, and these features will be examined in Chapter 3. Chapter 4 will be concerned with the CMEA's organization and its role during the past three decades. These elements are believed to determine the exogenous and endogenous conditions of SEI, which will be summarized in Chapter 5 together with an assessment of the integration achievements to date and an evaluation of how present plans for the future are shaping up in current policy debates.

4. A word of caution

Whereas Western integration has been pursued with the backing of massive official documentation and intensive independent research, SEI and the activities of its ruling organs remain largely shrouded in secrecy or conflicting evidence. Only the barest minimum of systematic information on the more challenging aspects of economic cooperation in Eastern Europe has been divulged. Consequently, a comprehensive analysis of the Council and its activities is still very difficult.

Apart from the absence of many facts and figures about SEI and the doubtful value or reliability of a large portion of the information that is now made available by the CPEs, attention should also be drawn to the more general state of the art. To anyone even marginally acquainted with the CPEs, it must appear platitudinous to emphasize that there is no coherent theory of socialist foreign trade or SEI. East European economists with few exceptions confine themselves to restatements and refinements of the basic postulates of Marxism-Leninism – mostly as interpreted by current apologists and protagonists of this doctrine – or to the rather narrow, more technical study of production processes related more to engineering and accounting than to economic analysis proper.

Happily, there are some outstanding exceptions to this dismal exegesis, but their contributions often lack a comprehensive analytical structure. This is at least as formidable a drawback to the Western economist as is the inapplicability of many conventional tools of standard economic analysis to the CPEs and their economic policies.[5] This means in particular that in the course of the study a proper framework for analyzing the CPEs will have to be formulated, even if at the risk of having the product labeled a bourgeois[6] treatise. But this may be a price worth paying as long as East European specialists refrain from providing logical models or the more informative and structured analysis underlying their sometimes incoherent defense of ideological precepts. The risk of stressing one aspect or another more than it really deserves is further compounded by the fact that the more interesting East European research efforts seem to be closely correlated with the degree of ideological loyalty of the political leadership of any one country. This may well explain why some arguments tend to be, for instance, "too Hungarian."

Whenever deemed helpful, this study will explore matters well beyond the simple description of actual or presumed facts about SEI, though it is not pretended that a coherent theory of this multidimensional process will be presented. If properly and imaginatively phrased, such a model or theory would certainly be highly valuable. However, it would appear that the Western observer, and perhaps the East European participant as well, does not yet have a full grasp of the many different facets of the SEI movement, even if confined to the rather restrictive, albeit broad, definition of integration embraced here. Although it is fashionable to condemn descriptive analyses for being too discrete, too time-and-place determined, the theories of East European integration formulated so far would seem to have failed singularly in responding with a tolerable error margin to the standards that were set for them (for instance, Korbonski 1970, pp. 946–949). The level of abstraction in this monograph will therefore vary from topic to topic, depending upon the degree of understanding of the central questions under discussion.

The purpose of this contribution is to assemble the relevant parts in an effort to attain a broader and deeper perspective on what SEI is all about. To the extent that new facts have been successfully unearthed and they have been placed in their proper setting, this study addresses crucial aspects of what a comprehensive theory of SEI should ideally look like: First, it should be able to test the actual progress of integration with respect to what the initiators had in mind, not (as in Korbonski 1970, p. 946) what the ideal formal model might terminally be; second, it should help to forecast the broad future of SEI; and, finally, it must enable the investigator to relate SEI to other integration attempts in an effort to avoid postulating a regional vacuum – as if East European affairs were completely divorced from developments elsewhere, especially integration schemes initiated in different social systems.

Strictly speaking, the CMEA spans three continents, yet the preceding reference has been exclusively to Eastern Europe as the region over which the CMEA is supposedly presiding. In what follows, the roles of Mongolia and Cuba in CMEA affairs will be touched upon only incidentally because these countries are too underdeveloped, too far removed from the center of power and decision making, and too small to play instrumental roles in SEI. Similar remarks apply to Albania, which has been an official member since February 1949, but ceased to participate in active CMEA affairs in late 1961, without however revoking formal membership, and Vietnam, which joined only in June 1978. Nothing essential will be lost by excluding these four countries from most of the discussions. The terms "CMEA," "Eastern Europe," the "CPEs," the "socialist countries," and the like will therefore be used interchangeably unless explicitly indicated otherwise (especially regarding the notion of CMEA as a geographical area enveloping the East European countries or CMEA as an international organization serving mainly the countries belonging to that area).

1

The initial framework of East European economic cooperation

Today, as in the past, it is still well-nigh impossible to pinpoint the exact reasons for the creation of the CMEA and the circumstances of its gestation in early 1949. The decision to establish the Council is usually explained as a retaliatory political act to Western cooperation efforts, masterminded by Stalin or his associates, rather than as a momentous agreement with far-reaching implications for the future stable development of the East European economies.

The problems that confronted the leaders of a great power in the turbulent world environment of the 1940s were extremely diverse and complex, and the end of the 1940s was unquestionably a very tumultuous period, for a variety of reasons. First, uncertainty about the fate of the East European societies was rampant, though various uncoordinated projects were devised to revive the still war-ravaged and underdeveloped countries. These attempts to come to grips with the fundamental problems of a large region, rather than with those of the somewhat artificially drawn national states individually, were perhaps one of the most hopeful signs of an otherwise rather dismal period. Second, a great many forces were at work leading ultimately to a division of the world into two antagonistic blocs as a result of the Cold War, which itself ensued from a series of more fundamental, but basically incompatible, political, ideological, and other objectives regarding the most desirable course of "historical development." It must be recalled that several voices were raised to defend and activate the process of establishing world unity through mutual aid. When these utopian appeals proved to have been in vain, the division of the world into separate spheres of influence and areas of quite different social, political, and economic systems was accepted as unavoidable, at least for the time being. This was perhaps the most disquieting result of the discussions about regionalism and the division of Europe. The partition of the world economy into "capitalist" and "socialist" camps was attained mainly by political means. The West European countries accepted substantial American economic aid and other accompanying influences to bolster their economies and to stabilize their political systems, and slowly made headway in laying the foundations of an interlinked economy under the protective umbrella of the United States. The East, under the supreme aegis of the Soviet Union, reacted with, among other things, the creation of the CMEA in January 1949 and the withdrawal from nearly all international organizations with which the countries involved (mainly the USSR, of course) had, or thought they had, ideological quarrels or substantial doubts (Kaser 1967, pp. 10–26).

The interpretation of the CMEA's founding at that early time as being one of the idiosyncratic manifestations of Stalin's imitative mind has remained an unsatisfactory explanation of why and how the common economic organization was erected at all. Admittedly, the Council itself and its members have not produced convincing proof to refute this sweeping explanation of the CMEA's history up to the mid-1950s. It seems, however, utterly futile to set up a multinational institution if it is to be denied any practical significance, and it is therefore logical to look for an alternative, perhaps intellectually more satisfactory, rationale without, of course, denying that the CMEA was an abortive attempt for it actually achieved little to overcome the particular problems of the member countries and the region as a whole. Under the prevailing economic, political, and strategic conditions, the Council could not have acted otherwise than eschewing the particular problems that the separate CMEA partners had to face, and no viable alternative was offered to the discouraging regional economic policies so characteristic of the interwar period. By the early 1950s, uniformity in national economic policies rather than diversity within a common polity had become the rule, and no doubt was left as to whose example was to be emulated.

This chapter does not analyze the specific motives that may have prompted Stalin first to accede to the establishment of the

CMEA, and then suddenly to debilitate the Council so that its practical role was reduced to virtually nil. It attempts rather to tackle several interrelated topics. Because the traditional explanation of the CMEA's creation in 1949 raises more questions than it answers, it may be fruitful to reexamine the key issues at stake, and ask what may have led to the setting up of a common economic institution. Anticipating the arguments below concerning the economic problems of the region, a second question emerges: If in 1949 there was sufficient economic and political justification for setting up an institutional organ that would slowly stimulate regional economic cooperation, what were its original goals and the common means agreed upon or, alternatively, which objectives and instruments of regional economic development were debated? Finally, why did the members not implement those early blueprints for joint action, but resolve instead to adopt quite different principles of economic interaction?

That the CMEA as a regional institution has had little, if any, practical significance and in itself has been of marginal relevance to the development of its members in the early 1950s will not, of course, be disputed here. There are, however, several hints that militate against the notion that the Council was created solely as a propaganda instrument to marshal support for the skeptical Soviet views on the real nature of the Marshall Plan, the heretic Yugoslav road to socialism, or other disquieting international events. It will be argued that the original objectives embraced by the CPEs, particularly the newly established socialist regimes, were much wider than commonly posited and that the common institution could therefore have played a powerful, positive role in the region's industrialization. It was only later that efforts to exploit the latent benefits of tackling the precarious economic situation of the region as a whole were foiled by the USSR. If so, why was the CMEA unable to live up to its original raisons d'être, why was it so inactive and trivial, and why were no attempts made to increase its significance until the mid and late 1950s?

Those looking for easy cut and dried answers will be disappointed. It would make for a neat argument were one able to point to one factor or another as central, but that is not possible, for the objectives sought at the time were very much intertwined. Indeed, it is still unthinkable to complete the puzzling history of the earlier phases of the CMEA, and much of what will be discussed below therefore belongs more to the sphere of speculation than to that of hard historical facts (see also Montias 1969, pp. 38–40). Furthermore, the nature of this book may give the impression that the CMEA's origin is discussed in the vacuum of economic rationality as the only yardstick of SEI; this, however, is far from being the intention.[1]

Anyone scrutinizing the background to some of the more recent disputes within the CMEA will find telltale signs of what may have taken place in the late 1940s. One cannot, of course, infer from these isolated pieces of information a compendious, or even a coherent, history of actual events. Nevertheless, it would seem appropriate to record all the available evidence and concurrences pointing in the direction of another interpretation of the CMEA's birth, even if some of the isolated bits of evidence adduced are liable to prove coincidental, irrelevant, or plainly false if and when all the facts become accessible.

The narrative outlined here can at this stage be no more than a tentative description of events. Even so, it is hoped that the points raised may stimulate a comprehensive reappraisal of the Council's genuine roots so that a more balanced history of the CMEA's original objectives and tasks may be compiled. The fact that such a history is long overdue and more than desirable has been acknowledged in both Eastern (e.g., Guzek 1972, pp. 22–23) and Western (e.g., Montias 1969) scholarly publications.

1. Motives leading to the CMEA's creation

There seems to be a consensus among observers from socialist and nonsocialist countries alike that the Council's origin should be sought against the backdrop of the following dominant features of international relations in the late 1940s: (1) the then-emerging division of postwar Europe into two antagonistic political blocs; (2) Stalin's perceived need to safeguard Soviet interests by consolidating Eastern Europe into a "protective cordon" and drawing the region into the Soviet sphere of influence; and (3) the countering of the organizational, strategic, and economic consequences of the Marshall Plan. The specific phrasing of these points may, of course, differ but the hard core of the elements singled out appears to be as stated. It is argued below, however, that a more complex system of forces may have been at work. To do so, it will prove helpful to recall several familiar historical events and to add a few circumstantial, but possibly highly relevant, elements to the discussion before introducing an alternative or supplementary rationalization of the Council's creation.

Economic regionalism, the Marshall Plan, and East European options

The basic incompatibility between the inclination of some East European countries to participate in the recovery program for Europe (ERP), openly displayed at least by Czechoslovakia and Poland, and Stalin's aims[2] concerning Eastern Europe and the Soviet considerations about the most desirable organization of postwar international relations, is the most frequently cited argument in the discussion about what may have led to the establishment of the CMEA.

It will be recalled that when the American secretary of state at the time, G. C. Marshall, announced the program for the reconstruction of Europe with substantial American aid on 5 June 1947, the consolidation of Eastern Europe had not yet been completed and certainly not yet perfected. The communist parties or Popular Front coalitions, especially in the Central European countries, though their influence was dominant, had not yet achieved final takeover and an undivided subservience to Soviet policies. Furthermore, the political leadership in those countries where political power had already been usurped by these left-wing coalitions was still not firmly entrenched. In any case, the people's democracies at that time could hardly be considered as submissive puppets, entirely subjugated to Stalin's all-pervasive influence, though "socialist Caesarism" was well on the ascent even in matters relevant to the gestation of the CMEA.

The destructive effects of the war and of immediate postwar events had bequeathed to the East European countries an unenviable legacy, perhaps worse than that of many West European countries. This situation was exacerbated by the economic backwardness of these countries, excepting some regions especially in Czechoslovakia and Poland (the problems of the later-emerging German Democratic Republic should, of course, be dealt with outside this framework). The new leadership would have to embrace imaginative policies to come to grips with a burdensome, unskilled agricultural overpopulation as a precondition for securing economic growth and forestalling a repetition of the turbulent events so pervasive in the interwar period.[3] In view of these legacies from the recent past, the prospect of foreign economic aid was naturally considered a welcome boost on the way to a better mobilization of the resources of the backward or still disturbed economies. In any case, the cost of economic stabilization and progress could in this way have been more tolerable than if growth were to result mainly from native talents and wealth.

Immediately following the announcement of ERP, Czechoslovakia agreed to participate in the Paris conference. Hungary and Poland left little doubt about their basic interest in following suit, inasmuch as Poland informed Washington that the country was favorably inclined toward participation in an all-European economic plan (Ferrell 1966, p. 121), and the Hungarian government made its decision to join subject only to Moscow's approval of such an important move (Lipgens 1978, pp. 16–17). Although the reactions of the other countries are less well documented, it would seem nonetheless that they were not completely averse to taking a second look (excepting Bulgaria and Yugoslavia, which outrightly denounced the American-inspired cooperation plan).

Unfortunately, the prospect of East European participation crystallized briefly as a result of confusing Soviet diplomatic messages and did not point toward a promising juncture in the East–West turn of events. The prolonged deliberations about the conclusion of a peace treaty and the future of Austria and Germany, and hence European cooperation, during the fourth session of the Council of Foreign Ministers in Moscow (March–April 1947) and Marshall's personal visit with Stalin in April 1947 (Halle 1967, p. 134) had left the firm impression that the USSR appeared to be interested primarily in stalling negotiations while Europe disintegrated economically. The Moscow conference proved to be a turning point in the West's postwar deliberations with the Soviet Union in that the American leadership felt its view confirmed that the USSR would thwart any cooperation program that would subject national policies, however mildly and benevolently intended, to "unilateral foreign influence." East European participation in such a Europeanwide program for economic cooperation would under the circumstances be most improbable, if not fully precluded (Yergin 1977, p. 299).

Notwithstanding these rather distressing signals, Moscow accepted the invitation to the Paris preparatory conference of foreign ministers (June–July 1947) to deliberate about the Marshall Plan. Molotov's stand at this conference, as his earlier one in Moscow, left little doubt that Stalin perceived the Marshall Plan as trespassing on the sovereign rights of the participants or, in other words, as unfair meddling in national affairs on the part of the United States (Molotov 1949, pp. 461–468). From these summit meetings, Stalin's stance, perhaps motivated by communist ideology, was perceived to amount in fact to a firm refusal to endorse any collective undertaking that could pose a threat to the Soviet Union's exclusive influence in Eastern Europe and increase Western Europe's capacity to resist communist penetration. The United States was steering exactly the opposite course in its foreign policy, but with the same goal of securing its sphere of influence, albeit that this objective was considered honorable because of concerns about safeguarding democracy. Collision was therefore unavoidable so long as both superpowers were committed to their strategies, and the revival of all-European economic cooperation buttressed by the infusion of capital and other assistance from the United States, under the circumstances, became an impossible proposition.

The subsequent course of events is well known: After first accepting the invitation to the Paris conference, which endorsed the creation of the Organisation for European Economic Cooperation (OEEC), Czechoslovakia and Poland withdrew their support and joined in the chorus that denounced the ERP and OEEC as instruments of imperialist exploitation violating the national sovereignty and other interests of the economies taking part in it.[4] Yet, in this critical period the overt and all-out political conflict, particularly between the USSR and the United States, which would come to be called the Cold War, presented itself as an imminent danger but not as a foregone conclusion.

Whatever the political weapons wielded to polarize the East European countries and to force them into foregoing Western aid, their initial enthusiasm for such a program derived not only, and perhaps not even mainly, from political calculation. There is little doubt that some countries wished to participate in regional cooperation efforts to speed up the progress of domestic recovery and economic development. A quick solution to their urgent economic needs required large-scale aid, if not from the West, then from some other source, possibly the USSR, although that country had to tackle a huge economic recovery problem itself. The motivations on the part of the United States for inviting the East European countries and on the part of the USSR for forcing rejection are, of course, a different issue altogether.

Aside from the immediate urge to reactivate the economies, the magnitude of the region's economic plight should not be underestimated, and certainly not neglected as it has so often been in the literature on the CMEA and the postwar turn of events in Eastern Europe. The interwar period had not been very promising from the point of view of economic, social, and political developments as such, nor from the point of view of regional cooperation and normalization of animated controversies inherited from the past. These lingering disputes, kindled largely by the strident nationalism of the successor states and the problems emerging from the abrupt liquidation of natural links with their former hinterland, had prevented the emergence of a bold regional effort aimed at getting the upper hand of the dislocations engendered by the First World War, the breakup of the great empires, and the sequence of economic crises, particularly the depression of the 1930s. Certainly, inasmuch as the East European countries were by and large competitors, they traded more with the West than they did among themselves. This was true in particular for Central Europe. Though some triangular complementarity had been established among the above region, the Balkan countries, and the West, the level of interaction fell far short of the degree of constructive cooperation that could have been achieved by a comprehensive endeavor to seek regional economic integration. In view of the postwar fusion of these countries under a single polity, the region's trade could have been expected to be governed from a single center, with as much mobility of capital and labor as the cost of structural redeployment permitted or defense considerations allowed (Montias 1966, pp. 63–64).

Although there are very strong advocates of the thesis that East European regionalism cannot be an effective policy because these countries are basically more competitive than complementary, several points may be put forward to justify the view that a balanced regional economic policy could exert a highly positive influence on the area's industrialization and reconstruction process (Basch 1943, pp. 408–419; Rosenstein 1943, pp. 202–211).

First, the arguments against regional integration are not convincing: Why should the competitive nature of most of these countries, their different levels of development, and the relative scarcity of a variety of basic primary goods in most countries necessarily and intrinsically abort a cooperative effort? Unless one were arguing the case of an autarchic regional policy completely severed from the rest of the world, on the basis of the theory of the positive and negative effects of integration there are more arguments in favor of cooperation than against, particularly in view of the postwar constellation of forces. It might be quite true that in static equilibrium some countries stood to lose more from curtailing traditional economic ties with the West than they could gain from adjusting themselves to a uniform regional policy. But neither the 1930s nor the 1940s provided much of an equilibrium!

Second, ever since the breakup of the Austro-Hungarian Empire, various proposals for regional integration had been launched. During and immediately after the war, several such schemes were in an advanced stage of preparation (e.g., the topical Czechoslovak–Polish cooperation plan and the various alternatives for a Balkan federation).[5] The fact that attempts to test these proposals were short-circuited, mainly by the USSR, should not prevent the observer from noting that the governments involved held high expectations of achieving a degree of recovery and durable economic progress through such channels. Some of these intended unions were certainly based on sound principles and could have entailed a much different path of postwar development from what actually emerged.

The postwar economic and political initiatives had given rise to newly conceived projects, which were discussed at preparatory negotiations and were carried to the initial stage of agreement. They promised a radical change in the trend toward autarky, which prevailed in the interbellum and tended to mar postwar recovery. The negotiations held out bright prospects of sound economic growth, particularly for those countries of the region whose natural endowment was limited and, in the event of parallel development patterns, would waste scarce resources. These projects surely encouraged the hope that, with the help of integration, each country would be enabled to focus on developing those sectors best suited to the prevailing conditions and to attain in those activities the highest technical competence, while relying on more extensive markets.

But just like the desire to join the Marshall Plan and other cooperation proposals launched by the West, all designs to promote regionalism without the USSR were nipped in the bud, apparently on Stalin's personal order (Kiss 1972, p. 15). Stalin is reported to have nurtured a profound distrust of the intentions of the East European countries. He apparently feared that if the region were to fuse the various economies and bolster mutual cooperation, it might lead to an anti-Soviet bulwark.[6] Indeed, joint efforts to come to grips with the most urgent of their common problems without the tutelage of the USSR[7] might have undermined the long-cherished Soviet interest in exercising hegemony over Eastern Europe. Would a regional policy with the USSR then offer an alternative? Most observers think not, on the grounds that Stalin did not want a regional economic policy as "His whole object was to hold the satellites down, but at arm's length. Unreliable and westernized, they must not be allowed too close" (Wiles 1968, p. 311). This, as frequently argued, also explains why Stalin balked at outright annexation, for which the USSR had the power but perhaps not the determination (Dedijer 1971, p. 101), and why he forced each country to entrench itself in autarky, thereby ignoring historical circumstances, the nature of Eastern Europe, and, generally, the concrete conditions and peculiarities of the various countries. This line of thought does not appear to be a convincing explanation of what took place in late 1948 and early 1949, although it might help to clarify various other features of the CMEA's inactivity later on and Soviet policies in Eastern Europe that were directed at subjecting the region to a stereotyped, instead of a creative, application of Soviet experience.

Political motives

Another line of thought sees the CMEA as a pure propaganda instrument (e.g., Agoston 1965, pp. 22–23; Wiles 1968, p. 311) to demonstrate an alleged unity in the socialist camp by creating an economic equivalent to the Cominform,[8] aiming among other things at isolating Tito's Yugoslavia (Dedijer 1971, p. 197). This was probably one of the considerations behind the CMEA's establishment, but certainly not the only one. I. T. Berend has stated in this respect that "The conflict with Yugoslavia . . . put an end to all the initial plans and endeavors for economic cooperation; its indirect effect was to foster adherence to autarkic principles" (Berend 1971, p. 14). Certainly, the Yugoslav affair and the initial confusion about the Marshall Plan, especially the Czechoslovak and Polish resolve to participate despite Soviet displeasures, indicated to Stalin that a dangerous diversity existed within his sphere of influence, which he would no longer tolerate in a rapidly deteriorating international environment with an incipient political crisis of major dimensions. Although the Marshall Plan debate and the Yugoslav affair may have compelled the countries to demonstrate overtly their political and economic unity, arguments presupposing only political motives behind the CMEA's creation seem one-sided and have come under strong criticism, even in some of the East European press.[9] Naturally, the CMEA could have become an effective political riposte to various disquieting international events only if it had been intended to follow up the political demonstration by action-oriented initiatives, especially in economic affairs (Berend 1968, p. 558).

Some observers have indirectly stressed the close parallel between the CMEA and the Cominform, especially regarding the main objective underlying the Council's foundation: the integration of the socialist countries into a solid economic bloc or the creation of a *Großraumwirtschaft* (Kis 1964, p. 104; Knorre 1961, p. 3; Korbonski 1964, pp. 5–6; Skubiszewski 1966, p. 547). Certainly, the Cominform was set up as a counterstroke to the challenge presented by the phase of mainly political diversity (Brzezinski 1961, pp. 58–64). Not unexpectedly, the socialist bloc could only be tightened by placing greater emphasis on all-round unity, and this could hardly be achieved in the political sphere if economic processes were allowed to proceed freely. But it is unlikely that one of the prime goals of the Cominform was control over economic affairs.[10] Whether Stalin intended at that stage to replace the postwar bilateral treaties by a fully fledged but gradual integration scheme as one of the Cominform platforms (as argued, for instance, by Kis 1964, p. 125; and Knorre 1961, p. 3) has so far remained an unconfirmed speculation. Similarly, the contention that the Council was set up as an equivalent of the Cominform without, however, being more than a provisional and temporary instrument of exercising control, pending the final shaping up of Soviet policy regarding the future of Eastern Europe (Skubiszewski 1966, p. 546), or that its calling was disruptive agitation in Western markets, paralleling the Cominform in the economic affairs of the socialist and other countries (Alexandrowicz 1950), cannot be based on solid information or even on genuine hints regarding the purposes of the Council.

Is it possible that Stalin was deceived by his protégés? Kaser has suggested that the Soviet option for SEI in 1949 was a natural extension of its domestic economic reform then contemplated (Kaser 1967, pp. 21–26), and P. Wiles sees the solution in the following rationalization of Kaser's arguments:

> Romantic as it may be, I find M. Kaser's answer wholly plausible. The CMEA was a carry-over from the aggressive, expansionist, forward-looking policy of A. A. Zhdanov, who had supported a forward, "Leningrad-type" policy in Europe and treated the communist parties of both Eastern and Western Europe as responsible, semi-independent, agents. ... The conclusion is therefore irresistible that its foundation was the last fling of the Zhdanov-Voznesenski policy, and that Stalin found himself saddled with an organ he had indeed allowed to be born, but could not personally work with. [Wiles 1968, p. 313]

This is reading at the same time too much and too little into Kaser's careful reconstruction of what might have prompted the CMEA's foundation. One can of course try to explain past history by the hindsight of subsequent events if information on the latter is ampler than on the former, as indeed it is in the CMEA's case. But it seems futile to rationalize the inauspicious beginnings of the CMEA by its inactivity up to 1954. Indeed, the question of why it did not function well is quite different, or at least it may be quite distinct, from that of why the Council was set up, barring the negligible possibility that it was not set up to function. And the limited documentary evidence that is available tends to exclude such a trivial motive.

Postwar trade and aid

Whatever the political and other conditions under which the East European countries could unfold their postwar identity, it is beyond doubt that they were ultimately drawn into the Soviet sphere of influence. A growing isolation from the Western world, a sometimes supine imitation of Soviet precepts, and Stalin's rapidly swelling suspicion of Western intentions made it hardly possible for the new Soviet partners to resume their prewar pattern of trade and economic relations. Yet, without such ties these countries could not hope to normalize economic activity, let alone attack the basic roots of their underdevelopment.

It should be recalled that a large share of East Europe's prewar trade had been cleared outside the region, especially with the German Reich. At the end of the war, a political and economic vacuum was left that neither Germany nor the West could fill, and that the USSR was all too willing to exploit under the circumstances. In short, the USSR helped to relieve the desperate shortage of food by grain loans, and concluded trade agreements for the supply of raw materials and other essential goods in exchange for whatever the countries had to offer. For them, there were no alternatives to the Soviet offer: "They had to choose between trade with the USSR on the terms offered, or no trade at all" (Dewar 1951, p. 2). Through reparation claims, control over key activities (e.g., the "mixed companies"), large-scale dismantling of factories, and regular trade agreements, the Soviet Union sought to acquire a dominant position in the economic activities of the East European countries, and managed to do so.

But these initial agreements and loans had been concluded to meet immediate requirements rather than as the beginning of a comprehensive cooperation effort. In 1947–1948, the Soviet share of Czechoslovakia, Hungary, and Poland's trade had fallen – it was just over 30 percent – and tended to dwindle further as trade with the West resumed (Brabant 1975; Dewar 1951, p. 97). If the USSR were to maintain its exclusive position in the economic sphere, an alternative policy would have to be formulated without delay. The need to change gear became particularly urgent during 1947 as the prospect of maintaining supremacy over the region tended to be eroded by the ERP and its ramifications. The Soviet Union was called upon to provide a retort and a palliative. To pacify the region, the USSR made a series of piecemeal gestures: Credit agreements were negotiated with Bulgaria, Czechoslovakia, and Yugoslavia; half the Rumanian and Hungarian reparation debts were written off; and so on (Lukin 1974, pp. 39–42; Nove 1970, p. 314). In sum, this first concrete reaction to the Marshall Plan debacle has a hastily improvised series of trade and payments measures, which is in the West sometimes referred to, with some exaggeration, as the Molotov Plan.[11]

East–West discords

In 1948 the fourth, and perhaps major, stimulus to the establishment of a common economic agency was provided by the ever-growing open antagonism between East and West. In addition to the problems of adversely developing trade trends and the attractiveness of American aid, the Soviet Union had to face the East European tensions that its interference in regional and other cooperation efforts had engendered. Under the circumstances, then, it seems logical to expect a program for mutual cooperation to be launched, possibly under the supervision of the Cominform. Yugoslavia's expulsion[12] from the latter and the economic embargo, which was stepped up at the time, must have further aggravated these tensions, and most likely brought pressure to bear on the USSR so that measures had to be taken beyond those normally within the scope of an interparty agency such as the Cominform.

Yugoslavia's excommunication occurred suddenly on 28 June 1948 after a sub rosa but nonetheless protracted and bitter debate on alternative roads to socialism. After the other East European countries had firmly pledged their solidarity with the Soviet position, denouncing Marshall aid and supporting the

Berlin blockade – a most effective kind of "reconnaissance in force" (Medvedev 1972, p. 479) and the first great test of the sincerity and resolve of Western unity – the West reinforced East Europe's isolation by means of the embargo and the cutting off of capital exports. As of 1 March 1948, American exports to Eastern Europe became subject to government licensing. The scope of the boycott was extended on 3 April 1948 by the statutes of the Marshall Plan, which implied that the ERP participants could not trade with Eastern Europe goods forbidden or subject to controls in the United States. This policy was formalized later with the creation of COCOM (Coordinating Committee for East–West Trade Policy). All this must have been particularly damaging to the three Central European countries that still relied extensively on trade with the West.

As argued by many East European writers, the boycott and export embargo were instrumental in spurring on the creation of the CMEA. Certainly, the postwar foreign policy initiatives embraced by the United States and abetted by most West European governments played an overwhelming role in the sense that they challenged the Soviet Union into inaugurating a countermove. Beyond that, however, the East is usually unable to explain the organization's origin, for Stalin and his protégés did little to solve the economic problems by means of a regional policy, apart from the diversion of trade from the West to the Soviet orbit, which coincided with the relative decline of the role of trade in these economies. But Western observers also seem to have drawn the wrong conclusions in that the first hostile moves from the West in the nascent economic warfare provided the USSR with a welcome argument used to reinforce its propaganda and to strengthen the display of patched-up unity exhibited by the CMEA's foundation. The smaller partners were hit far more vitally than the Soviet economy could ever be. Hence, this is one additional argument for a more positive approach toward the elaboration of a regional policy and the creation of a common organization to administer it.

Admittedly, the above arguments fail to fully solve the riddle of why the CMEA was set up. Certainly, the political motivation inspired by the perceived need to demonstrate unity under Soviet "guidance" against Western policies was of overwhelming importance. But the subsequent isolation of the communist world seems to strengthen the logic of gradually working out a joint economic policy for the region as a whole. The notion that also economic factors were behind the CMEA's creation certainly does not represent the traditional approach. Ironically, it is only in some recent East European reports that a stronger emphasis on economic arguments can be found. These will be summarized and interpreted in section 3 of this chapter, after settling yet another enigma of historical facts that remain hidden in inaccessible archives.

2. The founding date of the CMEA

It might be thought that such a trivial bit of information as the exact founding date of the CMEA could be unambiguously established, but this is unfortunately not the case. Why this is so is by no means clear. In itself, the precise founding date may seem an unimportant detail but, in view of the very different interpretations of what in fact germinated and when in 1949–1950, it is by no means superfluous to look again at the record and to build up at least some degree of consistency. This will be of some importance in reconstructing the economic aspects underlying the CMEA's creation.

Various writers have offered quite different specifications of when the CMEA was founded. A far from exhaustive sample of the Western literature yields the following: Weber picks 20 January 1949 (Weber 1971, p. 129), Köhler selects the 21st (Kohler 1965, p. 81), Kaser the 22nd (Kaser 1967, p. 11), Uschakow the 23rd (Uschakow 1962, p. 69), and Kiesewetter the 24th (Kiesewetter 1960, p. 52), whereas Pisar takes 30 January as the point of reference (Pisar 1970, p. 13). According to contemporary diplomatic observations (Foreign 1976, p. 4), the agreement creating the CMEA and detailing the objectives and instruments of SEI was signed on 18 January. It might be surmised that a survey of the specialized East European literature could straighten the record, but in this the researcher gets quickly disappointed. Even the CMEA secretary's latest history of the organization (Faddeev 1974b) fails to pinpoint a precise date![13] Other writers content themselves with a vague reference to January 1949, when the founding conference was held, or to April 1949, when the first Council Session was convened, if a specific date is included at all. The puzzle has not been completed by recent research. In fact, some of the latest accounts add to the confusion by proposing 5 January 1949 (Menzinskij 1971, p. 83) – the opening date of the Moscow founding conference – or 23 January (Mezi 1975, p. 60), when the conference participants allegedly adopted a resolution to create the CMEA that was subsequently published as the official communiqué (a point also endorsed in Uschakow 1962, p. 69). The matter has presumably vexed some East European specialists too. For example, apparently in order to square the founding date with the known conference (but whose sitting dates were revealed for the first time only in Faddeev 1967, p. 4), a Polish observer has stated that the conference was convened in Bucharest from 20 to 25 January 1949, hence the publication date of the founding communiqué (Rutkowski 1964, pp. 238–239)!

A simple pragmatic approach may help to dispose of the matter until a reliable, official insider's history of largely intramural events becomes available. However unfortunate, it must be assumed that no precise founding date is available. It is on the record that the communiqué disclosing the CMEA's creation was published on 25 January 1949 (*Pravda*, p. 2). The confusion about when the final decision to create the Council was actually taken is by no means confined to the Western observer. Ju. S. Širjaev states, for instance, that the "Moscow conference of representatives from the European socialist states accepted the declaration of the creation of the CMEA on 25 January 1949" (Sirjaev 1974, p. 5), thus postdating the resolve reported in Mezi 1975, p. 60. Whether these isolated bits of information suggest that the original conference, officially in session from 5 to 8 January 1949 in Moscow, was continued without formal deliberations cannot be proved or disproved.

In view of the above confusion, the simplest and most satisfactory interim solution for the problem would therefore seem to be to accept the publication date of the communiqué as the Council's founding date. Most Western specialists seem to go along with this proposition, but then err in the precise date.[14] Alternatively, one could also accept the opening date of the first conference – 5 January – dealing with the desirability of setting up a common regional institute as the founding date. This might be a satisfactory choice if Kaser's (Kaser 1967, pp. 10–41) and Čížkovský's (Cizkovsky 1971, pp. 54–61) accounts of the events, suggesting that the intention to create the CMEA was presented to the participants as a fait accompli,[15] could be confirmed. But there is considerable doubt that the CMEA was indeed a white rabbit pulled from Stalin's hat.

As to what actually took place between the end of the conference and the publication of the communiqué, no single convincing explanation has been suggested. Surely, further mutual consultations may have taken place. But Uschakow's suggestion that the interim was largely "a tug of war between the USSR and the other bloc countries on the expediency of such an initiative in general, and on the concrete shape of the future organization in particular" (Uschakow 1972, p. 13), is likely to be no more than unconfirmed and unverifiable speculation.

According to recently published contemporary diplomatic dispatches of the U.S. State Department (Foreign 1976, p. 4), the conference participants concluded a potentially wide-ranging treaty on economic cooperation on 18 January 1949. This treaty is purported to be the complete text of the agreement establishing the CMEA, which would tend to refute speculation about the conference's failure or the allegedly insurmountable division of views on SEI expressed there. Unfortunately, not much is known about this treaty, although it has been in U.S. diplomatic files since February 1949 (Foreign 1976, p. 4). Whether this document is a hoax, CMEA's founding document, or simply part of a projected comprehensive treaty then being debated, cannot be ascertained.[16]

It is of some importance to recall that the January conference was attended by the chief planners, rather than the political leaders. However, it seems highly unlikely that party and government officials were entirely uninformed about the imminent formation of a regional economic organization (Yugoslavia [Dedijer 1971, pp. 101–103] and the United States [Foreign 1976, pp. 1–9] were apparently abreast of events). Perhaps almost three weeks were needed to iron out political controversies. Or was it from the very beginning judged best not to divulge anything about the Council? According to Kaser, the founding conference was characterized by so much dissent about the Council's functions and tasks that it was deemed expedient to discreetly omit the founding date so as to mislead the outside world into believing that the CMEA was unanimously acclaimed. This could then have been a major propaganda stunt designed to counter the Marshall Plan and the ensuing embargo, and, presumably, also to create unanimous support for the blockade of West Berlin, the boycott of Yugoslavia, and the unification of economic forces to disrupt Western markets. However, a propaganda feat and a declaration of ostensible unity in economic and other affairs could have been achieved by less primitive means than the postponement of the disclosure on the CMEA's creation; and the organization of a common front with the overt purpose of disorganizing international markets and to sow the seeds of unrest in the world (Alexandrowicz 1950, p. 46) can hardly have been a major guiding force at the time. As to the results of this meeting, Kaser points out that:

> The debates on what should be established and how it should function were so protracted that the session had to be prolonged, and the discussions were finally deferred to a new reunion which, it seems, took place in Matrahaza, in Hungary. In order to prevent the revelation of the duration and the inconclusive debates, the *communiqué* omits a precise date. [Kaser 1966, p. 816]

The precise course of events may well have occurred as explained in Kaser's knowledgeable account. However, there is not a single confirmation, not even an obscure hint, of such a meeting. This does not, of course, disprove the above narrative. However, from recently released information, one may gain a somewhat different, but not necessarily contradictory, impression of both the January discussions and the preliminary statutes and other agreements drafted at this time. These sources of the events (mainly, Cizkovsky 1970, 1971; and Foreign 1975, 1976), unfortunately, shed no conclusive light on the degree of unity or disagreement at these meetings. It would appear, however, that there is sufficient evidence for arguing that some key points were deferred to further discussions, which could have been arranged to take place in Hungary. In any case, the points mentioned in connection with the outcome of the January meeting and the first official Council Session in April 1949 are identical. If the chronicle offered by Čížkovský can be relied upon, the March meeting in Mátráháza might have led to results that were approved by more members than indicated by Kaser. Let us investigate this evidence.

3. The aims and organization of the CMEA

For more than ten years, the official policy of the new organization was confined to the vaguely worded communiqué of 1949, which expressed the essence of the CMEA's tasks as follows: "exchanging economic experience, extending technical aid to one another, and rendering mutual assistance with respect to raw materials, foodstuffs, machines, equipment, etc." (Tokareva 1967, p. 44). The bold and aggressive nature of the Council as a countervailing force to the Marshall Plan and as an organ designed to obviate as far as possible the economic losses resulting from the West's boycott, was explicitly stated to be an integral part of the CMEA's tasks.

Naturally, the essence of the CMEA's goals as formulated in the quotation above is open to almost any interpretation. Indeed, it is no more than an extremely vague, if not abstruse, declaration of intent, which is very common in most of the friendship agreements signed between socialist countries (Richter 1968). But the communication indicated also that the CMEA's creation was agreed upon during the January conference on economic affairs held in Moscow in which the six founder members[17] (Bulgaria, Czechoslovakia, Hungary, Poland, Rumania, and the USSR) participated.

N. V. Faddeev, for more than twenty years the highest official of the CMEA, has detailed the tasks of the conference as follows:

The summoning of an economic conference from 5 to 8 January 1949 of representatives from the governments [of the CPEs] – on the initiative of several communist and workers' parties of the people's democracies and the Soviet Union – was of major importance for the development of economic cooperation.

In compliance with the decisions of this conference, the CMEA was created in 1949; this embodied new principles of international political and economic collaboration of the socialist countries. [Faddeev 1967, p. 4]

What were these new principles? According to most sources, no such principles were laid down, though some Soviet sources claim that the "goals and principles of the CMEA were agreed upon together with its organization in 1949" (Olejnik 1969, p. 79). In the absence of hard evidence it is difficult to confirm this.

In fact, even East European writers, including the CMEA's secretary (Faddeev 1966, pp. 30–31), tend to dismiss the idea of a goal-oriented blueprint having been drawn up in 1949, although the latest comprehensive official history (Faddeev 1974b) contains oblique references to "founding documents," such as a set of rules of procedure or an ordinance (*položenie*), that were drawn up by 8 January 1949 (see Brabant 1979). The communiqué of the twelfth Council Session in December 1959 (in Uschakow 1962, pp. 106–109) contains a passus specifying explicitly that the then-adopted charter replaced the earlier decisions regarding "goals, principles, and organizational forms of [CMEA's] activity." More commonly, however, it is argued, as in a Polish source, that what later materialized into official documents was "the result of historical practice" (Sandorski 1968, p. 571), not of intellectual or political forethought. But it seems hardly likely that the principal planners from the CPEs should have conferred for four days without reaching any decision on the future of intrasocialist cooperation, as most observers maintain. There are now several accounts warranting a more positive interpretation.

The earliest source surveying concrete proposals formulated as definite decisions appeared in 1949. According to C. L. Sulzberger's report (Sulzberger 1949), which is apparently based on the 18 January 1949 document referred to in section 2 of this chapter (Foreign 1976, p. 4), the various deliberations resulted in a pact concerning mutual commercial and industrial affairs extending over a period of twenty years. The agreement is said to have been signed in January 1949, but how and where it was endorsed or tacitly approved is not disclosed. But apparently it was "forced" upon the partners, thus possibly corroborating Kaser's account that the January conference was urgently summoned without giving the policy makers any hint of what was in the offing. However, four important facts cast some doubt on this last point. First, Yugoslavia seems to have requested permission to join such an organization in a note sent on 1 January 1949 – well before the founding conference – to unnamed Soviet leaders, who had presumably discussed plans for regional economic integration with their East European allies (Cizkovsky 1971, p. 59).[18] Second, the conference was chaired by M. Suslov, secretary of the Central Committee since 1947 and then, as now, chiefly concerned with interparty relations. This may be interpreted as a tentative confirmation of the aforementioned Cominform connection of the CMEA or at least that such an eventuality was discussed well in advance. Third, from U.S. diplomatic files (Foreign 1975, p. 933; 1976, pp. 1–9), it appears evident that plans for a common economic organization were widely discussed, albeit secretly, among communist leaders in the fall of 1948. Finally, though it is not known whether background material was available at that time or not, it appears highly likely that the Council's creation did not come totally out of the blue for reasons explored below. The previous plans for East European subregional unions, at least, must still have been extant and apparently played an important formative role at the time (Kiss 1972, p. 15).

According to Sulzberger's sources,[19] the various meetings apparently resulted in a series of specific decisions, four of which are of sufficient importance to be mentioned here: (1) The Council would develop a general plan for the coordination of the economic activities of the member countries; (2) the members would establish a common investment fund in gold or convertible currencies to the tune of 100 million rubles,[20] half of which would be contributed by the USSR, whereas the rest would be split up into equal shares by the other founder members; (3) this fund would be at the disposal of the "secretariat"[21] for financing projects of common interest; joint-stock companies would be established (e.g., between Czechoslovakia and Poland to exploit together the natural resources of Silesia),[22] but apparently on a different footing than that of the existing mixed companies, which had been formed on the basis of capital funds expropriated after the war mainly from German holdings and the national resources of several of the former hostile East European "host" countries; and (4) the Council would be entitled to detailed and full information and to send both observers and advisers to members, who would be bound by their advice.

Sulzberger's report reflects the essentials of the purported founding treaty, but there are some significant discrepancies (Protocol 1949). First, the document was drawn up by the six countries while assembled in Moscow on 18 January 1949. Second, the organization's task would be the coordination of the member economies within a general economic plan directed at "the consolidation and development in each country . . . in such a manner that [the economies] will no longer be competitive but will compose a homogeneous whole, complementing one another" (article 2). Third, the common fund would have to be established by 1 April 1949, and contributions could also be made in rubles. Fourth, Council Sessions would be held at least once every three months to discuss the economic situation of each member. Fifth, starting in 1950, the plans of the members would be drawn up "with the advice of the Council," and investment decisions not yet preempted for 1949 would have to be revised in accordance with the protocol and the advice of the secretariat. Sixth, the secretariat would have the authority to make any decision, subject to ratification by the Council at its first subsequent meeting. Finally, each member would have to submit every month a "detailed statistical situation report concerning production and any other documentary material pertinent to [its] economic and financial situation . . . for the preceding month" (article 9). Accordingly, the Council was viewed as the equivalent of the national governing body, whereas the "secretariat" was to emulate the national planning bureaus at the regional level with the intention of pursuing far-reaching supranational planning and control of the various member countries.

These details have never been corroborated in the specialized literature. M. Dewar mentions, without reference, that "in spite of unconfirmed reports of a twenty years' treaty concluded in Moscow at a secret meeting in May 1949, and the creation of a 100 million rouble fund to balance payments (in the first place to Czechoslovakia), there is not sufficient evidence to support such an assumption" (Dewar 1951, p. 5).[23] Kaser refers to this source as a rumor (Kaser 1967, p. 47). The contemplation of such a treaty has also remained unconfirmed by East European research, at least insofar as the specific details of the agreement are concerned. Yet, the "facts" or "intentions" reported above fit neatly into the economic arguments advanced here, and their overall implications, as distinct from specific details, can be supported by a few recent revelations about the CMEA's founding circumstances.

The most common East European representation of the 1949 events details simply that "the decision to create the CMEA was taken in January 1949 during the Moscow conference; . . . the organizational structure was agreed upon during the first council session . . ." (Ikonnikov 1969, p. 89), which is sufficiently ambiguous to confirm most skeptical or other opinions on the window-dressing effects of the Council's establishment. But Milan Čížkovský, a well-known Czechoslovak scholar, stresses that considerably more was attained. He maintains, for example, that there has been not only one operative set of statutes (those endorsed in 1959 and ratified in 1960), but that there have been in fact three such charters extant – not counting the revisions since 1962 (Cizkovsky 1970, p. 246).[24] Accordingly, the 1949 deliberations appear to have yielded more than is commonly supposed.

The genuine documents of the period under discussion, to the extent that the contemporary proposals and deliberations were recorded at all, unfortunately, are confined to central archives, to which access is apparently highly restricted, possibly because no one likes to be reminded of, what turned out to be, a discouraging stillbirth. From insiders' narratives of the Council's evolution (especially, Faddeev 1974b and Lukin 1974), it is virtually certain that a number of, possibly preliminary, agreements regarding the goals, instruments, and mechanisms of SEI were drawn up and adopted by 8 January 1949. In any case, in what follows the disparate bits of information will be pieced together without, however, pretending to attaining full consistency.

Both in 1949 and 1954, the CMEA members drafted statutes that were, at least temporarily, influential in charting CMEA affairs. Their common element appears to be the general statement that the coordination of the various national plans into a de facto regional plan should be the chief aim and task of the CMEA (Faddeev 1974, p. 13). Accordingly, the supreme goal of the CMEA from the outset has been integration by means of a bureaucratic coordination of the national plans of the members (Lukin 1974, p. 44), even though it is unclear whether this is simply paying lip service to present debates or a genuine reflection of historical events. According to the current CMEA secretary's history of events (Faddeev 1974b, pp. 59–64), it was only in 1954 that the CMEA's function was clearly defined in terms of what is now generally connotated as the coordination of national economic plans. The mechanism envisaged in 1949, in contradistinction to the 1954 redefinition, was apparently far more flexible, combining strict planning of key macroeconomic aggregates with a host of other coordination instruments, including the essentials of monetary and financial cooperation among sovereign states.

Attempts to mesh the various plans and to establish fruitful links between bilateral and multilateral cooperation efforts within the region (Lukin 1974, p. 46) were apparently made in early 1949, though not very successfully. G. L. Amundsen was told explicitly that the January preliminary statutes contained the objectives and procedures deemed necessary to come to a political and economic cohesion of the member countries (Amundsen 1971, p. 80). Also I. Friss, the late *éminence grise* of Hungarian political economists, has drawn attention to the apparent consensus prevailing in 1949–1950 that coordination of economic policies and national economic plans would be the main instrument to reach the definite objective of a solidly integrated economic bloc (Friss 1966, p. 104).[25] Similar ideas have been voiced by J. Szita (Szita 1968, p. 745). J. Sandorski acknowledges the existence of agreements on the forms that the future cooperation among the CPEs should take, but "without hoping for their immediate and complete realization" (Sandorski 1968, p. 571). It is perhaps useful to quote Friss *in extenso:*

During the first phase, approximately the first nine months, the member countries were very much concerned ... about coordinating the industrialization of the socialist countries. The members only stepped down when it became evident that, under the then-existing conditions, this road could no longer be followed, and then concentrated mainly on coordinating industrialization ... by means of foreign trade. [Friss 1966, pp. 103–104].

If another interpretation of the CMEA's origin is warranted on the basis of this admittedly veiled evidence, the above quotation raises three questions: When were these nine months, what plans existed, and what were the then-existing conditions that compelled the members to concentrate mainly on bilateral trade agreements?

Taking the April 1949 Council Session as marking the beginning of practical work (Mirosnicenko 1968, p. 84), Friss's dating would mean that the span of active work of the Council was extended up to the end of 1949 or the beginning of 1950. Unfortunately, not much is known about CMEA meetings in early 1950. The formal decision-making body, the Council Session, did not officially meet between August 1949 and late 1950, the precise date of the latter meeting remaining something of an enigma.[26] Kaser reports on a "highly secret" meeting of party leaders at Hollóháza (Kaser 1967, p. 234) in November 1950 to which there are no other known references. This second high-level meeting in Hungary apparently formulated the bases of the so-called revised medium-term industrialization plans, which slated very ambitious targets especially for heavy industry, and the closer cooperation in support of the Korean War effort.

M. Čížkovský provides another piece of unconfirmed, previously undisclosed, evidence. His narrative includes a reference to a 10 January 1950 meeting in Moscow. He refers to this as the "third session," but it is unclear whether this pertains to the Council, the Bureau, some meeting of party leaders, or what. Although rather important decisions were apparently reached there, the author concludes that "with this meeting, the activities of the CMEA were terminated for the next three years without, however, a final decision having been taken on the crucial question of plan coordination as put forward in the program accepted during the first Council Session" (Cizkovsky 1971, p. 56). If this hint is genuine, it cannot refer to a meeting of the official Council Session. But it tends to corroborate Friss's dating and may also support Kaser's speculation that the termination of the Council's activities ensued from fundamental disagreements about the actual ways and means of integrating the East European countries.

The second problem of the report by Friss can be partly solved by means of other sources, whereas the third was already tentatively settled in detail in section 1 and will be examined further in section 4. An examination of the Council's ostensible purposes and activities during that early period is now in order.

It is interesting that an unreferenced quotation by B. Kiesewetter confirms some points of Sulzberger's communication and some parts of what will follow below. According to this unreferenced information, the East European countries had decided "to coordinate their economic plans, to work out common investment and production programs according to the needs of each country and in respect of each country's natural and historical conditions" (Kiesewetter 1960, p. 52).[27]

The most detailed information about the Council's early history has been disclosed by M. Čížkovský. In spite of a few minor weak points in his exposition of the events, the interpretation of what may have occurred seems wholly plausible:

the prerequisites for organizing supranational unified planning were to all intents and purposes created as a result of the decision to coordinate the plans; the main goal was the gradual planned elimination of all attributes of the national economic units. Therefore, a supranational system negating absolute state sovereignty should have ensued. [Cizkovsky 1970, p. 254].

This is, of course, fully compatible with the attempts to impose unity on the area in the late 1950s and early 1960s, but it also brings entirely new elements into the discussion about the original intentions and decisions of the Council, as perhaps indicated in the purported "founding treaty" (Brabant 1979), referred to above.

According to this narrative, the Council's goals and instruments were agreed upon in 1949 on the initiative of Rumania and the USSR (Cizkovsky 1971, p. 54). This is a baffling statement because Rumania at that time did not figure prominently in the integration discussions, and it seems unlikely that it played a more important role in the CMEA's gestation than, say, Czechoslovakia or Poland.[28] Whoever initiated the Moscow meeting, the following points were in the minutes of the "founding session" – presumably January 1949 (Cizkovsky 1971, p. 55; Mirosnicenko 1968, p. 91):[29] (1) Consensus was reached about the construction of common plans on one aspect or another of the reciprocal economic relations of the members, as well as the coordination of the national plans so as to promote regional specialization and cooperation; (2) trade plans for important commodities were to be dovetailed; (3) plans to enlarge the transport and transit facilities were to be worked out jointly in order to keep pace with the growth of other economic relations; (4) directions for extending mutual aid to offset or to counteract the effects of the boycott and the discrimination of the capitalist countries at the behest of the United States were agreed upon in principle, if not in all details; (5) the institution of multilateral clearing and the perfection of exchange rates were considered crucial elements in the gradual implementation of SEI; (6) the development of all-round scientific-technical cooperation was to be envigorated; and (7) control of the execution of the planned cooperation was to be in the hands of the Council's Bureau. These points are essentially confirmed, albeit in fewer words and with less precision, by the authoritative CMEA historians (Faddeev 1974b, pp. 59–60; Lukin 1974, pp. 45–47).

During the first official Council Session (Moscow, 26–28 April 1949), in which economic, political, and government delegations from the members participated, the basic tasks of the Council were laid down as follows (Cizkovsky 1971, p. 55): (1) aspects of foreign trade to enlarge the scope of mutual interaction; (2) questions of trade with capitalist countries; (3) the issues of instituting regional prices, multilateral clearing, and the coordination of foreign trade intentions; (4) the coordination of economic plans, particularly of production plans for important industrial products and primary goods in short supply; (5) the continuous elaboration of solutions to key questions of economic reconstruction; and (6) questions of technical aid, scientific-technical cooperation, and standardization. Although not fully identical with the unsuccessful project of Polish-Czechoslovak cooperation, it should be pointed out, incidentally, that most of these issues closely paralleled it, even in some details (Spulber 1957, pp. 427–428). This casts further doubt on the aforementioned suggestion that the participants in the January conference were completely unaware of what was in the offing. The fact that none of the fundamental issues appears to have been settled at this early date does not necessarily disprove the very earnest desire, at least on the part of some members, to amalgamate Eastern Europe under the umbrella of a common, integrated economic policy.

According to well-informed sources, the only apparent result of this meeting was an agreement to establish a permanent "central working apparatus," called the Bureau of the Council, which would be supported by a technical secretariat. This forerunner of the present Secretariat was to consist of 38 specialists and 36 auxiliary members (Cizkovsky 1971, p. 56). How they would be able to settle the wide range of complex matters outlined above is baffling (Friss 1974, pp. 2–3), all the more so because these active functionaries would be allotted to three groups, supervising: (1) individual economic branches (metallurgy, mining, machine building, energy, light industry, transport, and agriculture); (2) single economic topics (questions of balancing trade in nonessential goods, finance, foreign exchange and trade, planning and statistics, and legal problems); and (3) specific aspects of bilateral consultations. This intended structure of the Bureau's secretariat (see below) would imply that on the average at most two specialists were to be responsible for any of the myriad problems listed above. It may be suspected, although there is unfortunately no evidence to verify the conjecture, that the permanent functionaries were probably slated to become the chiefs of research and administration with a subordinate staff located in the CPEs.

Rather than relying exclusively on the highest organ – the formal Council Session – which officially consisted of two delegates from each member country and a small staff of advisers (Faddeev 1974b, p. 64; Lukin 1974, p. 46), the first CMEA Session set up a Bureau of the Council, whose tasks consisted chiefly of preparing projects, proposals, and recommendations that were to be discussed during the plenary meetings of the Council. If these drafts were endorsed, the Bureau was also placed in charge of overseeing their implementation. Regular sessions were to be convened every quarter but, if need be, formal gatherings could be called more frequently on the request of any member (Lukin 1974, pp. 46–47). The Bureau also had the duty of overseeing the activities of the specialists and subordinate staff, who constituted the Bureau's secretariat (Cizkovsky 1971, p. 56; Fiumel 1967, p. 12). This was the only permanent Council organ until much later, and was composed of at least one representative from each member. According to one source, its authority was confined to taking decisions on "organizational matters" (Fiumel 1967, p. 13), although others seem to indicate that this organ was invested with a more far-reaching mandate (see above and Cizkovsky 1971, pp. 56–59).

In fact, it appears that the Bureau and its staff were originally created to perform the tasks eventually assigned, respectively, to the Executive Committee (created in 1962) and the Secretariat (established during the fourth CMEA Session in 1954). In other words, the Bureau was expected chiefly to prepare detailed background materials and recommendations for negotiations during the top-level policy meetings. According to Čížkovský, the following were the main traits of the Bureau's authority and activities. First, it was an executive arm of the Council Session, at whose request it prepared the formal meetings, directed the working apparatus, elaborated background materials for the plenary sessions, controlled the implementation of the Council decisions, and so on. Second, it was entrusted with the preparation of revised solutions to questions that failed to be resolved or endorsed by the Council Session. Finally, it was also called upon to direct and oversee the other specialized organs of the Council (e.g., the Committee for the Coordination of Trade with Capitalist Countries).

As reported above, the first Council Session had an astoundingly comprehensive agenda, and it is perhaps not surprising that apparently no concrete agreements could be reached on the very difficult problems at hand. Unlike the first Session with its excessively wide range of problems, the second one in Sofia (25–27 August 1949) seems to have endorsed a number of concrete solutions. The agenda contained: (1) questions of foreign trade and the creation of multilateral clearing, which was slated for introduction in 1950; (2) the most promising forms of scientific-technical cooperation, which was to be free of charge and worked out in bilateral commissions; and (3) questions of normalization and standardization of production, statistics, and the like (Cizkovsky 1971, p. 56). Although it is not said explicitly, it may be inferred that no acceptable solution was reached on the first topic, though a "first variant of multilateral clearing" had been discussed in detail; the meeting hammered out "the principal positions, which were to form the fundamental basis of instituting multilateral clearing and guaranteeing its normal functioning" (Mazanov 1970, p. 45). This suggests that the countries involved unanimously accepted the principle of multilateral clearing as the chief instrument for transacting future trade. Furthermore, Mazanov's note states that only a few details of the multilateral clearing scheme were left open to further deliberations. Unfortunately, as with so many of the documents of that period, no further details are available on how this multilateralization of regional trade and payments was envisioned to function. On the second and third points of the second Session's agenda, more information is available as specific recommendations were adopted regarding the free exchange of scientific-technical information and the norming and standardization of production, trade, and statistics to promote specialization (see Chapter 4). Also a few specific agreements were signed on specialization in ball bearings, the organization of railway freight shipment, and other "minor" issues (Lukin 1974, pp. 47–48).

The question of multilateralizing trade and related flows was again on the agenda of the mysterious "third" session of 10 January 1950. This was possibly a preparatory consultation for an upcoming Council Session dealing with the problems left over from the second Session; the meeting may have been adjourned abruptly because no unanimous agreement on the questions of multilateralization and plan coordination could be hammered out. The apparent result of this meeting was: (1) the acceptance of means by which mutual trade could be enlarged (on the Bureau's recommendation); (2) the exchange of information regarding the practical realization of multilateral clearing (the Bureau was requested to produce more on this problem); and (3) the coordination of trade with capitalist countries, for which a separate commission was set up as part of the Bureau. As reported, this seems to have signaled the temporary end of the CMEA's activity, though a definite agreement on the more fundamental questions of integration through the coordination of national economic plans had not yet been hammered out. With respect to this enigmatic session, Čížkovský adds that it "was certainly not known [at the time] that such questions [plan coordination] would no longer be discussed, or that the activity of the CMEA would come to a complete standstill for the next three years" (Cizkovsky 1971, p. 56). Because the Bureau was a permanent organ in charge of preparing the plenary session, it lost its official purpose in the early 1950s as no meetings dealing with substantive SEI issues were organized thereafter for a very long time and its small staff was further reduced (Lukin 1974, p. 53). But this does not imply that the Bureau – as distinct from the Council Session – was dissolved or reduced to complete inactivity.

In January 1950 it was by no means clear that work on the more fundamental issue of plan coordination would no longer be deemed necessary. According to the available evidence, in the first half of 1950 the Bureau continued to execute its mandate by revising the proposal on the principles and practice of plan coordination in preparation for the third Council Session, which following several postponements, was slated for May 1950, but was in fact not convened until November 1950. When this Session suddenly chose to restrict debate to questions of foreign trade – apparently in accordance with the decision to step up industrialization and armaments production – this appeared to be a totally unexpected move for the Bureau. One of the topics discussed, in spite of other, more important, items on the agenda, was the basis of regional price formation in the light of the rapid inflation of raw material prices on world markets (Huber 1974, p. 9), which resulted in the acceptance of stop prices for regional trade and eventually matured into the system of so-called socialist world market prices (WMPs).

Sometime in mid-1950 – note the outbreak of the Korean War on 25 June 1950, a conflict that appears to have played a crucial role in molding integration options (Kohlmey 1974, p. 31) – the Soviet Union abruptly ceased to support the Bureau's work program and general mandate. Henceforth, the Bureau's ostensible mission was divided into functions belonging to the USSR's sphere of interest and those concerning the other members. While the Bureau concentrated on isolated, relatively unimportant problems of cooperation among the remaining members (Lukin 1974, pp. 47–53), the USSR established its "embassy system" of meddling in the other countries' affairs directly and through bilateral consultations (Cizkovsky 1970, p. 249; 1971, p. 60). As a member of the CMEA Bureau at that time, Ausch confirms this as follows:

It may seem anachronistic to apply our *ex post* judgment to the period in question. It is, however, a fact that during the first months of the CMEA's functioning, its working apparatus started its practical activity on the basis of principles much similar to what seems adequate in our days. Stalin, however, intervened and, by referring to the principle of national sovereignty . . . put an end to the activities of the CMEA apparatus in this field. He proposed a different solution, resting partly on autonomous national decisions and partly on bilateral agreements. [Ausch 1972, p. 44]

For all practical purposes, then, the CMEA's activities came to a virtual standstill from mid-1950 to 1954. Although one commonly finds references to the Bureau's role in coordinating trade plans during that period, this seems to apply to the coordination of a few selected, important products because the actual elaboration of bilateral (and some trilateral) trade and payments agreements was reserved for bargaining sessions of trade commissions of pairs of socialist countries. The Bureau and its staff may have supplied some information and assistance to speed up these negotiations, but its role in the actual process of decision making on foreign trade seems to have been confined, indeed (Lukin 1974, p. 53). The Bureau's activities were on the whole probably restricted to rather unimportant organizational matters such as the standardization of trade and payments agreements, statistical uniformity, the working out of general conditions for delivery, and so on (Savov 1973a, p. 120; Lukin 1974, pp. 50–53). In I. Friss's sarcastic words: "Given but little rein to their fantasy, the functionaries of the [Bureau] advised each socialist country to cultivate rice, cotton, and to substitute rubber for Russian dandelions" (Friss 1974, p. 3).

4. The Council's nadir in retrospect

Looking back at the early history of the CMEA, it seems paradoxical that under Stalin the USSR certainly had the power, but apparently not the perseverance and possibly the will to enjoin substantial economic unity in Eastern Europe, if not outright annexation. As it transpired much later under Chruščëv, the USSR seems to have had the determination but not the power to impose the then-coveted regional cohesion.[30] East European integration, as defined here, has remained an elusive dream up to the present.

From the guesswork, conjectures, and contradictory evidence introduced above, one cannot but retain the impression that the CMEA's creation in 1949 continues to be a curious and largely unexplained manifestation of Stalin's postwar policy with respect to Eastern Europe. Did Stalin really wish to facilitate collaboration among the leaders of the area so soon after he had squashed all attempts at political and economic federation in Central and Southeastern Europe? Or did he wish to set up an ostensible counterpart to the Marshall Plan and the newly founded OEEC? Was it all window dressing designed to mislead the outside world about acrid intramural discussions, while Stalin continued to deal separately with his allies and to discourage strong contacts among them, especially if these might entail political consequences – a possible outcome of the dovetailing of long-term economic plans through bilateral negotiations? These are a selection of the many unsolved questions about the USSR's postwar policies. The above analysis of the record leads to the inescapable conclusion that no unequivocal answer can be provided until the archives of the frustrating and frustrated discussions of that period become available, if the gist of and the diversity spawned by these deliberations were put on paper at all.[31]

From some of the points developed in section 1, it is very easy to construct a plausible explanation of why the Council ceased to function so soon after its foundation. In fact, attributing the CMEA's creation to a combination of pure propaganda, the boycott of Yugoslavia, a show of apparent unity, the countering of the Marshall Plan and the Western embargo, and the like already presupposes the Council's futility because it is presumed that this institution was not created to deal with urgent economic problems. The absence of authentic documentary evidence does not, of course, disprove the existence of such motives, nor does it help to prove conclusively that the objectives were perhaps more economic in nature than is commonly granted.

In order to explain the CMEA's nadir, Wiles contends that: "Precisely because it was a formal body, established by treaty,[32] with a democratic constitution based on national sovereignty and international equality, Stalin did not much use the CMEA" (Wiles 1968, p. 314). This explanation raises two questions. First, the ever-present emphasis on sovereignty, democracy, and international equality in all future dealings between the USSR and Eastern Europe did not prevent Stalin – or his successors for that matter – from actively encouraging the emergence of asymmetrical relations in Eastern Europe. Second, the issue at stake is not *how* integration was allegedly organized. Stalin most certainly abhorred formalized democratic bodies with protracted debates by which the course of Soviet policy could be affected, however remotely, though there is just not enough evidence to support Wiles's conjecture that the Council was intended to become a fully democratic body overseeing regional integration. The real issue is *why* integration was not vigorously pursued and why the early tasks of the CMEA were abandoned so suddenly. In this respect, the preceding deductions are not very illuminating. The Ždanov-Voznesenskij type of argument, as presented by Kaser, is extremely attractive. Accordingly, the CMEA's efforts may have come to a virtual standstill for two reasons. First, the Council was created as a compromise to forces competing for economic control over the region, a temporary manifestation of disunity among the CPE leaders (Skubiszewski 1966, pp. 545–547). Pending the resolution of the political diversity, Stalin allowed the Council to proceed while he was facing the need to do away with both of his alleged opponents (A. A. Ždanov died in 1948 and N. A. Voznesenskij was arrested in March 1949) and their influence (as Gosplan director, Voznesenkij attempted to implement improvements in the Soviet economy; after his removal, some reform elements, such as the 1949 price revision, were indeed reversed). While market-type policies may have been perceived as potentially weakening central power, it is by no means certain that the young Gosplan director was removed solely because of his "heretical" economic principles.[33] Second, Stalin may have been unable to operate an apparatus that would eventually function on the basis of scarcity principles, rather than on political expediency, and therefore scrapped the CMEA's potential role in favor of tight bilateral consultations and direct controls. The latter is an attractive explanation, for it fits nicely into the pattern of Byzantine policy making so pervasive in the Stalin era.

Although the above approach would support the case for drawing up plans on the basis of comparative costs and multilateral exchange, among others, by means of common currency arrangements (see Kaser 1967, p. 35), there is just too little unalloyed evidence on the earlier debates to suggest that such a future was actually contemplated as the mainstay of the CMEA. In fact, it should be recalled that at least Czechoslovakia, Hungary, and the USSR had already embarked on detailed, strictly centralized, medium-term plans, which relied on direct assignments and controls. Furthermore, all other members were at the time frantically preparing the inauguration of medium-term planning (Polienko 1960, pp. 14–15). The proposals favoring efficient multilateral specialization may have made an important contribution to the broad outline of future developments in the region, but they can hardly have been conceived as the sole foundation for the formulation and implementation of plans.[34] To the extent that the reports quoted in section 3 are specific at all, the 1949–1950 discussions seem to have gravitated chiefly around the very involved problem of how to settle integration through plan coordination and trade in spite of embargoes, considerable differences in levels of development, and other inclement circumstances.

Considering the ideological importance of central planning, the debates of the late 1940s probably centered more on how to derive an integrated program from the coordination of national plans than on how to link the CPEs efficiently, although there is not enough conclusive evidence to support this logical inference. In any case, SEI through plan coordination or by means of market-type relations would have required careful preparation for which the general political, strategic, and economic environment at the time was hardly propitious.

The arguments developed here point to mid-1950 as the time of the decisive turn of events. Although Voznesenskij's ideas may have been debated during the January 1949 conference, there is no evidence to suggest that real market-type specialization was on the agenda at all during the 1949–1950 conferences. Also, it should not be forgotten that this founding conference was chaired by the orthodox Stalinist M. Suslov and that the participating economic chiefs (e.g., Imre Vajda, Hilary Minc, Ernö Gerö, and others) were aiming at total control of their respective economies. The topical discussions probably gravitated on how to organize economic relations among centrally administered economies. Because the debates were so protracted and requirements mounted for more heavy industry and armaments in support of the Korean War and in preparation for the expected third world conflict, which was deemed imminent and inevitable, Stalin probably halted all further discussions and reverted to the immediate postwar tactics of dealing separately with the East European countries (Ausch 1972, p. 44). In this climate, there was some ground for suspecting the reliability of the strategic cordon on the Western front in the event of a confrontation and, under the circumstances, it may have proved more effective to institute direct bilateral controls, rather than to prolong the search for regional integration on the basis of a rational division of labor.

Today it seems wrong, however, to conclude that SEI was originally scheduled to take root mainly through the coordination of long-term trade plans. Certainly, these agreements helped, if only indirectly, to lay the foundations of some of the main branches of industry of the CPEs, but it would be remiss to say that this was in fact what was contemplated ex ante. The first long-term trade plans were hardly more than a practical device to tie the individual countries to the immediate interests of the USSR in its quest for supremacy and hegemony over the region. In fact, detailed long-term trade agreements between the smaller countries do not seem to have existed at least until 1952, and even then they were not in the rigid and comprehensive format typical of more recent agreements (Lukin 1974, p. 50).

Whether at that time the countries simply found it expedient or inevitable to settle for a minimum of dovetailed cooperation by way of detailed ex ante bilateral trade agreements – perhaps a strategic retreat for fear of arousing domestic and regional political repercussions – is of little import to the gradual evolvement of intrasocialist economic cooperation. However, from a more systemic point of view, the issue is not uninteresting. The above analyses, which will be further elaborated below, have hopefully demonstrated that the efforts aimed at working out regional cooperation for all practical purposes foundered. In any case, it appears very presumptuous to characterize the Council's establishment in 1949 as "the necessary result of the formation of a new type of international economic relations and the natural culmination of the aspiration of the [CPEs] for very tight economic and scientific-technical cooperation and the intended emergence of all-round coordination of the national economic plans" (Barcak 1974, p. 4).

The main point of view advanced here may be reconciled with the more traditional, noneconomic interpretation of the CMEA's creation by distinguishing between the short- and long-term interests of the USSR and by recognizing the real economic needs of its partners. There is very little doubt that the USSR's short-term interests were vested in accelerated economic reconstruction and relentless industrialization at home on the one hand, and in ensconcing Eastern Europe into an ideologically and militarily strong bloc that would keep the West at bay on the other. These objectives could be reached partly by mobilizing all resources of the region and promoting Soviet-type growth. However, when it became evident that no coordinated plan serving the immediate Soviet interests could be harnessed, the embassy system of economic cooperation may have better suited the leading partner's real or imagined needs (Brezinski 1978, p. 30).

The long-term interests of the USSR in this matter of economic cooperation were most likely vested, as they are now, in the integration of Eastern Europe into a strong interwoven economic, strategic, and political union. These interests could have been better served by fostering genuine growth in Eastern Europe under the USSR's guidance than by total control over the East European countries, which developed in virtual estrangement from one another. To this end, efficient economic relations, not only in CMEA cooperation, but also within each of the CPEs taken separately, might have proved instrumental, and certainly of more lasting value than the autarkic economic policies that actually emerged.

5. Concluding remarks

Although much of what occurred during the early phases of the CMEA's history still remains enigmatic, an attempt was made to show that: (1) The Council's original mandate did not gravitate around the ostensible need for propaganda and the organization did not emerge solely as a result of imitative fervor; (2) active discussions about real economic integration continued at least until early 1950; (3) long-term trade agreements were not considered as the basic instrument and surely not as the only mechanism for the implementation of genuine integration among the CPEs; (4) throughout the period 1949–1954, the USSR permitted the Council's Bureau to deal with selected practical projects of minor importance, but admittedly not with the more fundamental questions of SEI; and (5) the virtual standstill of the Council was codetermined by exogenous events such as the Cold War, the Korean conflict, and the imminence of a new global military confrontation.

This chapter has hopefully provided a few important leads toward a more positive appraisal of the founding years of the Council, though the evidence is insufficient to conclude that the top-level negotiations at the time aimed at the creation of genuine integration in Eastern Europe. There is indeed neither the comprehensive archival material nor the adequate body of reliable circumstantial evidence to prove beyond doubt that the Council's creation was unconditionally acclaimed, as recent interpretations of the earlier decisions would have us believe: "The January declaration became an important historical landmark in the practical realization of the basic Marxist-Leninist idea of international unity – a close union and rallying of the workers from all countries who chose the course of constructing a new social system" (Sirjaev 1974, p. 5). The author of this quotation, presently the director of CMEA's economic research institute (see Chapter 4), may have confounded the actual policies in Eastern Europe with what might have been accomplished had the initial plans not been aborted. As shown in Chapters 2 and 3, the failure to inaugurate SEI was of singular importance in the economic policies pursued by the CPEs in the 1950s and continues to play some role in current discussions about SEI. Although it is certainly useful to reevaluate at some interval our perception of historical events, the above analysis has three more practical bearings for the rest of the study. First, in many of the current debates about the goals and forms of SEI, one can detect subtle, and at times abstruse, references to past experiences, and a better understanding of the latter's historical setting may therefore help to unravel sometimes baffling contemporary controversies. Second, many of the institutional "innovations" introduced or attempted in the CMEA since the early 1960s seem to bear close resemblance to projects that were hatched and debated at some length from the outset of the cooperation process in Eastern Europe, but could not come to fruition; or if given a definite shape in these inaugural discussions, they could not be implemented until more recently. Finally, a better understanding of what actually misfired during Stalin's reign may be highly instructive in formulating more appropriate policy alternatives even at the present, as will be investigated later on.

2

Salient features of domestic economic developments

The confused economic events dominating economic policy concerns in the East European countries in 1945–1948 were embedded more in apprehensions about countering the legacies of the war and postwar settlements, than in working out imaginative blueprints for steady long-term economic expansion. Nonetheless, the latter became of prime importance once the political situation in these countries was under control and the urgent problems of postwar reconstruction and stabilization receded into the background. How to combat effectively the economic backwardness and the burden of agrarian overpopulation inherited from the past, and to marshal all available resources toward this development goal became the focal point of political choice at the time.

Unfortunately, as described in the preceding chapter, the initiatives aimed at working out a common strategy to buttress rapid economic growth anchored to vigorous industrialization, preferably through joint efforts, foundered. As far as the tasks and forms of possible regional cooperation are concerned, the debates of 1949–1950 failed to clarify the issues at stake and offered but marginal ideas on how development without a broadly based cooperative effort could be achieved. Nevertheless, most countries lacked sufficient indigenous resources (both capital and skilled manpower) to accelerate autonomously the pace of economic development. A substantial amount of investment goods and many types of essential raw materials would therefore have to be procured from abroad. Furthermore, their internal markets were too small to warrant a dissipation of scarce resources into building up the foundations for steady growth in isolation. A more rational participation in world trade could enable these countries to exploit their natural and embodied advantages. Yet, owing to the Western embargo, the perceived precarious international political balance, and the severe foreign exchange constraint, the trade horizon of these countries was highly confined.

Although the immediate postwar intergovernmental trade agreements concluded with the USSR helped to relieve the most pressing shortages by providing for deliveries of essential products and some measure of tied credits, the ad hoc narrowly bilateral form of exchange was not conducive to the implementation of ambitious development programs that by necessity had to rely heavily on uncertain trade prospects. The disappointment over the inconclusive high-level discussions on regional cooperation must be placed in perspective against the above backdrop.

The first integration debates centered on the ways and means of coordinating national economic plans (probably also the formulation and implementation of individual plans), among others, with the assistance of instruments of financial and monetary policy. The multilateralization of regional trade, anchored to market-clearing prices and realistic exchange rates, was considered an institutional setting superior to the bilateral trade policies implemented since the war and, incidentally, also a powerful mechanism of galvanizing the rather dismal developments in the period between the two world wars. By suitably combining planning with instruments of indirect coordination, at least some of the leaders hoped eventually to draw together the disparate economies into an effective, closely knit community. Though no wholehearted support for such a comprehensive policy could be found, especially the smaller countries singly or in concert might have been expected to avoid taking energetic measures forestalling the emergence of a balanced, if informal, regional development program (Brabant 1976). However, the domestic economic policies launched with great élan in the late 1940s in fact were fully out of tune with integration requirements. To some degree, at least, this turn of events ensued from long-standing rivalry and suspicion among the leaders of the new CPEs, a historical heritage that was reinforced by Stalin's approach to cooperation.

What distinguishes CPEs from other countries are chiefly the implications of the political and ideological doctrines and convic-

tions of their leadership. In the economic domain, they led to
the emergence of a highly centralized economic model and an
interesting long-term development strategy. Although minor
variations in the implementation of strategy and model in the
several CPEs should not be ignored, the characteristic common
elements taken together represent the core of these countries'
departure from conventional development policies pursued in
MTEs. These common features, rather than the local variations,
are so crucial to a better understanding of the conditions for SEI
that both aspects of postwar development policies will be dealt
with in rather general terms (trade strategy and supporting institutions are examined in detail in Chapter 3). Section 1
presents the general framework of development policies. Section 2 discusses the salient features of the growth strategy
adopted first by the USSR and transferred later to all East European countries. The socialist model of central planning and its
implications are examined in section 3. Finally, the impacts of
the reform movement for strategy and model are outlined in
section 4.

1. The general thrust of development policies

In the immediate postwar period, Eastern Europe devoted most
of its energy to economic reconstruction, the consolidation of socialist supremacy in all parts of society, and the creation of a
climate receptive to major socioeconomic changes. By the end of
the 1940s, these countries were fully in the Soviet sphere of
influence – a process formally completed with the Czechoslovak
coup d'état of early 1948. As the power of the communist parties
became dominant, the social, political, economic, and nearly all
other societal aspects of these countries were gradually molded
into a framework that suited the postwar situation, characterized
as it was by the overwhelming influence of the USSR in Eastern
Europe and its dominating military presence there. Since then,
the region has been typified by an economic policy wedded primarily to rapid economic development through forced industrialization. Industrialization has played a key role in the concept
of socialist development, and the penchant for industrial growth
per se has been a very heavily weighted preference for socialist

policy makers in the sense that, during most of the postwar period, decision making about the overall allocation of resources became almost exclusively geared to the priority role accorded to industry, on which all CPEs were bent. Even now when more or less far-reaching reforms have been or are being introduced (see section 4), industrial growth in breadth and in depth still remains the central anchor of socialist development planning.

The central objective of economic policies in Eastern Europe since the institutionalization of socialism has been the elaboration of a more or less self-reliant economic complex. An apparently very important role in this choice was played by the imposing example of the previous successes in the USSR, as well as the dogmatic ideas that crystallized around these achievements. This proclivity for relative autarky should not, however, be equated with an explicit policy designed to sever completely all contacts with other economies, although at one time a narrowly defined self-sufficiency goal for many sectors of economic activity certainly permeated the socialist concept of the best allocation of resources. One of the weightiest tasks of economic policy in the CPEs is the creation of a well-balanced, widely diversified industrial economy that is relatively independent, directly as well as indirectly, of fluctuations abroad. The strategy adopted by the Soviet policy makers in the 1930s under circumstances in which there was apparently no other possible choice than that of autarkic development in order to provide for independence from the hostile capitalist world and to ensure self-protection, was for a long time the accepted example of how to achieve a mature socialist economy, regardless of the specific conditions for growth. This development concept was transplanted into Eastern Europe because it suited immediate Soviet interests and also because the chief mentor of economic policy in the other CPEs could not quickly adapt its own experiences and interests to conditions specific to Eastern Europe, that is, to growth circumstances that inherently differ greatly from those prevailing in the USSR.

To arrive at a proper assessment of the socialist development experience, it is instructive to distinguish between the characteristics of the economic model and the strategy for growth. Although these concepts are interrelated and elements of the two tend to overlap, it will prove convenient, although difficult, to treat them separately so that inferences for the present and future of SEI can be based on clearly defined reference points. This will also prove useful in clarifying the main issues of foreign trade and integration later on.

2. The strategy of economic growth

A growth strategy may be defined as a complex set of interrelated measures designed to mobilize and allocate economic resources with a view toward attaining one or more long-term objectives with the assistance of a number of proper policy instruments, institutions, and behavioral rules. By manipulating the policy instruments and by setting specific behavioral rules through new institutional arrangements, the architects of CPEs attempt to deploy economic resources in such a way that backward, agrarian countries or economies too dependent on "calico industries" will eventually mature into industrial strongholds. Communist doctrine distinguishes here between agrarian, industrial-agrarian or agrarian-industrial, and industrial countries. After the war, the first group included Albania, Bulgaria, Rumania, and Yugoslavia; Hungary, Poland, and the USSR belonged to the second group (with Hungary as industrial-agrarian); while Czechoslovakia and the German Democratic Republic were the only industrial ones.

Formative elements

The elaboration of a standard "socialist industrial basis" in each CPE, irrespective of its specific development potential, has gained a special meaning because it draws heavily on Soviet industrialization practice. Through force of circumstance, the experience of the USSR in the 1930s was held to be the archtype to which all socialist societies should conform. Even countries such as Czechoslovakia and East Germany, where the industrial sector in the presocialist period was already well-entrenched and quite extensive, were called upon to transform their capacities and reanchor them to a strong metallurgical sector, which functions as the motor generating rapid growth elsewhere in the economy. This striving toward a facsimile of Soviet institutions and policies, of course, differs substantially from the advice given to nonsocialist developing countries on the strength of Western economic experience.

Socialist economic organization and detailed target planning of the entire economy were first attempted in the USSR, where political expediency and ideological convictions took ascendancy over the semifeudal Russian society in 1917. Economic matters were not only largely untried, there was not even a modest theoretical model that could inspire the practical contractors of the socialist transformation in shaping the new society into a viable experiment. Though the Bolshevik political victory sought to give the Marxian doctrine a dominant, and at times a monopolistic, position also in the formulation of economic policy, the eclectic economic doctrine officially adhered to was of little practical help in modeling economic priorities. Owing to the scientific socialists' restraint of committing themselves beyond generalities with respect to the economics of the "communist society," the planners had to fill an enormous theoretical vacuum. Although this was certainly a formidable task faced by the Soviet policy makers, the problem surfaced anew when the new socialist countries were set up, owing especially to their substantial differences from the USSR in size, resource endowment, and level of economic maturity.

Although socialist economic policies have essentially been empirical – despite the dogmatic rationalization of practical affairs in theoretical discourses – the CPEs have been slow in adjusting themselves to the needs of actual practice especially once the previous success of Soviet development was rationalized into a formal socialist doctrine, whose theoretical validation is allegedly derived from the analyses and observations on economic development by socialist thinkers, including Marx, Lenin, and Engels (Zauberman 1975, pp. 2–5). Although the Soviet development doctrine was based largely on practical experience, this does not mean, however, that the relentless fostering of industrialization under central guidance in the USSR went uninspired by certain broad concepts and suggestions of the Marxian classics, whose analyses were congenial to the way of thinking in the first socialist state. The origin and key components of Soviet growth doctrine are usually expounded in terms of "development laws" to be respected and adhered to by all socialist societies. Before explaining them, it is worthwhile to digress briefly to clarify the general nature of an economic law in socialist thinking.

The concept of economic law

Economic laws play a key role in East European analyses of and reflections on economic and other events. Their formulation and meaning need to be understood in the context of the framework developed by the preceptors of communism, or borrowed by them from other thinkers, especially nineteenth-century positivism and Hegelian philosophy of history. According to their method of analysis, a law as a cognitive concept signals a general, internal, essential, and necessary relationship between two or more phenomena of nature, the human mind, the economy, society, and so on, which is presumed to be stable in the sense that it will be reproduced under identical circumstances.

Laws of economic development or production should, however, be differentiated from, say, legal prescriptions or physical laws. Instead of being normative (as in legal principles) or truly objective (as in physics), an economic law can only exist through human activity. Whereas the laws of production, for instance, are evidently everywhere the same, by themselves they are not at all laws of nature; some are steeped in technological requirements while others depend on limitations of human capacity and psychology, or they are conditioned by the prevailing institutional, political, and ideological environment. The essential feature of socialist development doctrine is that the socialist economy can dispense with the negative aspects of some laws of capitalism (such as exploitation and imperialism) and that man can and should master these phenomena of human nature in full awareness and in better understanding of his own behavior and role in historical development.

On the basis of historical materialism, Marx and his followers regard history and all human society as inherently determined by laws that, like physical laws, cannot be altered by human interference, though the economic laws of socialism are not deterministic: Historical development, while independent of human preferences, occurs through man's activity and man can, that is, he is free to, act according to or against these laws. A crucial aspect of this philosophy is that, in a historical dimension, man will reflect these laws and benefit from knowing them if he recognizes and masters them, and acts accordingly. This is what is meant by the "freedom to understand historical necessity." Through the knowledge and recognition of these laws, man will be able to transcend isolated and in some ways superficial appearances – a crucial step toward comprehending the inner essence of his own behavior.[1]

The laws of socialist doctrine are prescriptions of how society ought to develop to its own historical destiny as discerned by the Marxist-Leninist, at times changing, perceptions of historical evolution. This is an important point, for new laws or new interpretations of established ones are occasionally formulated to validate shifts in actual policies. Thus, the recently codified "law of the ISDL" and "law of SEI" differ appreciably from past formulations (and, incidentally, they are also at considerable odds with past practices). It can hardly be true that the present versions result exclusively from the constant enrichment of human knowledge of economic phenomena (as argued, for example, in Dudinskij 1970 and Ladygin 1973).[2]

Perhaps most important is that these socialist prescriptions are considered universally applicable, regardless of palpable differences and changes in knowledge, resource endowments, production capacities, and the like – all of which are supposedly subsidiary, if not altogether irrelevant, to the formulation of plans and concrete measures in observance of the basic laws of development. Acting according to these laws depends upon a recognition and understanding of historical necessity. But application of these principles to speed up historical development is quite another matter, and it is in this context that several knotty problems appear. Especially crucial for actual CPE policies, as distinct from more philosophical discourses, is that in molding and guiding economic activity, compliance with these laws ought to be based on one type of understanding only, notably that of the *primus inter pares*. The basic principles underlying the interpretation and application of these laws are still formidable forces to be reckoned with in understanding the at times quite convoluted interpretation and rationalization of actual policy measures, even though the formulation of economic policies in contemporary CPEs is now inspired by greater circumspection and characterized more by flexibility (Friss 1971, 1977).

The basic laws of socialist development

The intellectual foundations of the socialist development strategy can be outlined in three basic Marxist-Leninist propositions on economic development: (1) the eschatological goal of historical development, (2) the material-technical foundations of this development, and (3) the means by which the foundations can be gradually solidified. Though Marxian analyses were borrowed in support of empirically built-up principles in the Soviet Union, a brief restatement of the antecedents may help in understanding the ideological constraints under which the newly founded CPEs conceived their development path.

The distant, yet ultimate, objective of socialist growth is the realization of the so-called communist welfare state, a society in which each is rewarded according to his needs and each contributes according to his abilities. To attain it, even if only in a remote future, socialist policies must aim at as high a growth rate as possible, particularly by elaborating and extending the material and technical prerequisites of communism. Each CPE must therefore produce as large and as diverse a selection of products as feasible, so as to meet present and future needs to the greatest extent possible. In the immediate postwar years, this task was understood to imply that each CPE should aim at a relatively self-sufficient economy. Especially in the context of the "developed socialist society" it is now stressed that the diversity of output should be procured also through wider participation in international trade.

To embark on this growth path, the law of planned proportional development must be applied and adhered to. The communist welfare state will eventually be achieved, accordingly, by centrally planning, guiding, and controlling all-round growth in order to steer a smooth course toward the final objective. The qualification "proportional" needs some clarification. Unlike most nonsocialist theories of balanced growth, the doctrine of proportional development under socialism must be placed in the context of unbalanced growth, as propounded inter alia by A. O.

Hirschman (Hirschman 1958, pp 65–75), or of disharmonious growth, as outlined by J. Kornai (Kornai 1971, 1972). Actually, there might be some misunderstanding about the definition of what is balanced and what is not.[3] If the inherited economic structure is unbalanced, an unbalanced economic policy might be required to force the economy in the direction of the proper growth path of harmonious development. From development experiences of the CPEs, one may indeed conclude that the leaders have attempted to attain a high rate of growth by overcoming consciously and unconsciously induced disequilibria; the mobilization of resources to open up such new bottlenecks served to sustain the next growth phase.

One important instance in which socialist policy makers looked to Marx for support of empirically built-up principles is the third law, which says that the first department in the Marxian reproduction scheme should grow faster than the second; it also requires that growth of one component of the first department should at all times exceed that of the rest of the economy. A brief digression on Marx's model may elucidate this. Marx divided the economy into two principal departments: that of the means of production, or capital goods, and that of the means of consumption, or consumer goods. The sector of producer goods is further divided into capital goods for producing more capital goods and capital goods for producing consumer goods. According to this compartmentalization, maximal growth should be achieved through the faster growth of the capital goods sector with the side constraint that the production of capital goods for producing more capital goods should accelerate at least at the same rate. Without going into details, suffice it to state that this proposition rests on the belief that the expanding economy, as understood by Marx, depends critically on a characteristic increase in the "organic composition of capital," meaning that created factors of production will play an ever-growing role in sustaining steady growth.

In focusing on the strategic precept of growth propulsion, Marx's scheme of long-term growth – the first comprehensive modeling effort with some degree of rigor in the evolution of economic thought – articulated the Soviet stand on industrialization well. Translated into more familiar terminology, the socialist growth doctrine focuses primarily on the acceleration of a few crucial economic sectors especially as a result of injecting capital goods made possible through involuntary savings. Accordingly, growth efforts of the CPEs have been directed particularly at steadily enlarging the various sectors of heavy industry producing energy, metals, chemical products, construction materials, and machines. In this, the engineering sector – the industry of industries – has received particular attention as the backbone of socialist development.

Implications

Even though the development principles embraced by the architects of the CPEs are only a rationalization or justification of pragmatic choices, they in themselves suggest some momentous implications of actual economic policies. These features are important in view of the fact that a realistic interpretation of desirable policy measures was preempted by certain dogmatic ideas, which considered the road and methods of Soviet economic development to be the sole and eternally valid model of socialist progress.

First, the growth strategy focuses on the most important links in the process of developing backward economies. Under circumstances such as those prevalent in the USSR, the strategic choices could be confined to a narrow range of processes, and planning institutions and instruments (i.e., the economic model) would support this. It is therefore not surprising that the CPEs have generally opted for a dual technology: sophisticated production methods with a relatively high capital-to-labor ratio in the locomotive sectors, while other activities received much less attention or had to be operated on the basis of existing, outmoded technologies with a low capital-to-labor ratio. Priority development in selected sectors also calls for establishing large enterprises to capture economies of scale and the advantages of mechanization and automation. Moreover, available equipment must be operated continuously, whenever feasible, until beyond repair as by far the larger share of disposable investment funds is earmarked for extending industry in breadth, not in depth. This strategic choice has entailed a predominantly extensive course of economic development in the sense that growth is sought primarily from new ventures to attain eventually a "well-balanced" industrial economy.[4] Efficiency considerations as such are not important in the determination of the CPE's structure, an attitude that is reinforced by the chosen model.

Another implication of the strategy is the gradual improvement in the quality of human capital – a factor that is frequently neglected in appraisals of socialist developments. The lack of an educated and solid, technically trained labor force was a severe bottleneck in the period between the two wars and this could be surmounted either through formal education or by attracting unskilled labor to the factory and investing in massive training on the job. Because socialism calls for rapid development per se with full employment, the first alternative was initially not viable. Instead, industry absorbed labor indiscriminately, partly to lessen the capital constraint, but also because the factor was not considered scarce. This behavior has entailed a wasteful utilization of labor resources. Nevertheless, the policy has had its advantages as well. The rush toward a more or less self-sufficient economy has enabled the policy makers of CPEs to reap substantial social benefits from large-scale and diverse practical experience. Especially in the least developed CPEs, forced industrialization has enabled the socialist leaders to inculcate industrial discipline in those workers who only recently joined the pool of wage earners, mainly from agrarian activities. This has not only permitted the elimination of possibly severe sociological bottlenecks to further swift economic expansion, but has also enabled the policy makers to support extensive expansion by injecting capital and labor simultaneously, thereby shifting the production locus and deferring the decelerating growth prospects likely to occur when operating under diminishing returns from factor substitution.

Perhaps the most important implication, at least in the present context, is that in the new development programs inaugurated at the end of the 1940s, the possibilities offered by foreign economic cooperation and the bitter lessons of the years between the two world wars were not taken into consideration as, once again, the region reverted to autarkic development, in some cases buttressed by strident nationalism. Although this policy brought rapid and historically very significant industrial expansion, it could not avoid serious contradictions and tensions, which cast a shadow over many well-meant endeavors and impressive achievements, and hindered the full exploitation of these countries' development potential. If not a direct consequence of patterning development strategies after the basic laws, the lack of coordination of national growth efforts and the particular twist of the actual policies pursued emerged to a large extent from a myopic application of Marxist-Leninist precepts.

Because strategy and model are considerably interdependent, other implications of socialist development impinging on the strategy will be taken up after exposing the salient features of the organization and decision making in traditional CPEs.

An evaluation

Reflecting on the development strategy, it should be pointed out that the interpretation of the propositions on historical evolution is essentially relative. The analyses of Marx and Lenin do not tell the student much about the kind of economic policy choices the East European leaders made or were forced to make. Although those in command of CPEs usually take great pains to interpret and justify their actions by reference to Marx and Lenin, this is mostly no more than rationalization after the event. The goal of achieving communism, whatever its meaning, is something socialist leaders can make ritual obeisance to, but their real preoccupations have grown out of more immediate and practical problems, though adaptations to local circumstances and changing conditions, until recently, have had to be kept to a strict minimum, if such desirable deviations from the Soviet doctrine could be envisaged at all.

Eastern Europe after the war was indeed a very disparate region comprising several dissimilar countries. The relatively poor resource endowment, the narrow base of skilled human resources, the substantial differences in development level, and other circumstances ought to have led to a realistic adaptation of the Soviet strategy to local conditions or to the modification of the incidental features of the "laws" in conformity with objective "historical necessities" in the different countries. Instead, an uncritical transplantation of strictly ideological and power-political prescriptions begot considerable inflexibility and waste in the mobilization of scarce resources. This became most apparent in the smaller CPEs, especially those that had already attained an appreciable level of industry when the helm passed into socialist hands (Zauberman 1964). Substantial success, in spite of inefficiency, in the less developed CPEs, especially Bulgaria and Rumania, should not be excluded from the balance sheet (Montias 1967). The gradual disappearance of doctrinal rigidity in the formulation and implementation of growth policies, especially since the mid-1960s, would seem to be the most attractive feature of the economic reform period (see section 4).

The above does not intend to argue the case against industrialization or that socialist growth precepts should be discarded altogether; quite on the contrary. Under normal circumstances, fast and stable growth can only be attained through industrial expansion, provided natural resource endowments, capital and labor resources, consumption levels, and real trade opportunities are not ignored, as they were to a varying extent in the postwar policies. In this connection, it may be useful to distinguish between "extensive" and "intensive" growth, and to relate the socialist prescriptions for the acceleration of industrial expansion to evolving developmental conditions.

The Marxist-Leninist theses on development were formulated during crucial industrialization phases on the European continent, especially in England as far as Marx is concerned and Russia at the turn of the century for Lenin. Their formative environment was the overwhelming reality of the continuous creation of new production facilities. If adapted to local circumstances, there is in principle nothing wrong with pursuing fast capital accumulation in breadth. But where a strong industrial basis is already well-entrenched, the dissipation of funds in all sorts of economic activities without paying heed to the requirements of maintaining and upgrading the existing structure are unlikely to sustain stable growth for a long time.

Where should the dividing line between intensive and extensive growth be drawn?[5] In a theoretical model it can be put this way: It is rational to promote extensive development until the net return in terms of marginal value added for the last unit of expenditure in extensive activity equals the net return in terms of marginal value added from intensive activity. Given the diversity in Eastern Europe, it is intuitive that the net return curve from extensive growth in an underdeveloped CPE such as Rumania, where underutilized labor resources can be absorbed in new units, differs essentially in both location and slope from the same curve in already well-diversified industrial economies such as Czechoslovakia, where there are relatively few opportunities for resource redeployment. If only for that reason, the CPEs should have adopted differentiated development policies.[6]

In retrospect, one may conclude that an important place in the socialist growth strategy is given to amassing production factors in priority sectors, and to allocating most of the current "surplus value" not to present consumption but to the financing of the expansion of selected production sectors, at the expense of other activities (agriculture and services in particular). This implies that consumption in the CPEs could in principle not increase much, and that it could even decline for a few years, as in the early years of socialist industrialization. However, recent events in Eastern Europe have shown that a decline in real per capita consumption is no longer acceptable and there is fierce real wage resistance.

3. The economic model

A growth strategy must be buttressed by an appropriate economic model – the two twin components of the CPEs' economic system. A model in this context may be defined as the combination of institutions, behavioral rules, and policy instruments utilized to implement economic development goals, to assess more or less continually achievements against targets, and when necessary to initiate revisions in current goals. If the model has to support crucial components of the growth strategy according to which a community determines what shall be produced and how the bill of goods attained will be distributed, it is incumbent on the responsible policy makers to modify the model as economic development progresses and alters the size and structure of the economy and, hence, engenders "new" conditions for future expansion. It is especially important to enact timely changes in one or more of the institutions, policy instruments, or behavioral rules when key components of the growth strategy are reinterpreted.

From the salient features of the development strategy, it would seem logical that the CPEs intend their achievements to be assessed essentially in a dynamic perspective. For a traditional CPE, successful development critically depends on building up a development program with a coordinated succession of imbalances, entailing the fast transformation of an underdeveloped economy into a dynamic one. In the framework of general-equilibrium analysis, progress should be encouraged by parceling out production factors among different sectors with a view toward equalizing the social marginal productivity (SMP) from each activity. This notion, however, remains an "empty box" as long as no one succeeds in providing an operational definition and a pertinent measurement of SMP. The socialist strategy proposes a program based on disequilibria and sheer empirical ingenuity. Because a disequilibrium may be interpreted as an indicator of unequal SMPs, the continuous or discrete correction of disparities, perhaps by creating new disequilibria, may be viewed as an integral component of a much more fundamental adjustment process aimed at gradually narrowing sectoral differences in SMPs.

Induced economic disequilibria and empiricism are measures that may successfully stimulate structural change and rapid growth in underdeveloped areas. As the economy progresses and becomes more complex, however, the informal pursuit of disequilibria becomes a costly and inappropriate means of steering toward high growth. Socialist writers call this the gradual exhaustion of extensive growth opportunities and the signal for shifting economic policy in favor of a more intensive exploitation of resources by actively promoting gains in average labor productivity through better management methods, technical and scientific research, rational working methods, intensification of foreign trade, automation, and so on.

From the very beginning of socialist economic organization it has been accepted as axiomatic that socialism implies the effective control of the economy by society in pursuance of its objectives, particularly the full control of productive resources by means of an appropriate layer of institutions, behavioral rules, and policy instruments; in order to discharge itself of these demanding tasks, socialism also implies that the planned steering by the state of the course of economic life will permeate all layers of society. Since the embracement of socialism in the USSR after 1917, both features have exerted an overwhelming influence on practical economic affairs. If the strategy adopted by the CPEs can be properly understood only in terms of what the USSR aimed at during the 1930s, the same is true of the economic model introduced in all CPEs. It was transplanted from the USSR, in conjunction with the growth strategy, without essential modifications in spite of a radically different growth environment. In fact, even less ingenuity and originality were displayed in elaborating the CPEs' new model.[7]

The crucial components of the model of a traditional CPE can be summarized by the following eight characteristics of socialist economic policies.

1. To enforce a growth strategy, nearly all economic activities are brought under detailed central planning, and decision-making authority is vested in a complex administrative hierarchy.
2. All important production factors and institutions are nationalized or closely controlled by the state.
3. Collectivization is the dominant pattern of socialist agriculture, with the nominally cooperatively owned farms under close state control.
4. Fiscal, price, and monetary policies are subordinated to the realization of physical growth targets, especially those pertaining to forced industrialization. Prices are administratively set, often below market-clearing levels, and infrequently changed. Money is held passive, especially in the productive sphere, with the flow of funds adjusted by taxes, subsidies, and credits according to the allocation of resources previously earmarked in physical terms.
5. The rigid planning and organization of the productive structure is complemented by informal initiative at all levels of production and consumption.
6. Bureaucratization of economic activities ensues as production and its disposition are enforced by administrative allocation criteria or, in other words, by rationing of materials and central control over wage disbursements (both the total wage bill and its components). Managerial and worker incentives are tied primarily to the fulfillment and overfulfillment of centrally decreed production targets.
7. The CPE is to a considerable extent politicized as a result of the gradual evolvement of the Communist Party, inter alia, into an instrument of channeling production factors preferably into ac-

tivities corresponding to the economic and other goals of socialist society.

8. Internal economic activity is rigidly insulated from external influences and from the foreign economic relations of the CPE, and the actual or potential effects propagated by unavoidable contacts abroad are neutralized by means at the disposal of the planning center. Trade tasks are generally entrusted to special export-import corporations, who see to it that producing enterprises have no direct contact with foreign customers or suppliers, and their interest in the economic effects of foreign trade is deliberately kept weak.

Some of the salient features of the traditional model will be examined in some detail below.

Nationalization

In order to marshal all available production factors to the centrally set development path, all CPEs started their postwar economic expansion by nationalizing production factors and institutions or by bringing them under close central government control. Certainly, labor could not be conscripted as effectively as, say, capital, but even the human factor was centrally manipulated, regulated, and controlled to awaken the masses to an industrial and socialist mode of production, and to the more general objectives of socialism. Although labor mobility is in principle unhampered, frequent interference in the labor market and the imposition of encumbrances on free labor movement by the center have been common in the service of the exigencies of detailed planning and the material incentive system. Land was nationalized in the USSR but not in the other CPEs. Nevertheless the particular type of agricultural organization imposed assured the preeminent influence of the center on decision making in the collective organization.

After the consolidation of political and economic power, and the elimination of the most serious shortcomings stemming from the war and the internal power struggles, the production factors were assigned to the preferred type of economic development under guidance, among other things, of comprehensive, physically detailed central planning.

Central planning

Planning for growth means setting concrete targets of economic development, mobilizing sufficient resources to implement these aims as well as possible, and seeing to it that the actual economic agents will conform closely to central expectations. The instruments used in resource allocation and the important question of who determines the ultimate development objectives as an expression of society's preferences can be taken as substantial pointers in distinguishing between various planning systems. In a CPE it is the Communist Party that, in its capacity as society's vanguard, feels itself called upon to lead the country's subjects to their historical destiny. In reality, of course, the planning instruments and the overall development goals are set by the precepts of a select circle of party members (e.g., the Politbureau).

The allocation of production factors is essentially prescribed by central fiat. Socialist planning is authoritarian because the plan attempts to formulate instructions in such a way that the ultimate producer and consumer is left little or no alternative to their execution. That is, entrepreneurs in a CPE resemble more production managers than persons who make vital decisions on enterprise policies. Crucial questions such as what is to be produced, how production is to be organized, what inputs are to be made available, and the like, are in principle determined at the highest level of the plan hierarchy, normally specified as "norms" in the central plan, and are not answered by the foresight, risk taking, technical and managerial competence, and creative innovation of an entrepreneurial leadership.

Production and distribution relations in reality differ markedly from the picture that is subsumed under the ideal construction of a central plan and the implied parametric, technocratic behavior of the production units. This stems partly from the fact that there are various degrees of uncertainty the planners will have to come to grips with and partly from the fact that the activities of conscious persons cannot be reduced to the simple act of pulling a lever. Some scope, however confined, will have to be reserved for entrepreneurial decision making in the lower tiers of the plan hierarchy, because the planning center cannot possibly hope to cope with all details of the appropriate functioning of an increasingly complex economy, particularly in view of a variety of uncertainties about future economic activity.

Uncertainty in planning is bound to crop up because the plan has to be implemented by human individuals, not all relations can be included in the plan in the same degree of detail, and also there are difficulties inherent in forecasting accurately the complicated relationships of an economy. Actual events in such key sectors as agriculture, trade, and construction are essentially unpredictable mainly because the specification of some of these sectors' parameters is contingent on forces that remain largely outside the scope of the information at the disposal of central planners, and moreover beyond their control. Potential conflicts stemming from this uncertainty will have to be resolved either by adopting a rather flexible type of planning or, more realistically, by informal solutions carried out by the lower decision-making levels of the planning hierarchy. Furthermore, as the economy develops, its complexity increases and so will the magnitude of the problems stemming from planning in detail. In technical terms, one might put it as follows: As the technological matrix of interindustry relations contains fewer zeros, the process of convergence toward a consistent plan essentially slows down. Central administration by detailed physical planning becomes therefore much more arduous and time-consuming. This is one aspect. Another one is the uncertainty attributable to the fact that not all input-output (IO) coefficients can be specified exactly. Because the stochastic nature of some coefficients has wide repercussions on other activities as well, the degree of uncertainty of the plan will increase accordingly.

As a minimum objective, the central plan aims at consistency in production and distribution. The annual plan prescribes production, investment, and consumption for one year in partial fulfillment of a medium-term or perspective plan. The enterprise is instructed to adhere to a number of binding norms assigning in great detail the amount to be produced and its assortment; it also stipulates the appropriations of materials and capital and labor resources placed at the enterprise's disposal to attain these production targets.[8]

Although the central administrators regard the strict formulation of the central plan as the only possible outcome of responsible decision making, it is likely that the preferences and aims of the periphery of the plan hierarchy do not coincide exactly with those guiding the center. Such "local" interests are not necessarily confined to private income considerations or nonmonetary rewards. In addition, the entrepreneurial leadership or the associated party cells may wish to promote regional or local activities that are not quite compatible with the center's conception of current developments in the economy as a whole. If, for example, the enterprise plan fails to stipulate unambiguously all the variables and parameters associated with the relevant production and organizational processes, the enterprise and its various associated interest groups will be called on to fill in any gaps. It is highly unlikely that in so doing they will completely disregard their "local" interests, even if the perceived best interest of socialist society is their exclusive guideline. Similarly, such considerations will be of decisive importance when some of the plan assignments are internally inconsistent, as frequently happens. Friction is likely to arise, for instance, in cases where the plan calls for both profit maximization and output maximization as success indicators when, at the same time, the material incentives connected with the one considerably outweigh those related to the other. The ramifications and implications of local interest or pressure groups for the transformation of central plans into operative enterprise plans have not so far been investigated in as much detail as could be desired. The center's failure to assimilate fully the local interests of the lower levels of the plan hierarchy when formulating enterprise objectives has been typical of the traditional CPE.[9] Conversely, enterprise managers have not always behaved according to the overall philosophy underlying the plan, even if well known, because some of their rewards have remained outside the purview of the central planners (Wedel 1976, pp. 24–30).

Efficiency considerations

One of the few, if only broad, ideas offered by the Marxian classics to the architects and contractors of the CPE was that it should and could dispense with money. Except for a short period of the civil war in the USSR, socialist planners have steadfastly dissociated themselves from the concept of a nonmonetary economic system prior to the communist welfare state, although rationing of consumer goods was at times rationalized in ideological terms as a realization of the nonmonetary economy (see Nove 1970, pp. 201–202). Although this could suggest refuting the classics, the latter's guidelines nonetheless suggest an important implication. The Soviet theory of the central planning mechanism – and hence the foremost thought in the formulation of economic policy – crystallized as one resting on quantity-term calculations, as distinct from value planning. The plan is the expression of the center's goals in regulating economic activity. Without this being necessarily articulated, the accepted premise is that tools of indirect coordination of decisions are not sufficiently dependable in pursuing the CPE's objectives. The reason for this option might seem odd, although it is in fact straightforward enough, even if ideology is scorned. When central planning for fast industrialization was introduced in the USSR, at least three arguments may have been instrumental in motivating planners, by and large, to dispense with some essential components of planning for static efficiency by means of market-type instruments.[10]

First, centralized control and guidance were introduced in support of fast growth in priority sectors. In this, the character of the environment, especially its economic backwardness, was simplifying over a long period the processes of information, choice making, and control; and, in turn, the nature of Soviet planning and growth underlying it were enhancing the simplification. When an agrarian economy is being forcibly transformed into an industrial one, the strategic growth choices could be confined to a narrow range of processes, and the planning mechanism would support this. Also, in such an environment it does not matter much which particular industrial activities are selected for growth, if growth per se is the objective. Value indicators are certainly not very helpful in guiding decisions when, for reasons that are not mainly economic in nature, the policy makers have already opted for harnessing heavy industry as the core of economic expansion.

Second, because the socialist development strategy and its supporting model were introduced without taking due account of the specific factors of time and place in each country, it may be doubted whether market-type relations could have supported the implementation of the central objectives.[11] Instruments of indirect economic coordination ensuring static efficiency would probably have failed to generate the growth actually achieved for some indicators so dear to CPE decision makers (such as the overall rate of growth, the level of expansion of heavy industry, investment growth, and so on). The point is that the price mechanism would probably not have generated the same degree of success in fostering the preferred structural changes as attained under central planning guided by physical indicators and nonprice controls. The price mechanism would not have been sufficiently flexible and the economic agents unable to conform swiftly to the drastic adaptations required to bridge the abyss separating the presocialist and the industrial society.[12] If the situation finally attained corresponds to the targets planned and proves to be out of touch with real cost and benefit considerations, as it surely is in most CPEs, then market forces would indeed have failed to sustain it, and they probably could not have permitted it to arise in the first place.

Although these policy considerations may well have been subsidiary in selecting the adopted model, they nevertheless help to rationalize the knotty aspect of why value magnitudes were for such a long time simply ignored in favor of physical indicators. Even if relative prices were a reflection of real costs when the transformations were inaugurated, the CPEs could not envisage using these information channels, for policy makers did not even attempt to simulate decisions based on conventional allocation criteria.[13] With a few exceptions in handicrafts and part of agriculture, prices in a CPE mainly have an accounting function, in that they serve to aggregate physical magnitudes, and also a distributive function, in blotting up consumers' incomes.

Third, the introduction of central planning followed closely upon radical political transitions. Economic responsibilities were often entrusted to officials who had earned recognition in party politics, but were hardly familiar with the complexity of optimal economic administration. In such an environment, a physical yardstick (like x tons of steel) looked far more tangible than a value magnitude (like y rubles of steel), which could be manipulated in several ways.[14] Another important factor affecting the selection of economic instruments, as already alluded to, was the severe shortage of trained entrepreneurial ability in backward economies. If only a very small number of skilled managers are able to make decisions on the basis of socialist production objectives, and if central developmental preferences carry a lot of weight, it is probably preferable to allot only the smallest degree of freedom to individual production units; as a matter of practicality rather than of principles, then, the central plan tries to formulate as exactly as realistically feasible what each enterprise has to produce with given inputs expressed in nonprice terms. Failure to forecast accurately naturally implies that the executive echelons must take ad hoc remedial measures, but these do not necessarily blend with the objectives subsumed in the plan.

Instruments of indirect coordination

Socialist price policies are a case in point of the subordination of value criteria to physical targets in a traditional CPE. As a result of the central planner's penchant for rapid physical transformation and growth per se, prices in a CPE have never approximated real costs. Prices net of subsidies and taxes are, in principle, calculated by the center or its affiliated organs on the basis of average production costs in the branch as a whole plus a nominal profit mark-up.[15] These costs are defined as material and labor expenditures, without making due allowance for capital and land scarcities. Prices for consumer goods and services include in addition substantial taxes or subsidies; they are revised infrequently in order better to reflect market conditions, especially when consumer market imbalances become chronic. As a result, prices in a CPE are generally not good indicators of real scarcities, and their allocative function is therefore severely conscripted: Prices are used mostly for accounting and, to some extent, redistribution purposes. In that sense, socialist writers correctly emphasize that, as an instrument of economic policy in a CPE, prices differ essentially from the role assigned to them in MTEs. However, this nonscarcity feature does not necessarily imply that internal price formation in the CPEs has been irrational. Barring planners' unintentional errors, prices certainly have not been arbitrary in the sense that they have been selected randomly, for instance. On the contrary, they have performed functions that were logical in the context of the development objectives adopted, and as such they have had a rationality of their own. But they have not been rational from the standpoint of the efficiency of the allocation of resources in general, and value planning in particular.

The deliberate choice to deemphasize value planning through the price mechanism was carried over to nearly all familiar indirect instruments of economic policy and associated institutional arrangements typical of MTEs. In fact, the policy instruments and the supporting organization were simply to contribute to the realization of priority goals expressed mainly *in natura*. The role of these instruments has been narrowly circumscribed in the hope that they would not interfere with the execution of the physical plan targets, although they did to some extent.

Fiscal policies in the traditional CPE are almost exclusively concerned with indirect taxation – turnover taxes and subsidies – to assure some sort of equilibrium between demand and supply of consumer goods and to implement certain CPE goals. Turnover taxes are usually levied on consumer durables and subsidies are granted to basic necessities. The supply of consumer goods and services, as for most other goods, is largely determined by the plan, which on the whole fails to react swiftly to the revealed preferences in private and public consumption patterns. Prices are not used to help select individual options in the plan nor to achieve efficient allocation of resources. Direct taxation of enterprise revenues is largely redundant because enterprise receipts or gross profits are a major source of state revenue. Private incomes are normally not "actively" taxed because wages are directly controlled by the center and wages are the only source of monetary income of those not employed in agriculture or in the handicraft sectors.

With respect to monetary policies, it is enough to say that they have been passive. Capital investments, usually financed through the budget free of charge to the user, are undertaken without much regard for macroeconomic efficiency. Credit policy is designed to facilitate interenterprise transactions, that is, the implementation of planned exchanges. The lending institutions are simply expected to finance the centrally set investment or transaction targets, no matter how the latter are selected. A more active kind of monetary policy to equate private incomes with the value of consumer goods and services made available is applied sporadically to counter dangerous open or repressed inflation, and when unsatisfied demand may have potentially a far-reaching negative impact on labor morale.

Collectivization

An essential component of the initial phases of the socialist growth strategy is the mobilization of resources in the agricultural sector in support of industrial progress. According to the development theories elaborated by Preobraženskij and other left-wing Soviet policy leaders in the 1920s, the start-up of socialist growth could be financially facilitated by confiscating the agricultural surplus ("primitive accumulation") as a tribute to industrialization. Others, including L. Trockij, emphasized that the original socialist accumulation should be amassed through the self-exploitation of the working class (Ellman 1975, p. 260). Whether the tribute paid by agriculture actually financed industrialization is still a controversial topic.[16] Beyond doubt, however, is that the sector has played a crucial role in releasing labor for industrial activities and in stepping up its net marketed output for local consumption to feed the industrial labor force and for earning foreign exchange, which in turn permitted imports of capital equipment in support of industrialization. Industry, on the other hand, provided the means by which agriculture could be modernized and intensified.

To restructure agriculture and exploit it as an important contributor to the financing of the first stage of industrialization, enabling the policy makers to pursue it relentlessly, all CPEs, with the exception of post-1956 Poland, amalgamated landholdings into one type or another of Soviet collective. These collectives involved nominally independent cooperative ownership under close state scrutiny,[17] though other means (such as the fiscal policies advocated by Preobraženskij) could have been instituted to exact agriculture's tribute. In some cases, large landholdings were first expropriated ("dekulakization") and redistributed to the smallholder, though soon enough they were fused into collective exploitations, except in Poland after 1956.

Foreign trade and cooperation

An intrinsic component of the CPEs' economic model is the more or less complete separation of domestic economic activities from external influences. This choice might have been inspired by four considerations. First, the CPEs selected an ambitious growth path that had to be trodden without taking sufficient account of all relevant internal and external market conditions. Second, available resources were to be preempted for industrialization, and hence the need to avoid external leakage. Third, policy is made largely without the benefit of sophisticated plan techniques and pertinent micro- and macroeconomic policy instruments to guide and control plan implementation by indirect means. Finally, growth targets are generally not set after a careful search for efficient trade opportunities. For economies such as those of Eastern Europe that cannot be autarkic because of the cost of small-scale production and the acute absence of most primary goods from their resource endowment, severing domestic decision making from world criteria has had several crucial drawbacks, even if the aim of the CPEs has been to attain permanently high and stable rates of economic expansion, regardless of the static efficiency implications. Such economies ought indeed to formulate their objectives against the background of real external opportunities, at least those embedded in their preferred trade region, without necessarily confining growth exclusively to the directions suggested by static comparative advantage indicators.

External trade and payments, like other economic sectors, are under national control. A state monopoly of foreign trade and payments (MFT) tries to neutralize all influences from abroad, whether positive or disruptive. The nature of the CPEs' interaction with other economies has been more the desire for imports to pursue the set growth objectives than the pressure to exploit comparative advantages. An important point is that external trade, essentially, ought to result from a delicate choice between value indicators (e.g., differences between internal and external real costs). Because such efficiency indicators have not been available in the CPEs in the degree of detail required, effective criteria for trade decision making have been lacking. As with most other targets of socialist growth, trade was by and large conducted on the basis of physical needs and availabilities. A more detailed examination of this model component, a crucial feature in the determination of the internal conditions of SEI, will be provided in Chapter 3.

4. Economic reforms

Although admittedly not all relevant aspects of the growth strategy and economic model of traditional CPEs could be drawn into the picture, sufficient elements are now available to evaluate the appropriateness of the twin components of socialist development policies. Such an appraisal must necessarily be anchored to the degree to which the preferences of the policy makers in CPEs appear to have been satisfied, but not to what these countries could have accomplished under different policies and institutions. Indeed, the political bodies responsible for the control of society cannot remain uncommitted spectators of the natural evolution of the structure of needs and satisfactions, but must interfere with it. Although this is certainly also the case in MTEs, the economic role of the state and the ponderation of "state preferences" are much greater in CPEs, where in fact the state allocates economic resources with a view toward fulfilling a number of priorities of its own selection. If these were defined exclusively in terms of private preferences, then market-type criteria could be utilized as the crucial yardstick to gauge the CPEs' economic achievements.

The backdrop to the reforms

Considering the great value attached to industrialization and the establishment of a well-diversified economy, the evaluation of the CPE's performance and of most efforts to improve it falls into two categories: (1) the search for the nonessential elements of the growth strategy, particularly in connection with how extensive the economic structure should be and (2) a more precise definition and a more discriminating selection of the essential elements of the traditional model to support socialist growth. Such an evaluation should come to grips with new requirements imposed upon the CPE by the evolving political, economic, and social environment of concrete policy making.

As the record of economic development suggests, the strategy adopted and its supporting model have been very suitable for carrying out a consistent and radical transformation of a relatively backward economy into an industrial society, thus enabling the CPE to accelerate economic growth, to transform the economic structure, and to improve considerably the levels of living of the consumer. But it would be remiss simply to commend structural transformation without assessing its real cost. The same applies to the traditional model. A tightly centralized organization might have been the only possible platform that would support the coveted changes in a relatively short time frame. Factors such as turbulent times, inexperienced management and labor force, backward ways of thinking, and unproductive economic relations could well have prompted the course of forced industrialization under strictly centralized control in relative isolation from world market processes. But they hardly justify perpetuating the more incidental features of socialist organization once the above conditions wither or yield to the force of historical, economic, and political changes.

From the preceding section, it seems intuitive that there might be more than one model that could have shored up the socialist development strategy and different strategies could have been sustained by the centralized model. Each combination has its particular drawbacks and advantages, and distinguishing clearly between the implications of each possible linkage – even if somewhat superficial – should provide useful information. This means that when seeking to adapt the strategy and model, possibly in response to the disaffection of the ruling policy makers with past performance, it is essential to separate whenever possible the indispensable from the incidental components of model and strategy. Several questions should be addressed in such an evaluation. Were all elements of the model really required to yield the level of output attained? Were some of them necessary in the past but are they no longer needed? Are the actual level and composition of output still satisfactory in terms of current objectives regarding the CPE's future? Lastly, has the rate and structure of past growth been consonant with the policy makers' preferences?

Starting with the last question, there is little doubt that, over the years, the leaders of the smaller CPEs have been convinced, for several reasons, that extensive economic growth policies should be reconsidered once the essential components of the socialist "economic complex" are achieved. One important indicator of the growing need to redirect the growth strategy and to seek factor productivity gains rather than input growth arose in the mid-1960s, especially as a result of a growing labor shortage.[18] This constraint effectively marks the rapidly approaching end of the era in which the CPEs could raise industrial output simply by building new factories, expanding old ones, and pouring vast numbers of new wage earners into manufacturing. Owing to markedly lower growth rates and steeply rising capital–output ratios registered since the early 1960s, most CPEs (excepting perhaps the less developed members of the group where opportunities for absorbing labor, especially out of farming activities, are still considerable) have found their economy not performing up to expectations; even stepping up investment outlays leading, among other things, to an appreciable increase in the share of accumulation in the distribution of national income, in most countries, failed to sustain another round of high growth rates comparable to those experienced until the late 1950s.

The type of economic organization typical of a traditional CPE does not sufficiently safeguard against the emergence of a very bureaucratic society and the stifling rigidity of detailed planning. This danger evidently depends on the planning administration and the private and social interests of the executive plan tiers. It is uncontested, however, that central planners frequently selected development targets without adapting model and strategy to seminal changes in the evolving structure of the economy, and the growing capabilities and talents of the new managerial and entrepreneurial class. In particular, the growing sophistication of these economies has been invalidating the simplifying assumptions of the methodology of planning and running the economy, causing their obsolescence and making the need for more refined techniques and policy tools acute.

This problem has become potentially the most significant cause of growth retardation in the field of innovation and technical progress on account of the narrow confines for initiative and risk taking under detailed central planning. The reasons for focusing growth policies henceforth more on intensification than on simple additions to the factor input stream are doubtlessly very complex.

As an aggregate phenomenon, economic reforms actually are but one component of a multifaceted political, social, and cultural adjustment process that is likely to become a major factor stimulating further change in the system (Korbonski 1975, p. 8). As a result, it is well-nigh impossible to do full justice in a few words to the scope, extent, and evolution of the reform movements. Nonetheless, the reform blueprints of the 1960s incorporated a number of shifts in strategy and model that continue to exhibit a major significance in the current policy configurations of the CPEs, in spite of reversals incurred recently in the implementation of one factor or another of the process.[19] Though the reform aspects affecting the strategy and model are not neatly distinguishable, it will be instructive to separate them conceptually.

Shifts in strategy

With respect to the strategy, a dissipation of scarce resources over too many sectors is not an indispensable ingredient of promoting development according to the basic precepts of Marxism-Leninism, especially in the case of relatively small economies. Instead of seeking further extensive growth, East European policy makers have recently embraced various initiatives to encourage intensive economic expansion. By concentrating resources in selected sectors, gradually assimilating technological knowledge, and vigorously promoting new technology and management techniques, the CPEs may succeed in upgrading older ventures and in reaping substantial gains in average labor productivity. Coupled with judicious new injections of investments, the policy makers hope to accelerate growth, or at least to secure a more stable rate of economic expansion at a relatively high level.

Though the scope and intensity of these policy shifts differ considerably from one CPE to another, as a rule the priorities of the central planners have gradually become more realistic than what they were in the 1950s, aimed as they are now at achieving a more balanced and outward-looking economic structure. This conclusion would seem to be buttressed by the decreasing tensions between accumulation and consumption, between heavy and light industry, and, finally, between industry and agriculture that have characterized developments in the last decade or so in most, if not all, CPEs. Admittedly, these changes have been tentative in the sense that they have not yet culminated in shaping up an economy that is fully responsive to current conditions. This stems partly from the fact that since the late 1960s the CPEs have steadfastly avoided far-reaching changes requiring, among other things, the abandonment of essential components of the reform blueprints of the 1960s either through failure to implement contemplated moves or by abrogating shifts in midprocess. In some instances, a temporary retreat was dictated for fear of arousing domestic political trouble either because the reform tended to spill over into other layers of society's fabric or in view of instabilities in the reform commitment engendered by the tug of war between the proponents and opponents of economic devolution. Nevertheless, in spite of all the setbacks incurred in recent years (on which more later), the parts of the reform movement that have survived testify to the leadership's genuine concern about achieving a more balanced growth pattern, a less diversified economic structure, and a much more intensive participation in international trade. Recent experiments inaugurated in Czechoslovakia also buttress this claim.

Model changes

Questions concerning the economic efficiency of inward-looking, relatively autarkic economic development under rigid central planning gradually emerged as a focal point of economic and political debate in the mid-1950s, when the smaller CPEs slowly acquired a measure of sovereignty in economic affairs. These initially rather tepid discussions gradually matured in the 1960s into what has become known as the era of economic reforms, which impinged especially on the model of the small, trade-dependent CPEs. Inadequate incentives and scarcity yardsticks in these economies complicated a more efficient participation in international trade, which is so essential for small economies bent on mobilizing domestic resources for rapid growth. Overcentralization of decision making, excessively detailed central planning, inflexible materials-allocation procedures, the suppression of local initiative, unsound price structures, and overambitious development targets led to waste and inefficiency.

Although it is impossible to postulate a single reform model applicable to all CPEs, the various proposals formulated, but only partly enacted, contain a number of common features that, taken together, represent the hard core of the reforms and a significant departure from the traditional CPE. Naturally, in the reform blueprints the various countries put different stress even on these common elements because of the particular circumstances in which the reforms matured (such as level of development, degree of trade dependence, relative strength of the supporters and opponents of reforms). In addition, the reforms showed also appreciable diversity in extent, timing, speed, and reversibility of the proposed changes. The most important shifts can be divided into three groups according to their most significant impacts: (1) the organization of the economy, the devolution of economic administration, and the sharing of decision-making authority; (2) the improvement and the wider use of instruments of indirect economic coordination and administration; and (3) the role of external trade and economic cooperation.

The organization and planning of the economy
Even if the model and strategy of development had been appropriate at the time of the inception of the socialist economic system, it is intuitive that to maintain this quality revisions should have been formulated frequently to keep up with progress in domestic and foreign economic developments. One important instance pointing in this direction is the growing complexity of detailed physical planning for a fast-maturing economy. It bears stressing also that highly centralized physical planning is not an irreplaceable element of what is needed in support of socialist

development processes. Therefore, reforms in this context have been focused on the creation of a more practical division of administrative and economic duties between central and local levels. Moreover, important changes have recently been ushered in with the objective of activating an enterprise policy that facilitates "local" decision making by means of cost–benefit analyses without contravening the overall policy guidelines enacted by the center; such devoluted authority should also be able to cater to market preferences of domestic and foreign consumers.

However, even the most far-reaching of the reform models – the Hungarian – assumes an unswerving commitment to socialism, for instance, in the retention of public ownership of the means of production and the limitations on the distribution of income and wealth. Though all reforms have sought to a varying extent to widen the scope of market-type instruments in a CPE, they basically hold that market relations, if applied at all, should be complementary to, not a substitute for, extensive central planning. The latter should be concerned especially with the main proportions of the economy (such as the distribution of national income between private and public consumption, and accumulation, the rate of growth of the economy and its main sectors, infrastructural investments), while market forces should be applied primarily to achieve greater efficiency and flexibility in the allocation of resources.

Because this basic philosophy impinges on organizational matters, one of the essential aims of the reform was a substantial reduction in the number of norms or obligations imposed by the center, and concurrently, to yield ground formerly usurped exclusively by central planning to the efficiency calculus. In this way, it was hoped that inefficiencies stemming from, among other things, wasteful stockpiling of reserves, counterproductive spreading of capital resources, low quality of production, and the predominance of production push rather than market pull could be reduced, if not completely ruled out. Through a better sensing of private preferences and their role in final consumption, and an improved allocation of scarce capital and labor resources as a result of more direct, horizontal channels of communications, the central planner hoped to come closer to fulfilling the aspirations of the executive tiers. Finally, organizational changes were sought to integrate trade and foreign cooperation harmoniously in active support of intensive growth: Horizontal contacts between domestic and foreign producers should come to play a crucial role by assigning decision-making authority in trade matters to the units of information at source, including the actual production units or their immediate representative sales organizations.

In administering the economy, the reform included a tendency toward both the deconcentration of authority as well as the concentration of economic power. This is not a contradictory statement. Almost without exception, enterprises have been absorbed in or brought under the authority of much larger economic associations (also called unions, trusts, combined works, directorates, centrals, and so on). With the exception of Hungary (and as originally envisaged in the short-circuited Czechoslovak reform), where fusion could be decided by the individual units themselves, in all other CPEs this amalgamation of nominally independent enterprises has been imposed almost exclusively from above. Deconcentration has taken place in the sense that the ministries or central administrative tiers no longer try to shape enterprise policy unilaterally; enterprise associations have been invested with the responsibility of guarding the social interest of the firm, while the separate units have been granted much more latitude in formulating an appropriate enterprise policy.

Enterprises have been given a chance to seek out direct links with their clients and suppliers as a means of reaching the centrally prescribed targets and also to work out for themselves some of the norms previously dictated by fiat from above. The former rigorous central administration, by and large, still persists in the USSR but has been almost fully abandoned in most other CPEs. However, in most cases – except Hungary and to a limited extent also in Poland – this authority has now been vested with the associations; enterprises are still expected to act very much as before. This is not only true for internal production and consumption behavior. Although the MFT has so far not been abolished in any CPE, a very strong trend has emerged to provide room for direct contacts between domestic and foreign enterprises. In spite of these similarities in the fundamental directions of the economic reforms, differences across countries are still striking, particularly in the trade sector. In some CPEs, the associations are now in charge of trade decisions, while in others the individual enterprises or their selected representatives are permitted to take care of their economic interests abroad subject, of course, to central regulation and control (see Chapter 3).

In some CPEs, the separation of macroeconomic from microeconomic responsibilities has emerged as the most decisive element in selecting new channels of communication or in improving old ones, and in determining the centers of authority. Day-to-day planning in these economies has been delegated more and more to the lower planning and production authorities, implying that the basis especially of microeconomic decisions has been vastly expanded. Decentralization has made it possible to utilize at least part of the knowledge and experience of the actual producers and consumers, which facilitates decisions especially on nonpriority issues according to their actual situation instead of merely implementing the center's prescriptions. Nevertheless, decentralization is not always consistently adhered to and superior organs frequently interfere in internal enterprise matters to a much greater degree than they are entitled to according to the letter and spirit of official regulations.

In many CPEs central planning now guides and controls microeconomic decisions through instruments of indirect coordination, rather than by prescribing in detail how much of what the individual firm should produce with given resources. These instruments are thought of as basic tools at the center's disposal to ensure that too great a gap does not develop between the overall plan – which is a package of ways and means of carrying out development objectives in the medium and long run – and the execution of the short-term plans. In this sense, the planning board has been enabled to disengage itself from some of the detailed chores of instructing production units, in the hope that this will lead to a better selection of strategic decisions affecting the CPE's future. However, not all CPEs have been found willing or able to relieve their overcentralized administration, and some that did formulate such reforms in the 1960s have reversed the devolution process. This setback has arisen partly from the features of the economies concerned, but also from ideological and political misconceptions about the role of short-term considerations in long-term economic development – a misunderstanding of the fundamental interrelationships between politics and power on the one hand, and economic efficiency on the other. It should be added parenthetically that this devolution process has reached much farther in some sectors than in others. The reforms have had most impact in selected spheres of industry, for which they were primarily designed. In contrast, agriculture and the service sector have not been affected very much, at least not insofar as their organization is concerned, though in the 1970s the trend toward allowing greater latitude to private initiative in the service sector has been unmistakable. The much wider use of steering the economy by indirect means has, of course, also affected the nonindustrial sphere, including agriculture.

The role and scope of coordination instruments
When authority over economic decisions is no longer an exclusive prerogative of the central planner far removed from actual enterprise affairs, but a task divided among the several tiers of the CPE's economic hierarchy, the need for dovetailing the various actors' behavior becomes much more complex compared to when it was only a matter of coordinating physical yardsticks under traditional planning. From the macroeconomic point of view, it is of course not very rational to require firms to maximize profits, for example, when in fact enterprise profit is not even approximately indicative of economic profit. Similarly, from the private point of view, it is not an attractive proposition to blend in with overall policy targets when the material incentive and reward systems, broadly defined, suggest seeking other solutions as more favorable to the enterprise and its managers.

The economic reforms have not so far fully expunged the long-held premise that the utilization of tools of indirect regulation and coordination of economic processes in support of economywide objectives embraced by the chief policy makers are not completely dependable. Nonetheless, perhaps the most substantial, technicoeconomic aspect of the reforms has been the rather narrow concentration on streamlining the economic model, apparently on the assumption that a good balance between indirect methods of management and centrally controlled measures makes it possible to enhance the effectiveness of plan implementation and in addition motivates the executors to above-plan performance. Perhaps the pivotal tool of indirect coordination is an up-to-date system of relative prices capable of playing a constructive role in the allocation process.

Prices in a CPE can assume three functions: (1) an accounting tool for aggregating targets expressed in physical units and for controlling the performance of enterprises, associations, and ministries by synthetic value criteria; (2) a means of transmitting information between the center and the periphery of the planning network; and (3) a key parameter conveying information on real scarcities. In almost all CPEs, the price system is generally held to be a set of parameters for communicating orders from the center to the lower planning units and for controlling the performance reports submitted by these units. Only in some CPEs, especially Hungary and to some extent Poland, the new price systems are an important tool providing information on the state of a number of partial markets. However, in nearly all CPEs, market-balancing requirements are reflected to a varying extent in price fluctuations for most imports and domestically produced luxury goods, in addition to products of the peasant and handicraft sectors, while the role of prices is generally held down to that of accounting units.

Nevertheless, all CPEs have made an attempt to allot a more active role to prices in production and distribution processes, though these parameters are still mostly set by the center. In some cases, enterprises or their associations, under close supervision of the center, have some ability to revise prices from time to time in response to changes in domestic and foreign costs. It bears stressing, though, that in all CPEs, including those in which price adjustments are now a quasi-continuous process rather than a once-and-for-all major undertaking, price movements, as before, are narrowly circumscribed or fairly tightly controlled by the central pricing authority. In other words, price stability because of the need for a stable plan environment or for more social reasons has endured as a top priority of the CPE's economic policy.

Even in CPEs where prices continue to be fixed administratively, there has been a serious attempt to pattern prices more closely according to real production costs and, in some countries, also to pass on the approximate real cost of foreign trade.

Proposals to institutionalize scarcity pricing have not been received as favorably as outsiders might have hoped for. Instead, most price reforms have been confined to a recalculation of average costs, including a proxy for capital scarcity and import outlays. In some cases, central authority over price formation has been relaxed to induce balance between demand and supply and to maintain it better than in the past.

To attain market equilibrium, accurate prices are needed and the center must also see to it that prices are periodically adapted to fluctuations in demand and supply. Most reforms have therefore aimed at greater flexibility in price formation so that, as a result of more frequent recalculations of centrally set prices and the delegation of some authority over price formation to the lower levels, prices continue to convey meaningful information to the plan executors. Although at present prices do not accurately reflect objective economic conditions, especially after the cost explosion in world and CMEA markets of the mid-1970s, they undoubtedly have become a better indicator of real production costs than in the traditional CPE and, in some cases, they even react to changes in supply and demand in selected sectors. Capital levies, rents, and interest rates as formative cost elements have been recognized as permanent components of price calculation even when these categories do not yet accurately reflect the corresponding scarcity relationships. Because enterprises have partly gone over to economic accountability (*chozrasčët*) and self-financing, they have probably become more aware of cost conditions than before and will continue to bargain for greater latitude in their price-setting authority.

Although the price reform is the crucial element of more general social and economic transformations envisaged since the mid-1960s, it is by no means the only coordination instrument subject to reforms. Another important set of tools can be subsumed under the heading "credits." Instead of prescribing all inputs of capital to the enterprises by fiat, the state has now gradually allotted a more active role to banks, where individual enterprises on their own initiative can procure credits to finance improvements in their production structure and where consumers can obtain temporarily the means to purchase durable consumer goods. Key investment decisions (e.g., the construction of new factories) remain, as before, an exclusive prerogative of the central decision makers and are financed by the budget. However, investments for current production improvements and for the expansion of existing facilities are now partly a responsibility of the enterprise. Banks are expected to evaluate loan requests mainly on the basis of the real economic merits of the venture as seen within the overall credit guidelines issued by the center. Although a measurable share of decentralized investments is presently undertaken through retained profits and bank credits, the center and the banks frequently interfere, not exclusively on economic grounds, even in matters connected with self-financing, and bank financing is watched very closely by the center.

The amount and cost of credit is determined partly by an interest rate policy designed to guarantee greater economic rationality in the allocation of investment funds. The cost of these loans is now also borne by the enterprises themselves rather than by the budget, as was the rule before the reform. But the CPEs are still far from having an effective and flexible credit and interest rate policy, though recent changes in this sphere will probably be expanded and gradually improved.

With respect to current production, an important goal of the reforms is to adapt output more closely to demand by emphasizing financial indicators such as sales, profits, or profitability in evaluating enterprise performance, rather than gross or net output, cost reduction targets, and the like, which were the basic levers in the traditional CPE. In turn, managerial and workers' incentive systems have been revised to relate bonuses and premiums more directly to the new indicators and to have these wage-related disbursements paid out of enterprise profits.

To encourage labor productivity, enterprises have obtained greater flexibility, but by no means the exclusive right, to determine premiums, basic salary scales, personnel policies, and related labor matters. More extensive delegation of decision-making authority to the production units has been withheld, among other reasons, because the objective of full employment, combined with other social aims of socialism, are vital elements of the overall policy priorities of the CPEs. Under the defunct model, the central administration or its subordinates prescribed for each enterprise in detail the number of workers, sometimes even per category, the average wage norm per category, and the overall wage fund. Instead of many detailed prescriptions regarding employment, a trend has emerged to confine controls to a few norms and indirect regulators. In several CPEs, only the total wage fund is presently controlled, while in others average remuneration rates and their annual modifications are centrally regulated.

In the traditional CPE the enterprise could control profits only by reducing nominal production costs below planned levels, provided the firm behaved exactly as expected by the center. But profit as an indicator of enterprise efficiency was incidental to entrepreneurial decisions, as the rewards attached to profits were meager in any case, particularly in comparison with other success indicators (e.g., gross output). Now the enterprise can influence costs directly by a more careful selection of inputs and suppliers, by producing according to what the market can and is willing to absorb, and, in some cases, by using authority over price formation. Profit has now become a more meaningful decision-making criterion, partly because it is expected to play an important role in the determination of premiums and the more social advantages accruing to workers, and in the accumulation of funds for self-financing.

Foreign trade and integration

Transitions in the conception of the role of trade and foreign cooperation in the CPE's development and organization are perhaps the most important topics to be dealt with when considering the implications of the reforms for SEI. As briefly noted, foreign trade matters played a vital role in the pressure for reform, especially in the smaller CPEs, and continue to be at the forefront of the ongoing reform concepts. In several countries, this component is arguably the only surviving element of the intended reforms as regards both its strategic role in stabilizing and enhancing socialist development, and the way this sector can be harmonized with the domestic economy.

The overall impact of the national economic reforms clearly impinges on several dimensions of the CPE's institutional alliance within the CMEA framework. The reforms are bound to have important implications in the process of SEI for at least three reasons. First, the devolution of economic decision making will render it increasingly more difficult to hammer out far-reaching intergovernmental economic agreements and to implement them without serious prior consultation with the economic sectors concerned. Second, the emphasis on economic accounting would seem to make it harder to reach agreements acceptable to all CMEA members in the light of the substantial differences in the emphasis that the various reforms have placed on pursuing economic efficiency as a central, if not the only, yardstick of decision making. Third, the growing desire for modernization through innovation and technological assimilation can be satisfied to a significant extent only through a major expansion in trade and cooperation between CPEs and the developed MTEs. In view of these considerations, one would have expected the national reforms to have pressured for substantial changes in the CMEA's organization, transforming the institution from a simple clearinghouse for overseeing and promoting SEI to an active participant formulating policies conducive to the implementation of timely integration measures. Why this transition has not so far occurred will be detailed below.

5. Concluding remarks

From the brief outline of the evolution of the CPEs' economic policies and domestic institutions, it could be concluded that the leaders of Eastern Europe have been sifting out the essential elements of their socialist precepts from the more incidental practices previously justified on the strength of their inherited ideology or under the force of circumstance. In particular, preferences and allocation criteria are now established more along the lines of economic rationality to increase steadily the material-technical bases of their societies than according to the exigencies of overdemonstrating socialism and the rewards accruing to communist orthodoxy. Naturally, not all CPEs have come to this seemingly logical conclusion by the same reasoning, and most CPEs are still in the initial phases of bridging the gap between economic techniques and key policy responsibilities. But some countries have accomplished far more than others in promoting decentralization and economic rationality. Taking the two extremes, it seems fair to say that Hungary has advanced farthest in the direction of economic efficiency, whereas the USSR has hardly moved away from the typical features of the traditional CPE. This suggests that the analysis of the transition processes will remain a crucial factor in formulating realistic forecasts of future developments in Eastern Europe.

Ideological rationalizations of the ongoing transition toward the further improvement of the material and technical basis of communism have of late been dominated by the formulation of development goals and the introduction of policy instruments, institutions, and behavioral rules appropriate to the so-called advanced socialist society – a new component in the traditional Marxist-Leninist phasing of historical progress.[20] In some contrast to the vacillating policy innovations of the 1960s described in section 4, the reforms of the 1970s have been aimed at promoting "intensive economic growth," that is to say, the steady growth of factor productivity by adapting the economic infrastructure better to scientific and technological achievements, which is also a major preoccupation in the integration debates of the past decade. The trends toward pluralistic decision making and placing greater trust in the market mechanism have been reversed, and the chief concerns of the 1970s have been the adaptation of the centralized political and economic control levers to contemporary technological requirements. Without denying that some important elements of the original reform blueprints of the mid-1960s have been eliminated in the process, it is nonetheless the case that the reforms continue to inch forward, but now with much greater emphasis on the role of central guidance and control through comprehensive planning.

In spite of many important changes in strategy and model, the CPEs retain essential components of the command system: No CPE has as yet succeeded in patterning the branch structure of its economy in accordance with contemporary scientific and technological progress; the criteria of economic and technical efficiency still function imperfectly; it has not yet been possible to reverse the increase in capital–output ratios; intellectual and material resources continue to be underutilized; it is still more in the material interest of enterprises to confine themselves to fulfilling their production assignments than to aim vigorously at the smooth functioning of operations according to the long-term interests of their society. This is also true in the sphere of trade and international specialization, which will be examined in the following chapters.

3

The role and organization of trade

In discussing the conditions for promoting integration and the problems encumbering this process to date, the central issues revolve around the organization of trade and its place, especially in the context of planned economies. In an important way, foreign trade activities are, of course, an extension of overall domestic economic processes, and it is therefore open to question whether they should in fact be treated separately. It was decided to do so for several reasons. First, the foreign trade sector plays a pivotal role especially in the smaller CPEs. Second, the aspiration toward strengthening national independence – a weighty political consideration – has frequently played a decisive role in shaping strategies and setting up institutions affecting the scope and function of foreign economic cooperation in the CPEs. Third, by virtue of the peculiar postwar environment in which they were forced to unfold their identity, their inward-looking growth policies, and the antitrade bias embedded in their economic organization, the CPEs themselves have often treated trade separately from more exclusively domestic events. Finally, in spite of the hope for a tightly interlocked production structure, trade has been and will remain the chief vehicle for implementing SEI and, moreover, the most visible manifestation of its results and determinants.

In this chapter, the focus will be on the role and organization of trade, whereas the specific problems of CMEA cooperation, which are of course intimately related to the more general trade issues, will be explored in the next chapter. This division of the external economic aspects of the CPEs into general trade problems and intra-CMEA topics is somewhat artificial because such a large proportion of the CPEs' trade is cleared within their primary region. It is nevertheless helpful to split up the issues mainly because SEI can only succeed if measures are taken from below by the separate members in their own economies and from above through the channels of communication available at the CMEA level, regardless of whether or not the CMEA as an international organization will eventually be invested with supranational authority. This division of tasks is also justified in view of the special features of the CPEs' trade mechanism and policies, which have much wider ramifications than what is relevant for the CMEA region as a whole. A relatively high degree of autarky, almost complete currency and commodity inconvertibility, overall and structural bilateralism, price discrimination, and other features ought to be explained in the simplest possible terms for a typical CPE and then extended to the realities of Eastern Europe, especially intra-CMEA cooperation. This approach appears useful because integration is quite different from simple commodity transactions accommodated by traditional trade mechanisms, and systematic deviations from free trade in MTEs are on the whole less forceful and comprehensive than those implemented by the CPEs. In view of the singular effects of certain unique characteristics of the internal policies followed by the CPEs on the trade mechanism and behavior of these countries, it will be worthwhile to examine systematically those phenomena that actually differ substantially from the ones that stem from trade impediments in MTEs.

A simple model of trade decision making is examined in section 1, together with a brief outline of the place and role of trade in CPEs. The main focus is on the determination of the level and commodity composition of trade. The question of the geographical distribution of trade is also introduced in section 1, but its details are studied in section 2. Section 3 is devoted to an explanation of bilateralism and how its ramifications affect trade and economic activity. Section 4 explores the gradual emergence of structural or commodity bilateralism in CMEA trade – one of the most negative effects of the CPEs' trade policies. The implications of the economic reforms for trade behavior are summarized in section 5.

1. The role of trade in a traditional CPE

An attempt was made in Chapter 2 to show that, until recently, the growth objectives chosen by the CPEs imply an attempt to substitute continually and to a considerable degree new domestic production processes for traditional imports. Instruments, behavioral rules, and institutions embraced by these countries are designed to foster the realization of the growth objectives and the accompanying societal transformations within a framework that accommodates the nearly complete disjunction of domestic economic activities from foreign influences. On both accounts, trade was traditionally considered to be an auxiliary sector. Although helpful in carrying out the assigned tasks, foreign economic cooperation was certainly not treated as a, possibly main, generator of internal growth. On the whole, trade served chiefly as a means of fulfilling the overall development goals. This applied in particular to the smaller CPEs even though, because of market size, resource endowment, and level of development, the ambitious growth targets and domestic transformation patterns could not possibly be implemented without trade. Nonetheless, the volume of commerce was compressed well below levels that would have been warranted by comparative efficiency indicators. In the first decade or so of socialist policies, trade was largely determined by the volume of unavoidable imports and the need to earn the foreign exchange to acquire these goods.

One of the most significant policy decisions implemented soon after the countries shifted to socialist-type development is the nationalization of foreign trade through the creation of the MFT. This simply means that the right to engage in foreign transactions of goods, services, and capital belongs exclusively to the state; trade and payments are centralized under the strict control of a number of government agencies, which belong to two institutional hierarchies, themselves subordinated to the Planning Commission and the chief policy makers. The first one is the trade monopoly, which is composed of the Ministry of Foreign Trade, the foreign trade enterprises (FTEs), the customs administration, the Chamber of Commerce, and various

Table 1. *A simplified material balance: product* x *in plan year* t
(physical units)

Origin	Destination
Free and fixed[a] reserves (beginning of t)	Domestic consumption in t
	Final private consumption
Commodity production in t	Interindustrial use
Contracted imports[b]	Social consumption
From socialist countries	Contracted exports[b]
From nonsocialist countries[c]	To socialist countries
Other sources of supply	To nonsocialist countries[c]
	Free and fixed reserves (end of t)
Other imports	Other exports
From socialist countries	To socialist countries
From nonsocialist countries[c]	To nonsocialist countries[c]

[a] For example, strategic reserves of grain.
[b] Resulting from previous trade and payments agreements, including obligations stemming from specialization and cooperation protocols.
[c] This is usually further disaggregated into trade with convertible currency countries and other countries, sometimes according to whether the partners belong to the developing countries group or to developed market economies.
Source: Adapted from Grote 1973, p. 101.

other ancillary units. The second is the foreign exchange or valuta monopoly, which, in addition to the Ministry of Finance, encompasses the National Bank, the Foreign Trade Bank (where established) and other institutions such as financial research units.

The MFT empowers the state to establish its internal and external market relations in accordance with the requirements of the national economy as perceived by the government, to assert the priority of politics even in international trade ("commercial diplomacy"), and to protect the economy against undesirable fluctuations in external markets. Naturally, the state itself does not conduct trade operations. The MFT really means that authorization to engage in foreign transactions can be granted only by the Ministry of Foreign Trade within the policy guidelines underlying the plan and the targets expressed there; actual transactions are as a rule entrusted to FTEs and, in some cases, especially since the economic reforms, to individual enterprises or their associations.

Authority to engage in trade usually implies also the right to dispose of or to acquire foreign exchange, and the Ministry of Foreign Trade will therefore have to dovetail its decisions with those in charge of foreign exchange matters. The Ministry of Foreign Trade evaluates whether or not the proposed transaction fits in with the plan and indeed whether it is required at all to carry out the tasks stipulated in the plan. Until recently, all important trade decisions were made by the central authorities. The three basic issues in trade matters – what should be traded, where products should be traded, and to what extent should commerce be expanded – were basically resolved along with the formulation and implementation of the overall central plan. Details of how these operations were to be carried out, especially the selection of trade partners within broadly defined zones (see below), were delegated to FTEs. The implications of this type of decision making and organization will first be explored by means of an abstract model; it will then be expanded by including some specific features of the CPEs.

A diagrammatic analysis

The key planning instrument regulating short-term economic activity in the CPEs is the system of material balances, sometimes also referred to as balances of materials, equipment, and consumer goods (Grote 1973, p. 100). Briefly, a material balance is a record of available and required amounts of one product, product group, or type of production factor; it is the bookkeeping of the stocks and incoming and outgoing flows of a particular product or factor with reference to a given time period. A typical balance in its simplest form is depicted in Table 1.

Before examining a stylized version of the determination of

the level, the commodity composition, and the geographical distribution of trade in a CPE, it is worthwhile to look first at the central issues behind the complex interactions between trade and domestic activities with the help of a simple diagram, portraying the hypothetical decision-making sphere in countries bent on rapid industrialization per se. With the help of this simplification, which may be regarded as an ex post rationalization of the trade behavior of CPEs, particularly the selection of the absolute level of trade, a few crucial connections between the relatively low volume of trade of CPEs and their growth experience can be sketched. Problems associated with the commodity composition of trade and its geographical distribution will be studied later.

As argued in Chapter 2, although autarky was never an explicit objective in the sense that zero trade was certainly not a target of economic policies, trade aversion has generally been a very important implication of the overall policies pursued by the CPEs. In the stylized general-equilibrium model of international trade theory, autarky leads to suboptimal production and consumption levels, whereas completely free trade maximizes present satisfactions. However, the hypothetical world necessary for this proposition to hold is a highly unrealistic portrait of the actual complexities faced. Skepticism regarding the applicability of this theory to real-world decisions emerges not only on account of the existence of unemployment, monopolistic and other distortions, irrational price policies, and so on. The theoretical outcome of events is also unlikely to materialize in fact because no real policy could envisage an infinitesimal reallocation of production factors among economic sectors or even a complete dependence of consumption on foreign procurements of some products. Nevertheless, the general-equilibrium model with two countries, two production factors, and two commodities will be utilized here for heuristic purposes or as a point of reference to illustrate some important propositions or hints on the role of trade in a CPE.

It will be assumed that planners are aware to some degree of what can be produced with given resources, though they do not necessarily have all the information to map out a fully continuous production possibilities surface, which in theory might be as depicted by the curve *CC* in Figure 1. Instead, planners perceive

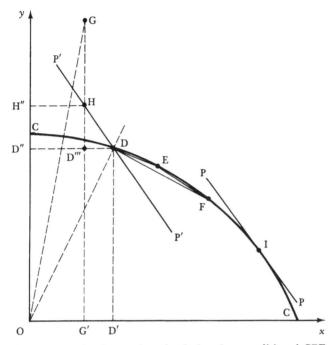

Figure 1. Production and trade choices in a traditional CPE.

their real production possibilities as a few discrete combinations indicated in the diagram by the three points *D, E,* and *F.* Whether these belong to the real production possibilities surface or not is a moot point. There is indeed some reason to believe that in the CPEs – as elsewhere – production factors are allocated suboptimally or, in other words, that the economies do not operate on but within the boundary of the surface. However problematic this may render a theoretical discourse or a comparison between actual economies and their hypothetical stereotype, for practical decision making it is much more important to deal with what the central planners or their counterparts in other economies in fact perceive to be the maximum output a combination of resources will yield.

The output combinations of *x* (foodstuffs) and *y* (investment goods) identified in the diagram by *D, E,* and *F* may have been found feasible production levels as a result of a first assessment of what planners view as alternative plan variants for the production side of decision making. Plan F might reflect the historically inherited production situation the planner is confronted with upon assuming control. D might be regarded as the most industry-intensive growth option (the most "voluntaristic" development path) that also envisages restricting consumption of x at or near the subsistence level (OG'). An intermediate development course might be E, where a "genetic" policy is pursued. The combination of the three points may be interpreted as part of the effective production possibilities locus here approximated by the broken chord DF. Socialist policy makers will now have to opt for one combination of outputs that serves not only current needs but also the long-term growth aims.

Let G indicate the combination of x and y that the central planner would like to consume, that is, he does not have a continuous surface depicting indifferences between various combinations of the two products but rather aims at one single basket. This extreme assumption on the form of the planner's preference function is not really needed to obtain the results explained below, but it simplifies matters. G might, for instance, be considered as the intersection of the ray OG, indicating the proportions in which the central planner hopes to distribute value added, and the vertical GG', depicting the minimum amount of x (OG') required for the population's subsistence.

If the socialist planner is shortsighted or opposed to the production of more foodstuffs than needed for subsistence, he might allocate resources in such a way that only D''' will be attained (surplus resources will, nevertheless, be concentrated in industries where their short-term marginal contribution will be zero). But he will probably not do so, as a larger amount of y (GG') is preferred than can be domestically produced. He will probably decide to produce a limited surplus of foodstuffs (say $G'D'$) and transform it into investment goods through trade. Such a choice can be substantiated simply by comparing rough transformation ratios in the domestic economy, as indicated by the chord DF, and the international price ratio PP, which suggests that trading x for y will increase the surplus available to alter the combination of production factors in the next planning period. Whether efficient internal prices are actually enacted is really irrelevant in the model, as such prices are not used to guide the allocation of domestic factors.

If the planner were a static optimizer, he should produce at F (the ideal case would be I) and engage in as much trade as feasible within the limits of his objective knowledge of production possibilities. Given the particular preference for y, he might decide to produce OG' of x rather than a more optimal quantity because he is convinced that the remaining factors should be fully used for domestic investment and that there should be a general shift toward producing more y domestically for social and other reasons that may have nothing to do with static economic efficiency as such.

If the planner decides to aim at autarky, he will select the most industry-intensive production point, D (also the consumption point), that he believes attainable. This will surely fall short of what the planner would like to obtain. In order to move closer toward the preferred consumption structure, the planner may resort to trade along $P'P'$ yet maintain production at D for reasons given above. He will trade $G'D'$ of x for $D''H''$ of y. If the planner were to set a consistent production-consumption plan, the preferred consumption bundle G would imply a considerable trade deficit. Because this is ruled out for reasons that will become more transparent later on, he will be obliged to change the "final product" combination G so that less y will be targeted than ideally preferred. He might arrive at this conclusion by means of the selection of production processes as indicated by the radius vector OD rather than those that would correspond to production points E and F or a combination of these processes.

At production point D the planner might prefer to minimize dependence on external markets and to promote rapid industrialization because of the imposed ideological precepts, conditions in outside markets (e.g., COCOM restrictions), concerns about coming to grips with the economic problems inherited, and other factors. The point is that the socialist planner as a rule decides to produce a much larger proportion of investment goods than what would be selected in an ideal MTE (which would be at I). It is true that the latter type of organization can generate in the short run higher consumption of both commodities, depending upon the preferences of the consumers, and that the CPE will be producing machinery at greater cost than on the world market. But it can be argued in turn that the dynamic effects of a larger output of domestically produced investment products and its accompanying externalities may well outweigh in the long run the immediate costs through advantages of having a larger domestic capital goods sector at an early stage: Learning by doing, economies of scale, external economies, the advantages of starting early, and so on may well argue in its favor.

The growing awareness of the real effects of trade in CPEs, once the above factors become less important, can also be illustrated in the diagram. At given world prices, the central planner might come to realize that at any point along $P'P'$ southeast of D the combination H (at which plan consistency with the production processes OD is generated) will remain attainable, yet the economy will not necessarily have to make full use of its resources. In other words, foreign trade can yield more machinery for investment than possible under relative autarky ($H''D''$), and in addition it will set free resources that, together with the extra machines, may yield a much higher transformation curve (or combination of a few points), shifting it in the northeasterly direction.

It is, of course, also conceivable that the CPE may try to become self-sufficient and that "a dialectical way to autarky" (Boltho 1971, p. 125) will be found by trading first and then retreating into self-sufficiency. But this course is not feasible for the smaller CPEs, and the USSR, which could pursue such a policy, has never held full self-reliance as a policy goal. It seems nevertheless instructive to consider this roundabout way to autarky as an ex post rationalization of the outcome of the policy aims that inspired choice in the late 1940s and early 1950s in all CPEs and of the USSR's policies in the mid-1930s (Holzman 1968, p. 281). Note, however, that a perpetuation of this course has been most emphatically rejected ever since the "New Course" of the mid-1950s (see below).

The above simple framework illustrates intuitively how the CPEs could have combined a desire for rapid industrialization through import substitution with a minimum dependence on trade. It cannot, of course, capture the dependence of the small CPEs on imports of primary and other goods. The key role of intermediate goods in the industrialization and trade policies of CPEs can be accommodated in a simple IO model derived from the balancing method of socialist planning.

A simple model of the CPE's trade behavior

The system of material balances is a rather primitive form of an IO table. But similarities exist, as the balance's origin is essentially a column and the destination side a row of a very detailed IO table expressed in absolute physical units. It may therefore be instructive to represent the CPE and its trade mechanism by means of an open IO model for which not all coefficients are known to the central planner. Because material balances are used in planning, and not only to accommodate ex post bookkeeping, most variables in the model below will be target variables.

A model of an open CPE should describe the planner's view of the economy and interactions with the essential structural stock and flow constraints imposed on the process of seeking a way to achieve centrally set targets. East European experience indicates that the mechanism by which planners harmonize foreign trade with the domestic plan is complex, sometimes inconsistent, and partially unconscious. In turn, the problem of analytically portraying trade decisions involves constructing a framework that enables the conversion of more or less simultaneous decisions made either during plan construction or conditioned by past developments, into an identifiable sequence or an algorithm of consecutive actions. The aim of the present model is to highlight this sequence of decisions rather than to depict in all details how trade problems are resolved in practice. To simplify the model, its planning horizon is restricted to one year, a condition that will preclude looking at the implications of specialization strategies per se. But the annual plan is still the chief institutional mechanism by which actual decisions are implemented, including specialization agreements.

The basic assumption of this model is that the planner is presented a set of production and consumption goals for which he must find a feasible plan within the constraints of the given economic structure and its components. The planner attempts to achieve society's short-term goals within a very restricted space. However, because production possibilities are not a singular point and the consumption frontier offers some substitutability, the planner can and must make choices within constraints, and his behavior must therefore be explicitly modeled to reflect his decision procedure.

It is assumed that the planner is given a vector of desirable net output levels, denoted q, which express the government or society's short-term preferences. This vector contains targets for domestic consumption and investments, including inventory levels. It is conceivable that the targets assigned are not all feasible under the given environment, and compromises will be necessary between, say, the government and the planner. However, certain targets of q (e.g., private consumption) will have a floor limit below which further compromises are deemed inadvisable.

The chief constraint is the inherited economic structure because it sets technological limits on substitutions, and sectoral and economywide capacity limitations on gross output levels $\bar{y}$ (the vector of capacity constraints is denoted $\bar{y}$). Though the total volume of labor, capital, and land setting upper limits on gross output is fixed in the short run, sectoral variations in the allocation of one or more of these factors will yield different combinations of gross output. Hence, $\bar{y}$ is a planner's variable and maximum output is a function of one possible allocation of production factors. The set of possible combinations of capacity limits will be denoted $\bar{Y}$. Interindustry relationships are captured by the matrix A of technological coefficients a_{ij}, indicating the sum of domestic and foreign inputs that sector j requires from sector i per unit of gross output y_j. Naturally, it is in the nature of the production process in complex economies that not all coefficients are fixed technologically and that the planner does not have a complete set of such coefficients at his disposal.

Finally, the foreign trade sector has to be constrained because of foreign exchange policy choices and the availability of foreign exchange (R). The volume of planned changes in reserves ($\dot{R}$) depends on the initial volume of exchange reserves, planned foreign loans, and government objectives for exchange reserves at the end of the plan period. Though it is not usually fixed absolutely because the CPEs can borrow abroad, it is here assumed that $\bar{R}$ is given and, hence, that conflicts between internal and external balance must be resolved not through ex post borrowing or lending abroad, but by domestic adjustments, for reasons that will be explained. Note that a positive value for $\bar{R}$ means that the CPE decumulates its foreign exchange; if $\bar{R}$ is negative, it signals that the CPE is bent on increasing its exchange reserves.

The planner's general problem now is to solve the system of interdependencies between supply (the sum of gross output and imports) and uses (the sum of intermediate uses, final consumption, and exports):[1]

$$Ay + q + x = y + m \tag{1}$$

subject to the constraints that gross output should not exceed the capacity limits implied by any permissible factor distribution:

$$y \leqslant \bar{y} \text{ for any } \bar{y} \; \epsilon \bar{Y}$$

and that the net surplus (deficit) of trade is at least as large as (not larger than) the intended accumulation (decumulation) of foreign exchange reserves:

$$p \, (m - x) \leqslant \bar{R} \tag{3}$$

The vector of foreign trade prices p and $\bar{R}$ are expressed as the domestic equivalent of foreign currency prices converted at the official exchange rate.

Because not all elements of A are known, the planner will attempt to construct a consistent, feasible plan by drawing up material balances on the basis of information collected from individual production units in response to tentative assignments. The planner checks for feasibility by calculating balances (b) of supplies ($y + m$) and demands ($Ay + x + q$):

$$y + m - Ay - x - q = b \tag{4}$$

The vector b contains positive elements for sectors in which total supply exceeds demand and negative elements for sectors in which the reverse relationship holds. Clearly, the negative elements are not feasible and the planner will have to seek another solution by changing some variables over which he has control (see below). At some point in the iterations, the planner will tend to set b equal to $(m - x)$, provided the foreign exchange constraint at equation 3 is satisfied. In other words, at some stage in the search for a feasible plan, the remaining negative elements of b will be added to the import plan while the remaining positive elements will be added to the export plan subject to satisfaction of the condition on the balance of trade.

How does the planner in such a stylized framework behave? In the model there are three vectors of choice: gross output y, the trade balance p $(x - m)$, and net output q. If one set of targets is fixed, say, by political priorities, the planner is constrained to search for a feasible solution by experimenting with different combinations of the two other variables. Given, for instance, q and choosing $\bar{y}$ will imply the trade balance, and conversely. Before narrowing down the choice among all feasible alternatives, which can be quite numerous under trade conditions, to a likely space, it is useful to mention a few important aspects of the CPEs, especially crucial to small open economies but not altogether irrelevant even to the USSR.

Observations on the behavior of CPEs show that in plan upon plan certain sectors are routinely targeted at gross output levels that cannot fully meet the needs of the economy, whereas certain others are normally slated to attain output levels well above domestic needs. In the first case, the planner apparently deems it advisable not to allocate production factors to those sectors in an effort to supplant imports because this would obviously be irrational or, in some cases, impossible. Similarly, a second set of sectors would appear to receive their factor allocations because the planner finds it natural to slate a certain level of exports for those activities, possibly because of specialization commitments. That is to say, the typical CPE has minimum levels of exports and imports known to some extent to the planner, and these levels are highly correlated with economic activity in one or more sectors. He could, for example, construct a set of minimum imports the economy could not dispense with. Thus the adopted technologies determining the configuration of A may allow for some substitution between domestic (E) and residual foreign inputs (MR), but not between E and basic imports (MM):[2]

$$A = E + MM + MR \qquad (5)$$

MM is a matrix of coefficients m_{ij} expressing the need for noncompeting imports. For a given level of gross output y_0 minimum imports can therefore be calculated from the system of balances $(MM\,y_0)$ to yield:

$$b_1 = [I - A]y_0 + (ma_1 - xa_1) - q_0 \tag{6}$$

where q_0 is the given set of final output objectives, ma_1 the vector of minimum import requirements, and xa_1 the vector of minimum export commitments. The balance of trade equals:

$$p\,(xa_1 - ma_1 + b_1) = R_1 \tag{7}$$

If this balance does not agree with the target for changes in foreign exchange reserves R, the planner will have to search for a different solution. If final output levels are kept unchanged, he has to continue to explore within the given constraints, and the second iteration will consist of setting new gross output levels equal to the old ones minus the incurred imbalances, which enables the planner to calculate new minimum import and export levels to yield new balances:

$$b_2 = [I - A]\,y_1 + (ma_2 - xa_2) - q_0 \tag{8}$$

and a new trade balance:

$$p\,(xa_2 - ma_2 + b_2) = R_2 \tag{9}$$

Feasibility will have to be checked and, possibly, the iteration process will have to be resumed. Would this sequence converge toward a feasible solution? Clearly, in the above model, where final output levels are given and the planner calculates gross outputs from responses of the lower planning organs, the outcome will depend especially on the shape of the feasible allocations contained in $\bar{Y}$ and other characteristics of the model. Whether a solution exists and how quickly it can be reached are matters that will not unduly concern us here (see Hewett 1976, pp. 167–170). The most likely outcome, however, is a conflict between the balancing requirement $\bar{R}$ and the set of final output levels q_0. With restrictions on gross output and limited alternative allocation possibilities, conflicts are bound to arise. Because the constraint of foreign reserves is not changeable by definition, some elements of q_0 must on balance be decreased. The process of arriving at a new set of final output levels q_1 depends on political negotiations, which probably set some trade-offs among the elements of q and lower bounds on some of its elements.

It should be added also that, if the planning process does not yield a satisfactory combination of gross and net output levels at the given constraints on the trade balance, the planner may resort to other practices that cannot be accommodated in this model. He may try to suppress inconsistencies, for instance, by reducing technological coefficients in an effort to curtail the demand for deficit commodities. The political bodies may also permit the planner to compress, at his discretion, the amount of goods not used for further reproduction (such as cutting private consumption or running down nonstrategic reserves). Although a discussion of the existence of feasible solutions and the special properties of reaching consistency is certainly most interesting, especially with the peculiar vector b in the model, such a detailed examination of phenomena that are not really germane to SEI falls outside the scope of this study. It will be assumed below that a solution exists without violating the balance requirement.

The role of prices and exchange rates in trade

Of considerable importance in assessing the role of trade in CPEs and the trade behavior of these countries is the balance of payments constraint. Before going into its more practical aspects and relating it to price and exchange rate policies, the validity of the proposition that CPEs aim at balancing current trade should be justified. Generally speaking, the central planner aims at balanced trade for the following reasons. In the event of a negative balance, the CPE will have little or no reserves of hard currencies or gold to fall back on, its own currency is not internationally accepted, its ability to arrange for ex post credits is limited, and it does not wish to become too dependent on unplanned capital flows as this might undermine the country's independence – a key objective of overall policy. This does not negate the fact that sometimes the CPE will arrange for borrowing abroad and thus increase imports beyond current export revenues. Sometimes too, as in the mid-1970s, relative price changes abroad are so drastic and unpredictable that the original plan can be adhered to only if unplanned credits are sought. The experience of several CPEs in 1974–1976 fits this picture rather well without, however, contradicting the general observation. Also large positive imbalances will be avoided precisely because the CPE's policy is anchored to the maximal exploitation of domestic resources for growth: The accumulation of hard currency reserves will not directly contribute to the rapid economic development of the internal economy or to the formation of capital within its industrial ventures.[3]

These observations are not intended to suggest that the planner works under an absolutely rigid foreign exchange constraint, but flexibility is evidently limited. Perhaps the overriding issue of striving for overall balance is the role of trade in the process of domestic industrialization – a point stressed in Chapter 2 but worth emphasizing once more here. CPEs engage in exports primarily to finance unavoidable imports. MTEs have, of course, a similar interest but there trade will be the aggregate result of individual actions in response to profitability of exports and imports as compared with domestic outlets. Government agencies in MTEs will most likely show more concern for the employment effects of international trade and will, therefore, tend to promote exports more than imports. In a CPE full or overfull employment is a permanent objective of national economic policy that is fairly well implemented, regardless of the particular trade strategy embraced at any given moment, and employment effects play therefore a much smaller role in the CPE's trade policies than balancing trade and acquiring imports. At times the CPEs have been obliged to resort to export campaigns because of balance of payments pressures generated by rapid growth, that is, ultimately to pay for rising imports (Holzman 1966, p. 240).

To explain more realistically how trade fits into the domestic economic activities of CPEs, it will be helpful to look at the implications of the balancing constraint for prices and exchange rates. From Chapter 2 it is clear that central planning operates without relying much on relative price comparisons, and domestic prices do not reflect real scarcities. For a closed economy, such a price policy implies an internal distribution of value added that differs measurably from what it ought to be according to the real contribution of the production factors. If the CPE wishes to open up its economy without allowing for potential price drifts, the internal autonomous price policy may yield an international redistribution of value added, quite contrary to the interests of the CPE. Users would prefer imports of commodities overvalued domestically and products undervalued domestically would be attractive to foreign users. Because internal prices do not express real relative costs, deciding on the basis of differences between actual internal prices and WMPs may imply considerable real losses, which could complicate or even jeopardize the implementation of the other policy objectives. Overvaluation of the domestic currency may, of course, explain the need for dispensing with price comparisons and the official exchange rate in central and decentralized decision making involving trade, and resorting instead to central controls (Holzman 1966, pp. 244–265). But such arguments are of marginal relevance in explaining and understanding why free trade cannot be permitted in a traditional CPE. Direct controls to ensure that foreign trade is planned and carried out in accordance with what is believed to be consistent with overall policies make the exchange rate a redundant instrument, for economic activities are not nearly approximately equally over- or undervalued and the CPE is bent on maintaining internal price autonomy. One of the key tasks of the MFT is precisely that of preventing an overvalued exchange rate to exert a direct influence on trade decisions and thus to avoid subsidizing trade for the benefit of foreign purchasers.

In a theoretical framework, the central planner will only be able to sustain price autonomy and some degree of trade efficiency at the same time if he is willing and able to impose a complex system of implicit or explicit taxes and subsidies on foreign trade prices, reflecting his preferences for domestic growth. To do so he should be able to base trade decisions on "shadow" prices or real cost differentials. Taxes will be levied whenever the foreign price calculated in domestic currency is below the internal price; subsidies are required whenever the reverse relationship holds on the import side. Exports must be subsidized whenever the domestic price is higher than the foreign price and taxed whenever the reverse relationship prevails. In other words, trade decisions should be based on real relative costs. In view of the planner's aversion to instruments of indirect coordination, it should not be too surprising to learn that differences between domestic and trade prices are neutralized largely by administrative means. Whether or not this will completely prevent an unintended redistribution of value added abroad will be discussed later. The fairly rigid separation of internal and external markets in the traditional CPE proceeds as follows. The MFT or its subordinate FTEs purchase the goods earmarked for exports at the internal price and sell abroad at the international price. Similarly for imports, which are purchased abroad at the foreign price but sold domestically at the internal price. As a result, exports and imports may yield bookkeeping losses or gains that do not necessarily represent the real "benefits" from trade for the economy as a whole. Subsidies and taxes are implicit in the sense that any loss (gain) incurred as a result of "price equalization" is compensated (siphoned off) by a special fund administered by the budget directors. A bookkeeping loss will result from exports if the value of exports expressed in domestic prices (p_d) exceeds the value of exports in foreign prices converted in local currency (p_w); in imports, a loss will result if the reverse relationship prevails. The MFT will show an aggregate profit from trade if:

$$x' \, (p_w - p_d) - m' \, (p_w - p_d) > 0 \qquad (10)$$

where x' and m' are the transposed export and import column vectors. Even if trade valued in foreign prices is balanced, there may be gains or losses incurred by the price-equalization account (for more details, see Brabant 1977, pp. 247–257).

Evidently, domestic and foreign trade prices may differ considerably because of currency overvaluation, tariffs, taxes, and subsidies, but the chief source of the differentiation is that domestic prices are set autonomously so as to suit the social, organizational, and economic features of socialist development policies. Incidentally, explicit but uniform tariffs are a completely redundant instrument in the commercial operations of such a CPE (but see section 2) and have in fact not played any perceptible role in trade decisions. Actually, until the 1960s, either no explicit tariffs existed or they were applied only in the bookkeeping of trade transactions.

Because of the virtually complete decoupling of internal and external markets, the balance constraint in the two models was specified in foreign price equivalents, which are defined here as the foreign export or import price multiplied with the official exchange rate actually used in bookkeeping operations.[4] Note, however, that the trade balance expressed in domestic prices may differ substantially in size and sign from the trade balance in foreign trade prices precisely because the official exchange rate is generally incapable of adequately relating domestic and foreign prices.

The CPEs generally embrace a set of multiple exchange rates to deal separately with a number of distinct foreign transactions (merchandise trade, noncommercial transactions, tourism, special transactions such as private remittances from abroad, internal exports, and so on),[5] and the rates have been set and modified at different points in time to suit particular interests. A crucial differentiation of exchange rates is needed for two important circumstances. First, the CPE maintains a dual system of domestic prices, because consumer prices are kept more constant than producer prices and they differ from producer prices by subsidies and taxes that can be quite substantial. Second, as examined below, prices in intra-CMEA trade differ both in level and proportion from WMPs.

Official exchange rates of the traditional CPE are set in terms of a gold parity and have been kept unchanged since 1961 for the USSR, 1962 for Bulgaria, and the early 1950s for all other CPEs, including Hungary (though there the official exchange rate, while still legally in force, is no longer quoted).[6] Their level bears generally no relation to the purchasing power of these currencies, nor do they express the real opportunity cost of earning foreign exchange. Even if they reflected on the whole a realistic purchasing power when they were established, as frequently claimed by East European writers (Brabant 1977, p. 293), changes in foreign or domestic prices have not been passed on in exchange rate fluctuations, at least until the early 1970s (see section 5). In the traditional CPE, the official exchange rate is generally a notional multiplier translating foreign trade values into domestic bookkeeping units. It has played some role in deciding upon the geographical allocation of trade with nonsocialist countries (see section 2), largely for a given set of export and import transactions earmarked in the plan. In countries where employee bonuses and premiums are tied in with the notional profit of the FTE, the official exchange rate has not been irrelevant altogether. Other rates, such as the noncommercial ones, have evidently exerted a much greater influence, especially on tourism and remittances from abroad.

As far as merchandise trade is concerned, the exchange rate played virtually no role until the economic reforms were ushered in. In fact, the planner has found it beneficial since the early 1950s to seek other means of assessing trade efficiency. But this point fits in better with the trade aspects of the economic reforms (section 5).

A preliminary assessment of the role of trade in a CPE

The models introduced here were designed to illustrate how a traditional CPE could determine trade. They are but a rough picture of the general processes underlying decisions about the level and the commodity composition of trade. Although there are several other versions of trade determination in CPEs, most models (for instance, Boltho 1971, pp. 68–127; and Hewett 1974, pp. 135–156) have focused narrowly, sometimes to an excessive extent, on optimality conditions in a general-equilibrium framework and hence presume heroic assumptions about knowledge, the computational ability of the planner, and a neutral environment without further ado. The analytical tools used here suggest that the essence of the material balance technique in the short run is consistency, that is, attaining a feasible solution that simultaneously satisfies to some degree the preferences of society's leaders, the trade balance requirement, and the restrictions on domestic resources, production capacities, and consumption. The short-term models illustrate how the level of trade and its composition can be selected once the activities included for operation and their level of gross or net output are selected, which may help to understand the management of the traditional CPE's foreign trade (Alampiev 1971, p. 22; Proft 1973, p. 126). The above framework can also dispense with the notion that the CPE's trade behavior rests chiefly on an "error theory of international trade" (Holzman 1976, p. 33).

To sum up, output targets or final domestic consumption targets in the traditional CPE are set mostly as a result of political choice, organizational expediency, or economic priority rather than on the basis of economic rationality. Although the influence of rationality in macroeconomic decisions, as explained, should not be minimized, the actual choice of what will be traded residually after satisfying basic needs results largely from the confines of reaching a feasible plan. Until recently, trade was not regarded as a possible growth motor and if a product could be produced at home, cost considerations played only an incidental role in weighing up alternatives.

The above models cannot cope with the third essential component of trade decisions, the geographical distribution of trade. From what was said it should be intuitive that the planner of a relatively open economy must in reality cope with several uncertainties: Can intended imports be secured at the right moment, in the desired quantities, and approximately at the planned cost? Can planned exports be disposed of at the anticipated return so that the balance of payments will not be unduly disturbed? These problems of planning trade for stable growth become even more restrictive because it does not suffice to earn foreign currency in the abstract to pay for a given import flow when the bill must be acquitted in a well-specified currency. Furthermore, price heterogeneity prevails because international markets are imperfectly integrated and the CPEs have adopted special rules for setting prices in mutual trade (see below). This implies that the constraint on the CPE's balance of trade or payments is in fact far more complicated than specified above, for the planner will have to come to grips with several regional or bilateral balances unless payment means can be procured exogenously by drawing upon gold and currency reserves or loans. Although such procurements may cushion adjustments in the short run, they cannot forestall them altogether because in the end reserves can only be replenished through exports.

2. The distribution of trade and its impact on trade levels

A key trade question is the selection of foreign markets. CPEs do not usually decide upon the geographical distribution of trade after a careful, patient choice between relative import costs and export returns in alternative outlets, even for commodities that the country would like to import or is able to export. In fact, the degree of choice here is subject to several additional constraints resulting from internal and external conditions, economic or others, delimiting the CPE's environment.

One of the principal factors restricting the CPE's choice of alternative trade partners stems from the organization of external trade and payments as it has been appended to the organization of detailed central planning. This form was chosen, partly for extraneous reasons (see below), but also because when a government pledged to the fast socialization of economic activities comes to power, one of its first acts is to create the MFT. Without state control over external transactions, comprehensive planning and control of domestic production, trade, and money would be impossible. The particular form in which this state control finds its expression in practical matters determines the passive role hitherto allotted to exports, because it demands that more attention be devoted to the fulfillment of the import plan as formulated on the basis of minimum requirements and the disequilibria of the material balances, than to the optimization of trade. As a result, socialist policy makers attach a lot of attention to trade planning as a basic tool attenuating the degree of uncertainty inherent in forecasting and engaging in foreign commerce.

Trade poses intricate problems for CPE central planning mainly because commerce is contingent on supply and demand forces that cannot be controlled by a single national planning center. Because socialist objectives envision rapid and stable economic development by concentrating resources especially in pacemaking sectors, they cannot rely extensively on trade. Import substitution, the planner's perceived requirement of stability, and the felt need for protecting the domestic economy against foreign disturbances will generally compress trade below levels warranted by efficiency considerations. Furthermore, excessive compliance with the requirements of socialist organization calls for rigid trade controls under the aegis of the MFT.

The trade-reducing effect of the planning institutions is by no means the only or even the principal explanation behind the CPE's relative disregard for trade. As noted, trade and other economic interactions between two or more nations is intricately bound up with the overall foreign policy of these countries. The traumatic experience of young Soviet Russia faced with threats from all countries plus the profoundly insular and nationalistic mentality of the Soviet leadership of the 1930s combined to dictate a trade strategy that was in fact not a strategy at all, but an attempt to cut links with the rest of the world. These formative experiences with socialist trade policies were crucial in shaping East European institutions and policies, and imparted autarkic characteristics in the development strategy that was imposed from outside. Though not all import-substitution endeavors succeeded, the fact that considerations about safeguarding national security and promoting autonomous development have permeated trade policies is crucial to a better understanding of the CPE's trade behavior and mechanisms. It will be shown here that there are additional, built-in features of the traditional CPE that have kept the volume of trade substantially lower than it would have been under a protective policy. Even if overprotection were completely disclaimed in the future without substantially remodeling the institutions, instruments, and behavioral rules, the CPE's trade volume would probably still be below that of an equivalent MTE, and the composition and distribution of trade would be very different.

To reduce the uncertainty surrounding foreign trade and hence to facilitate the implementation and fulfillment of domestic objectives, it is useful to obtain information about the trade intentions of possible partners. This knowledge can be acquired in several ways, but one of the most expedient means is by concluding formal trade and payments agreements as a comprehensive complement to the national economic plan. The economies willing and able to make such firm commitments are naturally those with a similar proclivity for forecasting and controlling trade, especially the other CPEs. The reason for this is rather simple. Western governments who enter into bilateral trade and payments agreements (BTPAs), for example, have no power to guarantee implementation, if the agreement stipulates detailed targets at all. Whereas the CPE can sign away part of its future national product in exchange for other goods, the political leadership in an MTE cannot do much more than foster trade with CPEs indirectly, especially by relaxing "extraeconomic" regulations because state trading is usually small and differently organized than in CPEs (Kostecki 1978, p. 202). MTE leaders can, for instance, open up their borders to exports and imports of particular products and can encourage contacts between private traders and trade organizations of the CPEs, but they cannot guarantee consummation of a transaction in the same way a CPE planner can. In particular, they cannot conscript enterprises to trade specific quantities or values. If anything, the trade agreement of a CPE with an MTE is therefore more a record of good intentions and of possible extraeconomic actions than a firm promise to buy and sell. With regard to the payments aspects of such agreements, MTE governments can do substantially more, for example, in accommodating clearing currencies, providing credits, and so on. Yet, owing to comprehensive central planning, payment means in whatever form are only incidental in eliciting market response in CPEs: The motor driving international transactions is indeed the agreement on the exchange of commodities for which payments must be arranged in one form or another.

F. D. Holzman attributes the extensive trade of the CPEs with each other at the expense of trade with other markets "in part at least, not to discrimination [by MTEs] but to the unwillingness of these non-bloc nations to adapt themselves, without a charge, to large-scale trade with the CPEs, under the CPE ground rules" (Holzman 1966, p. 25). This statement is essentially correct but does not go far enough: As the implementation of trade agreements between CPEs and MTEs has demonstrated, an MTE is not in a position to accommodate transactions in the rigid framework so typical of intra-CMEA agreements. It can be argued that even if an MTE were willing to adapt to CPE standards, it could not do so without violating some essential ground rules of the MTE system and the more general social values directly related to it. A valid case could be made for including contracts between CPEs and individual enterprises in MTEs. But such contracts have played a negligible role until very recently and pose problems quite different from those emanating from the BTPAs concluded between pairs of CPEs. The comments regarding the importance of trade contracts apply therefore mainly to trade with other CMEA members. A valid case could also be made for including the CPE's relations with the socialist countries largely ignored here. However, the analysis will disregard the other CPEs because they are relatively unimportant trade partners and, owing to economic as well as political reasons, their relations with the CMEA are much more unstable than the regional ties of the active European members.

The heavy reliance on intra-CMEA trade through formal and comprehensive BTPAs is a most important complement of the socialist domestic planning mechanism because, by so doing, the CPE buys stability in internal and external activities, if perhaps at the cost of flexibility in trade. Although the CPEs could have acquired more stability in trade by concluding ex ante agreements with all partners simultaneously, they have not done so for a number of reasons. First, it is undoubtedly easier to conclude an agreement between two partners than to settle all exchanges through multilateral negotiations. Second, the attitude of the USSR regarding trade with CPEs has generally favored bilateral rather than multilateral agreements as coping separately with each CPE seems to have better suited the USSR's political supremacy and hegemony over Eastern Europe. Third, the nature of domestic physical planning targets provides some rationale behind the choice of bilateral agreements. The CPEs' commitment to bilateralism stems essentially from this model's congruence with national planning as both are controlled by central planners, whereas in multilateral trading each country's trade balance could be affected adversely by the terms settled in its trading partners' commerce with each other. Also, the deliberate disregard of real scarcity indicators in planning makes it very difficult to offset bilateral balances through multilateral agreements.

A typical trade agreement for current transactions between any two CPEs contains a target for the trade level (exports as well as imports), the projected composition of trade by main commodity groups,[7] and a detailed listing of about four-fifths of what will be delivered and at what prices during a given trade period. Although the specification of the anticipated bilateral trade flows has probably become less rigid than it used to be in the early 1950s, all main goods are in principle still stipulated in the trade agreement. Within the agreed targets for turnover and commodity groups, excluding the commodity flows detailed, individual ministries can settle further details in the course of the period for which the agreement is in force. This means, for instance, that in principle a planned export target cannot be exceeded unless concurrently the parties agree upon supplementary import flows and that one partner's failure to honor its commitments will entail unplanned capital flows.

With the above as background, it seems fair to say that BTPAs are concluded, among other things, as a useful device for mitigating the uncertainty of foreign economic relations, as a way to attenuate fluctuations in international reserves and, in some instances, to dispense with reserves altogether, and, finally, as a convenient means of accommodating the ostensible administrative needs of the CPE. In view of this, it is somewhat easier to understand the transformation of the trade sector into an organizational framework that closely mirrors and complements domestic central planning.[8] So far so good. But is the particular type of bilateralism employed by the CPEs only a convenient organizational tool or is intra-CMEA bilateralism far more complex? Bilateralism is usually treated as one particular and somewhat peculiar form of preferential trading (Caves 1974, pp. 32–39) – a special type of trade discrimination. A number of complementary hypotheses will be investigated below to explain the East European variety of BTPAs. As demonstrated in section 3, the circumstances accompanying or giving rise to these BTPAs suggest that bilateralism among the CPEs is a very complex phenomenon that involves considerably more than simple organizational convenience or the express desire to discriminate.

To understand the drawbacks and advantages of bilateralism, it is useful to recall how trade decisions in MTEs are made. The optimal level, distribution, and composition of trade in the stylized MTE of general-equilibrium models of free competition are decided upon by exploiting fully the differences in relative costs between the home country and the outside world. The comparative cost doctrine underlying such an allocation suggests that a country can profitably extend foreign trade participation until internal relative prices tend to converge and become identical with relative WMPs. The classical doctrine of comparative advantage indicates how the ideal MTE should select the level and composition of trade so as to attain the best allocation of resources and the highest satisfaction of private and social needs. The determination of the geographical distribution of trade is usually not dealt with, as such a problem cannot arise in a model with two countries (the home country and the rest of the world) or in a model where foreign prices are assumed to be uniform. By extending the model to encompass "localized commodities," the theory can be brought a step closer to reality. Questions about trade would then be answered in much the same vein as above. In particular, the geographical distribution of trade would be determined by comparing relative costs of the home country with relative costs in all disjoint units of the outside world, that is, in all other regions with different cost structures. Exchange rates for all these disjoint markets in terms of the local currency would help to determine the volume of trade with each market.

In principle, trade decisions in a CPE should be made in much the same way as in an MTE as, indeed, the theory of trade of the ideal CPE should closely parallel the conventional general theory of international trade.[9] Difficulties start to crop up when an attempt is made to rationalize the actual trade behavior of a CPE. Admittedly, also the real MTE fails to behave in quite the same way as prescribed by economic theory, though it is doubtlessly true that trade decisions in an MTE are more in accordance with theory than is the case for the solutions adopted by a CPE.

Material balances as the principal planning instrument of a traditional CPE are drawn up so as to equate supply and demand, the latter being determined partly by the preferences of the political leadership and partly by the constraints emanating from production possibilities, consumption needs, and trade opportunities. The level and composition of trade result largely from the need for noncompeting imports, export commitments, and the relative shortages and surpluses revealed in the process of balancing the economy. To be sure, the geographical distribution of trade is, in principle, selected so that surpluses flow to the markets yielding the largest return and shortages are met by importing at the lowest possible cost, perhaps after allowing for differentiated tariffs. However, several exogenous constraints stemming from economic and other conditions typical of the CPE and its environment curtail the number of feasible alternatives that can be explored and hence the reduced likelihood of generating an optimal distribution of trade.

Ideally, trade contracts concluded by the CPEs as an integral part of the general economic plan should lead to the indirect coordination, not optimization, of the various national plans by dovetailing individual components of the CPE's trade needs. This desire to ensure more stability in trade through formal agreements is already an important restriction on the distribution of trade, as argued above. Other impediments to flexibility in determining the distribution result from the fact that the smaller CPEs are not completely free to choose trade with markets yielding the highest return on exports or entailing the lowest expenditure for imports. This stems from economic and political circumstances partly chosen by the CPE itself and partly imposed by whatever concrete geopolitical realities the CPE must cope with. The principal internal factor limiting the CPE's choice of markets is the administrative system of planning with material balances, which largely ignores or is unable to take into account real relative prices, and even precludes the creation of market-clearing prices.[10] This planning instrument's main defect with respect to the determination of the level and composition of trade consists of ignoring relative production costs, alternative production processes and trade programs, and the interdependencies between trade and investments. Apart from its failure to encourage optimal choice, a possibly more significant factor is the rather inflexible nature of this planning instrument (Montias 1959, pp. 242–251). Furthermore, the socialist growth strategy purposefully disregards alternative development paths that call for substantial trade participation. Finally, it should not be overlooked that the ideology dominant in the CPEs and its conflicts with other policies may preclude trade with certain countries or regions, notwithstanding obvious potential economic advantages. These obstacles are probably far more important in generating the distribution of trade than, say, differentiated tariff or exchange rate policies, though the latter play some role in distributing trade previously earmarked in the plan for nonsocialist countries.

The external conditions hindering the CPE's free choice of foreign markets may be divided into those imposed by the CPE's allies, who wish to control trade to maintain or to strengthen regional cohesion, and those imposed by other countries. Among the latter family of obstructions one should recall, for instance, the existence of strategic controls, quotas on imports from CPEs, open or hidden protectionism, and other such impediments to the free flow of goods, services, and capital.

This brief summary may underscore the view that intra-CMEA bilateralism is not the only hindrance to freer trade behavior and more flexible trade mechanisms in CPEs. Nevertheless, bilateralism both as a trade model and as a component of economic policy will receive much more attention here than any other of the obstacles named because it is regarded as the core of the problems dogging SEI and more efficient trade formation in general. Its specific characteristics will also help to define the variety and scope of instruments of indirect coordination that may be implemented to whittle gradually away the most negative effects of past and present policies.

3. Bilateralism and intra-CMEA trade

Bilateralism is but one form of general exchange controls. It is usually resorted to when countries face severe payments problems for which the more subtle forms of trade intervention and regulation (such as uniform or discriminatory tariffs and general commodity quotas) are no longer deemed adequate means of attaining the overall policy objectives in foreign trade and payments. Instead of managing trade on the macroeconomic level by indirect means, bilateralism is an instrument of a conscious policy of maintaining complete control over the foreign exchange market.[11] The difficulties of analyzing bilateralism in the real world stem from the great diversity of forms in which it has appeared, the amazing variety of motives behind its emergence,[12] and from the fact that such a trade policy is usually implemented by means of a considerably more complex network of measures than just declaring the home currency inconvertible.

BTPAs usually provide for financing current trade between two countries in the form of clearing credits, which are freely available for use by one country in making payments for goods and services from the other. Bilateralism is therefore normally concerned with the financial aspects of trade, especially as it is an endeavor to economize on scarce foreign exchange reserves.

Whereas fully unregulated, free trade cannot, of course, be permitted under bilateralism, the licensing schemes to guide real export and import flows, or the currency allocation schemes that accompany the special exchange controls, are as a rule administered by each country separately. Trade flows accommodated under clearing arrangements are by no means completely planned in advance and their shifts are responding to movements in the bilateral debit and credit positions of each country. In the arrangements instituted by the CPEs, however, the BTPAs are generally trade quota contracts that provide for the issuance of export and import licenses for specific types and quantities of goods and services both parties agree upon in advance.

In addition to trade obstacles emanating from the particular organizational form by which a bilateral trade policy is implemented, the trade level under bilateralism is usually also affected by motives other than those of economic efficiency and expediency. The chief impediment to a systematic analysis of intra-CMEA bilateralism is precisely that trade can no longer be conducted according to market forces, but is set in the central plan in the light of overall government policies, and there is no guarantee that central planners will endeavor to simulate market forces. Comprehensive control over trade leaves much leeway for the implementation of a number of foreign policy aims of which commercial diplomacy is perhaps the least injurious overt manifestation. In this context it becomes essential to "distinguish clearly between procedures of negotiations and the type of trading that is the object of such negotiations" (Condliffe 1940, p. 200), though this neat decoupling of the trade model from the policies it is designed to support may become blurred in the real world.

Although bilateralism emerges because of problems in foreign exchange markets, sooner or later, however, virtually every exchange-control system will lose its original rationale inspired primarily by monetary and financial considerations (e.g., to prevent capital flight and deflation). In the interferences with trade, protectionism, autarchy, and totalitarian control will gradually assume ascendency over the original aims, and they will eventually be used to further ulterior goals, not necessarily economic in

nature, if these were not at the root of the institution of bilateralism in the first place. And this ascendancy, as experience
proves, can persist quite long.

The definition and forms of bilateralism

Bilateralism may be defined variously (Brabant 1973, pp.
66–69), but here it will be taken to mean a foreign trade policy
designed to equate intended exports and imports between two
countries in such a way that unplanned transactions are avoided
or, at least, that actual transactions need not be compensated by
means of unanticipated capital movements. In a technical
framework, bilateralism as a trade policy may be defined as a
strategy optimizing a welfare function subject to the constraints
that no negative products can be generated, available resources
cannot be overdrawn, the processes finally used must at least
break even,[13] and bilateral trade imbalances over a mutually
agreed period of time cannot exceed a given magnitude, possibly zero. The result of this trade strategy is well-known: Reciprocal turnover will as a rule be compressed below levels that would
prevail under normal market conditions, as trade will tend to be
reduced to the export capacity of the weakest partner, after
allowing for price and income effects that necessarily accompany the reduction of absolute trade.

Such a trade policy may become very stifling if partners do not
initiate measures to coordinate their trade behavior and needs,
or if noneconomic motives prevail in selecting trade. Precisely to
contain the potential trade-reducing effects of bilateralized
trade, partners bent on maintaining intensive exchange, without
revoking other features of bilateralism altogether, usually embrace various refinements and ad hoc policy instruments that
will codetermine the outcome of bilateral trade negotiations and
the implementation of these contracts. It is this adaptation to individual needs that is responsible for the amazing variety of specific forms of bilateral trade policies and institutions, thus
seriously complicating generalizations.

A preliminary note: There is nothing inherently sinister or
even significant in seeking an exact balance of payments between two countries, even if it continues for years. The peculiar-

ity of bilateralism lies in the endeavor to achieve such balance at the expense of alternative trading partners. However, under the particular environment in which bilateral clearing schemes were promulgated after the war, the original focus was not on trade denial, but rather on how to attain some orderly exchange in a distorted trade world. In other words, bilateralism usually emerges in order to come to grips with an acute situation that results from multifarious trade restrictions and exchange controls brought about by large disequilibria in the world economy. As a symptom as well as a result of serious world economic derangements, it is a rather unsatisfactory solution for those difficulties, but the parties concerned may nevertheless seek ways and means of alleviating the strictures of rigid bilateralism, for instance by working seriously at mutually satisfactory BTPAs without infusing other policy goals in the negotiations.

The conclusion of BTPAs by pairs of governments is a normal phenomenon in the mutual trade relations of the CPEs, and such contracts serve several interrelated purposes. In the first place, it is hoped that a larger volume and a more appropriate composition of reciprocal trade will ensue from the BTPA in comparison with what would result from simply instituting exchange controls. Agreements usually provide for an immediate stimulus to trade, thereby facilitating economic reconstruction and consolidation – circumstances under which the adoption of bilateralism has become generally accepted. Following the last world war, West European nations turned to bilateralism and the financing of trade with inconvertible currencies chiefly for two reasons. First, it was difficult to acquire sufficient hard currency reserves given the general state of disequilibrium and the policy makers' reluctance to deflate economic activity. Second, BTPAs provided for financing trade with short-term credits, which would not have been forthcoming if trade had been conducted on a convertible currency basis. This prevailing concern about trade financing (Mikesell 1954, p. 436) certainly lurked also behind the East European BTPAs. As the economies returned to more normal conditions, however, the agreements were primarily used to stabilize trade at a desirable level so as to permit uninterrupted production and to avoid inadvertent relocations. In CPE trade there are, of course, other economic and weighty political factors behind BTPAs.

Bilateral bargaining in intra-CMEA trade has made use of several instruments and quid pro quos for assuring bilateral balance. Whether these instruments have emerged from the welfare and trade implications of the bilateral trade policies or whether the reverse is closer to the truth remains a moot question, though the first chain of reasoning is probably more realistic. Bilateralism has been maintained in view of the experiences in these countries in the period between the two wars, the need for trade controls under central planning, the favoring of a bilateral approach by the USSR, and the difficulties of multilateral trade negotiations for countries with inconvertible currencies and lacking firm criteria for measuring their own success in technical economic terms. Naturally, the gradual evolution of the present system of intra-CMEA bilateralism is a different topic altogether.

The formative elements of intra-CMEA bilateralism

In specifying the particular features of CMEA bilateralism, one should take a closer look at the reasons for the adoption of bilateralism and, even more, why it has been maintained for so long. The basic origins of CMEA bilateralism have not so far been the subject of systematic East European analyses of the recent economic history of the CPEs. Most observers tend to deal with single issues of this trade mechanism and policy, or confine their point of reference to the inconvertibility of the local currencies (as Garland 1977; Holzman 1966, p. 248; Wiles 1968, p. 254; Zwass 1974, pp. 44–45) or, more generally, to financial constraints on the external economic behavior of CPEs (McMillan 1975, pp. 5–6). It can be demonstrated though that bilateralism need not imply currency inconvertibility and that currency convertibility alone does not suffice to dispense with bilateralism as implemented in Eastern Europe. What is more important is the existence of commodity inconvertibility, that is, the situation in which nonresident holders of a CPE's currency can only exert their right to goods and services by passing through the entire planning hierarchy and obtaining clearance before being entitled to spend currency balances (Altman 1960, pp. 430–431), but this is certainly not the only explanation of intra-CMEA bilateralism (Brabant 1977, pp. 313–314).

F. D. Holzman has placed the issues on hand in a broader
perspective than most other treatments of CPE trade. He introduces the following reasons for the existence of bilateralism
and why adherence to this policy is still encouraged in the CPEs:
(1) Trade partners are unwilling to hold balances of CPE currency, (2) the CPE strives for overall trade balance, (3) the economically stronger nations obtain opportunities to improve their
terms of trade, (4) bilateral balancing is a carryover from the
general use of analogous techniques in domestic planning, and
(5) nonbloc countries prefer bilateral arrangements because of
balance of payments problems (Holzman 1966, pp. 248–250).
With the exception of the third and fourth arguments, Holzman
focuses primarily on given external conditions. It might be
argued *a contrario* that under the conditions prevailing in the
CPEs, the reversal of (1) and (5) would not greatly help to eliminate bilateralism, surely not in intra-CMEA trade where it is
most pervasive. Although Holzman's second point is certainly
valid, it is not very relevant: All nations are concerned about balancing payments, yet they do not ordinarily encourage bilateralism. It seems more convincing, as argued by the late Hungarian economist Sándor Ausch (Ausch 1972, pp. 155–166) to
refer in detail to the interconnection between trade policy and
trade mechanisms and their domestic counterparts (Holzman's
points three and four), and to place these relationships in perspective.[14] Because the present trade characteristics of the CPEs
are intricately interlaced with their domestic economic policies,
it bears to take a closer look at the following determinants of
CMEA bilateralism: (1) the socialist growth policies, (2) the
model of economic organization, (3) price policies, and (4) the
scope of trade with nonbloc partners.

The CPE's growth strategy

Though industrialization is not a panacea for all problems im-
peding economic expansion, it is now accepted that an appropriate industrialization policy constitutes the backbone of economic
progress for most countries. A steady expansion of the share of
manufacturing (where labor productivity is higher than in primary activities) in national product and a sustained increase in
productivity being induced by manufacturing in other sectors
through economies of scale, transfers of technology, different
input mixes, standardization, modern management techniques,

and so on will lead to higher output per capita and an increase in value added. By adopting a new economic path, the CPEs stressed the significance of the experiences of the industrially advanced countries in that machine building constitutes the industry of industries, providing as it does the capacity for sustained growth elsewhere. In addition to seeking growth per se, the custodians of socialist power also prescribed both the pace at which this economic progress should ideally be achieved and its environment, implying especially similar industrialization patterns in each country and minimizing the growth potential of specialization and participation in international trade.

The policy directed at a minimum reliance on trade in an effort to avoid the barriers to growth stemming from fluctuations abroad implied relative autarky, though trade was essential in eliminating bottlenecks to self-propelled growth. Initially, trade of the less developed CPEs resulted from the selected investment policies and the capacity to earn foreign exchange by exporting raw materials and foodstuffs. The developed CPEs in turn exported capital goods and imported primary products and foodstuffs. As development proceeded, further trade expansion was required to obtain continuously the inputs to operate the new processes and to dispose of part of the products turned out by these new ventures. These conflicting developments were not anticipated accurately in the formulation of the earlier development programs and in the elaboration of CMEA cooperation. Furthermore, the opportunities offered by alternative resource allocation, changes in the preferred output mix, and alternative trade markets were not extensively explored for a number of reasons.

Apart from miscalculations in planning and their repercussions on trade, an essential feature setting the stage for intra-CMEA developments is that the same factors that call for the expansion of imports of raw materials, foodstuffs, and fuels are also responsible for the much slower growth in supply, as agriculture and mining were until the late 1950s relatively neglected in the growth policies. If no alternative foreign sources can be tapped, the primary goods and foodstuffs offered on the CMEA market will eventually fail to satisfy the increasing demands of the members. In other words, the profile of postwar expansion has inherently engendered growing incompatibility of the CPEs' trade intentions. The normal response to such a classic divergence between demand and supply would have been price flexibility, concerted or unilateral adaptations of demand and supply, and the exploration of alternative markets. But such automatic adjustments have been precluded or substantially encumbered by the inflexible, dirigistic constraints of the economic model.

The socialist economic model

Central administration and control of all economic activities form the framework within which the strategy for structural change could materialize. Strict planning cannot hope to cope adequately with microeconomic price and cost considerations. Because central planning does not encompass the world, trade cannot be fully integrated in the CPE model. Nevertheless, voluntarism is to be avoided and trade therefore ought to be controlled and restricted to the bare minimum. Although specific processes for promoting production and investments for export goals have gradually been set up and extended, the operative plans have seldom, if ever, been drawn up after a patient assessment of the comparative merits of alternative production, consumption, and trade targets. Trade certainly widens the choice of "techniques" and, if effectively used, the number of plan variants that may add to the difficulty of drafting realistic plans. To short cut this complex iteration process and yet maintain trade indispensable to the fulfillment of other development goals, the planner felt compelled to resort to a dual structure of the CPE model.

The separation of internal and external economic processes permits the planner to support domestic price autonomy, economic stability, and central control. It also allows him to minimize the effects of foreign influences on central planning. As a result of the failure to adjust domestic prices intermittently to keep pace with the frequently profound changes in economic structure, the CPE is left with prices that cannot help to evaluate accurately the feasible range of internal and external trade-offs, even if desired only in scaling the potential future configurations of domestic and trade activities. In view of the preference for physical planning, trade plans have been rather rigid, and the degree of flexibility implicit in the trade targets fixed by overall policy considerations could hardly be exploited by the FTEs to maximum advantage, especially owing to the constraints imposed by the BTPAs.

Socialist price policies

The peculiar characteristics of domestic price policies in CPEs form an integral part of their model. Some crucial aspects of their external price policies can be attributed to internal model features as well, but the processes and practices of price formation in external markets certainly deserve separate treatment. Not only do internal prices fail to express real costs, the disparity between relative costs and prices among the various CMEA members is so substantial that trade has to be accounted according to yet another system of relative prices – the so-called socialist WMPs.

As a matter of principle and economic expediency, the CPEs decided early in their cooperation to adapt, within margins, prices borrowed from the main world markets for clearing their mutual trade. This principle was chosen because it proved impractical and unjustifiable ("the law of equivalent exchange") to clear mutual trade at domestic prices. Because the latter could not be used in merchandise trade, as distinct from the so-called noncommercial transactions in which domestic prices do play a role,[15] the planners had a choice between elaborating their own common accounting system or imitating the relative evaluations of the main world markets. They chose, in principle, a variant of WMPs: Historical WMPs of the principal world markets, usually for a five-year period, are averaged in an effort to eliminate conjunctural fluctuations; monopolistic and speculative prices are to be disregarded altogether. This selection arose mainly because an own, that is, an autonomous regional, price system (based, for example, on averaging domestic prices in the producer CPEs) might have disrupted regional trade as the divergence between domestic prices and WMPs makes arbitrage possible within the CPEs' opportunity to deflect trade to alternative markets, and would have induced windfall gains and losses unjustifiable for economies bent on marshaling domestic surpluses for further growth through trade.

In theory it seems reasonable to treat most CPEs as "small countries," that is, as partners in world trade who exercise but little influence on WMPs.[16] This is a valid first approximation, because most CPEs are rather small in terms of size and wealth, and their participation in world trade is almost "negligible." Hence, WMPs are in principle the real terms on which alternatives can be acquired through trade. Whereas CPEs generally are price takers in nonsocialist trade, the small country assumption does not seem to be particularly helpful in actual decision making. As the world's economies become more and more closely interlinked, not only physical goods are exchanged but also invisibles complementary to the former. This implies that a certain form of stability must be evident to persuade countries to specialize in trade and hence to engage in more than an erratic exchange of goods and services. The more reliable and intensive the CPEs' participation in world markets becomes, the more likely it is that actual WMPs are the real terms on which the CPEs can participate in nonsocialist trade.

However, during most of the postwar period the CPEs have not succeeded in promoting stable trade expansion with the nonsocialist markets for economic and other reasons. This factor is one of the chief reasons why when the CPEs suddenly have to switch trade to Western markets, they experience almost invariably a decline in terms of trade frequently entailing balance of payments problems, for which these countries have no automatic adjustment mechanisms (Holzman 1968a). This does not contradict the empirical fact that sudden changes in CPE supplies to world markets (or additional demands for that matter) do not greatly affect the general level of WMPs.[17] However, the overall insensitivity of WMPs to the trade of the CPEs is really irrelevant when this market is not fully competitive, particularly when it does not permit unhampered free entry. The point is that the import–demand elasticities in the world market for East European exports and, to some extent, the export–supply elasticities for CPE imports are relatively small, and hence the response of prices to quantities.

From the early 1950s the CPEs were induced to clear the larger part of their trade within the CMEA. This commerce was expected to be stable and mutually advantageous, not in the least with respect to prices. To realize these goals, the CPEs gradually adopted some special price-setting rules.[18] Until the end of 1974 the system worked as follows. At a certain point in time, under the sponsorship of CMEA authorities, the members agree to a reference period for the calculation of average WMPs. Comprehensive price lists for main world markets are prepared for a great number of products by the individual CPEs. In principle, the CPEs aimed at quinquennial price revisions, but there was no firm commitment to this rule in the Bucharest principles (see Chapter 4), nor were the reference bases revised every five years together with the conclusion of medium-term trade agreements.

Until 1958, CMEA prices were first patterned after actual WMPs and then stabilized in order to avoid the world inflation engendered by the Korean War boom. Minor adjustments were made in the mid-1950s, usually with reference to recent changes in WMPs. From 1958 to 1974, the reference price in intra-CMEA trade negotiations were fixed for a long period of time (during 1958–1964 they were derived from 1957–1958 WMPs; in 1965–1970 from 1960–1964 WMPs; and in 1971–1975 they were slated to be based on 1965–1969 WMPs but, in early 1975,[19] officially on the recommendation of CMEA's Executive Committee, this particular interpretation of the Bucharest principles was abandoned). Since 1976 average WMPs of the preceding five years are calculated annually. In any case, whenever the CMEA members agree to a general price revision, the data are collected for a relatively long reference period and are averaged in one way or another by each negotiating CPE separately. A new price basis does not, however, necessarily imply that all prices of all traded goods will be recomputed, nor does it forcibly change the basis of the calculation of starting prices (see below) for all CMEA members (Batizi 1978). Furthermore, these prices function only as the starting point in bilateral trade negotiations. Where there are valid reasons, starting contract prices are modified to bring them in line with the socialist principles of "equivalent exchange" and "mutual advantage." An essential requirement of these so-called socialist WMPs, in principle, is that they be uniform for all CPEs, though this goal has in fact never been realized, and not only because of the odd, fictive transportation surcharge (half of the transportation costs "saved" by importing from CPEs rather than from the reference MTE are added to the "starting price").

Apart from the weighty issue of whether these socialist WMPs are actually appropriate to the demand and supply forces typical of the CMEA market, it is equivocal whether actual CMEA trade prices have routinely been derived from past WMPs and, even more important, whether such prices could have been computed, not in the theoretical but rather in the empirical sense. Not the least important problem is how particular socialist WMPs are established, even if the CMEA authorities and their counterparts in the individual CPEs could document WMPs.

Whether the CPEs actually attempt to borrow "competitive" prices from Western markets or not is a moot question, especially because actual trade prices – incidentally, the only ones of importance to CPE policy makers! – are negotiated bilaterally on the basis of reference period documentation prepared by the national organisms in charge of hammering out BTPAs. Prices are agreed upon in bilateral negotiations and they generally diverge from those that would have prevailed in a competitive world. As a matter of fact, bilateralism usually entails higher absolute prices than free trade (Ellis 1941, pp. 320–321). Although this may leave relative prices unaffected, there is also good theoretical reasoning that would argue that the stronger bargainer in the negotiations can turn the bilateral barter terms of trade in his favor. Whether such discrimination in fact occurs in the CMEA where BTPAs are not instituted to reap overt gains from relative strengths in the negotiating process is a topic that has been debated so far inconclusively in the Western literature (e.g., Gajzago 1966; Hewett 1974; Marer 1969, 1972).

Nevertheless, the much-heralded simulation of the principle of competitive prices for intra-CMEA trade has in reality never been attained, for both logical and practical reasons (Brabant 1970, pp. 177–189). Intuitive arguments as to the problems of identifying WMPs and the evidence of recent quantitative research indicate at least that price uniformity has never existed and that in many cases WMPs have not been duplicated.[20] This is not necessarily inconsistent with the notion that the CPEs have endeavored to keep their trade prices tuned, with a lag, to basic trends in world markets (Hewett 1974, p. 110). It should also be mentioned that in recent years the starting prices have been applied only to regular BTPAs, whereas for specialized products, supplementary deliveries, and some very hard goods, actual prices have been derived from current trade opportunities with developed MTEs. More on this topic will be provided in the next chapters.

Regardless of the principles underlying price formation in the CMEA, one would expect, on the basis of logical and practical considerations, that some positive correlation must exist between the broad trends, as distinct from the actual level, of WMPs and intra-CMEA trade prices, if only because the CPEs have access to alternative markets. This is true particularly for "hardly comparable" goods, such as manufactures for which it is cumbersome to borrow prices directly, owing to the many different parameters that determine individual manufactured goods. For comparable products, such as fuels, many types of raw materials, and foodstuffs, one would expect a closer correspondence between world and CMEA trade prices, not only in trends but also in actual levels, and it is likely that averages of historical WMPs have been of some importance in CMEA price formation for such goods. As a result, until the revisions in the price-formation formula in 1975, the producers of primary goods in the CMEA were at a double disadvantage: Their unit export earnings declined in line with changes in real WMPs, whereas unit import costs increased, as during much of the 1950s and 1960s prices of manufactures in intra-CMEA trade tended to be fixed at the highest documentable WMP – relevant in fact for a higher quality product (Ausch 1969, pp. 124–126). This made it doubly attractive for the smaller CPEs to foster exports of manufactures, while at the same time reducing the export surplus, or increasing the import level, of primary goods and foodstuffs or diverting a large share of this surplus to finance trade with other markets. Nevertheless, the price disparity in mutual trade is limited because, even though the CPEs have some ability to discriminate against each other, they do possess a degree of bargaining power to sell or buy in third markets at current WMP levels, but this latitude is evidently not identical for all CPEs and not all members have explored it to the same extent. Also, one must allow for the socialist ideology of egalitarianism, which limits the scope for what might be considered price discrimination, which, as R. Caves notes, is in any case an ill-defined concept when prices and exchange rates do not reflect real costs (Caves 1974, p. 34). On the strength of all these arguments, CMEA prices cannot have been widely differentiated, though discriminatory price fixing has evidently played some role in clearing trade in much the same way as reexports, swing credits, long-term development credits, and other adjustments of bilateralism have been important in helping to attain bilaterally balanced trade in intra-CMEA relations (see below).

The distribution of trade

It can be demonstrated that redirecting some trade to nonbilateralized partners may considerably alleviate the negative effects of bilateralism. It was noted above that the CPEs have relied mostly on mutual trade and have not significantly diverted trade away from CPE markets. Furthermore, owing to the CPEs' trade policies and model, the possibility of optimizing the distribution of trade in the formulation of the plan has never been fully explored, for a variety of reasons, though the following points cover the most important economic features.

In the immediate postwar period, trade between CPEs and MTEs was restricted in view of political and economic factors. Rigid bilateral clearing adopted in CPEs and MTEs could not allow for the free choice of foreign markets. With some partners the CPEs signed no BTPAs at all, and as a result trade here tended to be erratic. Second, the more antagonistic the ideological and political conflict between East and West became, the smaller the chance for profitable trade, though the ingenuity of the business world can and did successfully dodge embargoes and other restrictions on trade. Third, the political aims of the USSR with respect to the other CPEs, though never outlined in any comprehensive way, effectively prevented intensive trade with the West, and even among the smaller CPEs themselves.

Once the dirigistic planning system was installed and forced industrialization held sway, trade with the West was further hampered. In fact, trade was diverted to the bilateralized area because MTEs are reluctant and unable to commit themselves to the extent desired by CPE partners, the commodities available for export in most CPEs found an easy outlet on the CMEA market, and the start of intra-CMEA cooperation contributed to the concentration of trade on CPE outlets, especially the Soviet market, by means of comprehensive BTPAs.

It may be observed, nevertheless, that since the 1950s the CPEs have gained sufficient autonomy and economic maturity to support a substantial expansion of trade with the West, which would be highly beneficial from the economic point of view. This situation has only materialized in moderately stronger trade ties in the last decade or so, mainly because the CPEs have been unable to satisfy Western demand, as their horizon was almost exclusively conditioned by the CMEA market, especially the USSR, and Western business largely lacked the incentive and experience to accommodate flexibly to the somewhat unusual, if not alien, world of CPEs.[21]

Specific features of CMEA bilateralism

The emergence of bilateralism as the dominant feature of the CPEs' trade policies may have been precipitated by a realistic evaluation of the chances of clearing trade at all in the uncertain postwar environment. Also, the need to control trade and the desire to isolate the domestic economy through the MFT may have been mingled with overall and regional balance of payments considerations. But the adopted trade policy and institutions have gradually evolved into a formidable construct that appears no longer warranted by either the internal or the external factors dominant in the earlier debates regarding industrialization. This does not imply, however, that the CPEs could at present unconditionally support free competition from abroad. Although one may acknowledge the CPEs' need for firm controls or even for being more protective than most MTEs, this does not necessarily validate the perpetuation of the rigid trade system. Whereas economic arguments favor the gradual replacement of bilateralism, other, more noneconomic, motives probably have had a strong bearing on the particular form taken by the individual trade policies and on the ineffectual measures introduced from above to replace local interests by regional objectives.

Whereas the inflexible planning system precluded effective trade optimization, even within the constraints of planning and bilateralism the CPEs do not appear to have done the best. In particular, they have not patiently tried to promote bilateral trade on the basis of real cost considerations. It can be shown that under bilateralism a collusion of interests of the partners to BTPAs and concerted action may lead to the introduction of trade policy instruments that can favorably affect trade turnover. Although such adjustment techniques have no place in a general-equilibrium framework, these typical features of intra-CMEA bilateralism were on the whole inspired by the need to improve trade efficiency.

The adjustment of trade criteria
To harmonize intensive trade with bilateral balancing, the CPEs have attempted to relax the restrictiveness of their trade mechanism by allowing, among other things, for reexports, short- and long-term credits, ad hoc price adjustments, and other like measures. Because such piecemeal measures will not necessarily improve the efficiency of the economies and may in some cases lead to the opposite of what would have emerged under free trade, they add a special dimension to BTPAs that further complicates the transition toward regional multilateralism.

The reexports referred to here denote trade flows expressly undertaken to balance trade with one partner by means of imbalances incurred with one or more others. If the main economic goal of bilateralism is to control the flow of goods and services from various partners, reexports may defeat this purpose, although it is a useful modification in that it permits trade expansion beyond levels feasible under strict bilateralism, without dispensing altogether with the requirement of balancing. However, reexports other than those called for by geographical or historical conditions (e.g., transit trade) may entail larger administrative and transport costs than direct trade. Whereas reexports would seem to be a frequent occurrence in intra-CMEA trade, information on its volume is highly unreliable.[22]

The demanding restriction of zero balance on bilateral trade flows has made the CPEs aware of the potential advantages of reciprocal borrowing and lending in financing regular trade, and such arrangements have taken place on the reasonable assumption that present imbalances can be reversed easily in future trade. Under the de jure agreements, interest-free swing credits at any time during a given trade period for approximately 2 to 3 percent of the contracted trade volume are available.[23] All CPEs have realized the importance of some sort of ex post multilateral settlement of accounts, even if BTPAs anticipate no imbalances. In spite of several official attempts to multilateralize trade, or rather payments, these formal agreements have not really affected the trade mechanism of the CPEs. It should be noted, however, that de facto swing credits have traditionally substantially surpassed the legal limits (Brabant 1977, pp. 66–102). If such unplanned practices are allowed for, then trade can indeed be increased beyond levels normally associated with bilateralism. Whether capital transfers improve or further distort allocative efficiency is not clear, because these loans are usually tied and, hence, are not necessarily channeled into the most rewarding activities. Swings are not attractive if they always happen to turn in favor of one country because imbalances are largely structural. The multilateral settlement of unplanned bilateral imbalances has not so far occurred because of the disparity in bilateral trade prices and the difficulty of satisfying the surplus country's demand from the deficit CMEA area. In any case, planned imbalances are still avoided precisely because swings represent a transfer of goods and services without a certain future return. Nonetheless, de facto swings have reduced the restrictiveness of bilateralism, at least for some CPEs.

Bilateral balance evidently depends on quantities and prices. In a competitive world, the main variable in the process of achieving bilateral balance is the quantity of commodities included in reciprocal trade, because prices are by definition predetermined. In CPEs external prices do not have much influence on the level or composition of trade, and are not important in domestic price formation. But to accommodate bilateral balancing, the CPEs have also resorted to discriminatory price-setting practices, although these have not necessarily been motivated solely by exploitation motives.[24]

In a competitive economy, countries will specialize in certain production lines in response to signals emanating from international trade opportunities, and "specialization" is the aggregate result of decisions made by individual microeconomic units. In CPEs, however, there is no direct interaction between trade and domestic decision making, and specialization results from key policy choices inspired by concerns about increasing the economy's level of efficiency in response to signals emanating from international trade opportunities and a host of other considerations. However, even if decisions are made in response to WMPs, the absence of reliable scarcity indicators within the CPE may considerably complicate the assessment of comparative advantages (see section 5). Unless such comparisons are made an organic part of routine policy making, a central vote to enhance the concentration of production factors in activities for which (according to the trade-offs of world markets) the country appears to be better suited than more traditional ventures, may entail a drastic redeployment of resources and hence a possibly sharp shift in production and trade profiles. The suddenness of the restructuring of trade may be cushioned by reaching prior agreement on the contemplated resource reallocation with potential trade partners ("agreed specialization"). However, because trade opportunities are evidently not identical in all possible trade outlets, the practice of bilateral balancing may fail to support the intended restructuring of resource allocation and indeed may even prevent its emergence.

Precisely because specialization agreements in the CMEA should not interfere with pairwise balancing, these contracts have had to be negotiated mostly with the goal of attaining bilateral "compensatory" protocols, trading off one specialized product against another by decisions affecting either the production processes subject to specialization or the distribution of outputs in the few known multilateral specialization agreements. Some recent agreements incorporate the principle that the price of components and parts should be expressed as a percentage of the overall price of the finished product, which itself ought to be determined on the basis of average production costs whenever these are or are expected to become lower than what average WMPs tend to indicate (Kormnov 1973a, pp. 13–15). Cases are also known where foreign price lists have been used to determine the relative prices of components and assembled items (Csikos 1975, pp. 316–317). The exchange resulting from such agreements will then involve the bartering of so many parts per unit of finished product. Such an arrangement may perhaps preclude disturbances in the delicate forces maintaining bilateral balance, but are hardly conducive to efficient specialization. The divergence from WMPs or uniform scarcity prices has permitted trade to be on a larger scale than would have been possible under strict bilateralism, although it should be noted that a comparison of empirical data does not necessarily confirm this. Also, especially in recent years, the notion of constant prices patterned after trends in historical WMPs has been applied much more loosely. In a number of cases, distinctions have been made between goods included in the regular BTPA, and hence settled at traditional prices, and noncontractual deliveries, in fact deliveries specified in a supplementary contract, whose prices are closely tied in with current WMPs and trade is sometimes paid for in convertible currencies.[25]

It is generally accepted that under bilateralism the price mechanism alone cannot function properly as the guideline of trade allocation and the role of the exchange rate, already reduced severely for reasons examined in section 1, is further immobilized especially for merchandise trade, which under divergent bilateral price-formation determinants implies as many different exchange rates as there are different price proportions. Even if price uniformity is maintained, the exchange rate is redundant, for trade has to be cleared with partners with whom a BTPA is available.

In order to counter the need for trade, parties to BTPAs may try to allow for the migration of labor, technology, capital, and natural resource endowments beyond what would occur under multilateral trade conditions. Technological knowledge has been diffused, at least until the late 1960s, at a token cost in conformity with the "Sofia principle" endorsed during the second CMEA Session (see section 3 of Chapter 1) or not at all. Although this generosity contributed to a reduction in technological disparities, the originator was not fully rewarded and found therefore little tangible incentive to share knowledge or to seek aggressively technical progress for export promotion. The possibility of labor transfers has more recently been explored, although the isolated cases so far known (e.g., Bulgarian workers in the Soviet lumbering industry) have contributed little to the gradual equalization of labor productivities. In any case, no permanent basis for resettlement has been worked out, and labor transfers remain ad hoc and exceptional.[26] Capital transfers have been more extensive, moving especially to the capital-short countries, though these flows have not been an integral part of a consistent policy aimed at reducing relative scarcities in the

CMEA area. Most capital transactions take the form of tied credits (and tied debts) that will help to reduce the relative scarcity of some products on the CMEA market. Such target credits have stimulated trade and specialization beyond what could have been accommodated under strict bilateralism, but it remains in doubt whether imposed capital mobility *in natura* is the best mechanism for the allocation of scarce resources. Whatever their defect, however, intra-CMEA capital and labor mobility has doubtlessly encouraged regional trade, because both types of transactions involve handing over services or commodities now in exchange for commodities to be delivered in the future.[27]

It should be remarked at this juncture that the CPEs reject free labor and capital mobility on socialist grounds. In principle, the export of labor is spurned because socialist leaders consider it their duty to attain full employment permanently: Anyone willing to work is entitled to a job in his own country. A purely temporary redeployment of workers in other CPEs is envisaged only in well-defined, isolated cases where these workers contribute both to the production potential of the host country and to the supply of knowledge, technical know-how, or commodities in their home country. Likewise, the desirability of direct investment abroad is repudiated because of the principles of sovereignty and nonintervention in the internal affairs of the receiving country. Only in some isolated cases, such as international banks and some international organizations examined in Chapter 4, is a special type of capital mobility permitted, whereas direct investment in the productive capacity of other CMEA partners is frowned upon.[28]

Institutional implications

As argued, the CPEs have not participated fully in world trade because of their development policy and the related institutional supports. But bilateralism itself has had implications for trade involvement. This position can be explained on the basis of several interrelated arguments, of which the most important are summarized below.

Strict bilateralism usually requires the separation of markets to maintain internal and external economic balance by competitive means. Admittedly, the bilateral trade policy in the CMEA has certainly not been the most important inducement behind the severing of ties between internal and external markets. The trade policy and model have permitted the CPEs to protect domestic policies and they have enabled at least some CPEs to export "new" products for which the exporter does not have a real comparative advantage and, hence, could not trade at a profit on world markets under competitive conditions (Alampiev 1971, p. 67). One further development of bilateralism necessary to allow for such flows, apart from those stemming from considerations about "fraternal cooperation," is the emergence of structural or commodity bilateralism in intra-CMEA trade (see section 4).

Since the mid-1960s, the CPEs have demonstrated a growing awareness of trade opportunities in third markets, though the expanding share of interbloc trade cannot mainly be attributed to CMEA bilateralism. The following may help to explain this. Because of the shift of emphasis from domestic development to trade, the CPEs have created trade, which has benefited third markets as well as CMEA partners. Second, the economic progress achieved over the past decades has called for setting a noticeably different level and composition of trade, and for exploring new trade partners. Third, the easing of tensions stemming from political controversies has made it possible for the CPEs to distribute trade over a more extensive area. Finally, intensifying the productive capacity of the CPEs necessitates new technologies, some of which can be procured only from outside the CMEA area. Nonetheless, an unquantifiable, but sizable, part of the new trade with nonbloc economies can be attributed to changing opportunities on the CMEA market and the restrictiveness of CMEA bilateralism.

In the early 1950s, difficulties in accommodating trade in BTPAs probably contributed to the diversification of each CPE's economy; the trade policy then followed has also had some impact on the selection of development targets later on. Growth of raw materials and fuels sectors has been inhibited, inter alia, because of the price policy in regional trade. One would have expected trade to shift gradually under the combined impact of specialization in manufactures within the CMEA and a diversification of supply sources for primary goods. However, specialization was not explored much until the 1970s and the CPEs have been reluctant to diversify their markets for imports of primary goods. Instead of gradually replacing bilateralism with a more realistic trade policy, the bilateral trade regime has been maintained together with the introduction of ad hoc trade inducements.

The industrialization policies pursued by the CPEs have entailed conflicts of interest in negotiating BTPAs. To maintain trade at high levels, especially the exchange of primary goods for manufactures, in an environment with almost inflexible prices, the producers of primary goods will normally insist on nonprice compensations or concessions. Tied sales, tied loans at a concessionary interest rate, larger swing credits, changes in the distribution and composition of trade, selling some commodities only against convertible currencies, and other such measures have been applied at one time or another in an effort to encourage exporters of primary goods.

The aggregate trade-inhibiting effect stems partly from the balancing constraint and the concrete organization of bilateralism, but depends also on other important factors. First, BTPAs are negotiated, implemented, and controlled by government agents, who are not exclusively motivated by economic criteria. For example, many regulations are required to ensure that the BTPA is not violated, and the associated direct and indirect costs are likely to be avoided for small and relatively unimportant trade flows. A concentration of trade in large transactions is a typical feature of bilateralism (Ellis 1941, p. 322) also found in intra-CMEA trade (Ausch 1969, pp. 111–126). Second, because for all practical purposes the bilateralized area is identical with the CMEA region, the CPEs will probably avoid transit trade that by origin or destination belongs to a nonclearing country and that might upset the BTPAs; if not completely precluded, the partners involved will most likely seek special regulation of such trade. Third, it is very difficult to fit services other than those related to commodity exchange into BTPAs, especially the CMEA variant, though such services can normally be an important source of financing merchandise trade. Fourth, the argument that, if confined to economic agreements, bilateralism does not inflict significant trade reduction because bilateral imbalances under normal trade conditions are usually relatively small (10 to 20 percent of trade between most MTEs), does not pass muster. The forced elimination of flows that are complementary to those subsumed to be "bilaterally balanced" and, therefore, the overall trade-reducing effect may be far more pervasive than what would be apparent at first glance from imbalances under free trade.

4. Structural bilateralism

Whenever bargaining and expediency in the implementation of bilateralism allow for the emergence of disparate relative prices in BTPAs, the role of prices in trade decisions becomes very precarious. The countries adhering to bilateralism must choose by way of prices and other yardsticks. One of these criteria, structural bilateralism, was pointed out above as one possible consequence of bilateralism in the sense that it may be advantageous for some partners to "force" the composition of trade away from what would prevail under multilateralism or overall bilateralism chiefly in lieu of price adjustments. This will enable some partners to promote commodities not otherwise exported, it permits a more extensive exploitation of arbitrage, and may improve the gains from bilateralized trade.

East European leaders have displayed an almost chronic obsession with the composition of trade in general and that of individual bilateral flows in particular. Although much desirable detail is still lacking, the level and composition of trade achieved by some CPEs with the aid of BTPAs does not appear to be commensurate with their economic profile. Certainly, whereas some of these exports may have emerged partly as a result of an honest effort to promote economic development through regional trade (though this is not necessarily the best course from an economic point of view), the larger proportion by far would seem to have emerged because some CPEs have deliberately distorted their export capacity by means other than those inherent in general bilateralism.

Structural bilateralism may be defined as an ex ante trade policy that aims at attaining overall bilateral balance by reducing trade imbalances in selected commodity groups and in some bilateral relations in support of an autonomous domestic development pattern. This trade policy variant therefore introduces new constraints on the distribution of trade and most likely also on its level and composition. How it has entangled intra-CMEA relations in recent years cannot be studied here in great detail (see Brabant 1973, pp. 118–155), though it will be useful to point out briefly the reason for the emergence of such a policy, the specific features of its application, and its most important implications.

Origins and application

The origins of structural bilateralism closely parallel those introduced for bilateralism. First, the properties of the growth strategy in CPEs help to explain the emergence and extent of structural bilateralism in intra-CMEA trade, inasmuch as virtually the same new industries have been nursed along in all members and inadequate provisions have been enacted to ensure both the future supply of raw materials and foodstuffs, and a market to absorb these parallel industrial products. Industrialization has therefore entailed a strong divergence in supply and demand, a feature that has not been countered to any large extent by price adjustments, trade diversion, or intra-CMEA specialization for reasons explained in the preceding section.

Second, socialist WMPs fail to represent the real opportunities for the CPEs individually or as a group, and are therefore insufficient guidelines for desirable developments, at least where prices de facto affect decisions and plan execution. Furthermore, "living by trading" is not compatible with normatively planned economies and barter trade has not helped to induce the planner to search for alternative growth patterns. Nevertheless, CPE policy makers have slowly reversed their antitrade attitude in search of a more active role for trade or, at least, for a less costly commercial policy. Because these countries continue to aim at the realization of independently formulated national goals rather than at the exploitation of regionwide advantages, comprehensive specialization cannot be effectively implemented, in spite of the negotiation of formal agreements to the contrary. In short, the model itself does not have the requisite flexibility to redress market disequilibria quickly, for instance, by means of price adjustments. Furthermore, the trade model has also exacerbated the problem as WMPs until recently have tended to induce the opposite of what would be needed to restore regional balance. Efforts to reformulate CMEA price policies, though proposed on several occasions, have not so far succeeded. Owing largely to inflexible fixed prices and redundant exchange rates, some disintegration of markets into a panoply of various degrees of "soft" and "hard" goods has emerged, as could have been anticipated (Frisch 1948, pp. 267–271), and further complicates decision making. This separation of regional commodity markets strengthens the bargaining position of the CPEs able to export hard goods, and there is little doubt that at least some members have exploited this, not mainly through prices, but by compensatory flows of commodities not really in demand in the partner country.[29] It is unfortunately impossible to estimate the extent of these tied sales, not even approximately.

Third, in spite of the overwhelming role of long-term planning for structural change, in trade the CPEs have been guided mostly by short-term gains.[30] Structural bilateralism could have been avoided if the central planners had worked in concert in molding the CPEs' economic structures according to regional requirements. Inasmuch as the pattern of trade in the early 1950s did not greatly interfere with domestic industrialization policies, it proved satisfactory. It is only since the mid-1950s (the "New Course") that market disequilibria started to be of concern. The sudden curtailment of investment expenditures and the sharp increase in providing tangible incentives to consumers – essential components of the New Course – tended to knock the bottom out of the intersectoral type of commerce within the bilateral framework. Instead of taking this as a strong hint to rethink development policies, the CPEs resorted to short-term measures such as imports of goods from non-CMEA partners, sometimes on credit, the extension of regional capital flows, and the polarization of intra-CMEA trade toward the USSR. In the late 1950s and early 1960s, the problems emanating from parallelism in economic structure and trade subsided temporarily as the new industrialization waves once again induced intersectoral exchange; but next to nothing was done to avert the recurrence of debilitating regional disequilibria.

Lastly, structural bilateralism has enabled some CPEs to fulfill noneconomic objectives. Not the least problem in socialist growth policies is the obsession with emulating advanced MTEs. Excessive attention to a diversified industrial basis and the expansion of the share of finished manufactures in trade have hampered the intensification of the CPEs' participation in world commerce. This largely psychologically motivated attitude has been called "technological snobbery" (Wiles 1968, p. 178), and may well be just that; but irrespective of its determinants, the attempt to foster trade in manufactures per se is a force to be reckoned with.

Implications

In comparison with bilateralism, structural bilateralism leads to a further segmentation of the trade market into noncommunicating units (Alampiev 1971, pp. 72–73). Goods will no longer flow to partners with whom a bilateral balance as such exists, but to where a contracted balance for the relevant commodity group has not yet been exhausted and to markets in which structural bilateralism is enforced less rigidly or not at all. The consequences for intraregional trade are very complex and, owing to the problems of drawing a clear distinction between the causes and effects of this trade policy, cannot be pinpointed or quantified exactly. As noted for overall bilateralism, the reasons for embracing special constraints on commodity group balances are usually reinforced through the introduction of this policy. The most important implications can be summed up as follows.

First, structural bilateralism further narrows the scope of specialization because of the stringent national controls and the relative unreliability of maintaining the existing composition and distribution of trade. Specialization will not occur spontaneously, though it may be enforced under the impact of the relatively strong position in regional trade of the exporters of hard goods if the weaker partners are not pushed into broaching alternative trade outlets. However, the CPEs have so far been reluctant or unable to engage in stable intersectoral specialization for organizational, economic, institutional, and strategic reasons. Intraproduct specialization, one of the paramount forces in the postwar expansion of the developed MTEs, is considerably handicapped in CPEs by the vexing problems of coming to grips with the intricate flexibility needed for producing on the basis of parts and components procured from various foreign sources within the traditional planning framework – a problem that is further compounded by price policies inadequately geared to CMEA market conditions. Another related factor, the technological backwardness of most CPEs, although mostly conditioned by the inflexibility of their domestic economic model, also stems from the absence of visible returns as a result of the free exchange of technical information. Though it greatly aided the industrialization efforts of the backward CPEs, the generous exchange of technical and scientific information is likely to be abused, as it may prove more reliable and perhaps also less expensive to acquire the know-how free of charge and use it indiscriminately for import substitution. At least some cases are known where also export promotion by the recipient of the blueprints has been actively sought, in spite of official agreements to the contrary (Bykov 1976, pp. 130–132).

Second, WMPs as understood by the CPEs have tended to favor the export of manufactures. The overt desire to expand the domestic industrial structure has therefore been reinforced by the selective imposition of commodity group balancing constraints. This may delay meaningful internal and external reforms as some CPEs find it advantageous to exploit further their bargaining position in spite of the longer-term implications. Structural trade policies may, however, persuade the weaker partners that more mutual specialization is the only means by which domestic industry can be supported in the long run, even though one or more CPEs can temporarily succeed in recouping on past mistakes by exacting "aid" in one form or another from the more developed partners. The ever-growing demand for Soviet exports of primary goods is likely to exert pressure on the CPEs to reduce the consumption of material inputs, to diversify their import markets, to upgrade their export profile, and, as a result, to seek far more specialization than in the past. However, it should not be forgotten that during the past years, the USSR has not tried very hard, or at least not very successfully, to force the other partners into serving Soviet economic interests. This is a very important point, although it is often neglected in discussions about SEI.

For most CPEs the most important market by far is the Soviet

Union, which accounts for about half to two-thirds of any CPE's intra-CMEA commerce. Furthermore, the USSR is a crucial deliverer of primary goods to and purchaser of finished goods from the smaller CPEs. Not infrequently, two-thirds to four-fifths of these countries' exports of finished manufactures, especially machinery, goes to the USSR. Should this large partner now resolve to enforce specialization, no CPE could choose to resist the painful process of retooling the domestic economic fabric according to specialization criteria. Although the USSR could have exacted a much greater degree of coordinated production and quality and cost consciousness in the smaller CPEs by being more demanding in regional trade, it does not appear to have brought significant pressure to bear on its partners. The proposition is therefore tempting that the dominant CMEA partner does not appear to have an overriding interest in promoting specialization, at least among the smaller CPEs (Brabant 1976).

Third, the disequilibria on the CMEA market have stimulated a search for nonprice compensation. One very important factor here has been the desire of the producers of primary products to obtain low-cost loans from trade partners to finance the expansion of productive capacity, thus increasing the potential foreign supply of such goods. Whether or not this has promoted a more efficient use of capital resources is an open question because so many details of these transactions remain unknown (Brabant 1971).

Fourth, the shortage of primary goods on the CMEA market, the barriers stemming from low currency reserves to purchase elsewhere, and the CPE's limited ability to compete effectively with Western manufactures in terms of design, quality, marketing, and service have made policy makers more aware of the real cost of trade. Some CPEs have tried to exploit their domestic resources further, in spite of steeply rising marginal costs and the relatively poor quality of endowments. Others have diversified their import markets for primary inputs. This must have exacerbated the CMEA problems, because a significant share of exports to the West consists of agricultural products and, in some cases, raw materials and fuels. The growing awareness of the opportunity cost of purchasing goods in MTEs and of the restricted exchange possibilities in the CMEA may have generated a more lasting effect, particularly on the scope of the reforms required to remedy the peculiar decision-making mechanisms and institutions in regional trade.

The gradual complication of intra-CMEA trade as a result of restraining intersectoral exchange has no doubt contributed to the malaise in regional trade and cooperation of the mid-1960s, and to the exploration of alternative means of promoting SEI. To that extent, structural bilateralism may have had a very salutary effect on the design of future economic policies and indeed it played an important and constructive role in the formulation of reforms.

5. Foreign trade reforms

Section 1 examined briefly how trade can be determined by means of material balances, but some questions were left unanswered. Although feasible trade combinations can be selected by means of this planning instrument, material balancing is of little help in assessing real trade opportunities in alternative markets. Even if the planner deliberately chooses to forego optimal participation in world trade, there is still quite a choice left. First, assuming that the CPE only imports noncompeting products set largely by the technological configuration of its economic structure, the planner still has a choice of several possible export combinations to pay for given imports, each of which will yield different results in terms of trade efficiency.

Second, the less dogmatic the adherence to independent development, the more the planner will be compelled to face domestic and trade alternatives. One particular instance of this was realized very early in socialist development: Should a CPE set up a vertically integrated metallurgical complex starting from iron ore and coal and ending in engineering products? Or would it not be more desirable to import, say, steel and transform it domestically into engineering products, especially if both iron ore and coal have to be imported? This celebrated question was first posed in 1954 in a seminal article (Liska 1954) discussing the soundness of the antitrade industrialization policies of the early 1950s. In this, East European economists rediscovered that the basics of standard trade theory remain applicable, if not in making strategic long-term decisions, then at least in solving partial problems.[31] Planners have since explored various possibilities for fostering trade without, however, completely abrogating the typical autonomous economic policies.

Because the level and composition of imports result largely from the chosen policy objectives, most CPE research has concentrated on export efficiency. Put simply, the partial problem is to minimize the export cost of a fixed import bill under given restrictions on production, trade opportunities, and consumption requirements. However, an average of domestic production costs as a substitute for true market-clearing prices can be very misleading in reaching trade decisions. A comparison of internal and external prices is not very helpful when the CPEs do not have scarcity prices and a meaningful exchange rate at their disposal, and may in fact entail considerable gains and losses for the economy as a whole.

In the process of trying to improve trade efficiency, CPE economists have devised an ingenious and apparently inexhaustible variety of partial and global trade efficiency indicators, relating a variant of approximate real domestic costs to returns in foreign currency. On the strength of such calculations, the CPE planner has slowly started to enact coefficients by which a variant of average domestic costs is related to average foreign prices (euphemistically referred to sometimes as "shadow exchange rate," but this is not a very helpful terminology).[32] Although it is questionable whether these experiments in assessing efficiency have played a significant role in selecting recent development targets, there is little doubt that the CPE planner has become concerned with the issue and that some of these efficiency criteria have been instrumental in solving partial problems of economic structure (such as within branches of industry) and in formulating decisions by the FTEs or the enterprises licensed to trade directly. Considerations about trade efficiency in deliberations about CMEA production specialization, especially since the late 1960s, have been widespread, though their role in the selection of actual projects remains unclear, partly because there are still many loose ends in these calculations that are rightly viewed as significant impediments to the further extension of the ISDL (see below).

Efficiency calculations have helped to mold the foreign trade component of the economic reforms. Problems with the central planning of trade were at least as acute as those emanating from the central guidance and management of purely domestic activities. Although the reforms were probably not mainly inspired by considerations about diverting trade away from the CMEA, nonetheless the restricted ability, especially of the developed members, to participate in East–West trade played a formative role in shaping crucial aspects of the reform. In addition to increasing the competitive position of the CPE in Western markets, trade intensification and specialization in their primary region as well as elsewhere were expected to exert a beneficial effect on the pattern and pace of development in all CPEs. This was especially pronounced in the Bulgarian, Czechoslovak, Hungarian, and, more recently, the Polish and Rumanian reforms.

Regarding the growth strategy, foreign trade and international specialization have by now acquired a pivotal position in planning the evolving structure of the CPEs, excepting perhaps the USSR. At the very least, trade has been perceived as a prime mover in stimulating technical progress, increasing factor productivity, and extending the effective range of domestic choices. Industrial expansion, once charted almost exclusively on the basis of autonomous decisions made in isolation, is now to be guided also by trade alternatives in CMEA and other markets. The crucial role of trade and cooperation in recent economic policies has been underscored well by the fact that the process of gradual change in enterprise organization and methods of planning and control has continued in the foreign trade sector, in sharp contrast to the slowing down or even regression of the transformation process in the early 1970s in most other parts of the economy (UN 1968, 1973). The crucial role of trade in stimulating steady gains in productivity levels has been underlined rather strongly in the current deliberations on the functioning of the "advanced socialist society," which to a significant extent must be integrated with the world economy.

As observed in Chapter 2, changes in the model have been forthcoming in some CPEs under the pressure of foreign trade, whereas in others changes in the forms of administration and management of the economy have themselves induced changes in the trade sector. Although domestic and trade reforms are interrelated and tend to overlap, this section largely abstracts from the more general aspects of domestic reforms.

By the late 1950s, the earlier sharp organizational separation of the trade sector from producers became increasingly difficult to perpetuate, especially owing to the need for stimulating trade in manufactures. The prolongation of the practically complete disjunction between trade and the domestic economy became also increasingly wasteful because of the growing participation in trade, rising levels of development and consumer needs, and the growing complexity of making sound economic decisions. The countermeasures formulated can be divided into the reinforcement of organizational links between trade and the internal economy on the one hand, and the strengthening of the role of trade prices in calculating and adjusting domestic prices.

Generally speaking, the foreign trade aspects of the reforms can be discussed under the heading of either partial reforms as enacted in most CPEs or of comprehensive reforms as in the case of Hungary, the aborted Czechoslovak model, and the Polish trade strategy of the 1970s. Partial reforms can take on various forms as they place different weights on: (1) prices and exchange rates, (2) the central regulation of trade, and (3) the specific operation of the MFT. Although such measures are loosely connected in the partial reforms, innovations in the trade sector are harmonized with each other and with internal changes in the comprehensive reforms. In other words, partial reforms amount to an "administrative streamlining" (Pryor 1970, p. 63) or a tune-up of traditional central administration, whereas the comprehensive reforms are an earnest attempt to reformulate economic policy and to restructure the supporting institutions, policy instruments, and behavioral rules accordingly.

Price and exchange rate reform

Forging a meaningful link between internal and external prices represents one of the crucial first steps both in the domestic price reform and in the trade system. As noted, in the traditional CPE the exchange rate is set arbitrarily and has virtually no influence, except chiefly in the sphere of direct spending by nonresidents. The East European reforms have not so far enacted new, more appropriate official exchange rates, although some CPEs appear to envisage this for the near future. In the case of Hungary, although not explicitly replacing the official exchange rate, commercial exchange rates have been instituted as an important policy tool; Rumania has slated a similar shift starting in 1979 (Cristea 1978).[33] Most other CPEs have contented themselves with the introduction of various conversion coefficients. In the CPEs with partial reforms, the role of these coefficients is much narrower than envisaged in the comprehensive reforms. In the former, trade results are allowed to influence major decisions by enterprises or associations, and in the calculation of domestic prices. Most price reforms have endeavored to narrow the gap between domestic prices and real costs, including export results and import costs, and to harmonize domestic prices with foreign prices at least to some extent; but there are still palpable differences. These changes have been introduced especially in Czechoslovakia, East Germany, Hungary, and Poland.

The conversion coefficients have not been set uniformly for all trade. Instead, the CPEs have calculated coefficients for major commodity groups or economic sectors, or for major trade areas or both. As a logical next step, the enterprise producing for export should actually receive the foreign price equivalent rather than the fixed domestic price. The same applies to imports, although here reforms have been far more conservative. These principles apply at least in their general outline to most CPEs, but they have been followed with relative consistency and to the greatest extent in Hungary, where pseudo-exchange rates for the two main trade areas – the ruble and dollar payment zones – came into existence in 1968 and were transformed into effective commercial rates in 1976. It should be added, however, that those parameters have not necessarily been applied faithfully and consistently in the formation of domestic prices.[34] Although the Hungarian planners have made an earnest attempt to enact drastic changes, recent abrupt shifts in WMPs and the ensuing revision of CMEA pricing principles have made it difficult to reconcile the goals of price flexibility with stability in domestic production and consumption. The "financial bridges" (i.e., the set of parameters utilized in relating domestic and trade prices) have had to be supplemented with target interferences by those guiding the microeconomic sphere. The inevitable conflict between the need for plan stability and using prices as a proper decision-making indicator is undoubtedly one of the major forces behind the comprehensive changes in price policy (such as the elimination of a substantial portion of government subsidies to consumer prices, and more frequent and larger price adjustments when warranted not only in the wholesale sector or at the level of producer prices, but also for consumer prices) presently being formulated for inauguration at the start of the next medium-term plan.[35] In all other CPEs, de facto multiple exchange rates prevail in the computation of the enterprise or association's trade results, or even in the formation of selected domestic prices. Although an important reorganization of planning and management processes was set off in the USSR in 1965, and this project was ostensibly reinvigorated in 1973, the changes to date have not yet greatly impacted on the trade sector, not even in the formation of domestic prices, which continue to be set by central fiat, although the periodicity of partial price adjustments has been increased considerably.

As one component of trade reforms, all CPEs (except the German Democratic Republic) have established multiple tariff schedules (usually differentiated into three columns: concessionary rates, preferential rates for countries granting the CPEs most-favored-nation treatment, and others). Inasmuch as the planning of trade has not been decentralized in most CPEs and the link between domestic and trade prices continues to be tenuous, these tariffs have had little, if any, impact on the level and composition of trade. They do not play a role in relations with other CPEs, but in trade with MTEs, the differentiated tariff levels have evidently impacted on the particular geographical distribution of East–West trade envisaged by the plan, especially in selecting individual trade partners; in clearing trade earmarked for developed MTEs and, separately, for other countries; and in some cases even in allocating nonsocialist trade without geographical restrictions.

The possible influence of prices and conversion coefficients on the reform of domestic and trade prices should not, however, be exaggerated. Although price adjustments influence the evolving structure of production, consumption, and trade, as a Czechoslovak economist pointedly noted, the "basic structural changes can only be attained as a result of programmatic structural adaptations in investment plans" (Knizek 1973, p. 4). In other words, prices will play a subordinate role in planning for structural transformation, even if intimately related to foreign trade.

To understand the variety of trade reforms, one should sharply distinguish between using trade results as a material stimulus for FTEs or production units, and integrating trade as a pivot for determining domestic allocation and assessing economic efficiency. Especially the former type of streamlining has been introduced as an incentive for producers or traders to promote export and import contracts with selected trade partners or to enhance trade in selected products. Enterprises in most CPEs are not entitled to pass on the trade results to the domestic market. If the entrepreneur is able to transmit real costs and returns of trade, his decisions on matters not covered by the plan will generally be confined to what he perceives as profitable ventures from his firm's point of view, unless the central authorities are willing to subsidize and able to tax, as the case may be; but experience gathered under the traditional model has proved that this perfect interference by the planner is illusory. In any case, the connection between internal and external prices continues to be very loose and indirect. The present situation in the CPEs would seem to be as follows.

On the export side, Czechoslovakia, Hungary, and Poland apply uniform currency coefficients or commercial exchange rates for each principal trade area. These parameters are periodically established on the basis of the average cost of earning foreign exchange in the relevant trade area (usually the ruble and dollar zones), especially for manufactures. In the German Democratic Republic, the direct influence of actual export returns encompasses most industrial enterprises and associations, presently being integrated into large trusts (*Kombinat*). In Bulgaria, this is confined to the state economic units who supervise individual enterprises in a particular branch of industry; the enterprise only receives the ex ante fixed factory price or the normative cost of production. Until recently, Poland applied several coefficients in the field of finished goods, particularly for machine building, chemical industries, and enterprises working on the economic accounting principle (*chozrasčët*). The enterprise obtains the actual export price or a fixed price negotiated with the FTE. For other sectors, agriculture and raw materials in particular, the planner attempts to take trade prices into account in fixing domestic prices. According to the December 1971 law, similar provisions apply in Rumania, with the variation that the enterprise will obtain a share of the positive difference between export returns and the national fiat price. The revisions introduced in 1979 are designed to relate foreign and domestic prices more directly, especially with a view toward promoting trade efficiency, though domestic prices, especially of consumer goods, will not be affected much (Cristea 1978). In the USSR, although some enterprises may benefit from exports on account of high quality or speedy delivery, the disjunction between domestic and trade prices is as a rule as wide as it used to be elsewhere.

With respect to imports, Hungary applies in principle the same regime as for exports, but policy makers are very wary of uncontrolled price changes and, as a result, resort to a differentiated policy of direct and indirect interventions. For products not subject to domestic price controls, actual import prices or an average of import cost will be transmitted in domestic prices. For many products (especially in the nonferro, textile, leather, and primary goods branches), the domestic price is subject to central price fixing, and import prices can exert pressure only indirectly when a new price is set. In Czechoslovakia, finished goods are in principle sold at import cost, whereas prices for raw materials and foodstuffs are controlled and "averaged." In Poland, import prices are directly felt in production and consumption in nonessential branches of industry. In Bulgaria, imports are sold at domestic prices if they do not account for a major proportion of domestic consumption. In the German Democratic Republic, import prices will impact directly the domestic price if there is no similar product produced domestically. If a major share of domestic consumption originates abroad, the import cost will be taken into account in setting domestic prices. Import costs have, however, a direct bearing on the users of engineering products and complete plants in particular. There is virtually no direct link between domestic and import prices in the USSR.

When and where import and export prices are directly related
to enterprise returns and price formation is unfortunately not
unequivocally clear. The best example here is Hungary, where
there are so many interferences with the effective transmission
of import prices (i.e., the sum of import prices converted at the
applicable exchange rate, customs duties, import tax, turnover
tax, and other financial bridges), that there is simply no straightforward rule that in effect encompasses the relationship between import and domestic prices. Whereas the direct influence
of trade results on domestic prices is not very extensive, its influence on the establishment of more flexible central prices cannot
be disregarded (Brabant 1977a, pp. 235–239).

Although it is undeniable that trade prices exert some influence on the formation of domestic prices in most CPEs, either
on the methods by which prices are calculated centrally or on the
direct gestation of prices applied by traders, producers of exports, and users of imports, the price system in all CPEs has on
the whole remained rather inflexible, though consumer prices
are more rigid than producer prices. The level of producer
prices and their changes over time are kept more or less independent of retail prices by various subsidies and taxes buffer-
ing socially undesirable shifts in the cost of living. Although assuring a high degree of price stability, which is aimed at for
social reasons with respect to consumer markets and for the sake
of plan administration in the case of producer markets, the rigidity of the administrative setting of prices has come into sharp
conflict with the goal of using prices more as one key allocation
criterion at all levels of decision making.

The dramatic price movements on international markets in
1973–1975 and their more recent transmission on the CMEA
market have accentuated the conflict between price stability and
economic efficiency. Inflation in Western markets has made it
increasingly cumbersome, especially for the trade-dependent
CPEs, to maintain present price levels indefinitely. Can this be
interpreted to mean that because of the economic reforms the
CPEs are no longer immune to foreign inflation and that perhaps they should retrench the remaining trade decentralization
features? The answer clearly depends on the type of economic
organization involved and the overall economic policies one assumes to be representative of the leaders' actions.

In the traditional CPE, as outlined in Chapter 2, the insulation of domestic from foreign prices through comprehensive price-equalization measures evidently enabled the CPEs to ward off direct inflation from abroad. Yet, if the terms of trade turn against the CPE or serious balance of payments deficits occur in the wake of external inflation, rising import costs will eventually have to be passed on to the economy. In appreciating the CPEs' immunity to the effects of external inflation, one should not confine the horizon to financial transactions (internally, the price-equalization account and, externally, the running down of currency reserves or borrowing in international markets). If external inflation is not conjunctural but structural, the CPE will not be able to avoid adjusting its economy to the situation abroad. Eventually, it will have to curtail domestic absorption in order to pay in real terms for the relatively more expensive imports. However, if the disturbances abroad are basically transitory, the MFT is capable of neutralizing their impact on the domestic economy, something which will be much more difficult to do in the reformed CPE. However, whether external inflation will affect domestic prices, if only indirectly and after some lag, depends very much on the planning institutions, instruments, and behavioral rules.

Especially in the reformed CPE, regardless of whether the transformations are partial or comprehensive, price stability is but one policy goal; others are full employment, internal and external balance, rapid output growth, and steady improvement in levels of living. Although these and other policy objectives also exist in the traditional CPE, it is now more unlikely that price stability will be sought indefinitely by administrative means because the other goals of the CPE may be affected indirectly. In principle a planner with full control over the CPE could neutralize direct price effects incurred in trade, but he will be reluctant to do so for all products and for a long time because the price stability goal will jeopardize attaining economic efficiency, especially if the latter is to be enhanced through the devolution of decision-making authority. Because improving efficiency is pivotal for reaching other policy aims, it is unlikely that the planner will seek indefinite postponement of domestic adjustments, including price revisions, though perhaps smoothed and introduced with a significant lag.

The increasingly vexing dilemma between price stability and efficiency has been resolved, for the time being, rather differently in the various CPEs. Although most countries have tightened the center's rein over decision making, also in trade, the depth of this retrenchment shows large variations. The CPEs placing a strong value on price stability have simply increased budgetary transfers, allowing only few price movements. Others, especially Hungary and Poland, have permitted price changes but have kept them, particularly retail prices, mostly within overall planned limits, which necessitates cushioning the trade impact by temporary, unanticipated increases in budgetary transfers. These CPEs have sought to ease the burden of domestic adjustments also by exchange rate changes or movements in conversion coefficients, staggered price revisions in successive annual plans a curtailment of import demand through credit control, export-promoting policies, and so on. However, all small CPEs have indicated that larger price changes will be enacted through planned revisions justified in view of shifts in real domestic and trade opportunities, and that the neutralization in the interim will not be perpetuated as in the traditional model.

Though on the whole producer prices have in recent years fluctuated more than consumer prices, the changes have been insufficient to cover rising import costs, and the export incentive arising from increased WMPs has had to be muted by various taxes or administrative regulations. It is somewhat ironical that developments in nonsocialist markets may become the major cause of dramatic changes in CPE price policies, although for social reasons these countries will continue to shield consumer goods prices from undesirable impacts emanating from foreign markets.

Planning reforms

Although in all CPEs there has been an undeniable tendency to reduce the number of physical norms imposed by the central plan and to reestablish contact between domestic and foreign markets, material balancing and central supply allocations have remained intact in all but Hungary and Poland. This proposition does not conflict with the fact that the gradual elimination of the nearly complete disjunction between trade and internal decision making continues to be of prime concern, even in the USSR. So far, the only noticeable influence is on the administrative link-up of trade with production or user. Foreign trade specialists in the ministries, branch associations, or individual enterprises are expected to play a major role both in drawing up the plans and in providing efficiency calculations on alternative trade processes. One evident change has been the reduction of the number of material balances denominated in physical units. Instead of detailed quantity assignments, the FTE as a rule now receives instructions on export tasks, import limits, or limitations on the imbalances expressed in foreign currency (generally separated into two categories, socialist or other trade). These instructions are still mandatory, if not for the FTEs directly then at least for the relevant ministry or association. The fact that the results of trade in FTEs or others authorized to conduct trade are now evaluated in foreign exchange equivalents constitutes an important novelty, though this does not necessarily imply that actual trade results can also be passed on to domestic prices.

Considerable differences continue to exist also in the effect exerted by the foreign trade results on the decision-making procedures of the producer, user, or relevant FTE. The more general expression of trade targets in foreign currency values does not, of course, imply that the trader is completely free in selecting partners or products to be traded. In all CPEs, trade plans, however aggregated, are assigned subject to limitations on the composition and distribution of trade. These restrictions are imposed by the relevant subdepartments of the Ministry of Foreign Trade either by administrative fiat, by instruments of indirect economic coordination, or tacitly (for instance, the FTEs are expected not to diverge too far from traditional trade patterns or from tentative official agreements). The perpetuation of BTPAs in intra-CMEA trade with all its ramifications for price formation and balancing restrictions has posed several knotty problems, especially for CPEs who expect the lower tiers of the plan hierarchy to make decisions on their own authority, as in Hungary. A whole set of "bridges" between artificial CMEA prices and WMPs on the one hand, and domestic prices on the other, has had to be worked out and periodically updated.

The monopoly of trade and payments

One of the first steps in changing the institutional functioning of the MFT, without however affecting its fundamental preeminence, was taken in the 1950s, when direct trading rights were granted to selected industrial firms or associations. Czechoslovakia, the German Democratic Republic, Hungary, and Poland have been pioneers in this domain. The decentralization of trade tasks by increasing the number of enterprises authorized to trade directly, although with palpable variations from country to country, has been one of the more conspicuous changes enacted by the reforms. In view of the importance attached to exporting manufactures, most of these new FTEs have been set up to take care of exports of machinery, transport equipment, consumer durables, and, above all, services for these products.

But no CPE has eliminated the MFT as such, nor have controls been relaxed much, not even in Hungary. Instead, the reforms have been designed to strengthen the role of the MFT, particularly the control of trade and payments, and the implementation of the overall economic plan. As a result, the competence of the MFT is now as comprehensive, if not as detailed, as before, a factor that must have been welcome when sharp adjustments in WMPs also threatened the economic stability of CPEs. Enterprises are subordinated to the ministry, which can issue compulsory instructions or plan targets, but these are usually rather elastic, allowing the FTE a certain freedom of action. The Ministry of Foreign Trade draws up the plan, it is entitled to issue legally binding regulations, and still grants permission or licenses for enterprises to engage in direct trade. It can also issue directives on what must be traded, especially with other CPEs, and on how the trade results will influence the domestic economy and the decentralized decisions of enterprises. Where centralization is still pervasive, one can witness at least a changeover from quantitative targets to sales' norms, particularly in export directives. However important and beneficial, these new arrangements do not yet add up to a new set of basic organizational principles needed to regulate what should be, on the one hand, the harmonic relationship between the producing enterprise and the FTE, and, on the other, the producer or FTE and the central authorities. Note also that the new guidelines have been worked out more fully in Hungary and Poland than elsewhere.

Cooperation abroad

The potential of trade and cooperation with MTEs played a crucial role in the formulation and implementation of the reforms. At least three CPEs (Hungary, Poland, and Rumania) have promulgated a legal framework regulating the creation of joint ventures that, it is hoped, will permit the acquisition not only of foreign capital but also of the know-how and technology needed to gain greater flexibility in trade and payments with advanced MTEs. Through these and other cooperation efforts, the CPEs expect to deepen and to facilitate their access to Western commodity and capital markets. Apart from those who have adapted their legal framework in matters of foreign property, the transfer abroad of earnings, the amortization of investments, the residence of foreigners, and so on, it must be mentioned that all CPEs have entered into major cooperation agreements with Western firms, though it is to be pointed out that the CPE economic systems are still far removed from permitting even a moderate degree of autonomy to local enterprise initiative in seeking profitable cooperation abroad.

As an outgrowth of the reforms, though not explicitly envisaged, the CPEs continue to look for more flexible modus operandi in trade and payments abroad. In recent years, there has been a significant reduction in the number of payments restrictions that CPEs have traditionally entertained with other countries. Bilateral clearing arrangements with advanced MTEs have been all but discontinued (except for countries as Finland and Greece, and then only for some CPEs), the number of clearing arrangements with developing countries has declined dramatically, and in many cases the CPEs have sought to provide for more flexible settlements in convertible currencies even if clearing arrangements are basically kept intact.

Also in the arena of East–West trade, the locus of formidable conflicts and so much antagonism in earlier years, the CPEs have sought to overcome ideological and political obstacles, among others, by joining international financial and trading organizations, by signing association or cooperation agreements with important trade blocs, and by generally improving the facilities for accommodating rapidly expanding interbloc trade and payments flows. The significance of these changes and their bearing on SEI will be looked at in greater detail in Chapter 5.

Cooperation between two or more enterprises belonging to at least two CPEs has been in the forefront of lengthy debates about the ways and means of fostering SEI since the late 1960s.[36] As to concrete results in terms of the role of common enterprises or the significance of cooperation agreements between the lower tiers of at least two different planning hierarchies, it is very difficult to draw an objective picture. The least to be said is that the CPEs have been sincerely concerned with the ways of enhancing SEI and the exploitation of various forms of regional cooperation other than direct merchandise exchange, not as an end in itself but rather as a supplement or complement to the traditional exchange of commodities and services. Judging from the recent literature, there are still numerous administrative, economic (Brabant 1977, pp. 279–293), legal, and ideological impediments. In fact, as paradoxical as it may seem, the era of economic reforms and, especially, the more genuine interest in international trade and cooperation has so far only marginally impacted on the formal and informal structure that is supposed to buttress the professed policy of SEI. Because decentralized decision making in trade is incompatible with the existing CMEA trade mechanism of fixed prices, commodity and general bilateralism, inconvertible currencies, and like factors on the one hand, and also conflicts with the existing institutional framework for enhancing regional interdependence on the other, one would have expected a determined effort to reform the CMEA framework in parallel at least with the largest common denominator of the national reforms. The intricate rationale behind the absence of such transformations will be explored in detail in Chapter 4.

6. Concluding remarks

In retrospect, it seems fair to observe that the trade system of the CPEs has evolved from being a simple appendage to the model and an incidental feature of the growth strategy to a pivotal economic activity in contemporary CPEs. But the situation has not yet settled down, as the foreign trade sector continues to be in a greater state of flux and subject to more experimentation than the other aspects of the reforms. Because not all CPEs have worked toward reforms in the same way or introduced the same degree of scope and depth in the changes they implemented, one finds a more differentiated situation than the former uniform landscape of rigid dichotomy, especially with regard to the influence of trade on domestic decision making and price formation. Whether this diversity facilitates or hampers progress with SEI is still unclear. Each CPE has made a serious effort to formulate its development goals and to pattern the underlying organizational structure in accordance with what the national leadership perceives to be warranted by domestic circumstances. Although this lack of coordination of reforms is deplorable and may in some cases be quite serious from the point of view of SEI, it is somewhat disconcerting that in the current literature, particularly the Soviet and East German, there is such a strong emphasis on the need for uniformity rather than diversity in planning methods, organization, and control, a subject that will be further explored in Chapter 5.

Paradoxically enough, although foreign trade matters have been in the forefront of the debates about reforming the traditional CPEs and their mutual relations are so important in trade and payments, nothing much seems to have been altered in intra-CMEA relations. The reasons for this state of affairs will be examined more closely in the next chapter.

4

The evolution of the Council

As an institution initially created to promote SEI, the CMEA could not live up to the high expectations of at least some of the postwar leaders of Eastern Europe. However vaguely the intentions were formulated at the time, from Chapter 1 it appears that most of the policy makers of the small CPEs expected their economies to be drawn into a regional policy that would help to forestall a repetition of the fragmented policies so characteristic of the period between the world wars. There were also several indications that by joining forces and by combining available resources, thus dovetailing the process of economic reconstruction as a start-up for a comprehensive regional development strategy, these countries would have a better chance of surmounting underdevelopment. Unfortunately, contrary to what might have been expected, the Council was established before a definite program of action delineating the scope of its active involvement in fostering cooperation could be agreed upon, it had no charter defining its authority and obligations, and it was not provided with an adequate institutional framework to support regional economic cooperation. Perhaps the most significant factor behind the Council's inactivity in the early 1950s is the fundamental disagreement among the political leaders of the CPEs on the most expedient strategy of regional development, and how mutual consultations and joint programs could stimulate this. Of course, the power-political environment and the shortsighted interests of the USSR should not be brushed away.

Although certainly much can be said about the organization's history, and it might be constructive to speculate about what could have materialized had the socialist leaders been more perspicacious by showing sincere concern for the economic prob-

lems of the region as a whole rather than those of each nation individually, the objective of this chapter is slightly different.
Because the Council's activities in the 1950s were only marginally relevant to the economic preoccupations of the members,
the focus will here be largely on the more recent period for, in
the past decades or so, but particularly in the 1970s, measurable
movement toward greater economic integration under the
Council's auspices has been noticeable.

This chapter will be concerned with the organizational infrastructure of the CMEA, the policy documents setting forth the
transformation of the official doctrine on regional cooperation,
the Council's role in promoting SEI, the members' attitude toward harmonizing Eastern Europe, and a brief exploratory assessment of the effects of SEI on the members. By proceeding in
this way, the background to the conditions under which the
CPEs can foster SEI will gradually be completed. The focus will
therefore be primarily on topics of present and future interest.
In order not to lose sight altogether of a historical perspective,
section 1 offers one possible periodization of CMEA events and
discusses briefly the issue of membership. Section 2 outlines the
Council's organizational structure. The background, purposes,
and implications of official policy documents are summarized in
section 3. Finally, section 4 evaluates the overall achievements of
SEI to date, but more details on this will be provided in the next
chapter.

1. Stages of CMEA cooperation and membership

The following schematic representation of the CMEA's evolution may be helpful in placing the discussion to follow in a
proper perspective.

1949–1950: Active discussions about the goals, scope, and instruments of SEI take place and the nucleus of CMEA's organizational links is institutionalized, without however resulting in an
accepted program of regional development goals, common instruments, and principles of cooperation. In other words, as an
international economic organization, the Council was created in
a legal and institutional vacuum, and it was oddly enough not
rescued from this legal limbo for more than a decade.
1950–1954: An inward-looking economic policy is imposed upon

each CPE. Although the USSR acts as catalyst of both economic and other forms of cooperation, it effectively prevents multilateral contacts among the CPEs. The CMEA's role as an institution dealing with cooperation is negligible or, at best, is confined to providing aid in the drafting of BTPAs; studying some questions of industrial and nomenclature standardization; and analyzing isolated topics of genuine cooperation other than simple trade exchanges, particularly production specialization.

1954–1956: Interest in regional cooperation is revived in an effort to stem the immediate impacts of the New Course in the economic policies pursued by the separate CPEs, to come to grips with the more fundamental problems of the growing wastefulness of duplication of work through parallel economic development, and to cope with the increasingly diverse needs of the members. Toward the end of this period, the first serious specialization agreements are signed, the CMEA institutions are enlarged and given a more explicit mandate, and the Council's authority in charting practical work toward future cooperation gains general acceptance.

1957–1961: A period of reflection on how production specialization and more general economic cooperation can be set up effectively in the wake of the serious economic disagreements brought to the surface, especially during the 1956 events in Hungary and Poland. However, implementation of the salient points of agreement is precluded by the new, once again, uncoordinated industrialization waves sweeping the CPEs. The drive toward the institutional reinforcement of the Council is resumed after 1958, and top-level discussions about the principles of the ISDL and how to implement it take place.

1962–1964: The acceptance of the principal document underlying the ISDL triggers off a serious dispute about regional specialization, the goals of CMEA cooperation, and the role of the common organization therein. The basic institutional structure is further enlarged and strengthened. But at that point the pressure to pursue organizational consolidation and policy innovations seems to have overreached itself, and in the face of the Rumanian obduracy on the creation of supranational planning, it is decided informally to place more trust in the further exploration of bilateral cooperation.

1965–1968: A period of reflection on promoting the ISDL and its possible alternatives. Active cooperation proceeds mostly on the bilateral level and largely in response to pressing necessities arising from the concrete economic conditions rather than as a result of a well-thought-out plan of mutual cooperation. This stems partly from the fact that each CPE gradually starts looking for or is already experimenting with its own national economic reforms, which show various degrees of detail and comprehensiveness. The debate on the roads to SEI centers in particular on regional planning policies on the one hand, and the utilization of instruments of indirect coordination compatible with the devolution of authority over decisions in the internal economies on the other.

1968–1971: Lively discussions on strengthening SEI with widely divergent outlooks take place during the consolidation phase that follows upon the 1968 events in Czechoslovakia and their impact on the other CPEs. The goals and means of SEI are finally laid down and agreed upon in a comprehensive policy document. Further institutional reinforcements are introduced to support international, as distinct from supranational, cooperation within Eastern Europe.

1971–1975: The CPEs search for what SEI can be understood to imply and for ways and means of exploiting effectively joint consultations on matters of common interest, especially on policy intentions, making fruitful use of the closer coordination of national plans, and generally elaborating a mechanism of SEI to prop up policy intentions. Further institutional reinforcements are mostly confined to the establishment of regional economic agencies put in charge of very specific tasks, mostly in the field of scientific and technological cooperation, but also the coordination of selected enterprise policies. The questions regarding to what extent money and finance should play an active role in guiding the process of SEI, what room will be preempted for plan coordination and joint planning, and how planning should be harmonized with instruments of indirect coordination remain basically unresolved. Whereas the deadlines of most of the targeted changes in monetary and financial cooperation are ostensibly heeded, the changes introduced are low-keyed, and interest in these indirect coordination instruments is evidently declining. But also plan coordination gets bogged down in numerous matters of principle and in a number of practical obstacles.

1976–present: SEI gradually loses its very ambitious outlook. Instead, the CPEs resort to target cooperation, in addition to traditional commerce and scientific-technical cooperation. This toning down finds its expression in two significant policy shifts: the conclusion of a multilateral plan of specific integration measures synchronized with the current medium-term plans for 1976–1980, and the formulation of so-called target programs for concrete actions in five crucial fields of cooperation that will increasingly necessitate the harmonization of economic policies in selected activities.

Naturally, a periodization of the developments of intra-CMEA affairs is bound to include some rather arbitrary divisions. The sketchy outline proposed here follows closely the evolution of CMEA's institutional structure and the elaboration of seminal policy statements. Several recent East European views of the CMEA's evolution (e.g., Alekseev 1974; Proft 1973, pp. 25–27) prefer a four-tier division: (1) the gradual development of multilateral cooperation (1949–1958); (2) the deepening of production cooperation (1958–1962); (3) the acceptance of plan coordination as the principal method of intra-CMEA cooperation (1962–1969); and (4) the development of SEI (present phase). But this division is by no means the standard accepted by most observers. Furthermore, the loaded terminological subdivisions, patterned after profound shifts in the political interpretation of CMEA's evolvement, is rather arbitrary and much too vague to place events or institutions in their proper historical setting. To appreciate the CMEA's accomplishments to date and the goals, instruments, and other means of SEI it will be more useful to keep in mind the broader outline above, which is less sweeping with regard to the rather controversial interpretation of terms such as integration, plan coordination, specialization, and multilateralization.

As defined in the introduction, the CMEA is understood as an agency enveloping some shared concerns of the seven active European members. Though the potential significance of widening the Council's horizon to accommodate in one form or another countries from other parts of the world and to cooperate with other international organizations is not looked upon with disdain, it is evident that SEI is concerned almost exclusively with the particular issues of East European cooperation – as indeed it was enshrined in the original (1959) charter. The European region is also likely to remain the focal area in which SEI will have to mature before the Council, and its active developed members can start tackling new problems that are bound to arise when other economies, especially those remotely linked to Eastern Europe or backward countries, are coopted and drawn into the sphere of CMEA's practical activities. But to the extent that other countries are or will become involved in SEI, it is useful to discuss briefly the various types of association presently available to nonmembers.

According to article 11 of the Council's statutes (Tokareva 1976, pp. 12–13), other countries may be invited to participate in the CMEA's activities by concluding special agreements.

Legally there are only members and nonmembers (Morozov 1977, p. 110), but from a more pragmatic point of view there are presently, broadly speaking, four separate degrees of attachment to the CMEA organization open to individual countries: full membership, limited participant, cooperant, and observer status. Although the latter three terms are not unambiguously defined, they do tend to suggest the descending degree of involvement open to nonmembers.

At present the CMEA comprises eleven full members: The seven active European members were joined in February 1949 by Albania, though this country ceased to participate in CMEA activities as of the end of 1961 without revoking formal membership; the German Democratic Republic joined in September 1950, Mongolia in June 1962, Cuba in July 1972, and Vietnam in June 1978. Full membership will be granted only to countries willing to subscribe to the aims and principles of the CMEA and to abide by the obligations and rights ensuing from the organization's charter. Although not explicitly stated, in view of the accompanying definition of the aims and principles of the CMEA, it would seem to be a prerequisite for membership that the applicant be socialist, as the charter requires that members favor "the development of [SEI and] the planned development of their national economies" (Tokareva 1976, p. 6), as well as adhere to the principles of the ISDL, socialist internationalism, and fraternal mutual assistance. Although the precise meaning of planning is left unspecified, it probably signals that membership is effectively reserved for CPEs (Klepacki 1975, p. 48). The requirements deriving from the ideological precepts underlying the CMEA in effect buttress this potential membership sphere. Thus, for example, the lack of "proper" planning instruments was used as an excuse in turning down Yugoslavia's request in 1959 to be readmitted as an observer to the Council Session (Uschakow 1962, p. 10)!

Full membership does not, however, call for participation in all CMEA activities. According to the "interested party provision," now also formally embodied in the latest version of CMEA's charter, members may elect to participate in specific CMEA projects or stand aloof, as they choose: "All recommendations and decisions of the CMEA organs can be adopted only with the consent of the interested member countries. . . . [They] do not affect countries who have declared themselves as having no interest in the question concerned" (Tokareva 1976, p. 8).

"Limited participant" is very much like the status of the "interested party provision" for full members, although cosmetically and legally the situation is, of course, quite different. Yugoslavia is the only country with this status; it cooperates in the work of a majority of the Council's Standing Commissions and in a number of other CMEA organs within the framework worked out in the agreement signed in September 1964.

The collaboration of most nonsocialist countries with the Council, if formal ties are sought at all, is normally regulated by a cooperant status, which was first granted to Finland in 1973; Iraq and Mexico followed suit in 1975. Many other developing countries (such as Angola, Ethiopia, Kampuchea, and Laos) have apparently shown interest in obtaining some type of association with the CMEA. Relations under the cooperant status are normally entrusted to bilateral joint committees, in which representatives from the cooperant and interested CMEA members participate. In principle, any topic of mutual interest can be retained for discussion or negotiation.

Traditionally, all nonmember CPEs are invited to participate in the CMEA bodies as observers, although China, Cuba (before 1972), Mongolia (before 1962), North Korea, and North Vietnam (now as Vietnam a full member) have not always sent delegations to the Council Session, and the level of importance of the delegations has varied considerably. Recently, Angola, Ethiopia, Kampuchea, and Laos have also taken part as observers. Observer status would seem to be no more than a diplomatic tool and a channel for exchanging information of mutual interest.

Membership in the above context has been discussed with reference to the strictly official organs of the Council as defined in section 2. Because a large number of international organizations established by some or all CMEA members have legally an autonomous status and by their charter not all require the same degree of ideological and sociopolitical commitment as a precondition for membership, as does the CMEA charter, it is in theory possible that non-CMEA members can join one or more of what will be termed here "CMEA-affiliated organizations," without acceding to the CMEA. This is said to apply especially to "some developing countries which have adopted certain elements of

economic planning" (Klepacki 1975, p. 51). However, further
details of the membership issue will be left to the legal specialist.

2. The Council's organization

As a regional economic organization, the CMEA has evolved
from a very simple institution investigating a few problems of
common interest to a very large organism comprising an exceedingly complex hierarchy of official and unofficial channels of
communication. Not all tiers of the CMEA can be examined
here, if only because not much is known about their contribution
to SEI: Before surveying the key echelons, it is necessary to settle
a very important issue regarding the degree of authority and autonomy enjoyed by the formal CMEA institutions.

Although it has no official place in the CMEA's formal hierarchy, the most important "CMEA organ" is the occasional gather-
ing of heads of state and party secretaries of the CPEs. Officially,
this informal organ is called the "Conference of First Secretaries
of Communist and Workers' Parties and of the Heads of Government of the CMEA Member Countries," but this cumbersome title will be condensed here to "Conference of Communist
Parties."

Top-level meetings of this organ have been convened more or
less regularly since 1958, although most of the summit political
meetings of the immediate postwar period, as those reported in
Chapter 1, should properly be included here as well. In the current East European literature, this organ's origin is normally
dated as May 1958, when important decisions specifically related
to the ISDL and the CMEA's role therein were adopted
(Amundsen 1971, pp. 151–153; Gamarnikow 1971, pp.
217–219; Kaser 1967, p. 85). Owing to the informal nature of
the Conference of Communist Parties, the range of possible
topics for debate is in principle very wide and not necessarily
confined to regional economic cooperation issues. However,
some sessions have been exclusively devoted to the goals, instruments, and problems of SEI, and decisions reached there
have been of critical significance to the evolution of regional economic policies and institutions. In fact, "fundamental decisions"
of the formal CMEA organs are usually reached by a Council

Session convened shortly after the meeting of the Conference of Communist Parties or when both coincide,[1] for it is here that the directions and basic principles of the CMEA's activities are programmatically charted. As noted by the Bulgarian economist M. Savov, "some of the Sessions have had an exceptional significance for the activity of the CMEA. This concerns in particular the Sessions which coincided with the [Conference of Communist Parties] or when they took part in the Session" (Savov 1973, p. 54). Although the decisions of these meetings have formally no binding character for the CMEA organization and hence SEI, they are routinely confirmed by the appropriate bodies of the CMEA. However, in view of the "role of these parties as the leading political force [of the CPEs], the directives adopted by the conferences are in fact binding and the appropriate organs of the organization are only called upon to give them formal legal force" (Klepacki 1975, p. 50). This observation underlines very appropriately the status of the CMEA: Although nominally independent, this organism does not really possess autonomy in making decisions or even in implementing them in practice.

The current (1974) version of the CMEA charter singles out the basic organs of the organization as the Council Session, the Executive Committee, the Council Committees, the Standing (or Permanent) Commissions, and the Secretariat (Tokareva 1976, p. 8). In addition to these pinnacle levels, the Council has a large assortment of special-purpose organs such as Institutes, Conferences, and Affiliated Organizations, whose official links with the Council are not always crystal clear. However, in none of these formal echelons, including the top Session, is vested any decision authority whatsoever, and in that respect the CMEA resembles far more such intergovernmental institutions as the Economic Commission for Europe in Geneva than, say, the European Communities in Brussels, even if the latter's supranational powers have been severely whittled in recent years. Indeed, in the CMEA framework the national communist parties or governments have not only the final power to endorse or to reject recommendations on principles and instruments of SEI, they also frequently interfere in ongoing discussions about these fundamental topics. This fragmented localization of power over SEI is a formidable impediment to dovetailing the member economies effectively, even if all partners were sincerely bent on fostering SEI. Given that the national power centers have many other tasks of more immediate urgency, it is certainly not surprising that at times matters of basic cooperation tend to be relegated to a nonpriority status among the wide range of focal policy issues. Nor is it by any means a coincidence that rather scanty attention has been devoted to the opportunities for multilateral economic cooperation within the CMEA framework, at least until the late 1960s.

Realizing the somber state of intra-CMEA affairs and, more generally, of socialist international commitment to economic cooperation, Chruščëv in the early 1960s called for bringing party heads, government leaders, and responsible officials into closer contact with the CMEA's actual work in an effort to acquaint these decision makers with the most weighty regional problems and to elicit a more responsible chord in getting SEI off the ground (Uschakow 1972, pp. 32–33). Although the national political chiefs did indeed get involved much more intimately in the myriad aspects of SEI – the two fundamental policy documents on the ISDL and SEI were approved first by the Conference of Communist Parties and only subsequently endorsed by the basic organs of the CMEA – they have so far refused to delegate any authority to the higher CMEA echelons; in fact, the CMEA's "supreme organ" – the Council Session according to article 6.1 of the charter – can do not much more than rubberstamp the general policy line and specific decisions of the real pinnacle body.

Despite the Council's apparent lack of authority and very restricted autonomy in charting SEI, it seems nevertheless useful to draw a rounded picture of the various formal CMEA echelons and to elaborate somewhat on each organ's tasks and role in SEI. The overall hierarchical structure of the CMEA is schematically represented in Figure 2. Further details of this organigram will be introduced as needed.[2]

The Council Session

As the highest official organ, this deliberative body comprises gatherings of government delegations selected by each member country at its own discretion and includes at least one perma-

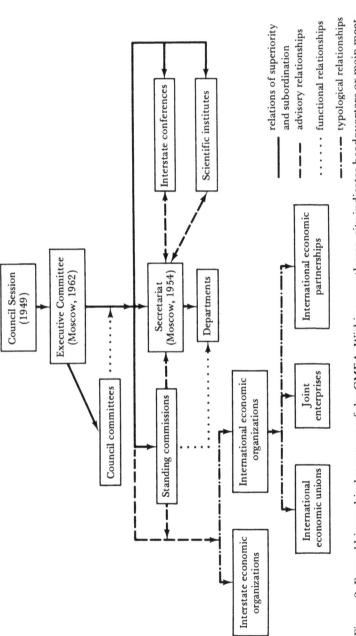

Figure 2. Formal hierarchical structure of the CMEA. Within parentheses, city indicates headquarters or main meeting place; date is that of founding.

nent representative. The permanent representative is in charge of relations between the Council and the members in between Council Sessions and is normally a deputy premier. When in session, the national delegation is usually headed by the permanent representative. However, the more important the topics on the agenda, the more likely that top decision makers of the individual CPEs, possibly the first party secretaries, will attend the meetings and lead the national delegations. In fact, since the twenty-fourth CMEA Session (Warsaw, 1970), the national delegations are usually headed by the prime ministers of the members (Faddeev 1974b, p. 70), though this has not always been the case (e.g., Cuba and Rumania). According to current provisions, this organ meets annually,[3] whenever possible during the second quarter, in one of the capitals of the CPEs in rotation according to the Cyrillic alphabet. An extraordinary or special Session can be summoned if at least one-third of the members request or consent to such a convocation, which will normally be held in Moscow.

The function of the Session is the examination of the fundamental problems of SEI. It also directs the activities of the Secretariat and subordinate organs. New official organs – as distinct from the other, "affiliated" organizations discussed below – may be set up by unanimous decision of the members of the Council Session. Whereas by statute the Session has very broad powers, it can in fact merely make recommendations on other than purely organizational matters, which become effective only if adopted by all interested individual governments in accordance with their own legal procedures.

In accordance with the rules of procedure of the Council Session (Tokareva 1976, pp. 19–31), the organ can make recommendations on matters of economic, scientific, and technological cooperation, as distinct from decisions on organizational or procedural issues. Interested members are obliged to consider these recommendations. Within sixty days after the Session's closure, "interested members" are obliged to inform the Council's secretary of the "results of the consideration by the government or other competent agencies . . . of the Session's recommendation." The endorsement of a recommendation entails the obligation to heed it. However, such recommendations cannot be implemented directly; they constitute in fact only the starting point in the process of plan coordination, with the emphasis being shifted to bilateral relations (Wasilkowski 1971, p. 43). Once accepted, the Council recommendations are normally implemented by means of bilateral and multilateral treaties or other types of agreement that outline the obligations and rights of those members that have indicated their willingness to participate in the proposed measure.

The significance of the various Council Sessions has varied considerably and depends largely on the attendant circumstances. In the current East European literature, the following meetings are regarded as having been especially significant: the second (Sofia, 1949), on questions of trade agreements and the free exchange of scientific and technological information; the fourth (Moscow, 1954), on problems of plan coordination and the institutional reinforcement of the CMEA; the seventh (Berlin, 1956), on specialization, especially in machine building, chemical, and metallurgical sectors; the ninth (Bucharest, 1958), on principles of regional price formation, the further institutional strengthening of the Council, and more topics of specialization; the sixteenth (Moscow, 1962), on institutional and programmatic changes in connection with the acceptance of the document on the ISDL and the agreement to create a common bank; the twenty-third "special"[4] Session (Moscow, 1969), on principles of specialization and SEI; the twenty-fifth (Bucharest, 1971), on the acceptance of the basic integration document; the twenty-seventh (Prague, 1973), on questions of plan coordination and the elaboration of multilateral specialization programs, which were actually endorsed during the twenty-ninth Session (Budapest, 1975); the thirtieth (Berlin, 1976), on establishing target programs as pivots in deepening long-term integration; and the thirty-second (Bucharest, 1978) and the thirty-third (Moscow, 1979), which endorsed the five target programs.

The Executive Committee

This highest executive organ was set up in 1962 to replace the Conference of Representatives of the CMEA Member Countries. It is a nonpermanent organ that is convoked regularly and relatively frequently (at present at least once a quarter, but in earlier versions of the charter, a frequency of at least once every two months was called for), and it is composed of high-ranking officials, normally the permanent CMEA representative, who is at least a vice-chairman of the Council of Ministers. It is normally in session in Moscow, although this is not mandatory. The Executive Committee is the main organization entrusted with elaborating policy recommendations and supervising their implementation in between Sessions. The functions of this organ include also the supervision of the work on plan coordination and scientific and technological cooperation, and guiding the research and deliberations of the Standing Commissions and of the Secretariat, which it controls. It can make decisions within its competence, that is, its own organization and administration.

Its founding in 1962 was in fact one of the essential measures that were expected eventually to lead up to the projected supranational planning agency then in the offing (see section 3). However, as a result of the ensuing debate on the means by which closer cooperation was to be achieved and on the goals of the ISDL, it never matured into a supranational planning board. Its Bureau[5] (replaced in 1971 by the Planning Committee) was a working organ composed of the deputy chairmen of the planning offices (the present Committee is composed of the chairmen) on a level comparable to that of the Standing Commissions. The innovations introduced in 1971 and 1974, that is to say, attaching Committees on fundamental general economic problems to the Executive Committee and above the Standing Commissions, have probably considerably strengthened the authority and importance of the Executive Committee.

The Secretariat

This is the only permanent CMEA organ. In spite of what their name might suggest, the Standing Commissions have no independent permanent secretariat, research units, or administrative staff. Such is only the case for the Council's Secretariat, which has been headed since the CMEA's inception by a Soviet citizen (since 1958, N. V. Faddeev has been the highest civil servant of the CMEA). The Secretariat is headquartered in Moscow in a futuristic skyscraper on the bank of the river Moskva. The secretary has several deputies in the upper echelon, in fact on the level of senior international civil servants, and oversees a staff of professionals recruited from the various members. The Secretariat is divided into a number of departments, generally corresponding to the Standing Commissions and several other staff agencies (Faddeev 1974b, pp. 80–81), which undertake much of the preparatory and staff work connected with policy recommendations and their implementation. These units are also responsible for much of the background work required before other CMEA organs can begin to examine effectively the problems within their purview.

According to article 10 of the charter, the Secretariat is officially responsible for organizing and contributing to the meetings of the other CMEA organs (in particular, the Council Session). It also guides the implementation and execution of recommendations and decisions taken by itself and the other Council organs. Officially, it has generally the same functions as the rather administrative obligations entrusted to the secretariats of conventional international organizations (such as the Economic Commission for Europe in Geneva); in particular, it is not empowered to enact and enforce recommendations to the member states on its own initiative. In short, it prepares the recommendations and decisions of the other organs, and molds them into a practical form. Even with these limited objectives, the Secretariat may still play a crucial role in charting the course of SEI (see below).

Council Committees

The first of these organs were established in 1971. The Committees generally have a much wider jurisdiction and greater prerogatives than those held by the Standing Commissions because they have the right to influence the work of other CMEA organs and agencies in accordance with prescribed uniform principles and methods of instruction. More important, they are also empowered to set priorities and make assignments accordingly, and the work of the Council's agencies must be molded in agreement with these priorities.

So far three Committees have been created, each charged with the duty of assuring the comprehensive examination and multilateral settlement of major problems of SEI, especially in the fields of economic, scientific, and technological cooperation: the Committee for Cooperation in Planning (1971), the Committee for Scientific-Technological Cooperation (1971), and the Committee for Cooperation in Material and Technical Supplies (1974). All Committees are headquartered in Moscow, where they also normally meet, though this is not compulsory.

The Planning Committee is perhaps the most important of the three and possibly of all other CMEA organs, with the exception of the Session and the Executive Committee. The members of this Committee are indeed the chairmen of the all-powerful national central planning offices, and thus also have direct access to top government and party leaders. Deputy chairmen of the national planning offices act as the permanent operating body of the Committee and form its Bureau. Were it not for the fact that also its recommendations are subject to approval by national government and party authorities, the Planning Committee would be in fact, if not in name, CMEA's supranational planning office – a goal that several CMEA members have coveted for almost two decades, so far meeting stiff opposition on the part of some other countries, especially Rumania. The list of the Planning Committee's tasks is long and tedious (Bajbakov 1976), and potentially envelops all planning problems dealt with in national planning bureaus. However, practical work would seem to have been narrowed down to more specific projects such as those underlying the Concerted Plan of Multilateral Integration Measures currently being implemented and the preparation of the Target Programs of Long-term Cooperation (see below), which are now being formulated together with the coordination of the next medium-term plans (1981–1985) of the member countries.

Perhaps the most active Committee is the one in charge of scientific-technological cooperation, which supervises some fifty-six research and cooperation centers located in the member countries, where the actual groundwork for the coordination and application of scientific and technical work is concentrated. It is also in charge of the Center for Scientific and Technological Information, the Interstate Commission for Calculating Techniques (both in Moscow), and the Council for Environmental Protection and Improvement (in Berlin). In addition to the coordination centers, the Committee is also assured of the collaboration of a large number of scientific institutions and other organizations participating in basic and applied research (Kirillin 1977, pp. 32–33).

Finally, the Committee on materials and supply problems deals with issues related to the harmonization of demand and supply, especially of scarce materials, and it elaborates measures to alleviate persistent disequilibria, to recycle secondary and waste materials, to computerize inventory control, and to foster better management and organization of material and technical supplies (Dymsic 1975).[6]

The Standing Commissions

The Standing Commissions are among the oldest of the CMEA organs and are organized along economic branch lines or according to major overall economic problem areas. Since the early 1960s, each has been paired with a department of the Secretariat. If need arises, joint working groups of two or more Commissions are set up to examine issues that cross branch boundaries or to find solutions to common problems. Each Commission theoretically has its permanent headquarters in one of the members and is chaired by the home country's minister or highest civil servant of the relevant branch, though the Commission can be convened in any CPE and the actual work program is carried out in the Secretariat in Moscow or under the supervision of one of the Secretariat's departments in the member countries.

As with the other organs, the Standing Commissions can make only recommendations, which have to be approved by the Executive Committee and presented to the formal Council Session. But measures become effective only after ratification or approval by the interested members. Each Commission usually consists of one or more sections or permanent work groups, temporary work groups, and scientific-technological centers. In addition, the Commissions entertain "advisory" relationships with relevant affiliated agencies, even if these are legally autonomous institutions and, strictly speaking, are not CMEA organs (Brunner 1976, p. 22). The presently existing Commissions are shown in Figure 3, together with their location and the dates they were established.

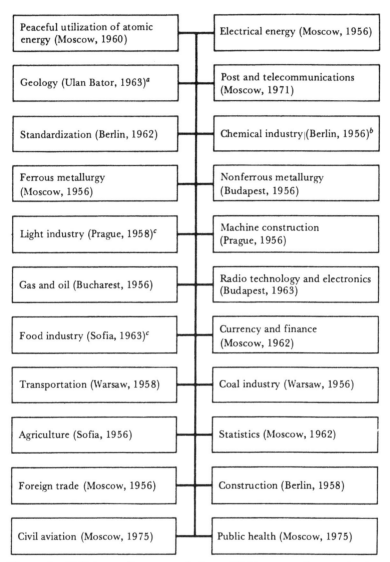

Figure 3. CMEA standing commissions. Within parentheses, city indicates headquarters or main meeting place; date is that of founding. (a) Created in 1956 in Moscow, abolished in 1958, and re-created in 1963. (b) Includes the commission for timber and cellulose, which was independent from 1956 to 1958. (c) Created in 1958 as the commission for food and light industries; the commission for food processing was established separately in 1963.

The Standing Commissions, together with the Committees, are the real working organs of the CMEA. They were set up first in 1956 to replace the ad hoc working parties and subdivisions of the Bureau and later of the Secretariat. Their number and field of authority has fluctuated a good deal, but would now seem to be more or less stabilized. Starting with twelve branch Commissions in 1956 (agriculture, chemical industry, coal, electrical energy, ferrous metals, foreign trade, engineering, nonferrous metallurgy, forestry, oil and gas, timber and cellulose, and geology), four more were added in 1958 (construction, economic questions, transportation, and food and light industries), while at the same time three of those created in 1956 were abolished (timber and cellulose, forestry, and geology). In 1960 the Commission for the peaceful utilization of atomic energy was founded. In 1962, four more were established (statistics, standardization, currency and finance, and the coordination of scientific and technological research). The Commission for geology was revived (with headquarters relocated from Moscow to Ulan Bator), the food industry was separated from the Commission for food and light industries, and a further Commission for radio-technology and related electronics industries was created in 1963. Then the formal organization was stabilized in the wake of the serious dispute about the basic principles of the ISDL. In 1971, the Commission for post and telecommunications was set up, while several others were abolished following the creation of the two Council Committees (the Commission for economic questions was apparently superseded by the Planning Committee and that for scientific-technological cooperation by the corresponding Committee). In 1975, two new Commissions were created: civil aviation, which was detached from the transportation Commission; and public health, from scientific-technological cooperation. This means that there are at present twenty-two Standing Commissions.[7]

Standing Commissions can be grouped into branch units and general economic organs. The sectoral ones are divided over the various member countries, whereas the general Commissions are all located in Moscow, excepting the one for standardization, which is in Berlin. Each of the branch Commissions is headquartered in one of the various members, usually selected on the basis of the particular importance of the relevant economic sector(s) for that country. But all the important general Commissions and Committees, which really mold the framework and select the guidelines for overall economic cooperation within the CMEA, have been concentrated in Moscow. This geographical distribution is not a trivial matter, as much of the range and quality of the work performed depends on the initiative and imagination of a Commission's chairman and the senior officials or ministers of the respective industries who head the Commission's activities and set their work schedule. The role of a particular Commission in improving production specialization and promoting SEI is substantially larger the more experts and scientists happen to be involved, the more technical the nature of their assignments, and, last but not least, the greater the initiative and clout of their chairman.

The national delegations in the Standing Commissions are typically headed by the ministers of the respective field or at least by senior civil servants of the appropriate ministries or institutions. The Commissions are in session at least twice a year, usually in Moscow, since their secretariats were transferred to the corresponding sections of the Council's Secretariat in 1962, presumably partly in anticipation of the imminent creation of a supranational planning agency at the Council level (see section 3).

Conferences

Officials of the CPEs in charge of specific economic, scientific, or technological affairs often find that they share a number of common preoccupations. To discuss such shared issues and exchange experience, a number of interstate conferences have been institutionalized. These organs are not empowered to make recommendations, let alone make decisions, as they have largely consultative, organizational, or coordinating functions. The Conferences recognized as CMEA organs number at present seven:

1. Conference of Ministers of Domestic Trade (1968)
2. Conference of Ministers of Labor Affairs (1974)
3. Conference of Heads of Technological Inventions and Patents (1971)

4. Conference of Price Office Chiefs (1973)
5. Conference of Representatives of CMEA Members on Legal Questions (1969)
6. Conference of Water Administration Heads (1962)
7. Conference of Representatives of Freight Transport and Shipping Organizations (1951), which supervises the Bureau for the Coordination of Ship Charters (1956)

These seven Conferences are generally organized as "permanent organs" (presumably because they have a statute and are convened on a regular basis, usually twice a year), and are subordinated in an advisory capacity to the Executive Committee or its specialized Committees (Faddeev 1974b, pp. 82–85). But there are in fact many other meetings convened on a more or less regular basis and in cooperation with or under the aegis of the CMEA, especially on theoretical or academic topics (see Trend 1975, p. 7). Though Conferences are purely consultative, they have at times led to the establishment of more formal CMEA institutions.[8]

The official Conferences can be separated into two categories: those that study special economic or other problems (e.g., prices and domestic trade) and those that supervise the operation of quasi-permanent tasks (e.g., the administration of shipping transportation). As an example, the Conference of shipping directors, created by the Council's Bureau in October 1951 (Lukin 1974a, p. 399), coordinates the shipping activities of CPEs abroad, organizes common passenger and freight services, elaborates propositions on the unification of shipment conditions, and so on. Although such largely administrative tasks could have been entrusted also to the Standing Commissions, the CPEs decided otherwise. One important reason for this chronic aversion to delegating duties in general is that committal of authority to the formal CMEA echelons implies in itself the transfer of power from the national to the regional level, whereas the relatively loose framework of a conference can meet the need for consultation and exchange of useful information and experience without in any way implying a further commitment to the transferring of decision-making authority. Also, the formal CMEA channels of communication appear to be top heavy, inflexible, and entrenched in the established bureaucracy, and are therefore not in a position to deal effectively with specialized issues as need arises (see below). In view of the importance of some topics, especially pricing and legal affairs, it is nevertheless somewhat surprising that the CPEs have not yet been willing to establish higher-level organs to deal with these crucial issues of SEI.

Institutes

The CMEA institutes, which are considered CMEA organs and are not fully subordinated to the Standing Commissions or the Committees (as is the Dubna nuclear research facility), number at present three: the Standardization Institute (Moscow, 1962), the International Institute for Economic Problems of the World Socialist System (Moscow, 1971), and the International Research Institute for Management Problems (Moscow, 1975). These organs are really concerned with the more theoretical, but possibly fundamental, problems of international cooperation rather than with the implementation of desirable or approved cooperation initiatives.

Standardization and unification of measurements, tolerances, profiles, complete products, and so on can certainly facilitate the transfer of commodities and services across the region, and even more of components and parts. From its inception in 1962, the Standardization Institute's mission has been the establishment of common scientific, technical, and industrial standards, especially for industry, agriculture, and science. But its role appears to have been more latent than active until the early 1970s, when the Complex Program called for greater standardization. Its authority has been immeasurably enhanced by the ratification, in 1974, of the protocol on technical standards. In essence, this document calls for compulsory adherence to CMEA technical standards as they are announced at regular intervals by the Standardization Commission (Smith 1977, p. 161), and the members (excepting Rumania, which apparently has not yet approved) must instruct their industries, design centers, laboratories, and so on to adhere to common CMEA standards within a certain time frame following approval of the Commission's recommendations, which are normally prepared by the Standardization Institute.

The Institute for the study of CMEA economic problems is more or less a general research organ overseeing some work on basic economic and other topics of SEI. The role of prices in trade and specialization, for example, can here be considered against a much wider background than was formerly possible in the now defunct Commission for economic questions. Although its activities have certainly placed the problems of SEI into perspective, the Institute's influence on the decision-making process in the CMEA does not appear to be very large. But it probably fulfills a perceptible role in preparing vast amounts of background information for more political and action-oriented debates in the higher-up levels, and in that sense it may play a very important function in enhancing the potential for SEI.

The Management Institute deals with the promotion of scientific management methods, including computer simulation of complex management processes; the prognosis of future developments in managerial duties and how present management should be gradually prepared for this transition; and, generally, with the theoretical analysis of "philosophical, social, economic, legal, mathematical, and cybernetic management problems" (*DDR Aussenwirtschaft*, 1977:51, p. 1). This Institute is of recent origin, and further details on its operations and role in SEI are lacking. Some recent surveys of CMEA's organization (as Organy 1978) omit this Institute altogether.

Though all Institutes are headquartered in Moscow and staffed with specialists and academics recruited from the various member countries, in fact these organs are especially responsible for the coordination of research activities undertaken by academic scholars and government specialists in the individual CPEs. In addition, these institutions frequently organize scientific and technical conferences within their field of competence. In that sense, although certainly important coordinating organs, where comprehensive scientific-technical information is assembled, these Institutes are by no means the real think tanks in charge of working out plausible alternative roads to SEI, various options for solving fundamental economic and other problems pertaining to regional cooperation, or issues about how the independent economies could be harmonized.

Sundry common organizations

Crucial to the gradual realization of SEI are a large number of other agencies, whose precise affiliation with the official CMEA echelons is not always quite clear. For practical reasons, these organs are referred to here as international economic organizations (IEOs) or affiliated agencies, though not all are really entrusted with economic duties, and the notion of IEO is therefore interpreted somewhat more broadly than stated with special emphasis in the Complex Program. Before specifying some of the characteristics of the more important IEOs belonging to this group, an attempt should be made to partition this by now vast number of institutions into meaningful groups for further discussion and to look into the possible explanation for their existence.

In view of the predilection for comprehensive planning and central regimentation in the CMEA and its members, the very rapid proliferation of these IEOs, especially in the first half of the 1970s, is a somewhat peculiar phenomenon, and the rationale for their having been established is not always very clear. Thus, of the forty-eight IEOs reported in 1974, twenty-five were founded after 1970 (Zschiedrich 1975, p. 1678). Why set up IEOs at all, especially in the rather loose form they have assumed recently, if the primary instrument for formulating, implementing, and enhancing the SEI processes will be joint planning and plan coordination? There are probably many possible answers, but the following would appear to be the most convincing. First, from the point of view of getting tasks executed, the creation of decentralized organizations in one form or another may accelerate the introduction of specific and well-defined integration measures on which there is no disagreement among the participating members. Second, such decentralized institutions may also help to give an operational format to matters settled at the stage of "willingness" or general principles, possibly because at the high level that such topics are ordinarily discussed there is a lack of vital information on details, and enlarging the technical sophistication of the negotiating teams by coopting various knowledgeable lower-level specialists or practitioners would prove rather cumbersome. In other words, just as the individual CPEs have felt the growing need for decentralization and coordination, the CMEA organs themselves cannot possibly hope to cope with all details of SEI (see below). IEOs are expected to broach possibilities for promoting cooperation that cannot even be explored or accurately gauged by the formal CMEA levels (Zschiedrich 1975, p. 1682), or to cope with a particular set of issues that otherwise would absorb too much of the debates in established organs (for instance, Intermetall and the ball-bearings organization grew out of special work groups of the corresponding Standing Commissions). Third, in spite of the official acceptance of the "limited interest" provision, the CPE policy makers are generally reluctant to create official organs in which some members (barring Albania and the non-European CPEs) are not willing to participate, even not pro forma.[9] Fourth, although IEOs are ostensibly independent institutions, the participating CPEs keep a tight rein on their activities. An explanation advanced in an East German source may shed some light on why some IEOs were created, as well as illuminate the inflexible bureaucratic organization of the formal CMEA organs:

> International specialization and cooperation in certain relevant domains [now preempted for IEOs] can be advanced much more quickly and effectively than is possible . . . within the framework of the Standing Commissions or other permanent CMEA institutions as the case may be. This starting point for a [particular] realization of common planning has emerged as a result of a certain temporary contradiction between the stormy development of the factors of production and the rather strong resistance to change (*Beharrungsvermögen*) of the organized forms of the [ISDL]. [Proft 1973, p. 141]

Also, as indicated by a number of CMEA specialists, these common ventures should be seen as experiments of or laboratories for SEI (Kormnov 1972, p. 314; Lehmann 1973, p. 1318), possibly because of the excessively lengthy and involved deliberations typical of the official CMEA channels. Finally, major aspects of the economic, trade, and financial problems of these common ventures cannot yet be given a comprehensive, general solution within the CMEA organizational framework and, in any case, their independence does not set a precedent for the attitudes toward the CMEA as such (Ptaszek 1972, p. 5).

However expedient this trend toward setting up new institutions may ultimately prove to be, some voices have already cautioned against an unchecked multiplication of isolated organizations, and hence the further devolution of formulating and implementing regional specialization (Alampiev 1971, pp. 81–83). Others, however, keep acclaiming the IEOs as the basic, genuine "long-lasting forms of intra-CMEA cooperation" (Morozov 1974, p. 95). Whatever current official policy amounts to, it is indicative of the still lingering ambivalence toward these institutions that few new ones have been added in the past four or five years, in marked contrast to the expansionist trend of the early 1970s.

How to organize this vast number of institutions? A precise typology is difficult, if not impossible. The Complex Program, as indicated in Figure 2, distinguishes between interstate economic organizations (*mežgosudarstvennaja ėkonomičeskaja organizacija*) and international economic organizations (*meždunarodnaja chozjajstvennaja organizacija*). The first type of organization has no independent financial status because such IEOs are funded through the budget of the participating CPEs, whereas the second group is intended to be financially independent. Also, the first group is subject to public law, whereas the second one falls in the sphere of private or civil law. However, according to the Executive Committee's framework recommendations of 1973 (Tokareva 1976, pp. 118–138), and its model statutes of 1976 – not yet officially endorsed by the members and, according to one source, contrary to expectations "will not become in the foreseeable future binding . . . on the members" (Valek 1978, p. 39) – this distinction based on legal status is no longer tenable. Although the Complex Program further divided the international economic organizations into joint enterprises and international economic associations or unions (*meždunarodnaja chozjajstvennaja ob"edinenija*) – both subject to private law – more recent documents add a third component, namely, the international economic partnership (*meždunarodnoe chozjajstvennoe tovariščestvo*), which is created not according to public or private law, but rather loosely on the basis of international law (Scheller 1978, pp. 5–7), and the application of which is not quite clear.

Joint enterprises can own property, are subject to civil law, operate on the basis of economic accounting, and are fully liable through their property for their obligations. The international economic associations, though financially autonomous, are cartel-like groupings of autonomous enterprises of the various CPEs, which retain their independence in legal, property, and organizational terms. They are set up mostly for the purpose of coordinating the production and specialization activities of the member enterprises, whereas joint enterprises are really production units not unlike an embryonic form of the transnational corporations in the nonsocialist world. Partnerships have an even looser status, and are primarily intended to coordinate the activities of government bodies (there are now two partnerships: a repair service for petrochemical operations and a water purification service). Whereas partitions based on such organizational and legal principles as above may certainly be useful and have already received some legal recognition in Eastern Europe, it will become apparent that they cannot properly accommodate all IEOs of relevance to this study.

CMEA organs have worked out a model statute for these IEOs and common financial and managerial regulations (CMEA 1975), in which the above partition is legally written down. More recently, however, many CPE specialists have argued for a more differentiated approach, though tinted by the proponent's particular bent: The jurists have centered their efforts above all on questions of membership, legal autonomy, CMEA affiliation, and property questions, whereas the economists have devoted their attention in particular to the methods of production integration through IEOs and the place of these institutions in the independent planning process of the members. Jurists have spent lots of energy on deciding when an IEO is a proper CMEA organ or not – an issue that is still unresolved – and how it fits into the gamut of integration channels, national and regional. From a narrow juridical point of view, one may indeed question whether the Council itself is legally entitled to create autonomous organizations such as the IEOs because its authority is restricted to the issuance of recommendations (Caillot 1971, p. 279).

Although regulating in civil, public, or international law the precise status of each IEO is evidently pertinent to the smooth functioning of these units, from an economic point of view it is not very helpful to know unambiguously which institutions are proper CMEA organs according to their statutes and which are not. The degree of involvement with official and unofficial integration activities would seem far more important, especially in view of the fact that no IEO can be set up without the participation, approval, and supervision of the national governments, and most, if not all, IEOs have concluded formal agreements regulating their participation with official CMEA hierarchical levels, usually through the offices of the Executive Committee. It is therefore quite obvious that a clear-cut distinction between the proper CMEA-affiliated IEOs and others is virtually impossible and rather immaterial to the purposes at hand.

For the economist it is more important to address three sets of problems. First, how do IEOs fit into the chain of command of largely autonomously planned economies? Second, what role is allotted to the IEOs in the formulation of integration measures, and, more important, how should IEOs help to implement these measures? Finally, to what extent, if any, have the IEOs contributed to the enhancement of SEI and how can their future role be seen?

Figure 4 is designed to act as a comprehensive guide in placing individual IEOs, though not all such organs will be discussed here.[10] The largely functional classification introduced here is intended to encompass virtually all instances of governmental and nongovernmental institutions between two or more CPEs that are set up to promote the realization of integration regardless of their legal affiliation with the CMEA.

The various levels depicted in Figure 4 can be explained according to three criteria: the economic functions of IEOs, their financial autonomy, and the level of national participation in the IEO.[11] Following the financial criterion, one should distinguish between autonomous units functioning on the basis of economic accounting; ventures financed permanently from the budgets of the participating CPEs; and institutions financed temporarily from the national budgets, but which are expected to be placed on economic accounting after some transition. Though several tiers would seem to be based on economic accounting principles, most IEOs are full budgetary units entrusted with coordination tasks, rather than autonomous production ventures. In several instances, East European specialists have advocated "taking the necessary measures to let these organizations gradually finance themselves by retaining profits from their operations" (Constan-

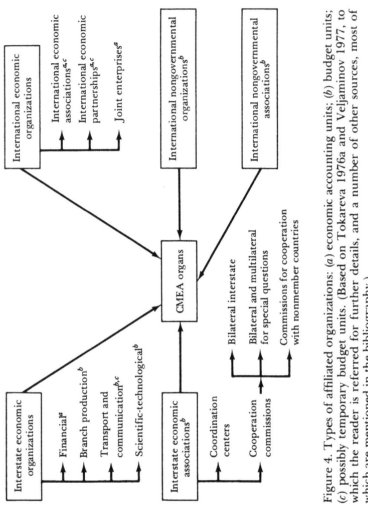

Figure 4. Types of affiliated organizations: (*a*) economic accounting units; (*b*) budget units; (*c*) possibly temporary budget units. (Based on Tokareva 1976a and Veljaminov 1977, to which the reader is referred for further details, and a number of other sources, most of which are mentioned in the bibliography.)

tinescu 1973, p. 77), but so far this advice has not been heeded, as the CPEs have largely failed to disengage their central planning organs from direct involvement in IEOs; even in those institutions that have the self-financing principle enshrined in their charter, results to date have been disappointing (Fischer 1978; Spiller 1978).

According to economic functions, it is useful to distinguish among common enterprises producing goods or services (e.g., Haldex), common ventures providing banking (e.g., IBEC) or transportation services (e.g., Mir), organizations entrusted with duties directly related to the coordination of research and the preparation of technical-scientific recommendations on specialization measures (e.g., Interchim), units placed in charge of production coordination or of organizing sales in addition to coordination of research (Intermetall), and all other coordination units, particularly trade and cooperation commissions. Some of these IEOs will be briefly examined below.

Financial institutions[12]

Although domestic economic affairs of the CPEs are traditionally managed without relying extensively on money and finance (see Chapter 2), on the international level it has proved imperative for these countries to face up to the necessity of accommodating monetary relations, particularly because there has not so far been a supranational planning agency or an appropriate common plan, and CPEs are reluctant to engage in "nonequivalent exchange." To meet these needs, two financial institutions have been set up that, at least on paper, provide for the gradual emergence of a regional capital market in the CMEA.

In 1964, the International Bank for Economic Cooperation (IBEC) started operating as an organization expected in due course to assume duties similar to those performed at an earlier juncture by the European Payments Union for the West European countries. In addition, it was decided to create a special socialist currency unit, the transferable ruble, which is nominally set equal to the Soviet internal ruble, but is emitted only in response to temporary or more permanent payments imbalances of the CPEs with regard to the CMEA region. Except for its role as a bookkeeping unit, the transferable ruble plays no role whatsoever in the integration process (Brabant 1977, pp. 108–116;

1978a). The bank's goals were impressive at the outset: (1) the gradual multilateralization of intra-CMEA trade and payments; (2) the elimination of the stifling system of BTPAs; (3) providing short-term credits to accommodate bilateral imbalances, to bridge seasonal disequilibria in trade, and to help cure structural payments problems; (4) the management of special funds for financing joint investment ventures; and (5) the easing of structural problems in trade and cooperation with third countries. There is very little doubt that in a narrow, technical bookkeeping sense, IBEC has played a significant role in providing accommodating loans in transferable rubles to the CPEs. It has also been instrumental in channeling capital funds acquired in Western money markets to its members. But with respect to its main function, namely, the substitution of regional multilateralism for bilateralism and the gradual bridging of the formidable gaps between intra- and extra-CMEA commerce, among others with the aid of the transferable ruble, the bank's operations during the past fifteen years have been a dismal failure. And until fundamental reforms in the planning systems of trade of all the member countries can be implemented, IBEC itself cannot even be expected to become an active participant in the process of SEI.

As is well known, the bank's charter and accompanying protocol on multilateral settlements did not touch upon the old barriers to the gradual multilateralization of regional trade and payments. First, to offset imbalances multilaterally, the members simply conclude supplementary BTPAs, even in the case of ex ante multilateral compensation. Bilateral positions rather than IBEC's technically multilateral accounts are the driving force of regional trade. Second, the revolution in trade practices that was expected from the multilateralization of payments did not materialize because IBEC's founding was not followed up by a relaxation of the formidable forces separating the CPEs' domestic markets from external relations. Third, in the wake of the serious dispute about the principles of the ISDL, the bank was never called upon to assist in the financing of joint ventures. In consequence, the bank has reverted more and more to its role as a technical clearing agency, granting loans – in fact, taking note of explicit or implicit lending and borrowing of the members – to offset unplanned bilateral imbalances, without, however, spurring on the anticipated expansion of trade and specialization. The only area in which the bank seems to have been quite successful is its participation in the Eurodollar and Eurocapital markets, especially to transmit Western funds to its members, although it was not primarily created to engage in such financial arbitrations.

The International Investment Bank (IIB) started operations in January 1971 with the overt goal of partially financing investment projects conceived within the specialization strategy of the ISDL or SEI. Although the structure of the IIB as a financial organization is far better than IBEC's, it cannot perform wonders in promoting CMEA-wide coordinated investment policies. Each CPE is still free to decide whether to curtail or to imitate production processes such as those financed by the IIB. In fact, the bank itself cannot select projects and the funds at its disposal amount to only a small fraction of total CMEA investments. Because the bank's funds are to be tied to specific projects for five to fifteen years, IIB's actual role in the coordination of investment strategies through its own financial resources will remain incidental. It is, nevertheless, useful to mention here several noteworthy elements of the founding and operation of this institution: (1) It has a substantial amount of subscribed capital (over one thousand and seventy-one million transferable rubles), 30 percent of which is in gold and convertible currencies: (2) majority voting, albeit a three-fourths majority, is allowed on important operational questions; (3) the bank has clearly delineated guidelines regarding the projects to be supported, although the criteria of project selection and evaluation are not precisely defined; (4) commercial interest rates are applied; and (5) the bank is empowered to augment its resources by floating bonds on nonsocialist markets, though this has not yet occurred.

IIB's role in furthering regional specialization should be seen primarily against its ability to channel funds borrowed in Western money markets into CMEA projects. Loans denominated in transferable rubles have by and large remained unconsummated, owing to the problem of acquiring appropriate goods and services outside regular BTPAs. As explained in detail elsewhere (Brabant 1977, pp. 232–241), most of the disbursed commitments – as distinct from nominal loans – have been financed from outside funds.

But the bank may exert a positive influence on SEI by indirect means. Thus, although its own or borrowed funds are too limited to enforce the coordination of investment projects and policies of the member countries, successful financing of a jointly coordinated venture, such as the Orenburg gas-condensate plant and the associated Sojuz pipeline, may demonstrate to all interested CPEs that closer harmonization of national economic policies and plans is definitely beneficial to all concerned. This in turn may prod the members in the long run to relax several other obstacles currently severely hemming SEI (see below).

Joint enterprises

A very promising type of IEO – at least in theory – is the creation of common enterprises with an own capital fund, an independent status (naturally, within the overall policy objectives of the participating CPEs, especially for the host country), management on the basis of profitability criteria, and the provision of commodities in surplus demand on the CMEA market. The first such enterprise, Haldex, was created in 1959 with Hungarian and Polish participation in terms of capital funds, technology, and specialized machines. It was then greeted as an important pilot venture soon to be followed by many more. However, the Hungarians and Poles were pioneers, not because they wanted to create a joint enterprise, but precisely because there was no other elegant way around the official Sofia doctrine of free exchange of scientific and technical know-how, which the Hungarians were very reluctant to adhere to in this instance. Hungary was looking for a way to capitalize on its technological advantage in extracting coal and construction materials from slag heaps. Despite the extremely complicated accounting system agreed upon to maintain "equality of partnership" and economic accounting tractable for both partners (e.g., sixty-two ad hoc exchange rates had to be worked out!), the Hungarians were in the early 1960s bent on emulating their first venture, especially in Czechoslovakia and the USSR. Subsequent efforts in that direction foundered because of "the extremely complicated system of accounting required under the present internal and external mechanism" (Ausch 1972, p. 210), among other things. Likewise, Czechoslovakia and Poland were in the mid-1960s actively negotiating the creation of a joint enterprise for the production of tractors and other agricultural capital equipment, but it proved impossible to arrive at a commonly acceptable format (Cizkovsky 1968, pp. 292–293).

At least three other joint enterprises exist at present.[13] The cotton-spinning mill Przyjaźń (1972) is a joint East German–Polish venture in Zawiercie (Poland). To extract and enrich copper and molybdenum deposits in Mongolia, the Soviet Union and Mongolia founded Ėrdėnėt in 1973. In the same year, these two countries created Mongolsovcvetmet to organize geological prospecting in Mongolia, to enrich ferrous ores, and gradually to enhance Mongolia's ferrous metallurgy. Given the rather hesitant approach toward joint ventures, it would seem that the CPEs do not intend to enhance SEI mainly through the establishment of joint property – whatever its legal implications – in independent enterprises, and joint ventures will remain the exception rather than become the mainstay of company cooperation in Eastern Europe.

International economic associations

Between 1972 and 1974, eight legally independent international economic associations were created for the coordination of research, production, and sales of nuclear machine construction (Interatominstrument), textile machinery (Intertekstil'maš), atomic power stations (Interatomėnergo), photography (Assofoto), measurement equipment (Interėtalonpribor), artificial fibers (Interchimvolokno), household chemicals (Domochim), and electrical installations (Interėnergoremont). A few more have been added since (Valek 1979), but the new ones belong more to the branch-technical organizations (see below). Some of these institutions are bilateral ventures like all joint enterprises that are actually engaged in material production, whereas others involve most, if not all, CPEs. They are separate from the joint enterprises in that international economic associations are really cartel-like institutions with the participating enterprises from two or more CPEs keeping their own separate identity. In view of a number of legal and economic problems (see below), the activities of these IEOs have been severely confined mostly to research, development, and production coordination. In some cases, even such tasks have had to be scaled down, and actual operations of the venture postponed until important financial and management issues can be settled (e.g., Interatomenergo's activities in the current five-year plan have reportedly been taken over by the Soviet participant, pending a thorough reexamination of the proper organization of that IEO). In a number of instances, the present activities of these organizations have been severely compressed until more comprehensive planning can be worked out in the near future (Lehmann 1977, p. 22). It is hoped that some vexing obstacles can be removed soon so that IEOs will be able to assume their proper place in the process of SEI, perhaps starting with the next medium-term plans, but the outlook does not appear to be very bright (Valek 1978).

Branch-technical and transportation organizations
From the practical point of view, that is to say, in facilitating the cooperation among the CPEs under existing conditions, the branch-technical and transportation IEOs are perhaps the most significant IEOs, numbering presently more than two dozen. The most important transportation organizations are the unified power grid (Mir, 1962), the common railroad wagon pool (1964), the joint container pool (1976), the coordination of port activities (Interport, 1973), the coordination of ocean and river shipment (Interlichter, 1978), and the network of oil and gas pipelines (including Družba [1958], Bratstvo [1974], Sojuz [1975], and their extensions). Of the branch-technical IEOs, the ball-bearings organization (Polish acronym Interpodszypnik [1965]; Russian reference is usually the abbreviation OSPP); the coordination of surplus rolled steel products and excess rolling capacities (Intermetall, 1964); the specialization of low-output, high-value chemicals (Interchim, 1969); the coordination of agricultural, especially horticultural, machinery (Agromaš, 1964); the coordination of electrotechnical equipment (Interelektro, 1973); the oil and gas exploration venture (Petrobaltik, 1975); and the units concerned with internal transportation equipment (Intransmaš, 1964) are perhaps the most important.

The Council's role in SEI

The above survey of the tiers of the CMEA hierarchy and its affiliated institutions suggests that the CMEA has, at least on paper, the necessary organizational machinery to deal with a

vast array of concrete problems arising from regional cooperation and the coordination of the members' economic development efforts. To appreciate the role of the common organization in the enhancement of SEI, it is useful to discuss separately
the official Council organs and the affiliated organizations. The
issues touched upon here in a preliminary way will be placed in a
more comprehensive context in Chapter 5.

The role of the Council organs

Although the Council's official organs have undoubtedly helped
to bolster East European cooperation, especially since the late
1960s, it is very difficult to assess, even approximately, their contribution to the progress that has been attained so far. As long as
the CPEs will hold on to their prerogative of formulating national economic plans autonomously and embracing uncoordinated policies, the CMEA organs will have to eschew the most
crucial issues embedded in the independent planning systems of
its members. Instead of acting as a de facto regional planning
agency, the formal CMEA echelons can bear on the integration
process indirectly, first, by collecting, analyzing, and disseminating pertinent information; second, by providing a forum for
a regular exchange of views among top-level policy makers,
planning practitioners, or those engaged in carrying out integration processes; and, third, by generally fostering the emergence
of an atmosphere congenial to a dispassionate analysis of SEI
opportunities and assessments. Actual progress with SEI can,
therefore, be attained largely through practical steps taken by
the members separately or in unison through various joint commissions. Within these limitations on its terms of reference, the
Council can nevertheless accomplish appreciably more than
what appears to have been forthcoming so far.

Perhaps the central organizational problem hemming the effective functioning of these organs is that they continue to be influenced by the legacies of the postwar, Stalinist views of proper
international socialist relations either because these played a formative role in the gestation of the Council levels or because the
existing organs persist in discharging themselves of their tasks in
the Byzantine spirit so characteristic of postwar socialist relations. This proposition can be explained on the basis of several
instances of potential and actual conflict.

Clearly, the Council Session, the Executive Committee and its associated Committees, and the Standing Commissions should be the pinnacles charting basic policies and principles of SEI. More practical cooperation matters should be delegated to those in charge of concrete problems. Experience shows, however, that this is not always so. Even the Session does not have the power to settle matters without the explicit endorsement of member governments. Not only does this delay effective deliberations and raise ambiguities, it occasionally seriously hampers or even paralyzes the transformation of agreed principles into practice because the governments concerned have never committed themselves to a broad operational integration mandate to be executed by political deliberations at CMEA level. Overcentralized and fragmented decision making is therefore a serious obstacle, and the CMEA organs have not so far been bold enough to test the limits of this proposition. Lukewarm enthusiasm for SEI on the part of some CPEs has for years stalled progress even in matters that by themselves are not controversial exactly because more precisely defined guidelines are not available and no CMEA organ seems willing or able to fill the void, even if only on an experimental basis.

The guiding principles of national sovereignty and national interest in the community's activities, for example, have until recently been interpreted very rigidly and, in some cases, rather chauvinistically. It was only in 1967, after several years of intensive debate, that the thirtieth session of the Executive Committee finally reached a tentative recommendation to the effect that deciding upon the principles of unanimity and interestedness should be interpreted less rigidly. This principle was later slightly toned down and incorporated into the Council charter of 1974. A country not interested in a particular project is henceforth permitted, and in fact invited, to withdraw from the deliberations, but is no longer expected to be in a position to halt the progress coveted by the interested CPEs (Franzmeyer 1973, pp. 53–55). This is true in principle, and the positive contribution to the more effective deliberation on community affairs emanating from the revised "interested party provision" should not be exaggerated. If a particular member is really uninterested either in participating or in the establishment of the proposed venture, it may still prove adroit to be officially "interested" and stall further progress by more subtle means than

the official veto! The Complex Program sought to broaden the
concept of interestedness by requiring the actual participants to
commit themselves to the cooperation project in principle as well
as in its implementation (Ruster 1977, p. 35), thus foiling attempts to hollow out agreements from within. Unfortunately,
this stronger version of the interestedness provision has not so
far found its way into the charter and, judging from the record,
does not appear to have played a major role in practical CMEA
affairs. It is symptomatic, for example, that in spite of the revised principle all active member countries are participating in
the CMEA's official organs with, as noted, only two exceptions.
Matters on which unanimity cannot be polled are either tabled
or have to be resolved through the creation of IEOs in one form
or another.

The above comments are not meant to convey the impression
that the Council's contribution to SEI has been negligible. Indeed, from a practical point of view the landmark measures introduced since the inception of the Complex Program, including the coordination of medium-term plans and the Concerted
Plan (see section 4), could not have been settled without the
Council's channels. Similarly, the codification of cooperation
principles, production standards, and a host of other practical
matters, has been immeasurably assisted by the Council's organs.
Whereas most specialization agreements have been hammered
out on lower planning levels, a number of Council organs have
nevertheless played an important role in paving the road for
such contracts, especially in cases where these agreements envisage the development and production of technologically advanced products.

The organs mostly responsible for this progress are arguably
the Council Committees and the Standing Commissions. With
the Council Committees, the CPEs have high-level regional echelons for dealing with crucial topics of coordinating overall national plans, for finding ways and means of attaining greater
consistency in production and consumption, and for furthering
economic development through concerted efforts aimed at
prompting and disseminating economic, scientific, and technological information. Similar observations apply to the Standing
Commissions, though here propositions regarding common
measures for general economic cooperation, production special-

ization, and synchronizing scientific-technical research are usually more target-oriented. An analysis of the available information on the various meetings of the Commissions and Committees shows that it is here that concrete propositions on common activities, bilateral as well as multilateral, are worked out, that the exact field of activity of the CMEA organs is detailed, and that huge masses of detailed information and documentation on the relevant economic sector(s) or more general economic and organizational matters are collected and distributed. It might be expected, as a result, that recommendations for trade and specialization worked out by these levels could be based on more detailed information and thus on the real possibilities for dovetailing cooperation between individual CPEs. But, as experience shows, these august fora by no means guarantee that all or even the most crucial recommendations will be implemented. Judging from what has evolved in the field of concrete coordination in production, perhaps the most important Standing Commissions are those dealing, directly or indirectly, with fuels, energy, chemicals, metallurgy, and transportation, for it is in these sectors that measurable progress has evidently been accomplished. Naturally, these achievements could not have been recorded without the more general cooperation work of the Commissions for foreign trade, standardization, and, especially, currency and finance.

In the light of their terms of reference, the Institutes and Conferences are largely consultative organs, whose influence on SEI is even more indirect. They do contribute appreciably to the work performed by the Secretariat. By its very nature, the Secretariat can accomplish little more than technical, preparatory work to facilitate deliberations on major policy issues elsewhere, to highlight the entire range of topics to be tackled by those in command, and to smoothen whenever possible the implementation of practical steps in response to political agreement on principles. In that sense, the Secretariat's role, and incidentally that of its chairman, is potentially far more important than the official stipulations of its tasks in the charter would tend to suggest, and should be seen in the following framework.

The gradual cultivation of an East European "community spirit" must emerge within and on the initiative of the Secretariat, naturally while fully respecting its official mandate. So far this seems to have been notably lacking, and not chiefly because of the Secretariat's lack of latitude in settling the many outstanding problems of intra-CMEA cooperation and SEI. The principal reason for this regrettable state of affairs is that in almost all other official organs of the Council there is no permanent community staff. All Standing Commissions, for example, when in session consist of ad hoc delegates from the CPEs, and they are expected to represent the interests of their country rather than what they might perceive as the interest of the community as a whole (Franzmeyer 1973, pp. 47–55; Machowski 1970, pp. 285–289). This is naturally not unrelated to the ambiguous commitment of the CPEs to genuine integration.

Against the background of the functions and staffing policy, the Secretariat and the Institutes do not yet embody an influential class of dedicated public servants concerned about the CMEA and able to leave a lasting imprint on SEI. As for most other civil servants employed in the CMEA (except a few top-level administrators), personnel is not permanently detached from comparable national offices: Most international civil servants in the CMEA will complete a tour of duty of approximately five years and then return to their former occupation in the home country.

The role of the affiliated organizations

Unlike most of the official CMEA echelons, the IEOs are assigned concrete integration tasks, even if only coordinating parallel activities of the participants. Unfortunately, many IEOs are of recent date and have not so far been able to assume their statutory obligations in view of inhibiting planning, legal, and organizational obstacles (Valek 1978), about which more below. Also, many facts and figures are kept shrouded in secrecy or are divulged only in rather vague terms. One must therefore be generous in giving the IEOs some benefit of the doubt when looking into their actual or potential contribution to SEI.

Without minimizing the role of the IEOs in fostering SEI, it is worthwhile to observe that these organizations do not yet cover the decisive branches of industrial activity in the CPEs, they are not fully independent in tackling their assigned tasks, and their influence on the participating CPEs should not be exaggerated. In particular, as a well-informed Soviet specialist noted in the early 1970s, these organizations have not been created with a view toward enhancing the criteria for realizing international production specialization and contributing measurably to the coordination of planning and trade of the CPEs (Kormnov 1972, p. 320). His views have been borne out since, inasmuch as none of the IEOs established since the approval of the Complex Program has been able to take up its tasks in production and marketing in the CMEA or elsewhere (Ficzere 1978, pp. 18–19). Without delegating at least some trade tasks, the IEOs cannot become financially independent (Biskup 1978, p. 11), and an evaluation of their performance will hence tend to be distorted because of the pressures exerted by national government through their budgetary allocations.

In order to establish a reliable guide to the IEOs' role in the integration process, one would require information that so far has been accessible only to a few CPE insiders. An evaluation by an outside observer, such as this writer, must therefore rely largely on impressionistic statements occasionally aired in the specialized literature. There one encounters very optimistic pronouncements alongside quite weighty complaints about the still numerous unsolved fundamental problems pertaining to the creation and management of these common ventures. The problems are sometimes technical, but most are of an organizational, legal, or economic nature, not to mention persistent bones of contention rooted in political and ideological debates or lingering controversies that hamper the activities of the IEOs.

Perhaps the most important obstacle to the effective operation of IEOs is organizational in nature. Because by definition these organs belong to enterprises or governmental agencies of the members, how to coordinate the activities of the IEOs with the national plans of the participants, especially of the host country, poses intricate problems. The flexibility needed for the effective exploitation of the IEO's potential advantages will come into sharp conflict with the perceived need for rigid controls, especially on the part of the host's planning center. Even if the IEO's activities are confined simply to seeking ways and means of coordinating the production activities of the members, formidable organizational problems have to be solved (Lehmann 1977).

Some of the weightiest impediments to the internationalization of effective production processes, as distinct from the exchange of technical and scientific information and experience, stem from ideological reservations regarding international factor mobility, ownership of the means of production, and so on. Although these issues may entail formidable philosophical questions, in themselves they should not prevent the IEO, once established, from working well. The related legal problems of socialist ownership are, however, many, owing especially to the fact that the CPEs have their own legal systems that are not mutually consistent and are not capable of dealing fully with international legal topics (see below). The creation and operation of the IEO must therefore be reconciled with these numerous legal obstacles. Efforts are undertaken to harmonize the various laws and to adopt "model statutes" for IEOs, but so far experience has shown that ad hoc agreements are the only sure way of establishing the IEO at all.

The economic issues associated with the effective exploitation of the IEO's potential are also vexing.[14] Because the CPEs have no scarcity pricing; price-formation, wage, profit, fiscal, and material allocation regulations of the various members differ perceptively; no effective exchange rates are available; foreign trade is subject to strict bilateral balancing and other rules; and so on; the problems of operating IEOs and evaluating their performance quickly become intractable and at times elusive as well. In that sense, the apparent indefinite deferment of solving the monetary and financial topics of SEI, even in the weak form outlined in the Complex Program, has rendered the target-oriented exploitation of IEOs appreciably more cumbersome.

The issues enumerated above are only a brief selection of what inhibits faster integration progress, and these problems will be looked at in greater detail in Chapter 5. However, a preliminary assessment of the IEOs' contribution to SEI may be drawn up by distinguishing between ventures such as the power grid, where international collaboration has a rather simple objective, and common units, where the responsibilities are much more formidable and diverse. Of the latter type, the creation and management of the research-oriented IEOs, especially the interstate economic organizations, are also much less complicated because these units are mostly financed by the budgets of the participating governments, they have no saleable output, and there are relatively few inputs needed (most expenditures are for wages and administration). But when it comes to the ordinary production enterprise or to ventures that should directly impact on productive activities of other enterprises, especially the economic associations and joint enterprises, a clear delineation of legal position, planning affiliation, accounting bases, ownership rights, pricing policies, and so on is vital. The lack to date of unambiguous rules on economic, legal, and organizational principles and procedures circumscribing the status of such production units has made these IEOs none too attractive (Lehmann 1977; Valek 1978), although there is little doubt that some of them, such as Haldex, have been quite successful in spite of the formidable organizational and financial hindrances.

From among the variety of IEOs, perhaps the largest contribution to SEI has been made by the branch-technical and transportation organizations because they fill a badly felt void that no single CPE alone can hope to cope with. The financial institutions do what they can within the tremendous limitations of the CPEs' trade system. To the extent that details are available, the joint enterprises appear to satisfy the participants within the narrow sphere of pragmatic objectives sought. For all practical purposes, however, the international economic associations have not been enabled to execute their original mandate, and largely confine themselves to the coordination of research and production profiles of the participating enterprises. It must be pointed out, however, that the research and development efforts of these units as well as in the other interstate economic organizations, if successful, may lead to sizable integration effects in future plan periods, provided that the members will be able to "coordinate their conception of long-term future economic structure and to work out the strategic directions of development of individual sectors" (Lehmann 1977, p. 36). But it is now disconcerting that no efforts appear to be made to effect a cost–benefit calculus (Fischer 1978) that would enable CPE policy makers to gauge the real contribution of these units to the improvement of economic efficiency in the region.

Although the IEOs appear to have contributed to SEI far less than what was originally anticipated in the early 1970s, one should at least acknowledge that their existence itself may be assisting the ongoing clarification of problems encountered in the day-to-day operation and long-term planning of common units.

To the extent that they are allowed to assume their projected activities, the IEOs may indirectly exert a positive influence on the course of specialization by helping from below the elaboration of central initiatives directed at working slowly but steadfastly toward a more satisfactory solution. The Standing Commissions and Committees could hence be entrusted with more basic integration aspects. In that sense, the IEOs are potentially one of the more interesting forms of regional cooperation because they bring into direct contact with each other those immediately responsible for the national coordination or even the production of specific types of products in the various CPEs, and act therefore as "laboratories for introducing socialist methods of planning the economy and . . . economic accounting" (Bautina 1973, p. 78).

On the strength of the operations of Intermetall in the late 1960s, E. Hewett concluded that the interstate economic organizations, according to the terminology introduced in Figure 4, are "the 'super' standing commissions" of the CMEA because they are "empowered to do everything a regular standing commission can do and, in addition, they have the power to make binding decisions in more substantive areas" (Hewett 1974, pp. 10–11). As experience has shown, however, this sweeping statement is much too positive an interpretation of the real significance and role of these IEOs, although their legal status may signal differently.[15] Officially, they are entitled to iron out important aspects of specialization in one branch or another, although in practice all plans and proposals must be approved by the national governments or the supervising ministries (Caillot 1971, p. 239), which ushers in right away the conundrum of decentralization. Moreover, if majority decisions are made at all, the dissenting members will not be bound (Fiumel 1975, p. 14), which leaves the execution of the entire project in doubt. After a disappointing start (Cizkovsky 1968, p. 294), Intermetall nevertheless appears to have played a highly constructive role in the reciprocal exchange of rolled steel products,[16] especially by assuring better utilization of spare production capacities in the member countries and fostering specialization in metallurgical products (Matevosjan 1975). It has also broadened its horizon as a result of its reportedly highly positive role in prodding the CPEs into joining forces when projecting additions to productive capacities with a view toward the needs of the community as a whole.[17] But it does not appear to have succeeded in emulating in the CMEA region the former Coal and Steel Community in Western Europe, which was one of the main considerations in its gestation (Cizkovsky 1968, p. 294).

Another rather successful cooperation venture is Interchim, which seeks to harmonize research and production of low-output, high-value chemicals in the CPEs. Although the signatories committed themselves in the bylaws to a phased transition toward self-financing by applying realistic charges for specific services rendered and, possibly, by marketing abroad some of the venture's accomplishments, the organization has so far focused its activities primarily on research and development, production specialization, and assisting the rational allocation of new capacities with a view toward eliminating deficits in a number of chemical products (Weber 1975).

The future role of the Council
To promote and encourage the effective functioning of the CMEA echelons, it would seem inadvisable to add on new institutions, as appears to have been thought productive since the 1960s. The weight of revisions in the internal planning bureaucracy of the CPEs in conjunction with judicious modifications in the mechanism of regional cooperation would seem to be far more important for enhancing the role and effectiveness of SEI. In that respect, it is symptomatic that the organizational and other internal reforms of the CPEs have not so far affected the Council's operations. The CMEA's role as a central clearinghouse for overseeing and promoting SEI has remained largely unchanged since the 1950s, despite the fast expansion of the organization's formal structure and the codification of many cooperation principles in response to changes in the economic and political environment. It is now ironic that such decisions typically do not touch upon the obstacles embedded in or ensuing from the internal organization of the participating CPEs.

For instance, party and government *apparatčiki*, who are steeped in the traditional planning system, are unlikely to enter the regional organizations suddenly imbued with the SEI spirit. It is in this light that one should appreciate the provisions in the Complex Program and a score of critical comments on the

CMEA in the East European literature. The program states explicitly and unambiguously that the members should take the necessary steps to enhance the further role of the Council in the process of SEI (Tokareva 1972, pp. 100–102). However, although there has undeniably been a sharp increase in organizational links between the Council and member governments, variations of the admonition of an influential Hungarian policy maker that "the Secretariat of the CMEA could even be justifiably expected to take a more energetic position on the economic situation of the nations or on certain concrete problems of cooperation" (Szita 1971, p. 41), do crop up with some regularity in the specialized literature.

Since the approval of the Complex Program, the member countries have sought to improve the CMEA's operations, though details on what may eventually materialize have not so far been disclosed. Already during the thirtieth Session (Berlin, 1976), some of the CPEs, especially Rumania, commented prematurely on intramural preparatory suggestions for organizational improvements, and the communiqué of this Session includes a revealing paragraph. The Executive Committee was explicitly instructed to prepare a number of concrete, action-oriented proposals for "improving the Council's work and ameliorating the style and methods governing the operations of the Council's organs" (CMEA 1976a, p. 51). Such recommendations as could be formulated were anticipated to be tabled at the thirty-first Session (Warsaw, 1977), but no concrete actions have thus far been endorsed, possibly implying that, if the topics were on the agenda, the members could not reach consensus. The issues involved reportedly include a crucial change in the charter to the effect that the CMEA voting rule, now anchored to unanimity of interested members, would be replaced by majority voting. Accordingly, any decision adopted by majority would henceforth be binding on all members, including those that voted against or abstained. This potentially explosive draft recommendation was apparently on the preliminary agenda of the recently concluded thirty-second Session (Bucharest, 1978) and thirty-third Session (Moscow, 1979), but no "recommendation" has so far been reported, and the communiqués avoid the issue altogether. In any case, it seems doubtful that the long-heralded principle of unanimity would henceforth be relinquished also for fundamental issues. It is perhaps more likely that something akin to IIB's voting system (Brabant 1977, pp. 210–211) would be extended to the Council and its agencies as a routine principle – not altogether an undesirable move. If so, operational questions of SEI, as distinct from fundamental topics, would accordingly be decided by majority vote. This could be a very powerful instrument for promoting regional specialization broadly defined, though there is unfortunately no hard evidence regarding the implications of such a change for the harmful ratification rule. It is doubtful that the CPEs could be found prepared to abandon the important prerogative of ratifying Council "recommendations," even if only for operational aspects of SEI.

Some members, notably Rumania, hold that in recent activities the Council has already trespassed its statutory mandate, and hence that there is a "need for orientating CMEA's activity towards the achievement of the aims for which this organization was created" (Stoian 1978, p. 31). Its nature and purpose, as embodied in the charter, should be maintained and strengthened with a view toward facilitating "the planned development of the national economy, the intensification of economic and social progress in each country, the growth of labor productivity, and the narrowing and equalization of the economic levels" (Stoian 1978, p. 31). Stoian adds that this must proceed against the background of the "exclusive and inalienable" right of sovereignty and independence of each CPE to map out its own socio-economic development.[18] For all practical purposes, this simply means that Rumania and possibly some other CPEs will persist in denying a delegation of decision-making authority to the Council in the foreseeable future.

3. Official principles and methods of SEI

Since the early 1960s, the CPEs have made a serious attempt to underpin their regional organization and cooperation efforts with policy documents, apparently with the aims of encouraging more positive Council activities within well-defined guidelines and of streamlining the process of SEI. Parallel to this, many specialization and cooperation agreements have been concluded, and the CPEs have been searching for ways and means of facilitating the regional mobility of goods, services, and production factors. Special attention should be devoted to two challenging documents on the goals, principles, and methods of SEI, because they have given rise to so much discussion, sometimes even to bitter and acrimonious debates, but also to sincere reflections on how to come to grips with the intricacies of dovetailing modern interdependent economies. The more interesting points of these documents will be set forth in conjunction with some of the background to the principal ideas behind them.

The principles of cooperation in the 1950s

Until 1962 the CMEA does not seem to have had a commonly agreed (and published!) policy on how the ISDL was to evolve. The only available documents from which one could infer official intentions were the vaguely phrased founding communiqué and the Council's official charter of 1959, which clarifies its legal organization.

The founding communication was not very informative about the structure, purposes, principles, and methods of the newly created organization, as documented in Chapter 1. The common call for "exchanging economic experience, extending technical aid to one another, and rendering mutual assistance with respect to raw materials, foodstuffs, machines, equipment, etc." (Tokareva 1967, p. 44) could be, and was in fact, interpreted according to whatever best suited the prevailing views on socialist international relations, national economic development, and regional cooperation. More specific tasks failed to be agreed on or, at least, they were not codified at that time. The scope and content of socialist cooperation tended to be defined implicitly as a result of practical actions, or "historical experience" in current phraseology, taken largely outside the scope of the regional institution, although there may have been commonly agreed, but unpublished, goals, mechanisms, and principles of regional economic cooperation (as discussed in Chapter 1).

The potential of the Council was unexpectedly immobilized when the USSR perfected its rather involved embassy system of dealing separately with the CPEs – a very effective expression of the USSR's intransigence with respect to SEI. And the other CPEs, supine as they were at the time to Soviet advice, failed to check the encroachment of the USSR's supreme role in virtually all areas of regional contacts. Although the small CPEs organized their own efforts to ward off the worst implications of independent development, they in effect stifled whatever possibilities for intercountry cooperation could still be mustered (Brabant 1976).

Instead of focusing on the chief tasks of SEI, the Council's Bureau concentrated on aiding the clearing of bilateral trade, the standardization of trade contracts and statistics, facilitating regional transportation, minor administrative tasks, and a few areas in which stimulating regional cooperation and production specialization was "obviously" advantageous for all concerned. In view of the postwar changes in Eastern Europe, one may surmise that the bilateral type of cooperation embraced to facilitate trade could also have been implemented without the CMEA's existence. Because the Council did not undertake anything to support this rather odd system of economic relations, the regional organization in fact did not exist until about the second half of the 1950s, when it was revived and finally obtained a charter in which more details were stipulated about its principles, methods, and goals.

The third phase of the CMEA's history, according to the periodization of section 1, was initiated as a result of the complex conflicts of interest aired during the so-called New Course. Following Stalin's death and the wrangling over his succession, fast industrialization per se as the goal of resource mobilization was temporarily abandoned in favor of a more balanced growth concept. This fundamental policy shift entailed serious conflicts, not only because of the transformed development concept but precisely because the move caught planners unaware. Conflicts in regional trade were particularly marked. The sudden change in industrialization policies in 1953–1954 diversified the aggregate demand for fuels, raw materials, and foodstuffs and reduced that for manufactures, especially industrial machinery. This had considerable practical implications for both the exporters of machinery and the importers of primary products, and upset particularly the trade prospects of the developed CPEs. Orders placed in these countries for capital equipment, for example, were canceled as investment plans in the purchasing countries were drastically scaled down. The potential exporters of foodstuffs, fuels, and industrial raw materials had to honor their new commitment to the improvement of domestic consumption levels and did not feel compelled to export in order to pay for imports that were no longer required. The situation was aggravated by the sale of the joint-stock companies, which suddenly strained the balance of payments of the former belligerent countries.

A more positive appreciation of trade arose as a result of concerns about the long-run effects of import substitution and the attempts to raise economic efficiency through production intensification. To maintain regional stability, mutual cooperation was looked upon more favorably, especially by the USSR, as one pivotal channel for promoting the objectives of the New Course. But economic affairs were certainly not the only force behind the renewed interest in regional cooperation and the first signs of the CMEA's renaissance. Not the least important of the stimuli activating the CMEA came from outside the region. The West European countries sharply reduced the embargo restrictions on trade with CPEs, thereby exacerbating the intra-CMEA inconsistencies in trade intentions, which increasingly strained regional relations. Under the prevailing circumstances, the Council could do next to nothing to alleviate the structural conflicts in the short run, for these basic incompatibilities could be mitigated only through the better dovetailing of development plans for the second half of the 1950s and beyond.

The first serious efforts directed at reviving the Council and at stimulating regional cooperation outside the confining straitjacket of BTPAs were made in the mid-1950s. Under impact of the rapidly growing critical examination of traditional policies, the several Council Session meetings of the mid-1950s focused particularly on deepening production specialization, especially in branches in which the CPEs had been seeking very similar, if not completely identical, industrial objectives. Preliminary agreements on specialization in key branches of machine building and metallurgy were settled in 1954 (Gora 1974, p. 33), thus underscoring the swift change in policies. This was also demonstrated by the fact that the members reportedly agreed to a fundamental shift in the original goals, mechanisms, and principles of regional cooperation (Faddeev 1974a, p. 59), which may have transpired into revised statutes (Cizkovsky 1970, p. 244), whose contents have never been disclosed in detail. But these largely political specialization agreements were concerned basically with principles of deepening regional production cooperation and were not derived from a fundamental search for a better allocation of resources in the region. It took the CPEs until 1956 before actual contracts were completed. In the wake of the 1956 events, however, renegotiation of important provisions was deemed opportune, presumably also because the preliminary agreements did not amount to a clear-cut set of guidelines on which production specialization and trade decisions could be based. In spite of renegotiation, current evaluation of the implementation and effect of these contracts (and, incidentally, of later protocols as well) is none too favorable, as will be examined below.

Under impact of the New Course, the frustrated attempts to implement feasible specialization agreements, the explicit challenge to the USSR's supremacy over all communist states, and the growing unification attempts in Western Europe, the CPE leaders also sought to reinforce the Council's institutions and to codify principles of cooperation in a joint policy statement on the ISDL.

Being formally without a clearly defined and agreed purpose, and without official statutes until 1959, when the basic ideas behind the CMEA were recorded for the first time (Tokareva 1967, pp. 45–54),[19] the CMEA as a regional institution was sort of a unicum among international organizations (Szawlowski 1963, p. 676). The first official charter, which was ratified in 1960, has been revised on several occasions (incidentally, in an unlawful manner because Albania did not approve and was not invited to do so) to enable non-European CPEs to participate, to shift the policy goals from simple cooperation to integration, and to enshrine new legal or other concepts. Nevertheless, the basic idea guiding the Council's mission has remained:

to promote, by uniting and coordinating the efforts of the [CPEs], the planned development of the national economy, the acceleration of economic and technical progress in these countries, the raising of the level of industrialization in the ... less developed countries, a continuous increase in labor productivity, and a steady improvement in the welfare of the peoples of the member countries. [Tokareva 1967, pp. 45–46]

This general task is specified further on in the document. The members are expected to promote gradually "the most rational use of their natural resources" and "to accelerate the development of their productive capacities." These goals are to be attained by means of the coordination of national economic plans, the comprehensive examination of the economic and scientific-technical problems of the CPEs, and the implementation of common ventures in any endeavor of interest to all or a majority of the members.

The charter is not entirely unambiguous as to the preferred areas in which the members should endeavor to foster progress: Should considerations of common or national advantage prevail in steering decision making? Certainly, the emphasis on full equality of rights, national sovereignty, national interest in carrying out common projects to mutual advantage, and friendly assistance can be found as general guidelines in most documents issuing from Eastern Europe. But this is generally not much more than paying lip service to the de jure organization of Eastern Europe, and is not always a reflection of actual political and economic realities.[20] It is stated explicitly in the charter's preamble, however, that the signatory states are "fully determined henceforth to develop all-round economic cooperation by consistently putting into practice the [ISDL], in the interest of building socialism and communism in these countries" (Tokareva 1967, p. 45).

But the CMEA as an international organization motivated by these general objectives can only hope to acquit itself of the concrete tasks involved within rather restrictive boundaries, especially because the Council is not empowered to issue binding instructions on the substantive matters of plan coordination and production specialization. In this connection it should be recalled that the members also agreed to "ensure the fulfillment of the recommendations" (Tokareva 1967, p. 46), a noble principle but hardly an operational modality of great practical import. As noted in section 2, decisions can only be made on organizational and procedural questions. Both the recommendations and decisions have to be approved unanimously and in recent years by consensus of interested members, a provision that has probably entailed technically involved problems as it is not explicitly defined when a member is "really" interested and when not in any matter under consideration. Similarly, the continuing formal membership of Albania may pose some complicated legal tangles, but they need not concern us here.

The principles of the ISDL

The CMEA's statutes cannot be regarded as a clear-cut statement of policy actions to be implemented or of policy intentions on which the members would act in due course, nor was this the most appropriate place to make public such actions and purposes. A more specific document on the goals and purposes of the CMEA and the principles and methods of SEI is the "Basic Principles of the International Socialist Division of Labor" (reproduced in Tokareva 1967, pp. 23–39, and in English in Kohler 1965, pp. 377–395), commonly referred to as Basic Principles, which was signed in 1962 and has since led to so much debate and wrangling over the Council's operations and the future of East European economic cooperation, though not to incisive action.

The Basic Principles too stress the inviolability of national sovereignty, mutual advantage, and so on. Interestingly enough, though, for the first time East European leaders put very strong emphasis on the need of each CPE to map out development plans according to its concrete conditions, while fully respecting the political and economic goals set by the leading communist parties and the needs and potentials of all socialist countries as a commonwealth (though, incidentally, only the CMEA members endorsed the document).[21] It is asserted further that "the new social system makes it possible to combine organically the development of [each CPE] with the development and consolidation of the world economic system of socialism as a whole," and that "the strengthening and widening of economic ties among the [CPEs] will promote the realization of an objective tendency which was outlined by V. I. Lenin: the creation in the future of the world communist economy directed by the victorious masses of the proletariat according to one plan" (Tokareva 1967, p. 24). This, in accompanying and subsequent analyses, clarifications, and statements (especially Chruscev 1962) was interpreted as a definite signal to the effect that, in the very near future, regional cooperation and SEI would be formulated and implemented according to a single, uniform economic plan, but this "momentous decision" may have been inspired by substantially differing goals of the CPEs. In any case, the chief merit of this document certainly is not the articulation of the specific instruments for promoting regional economic advancement and for blending primarily nationally oriented plans.

The objectives of the ISDL are much more clearly defined in this document than in any other official policy statement:

> The planned [ISDL] contributes to the maximum utilization of the advantages of the socialist world system, to the determination of correct proportions in the national economy of each country, to the rational location of production factors with respect to the socialist world system, to the effective utilization of labor and material resources, and to the strengthening of the defensive power of the socialist camp. The division of labor must guarantee each [CPE] a dependable market for the specialized products and the supply of the necessary raw materials, semifinished products, equipment, and other goods. [Tokareva 1967, p. 25]

This presumably indicates that the ISDL is to be aimed at the best allocation of resources in the region so as to optimize regional as opposed to national tasks, without, however, overlooking the legitimate developmental interests of the separate CPEs. The tendency to create a self-sufficient complex in each CPE in breadth and in depth at the expense of regional specialization and the attempt to impose one-sided international specialization are recognized as counterproductive policies, not only for the individual CPEs pursuing them but also for the community as a whole.

International specialization according to comparative advantage is very much the theme underlying the Basic Principles. To attain a more efficient and, in the end, optimal regional economy, plan synchronization as the basic instrument for enhancing socialist cooperation should be considerably improved and perfected. Bilateral and multilateral harmonization of intentions should contribute to the formulation and implementation of the ISDL. But nowhere in the document is it stated how the CPEs shall assess comparative advantage as the basis upon which planned specialization is to be promulgated. Incidentally, although the document frequently employs the term "international specialization," the authors in fact appear to refer to "regional specialization," which in context may suggest that the

CPEs should aim at the development of an autarkic regional policy. The close union of the CPEs within a single planning framework is considered a mandatory objective because of the "objective laws of economic and political developments." It will be a potent factor in encouraging "the intensification of the production in all the countries of materials scarce in the socialist camp, taking into account natural and economic conditions" (Tokareva 1967, p. 29). This tendency to restrict the horizon to the socialist region is brought out also in the emphasis placed on the institutionalization of regional multilateralism and the gradual elaboration of an own CMEA price system.

The most important goal expressed in this document is implied by the strong stress placed on implementing the ISDL through plan coordination. This instrument should in the future presumably be replaced by a common uniform plan drawn up by a supranational planning agency invested with adequate powers of decision making. Eliminating the problems of bilateralism and correcting inconsistent prices were explicitly mentioned as important tasks; multilateralism and appropriate scarcity prices were to serve as the main catalysts for furthering CMEA specialization. Although the document pays lip service to the national interest of the CPEs, it was this call for commonly solving common problems, not only in trade and joint ventures[22] but also in economic development in general, that was at the forefront of the discussion that was triggered off shortly after the document's approval.

It is perhaps needless to explain here why virtually none of the above and other components of this program loaded with intentions were carried out and why many of the proposals were slowly being brought backstage, shelved, and replaced by the incipient discussions about national economic reforms, the role of trade with MTEs in the intensive growth strategy to be elaborated, and the initiation of SEI. Let it suffice to recall here that it is not clarified in the Basic Principles how these largely political intentions were to be realized either in general or in specific detail; no methodology of plan coordination, specialization, multilateralism, and pricing, to name but a handful of crucial issues, was offered or referred to. This means presumably that the Council and its members were expected to start serious work on solving the key components of the ISDL soon after the adoption of the program. But the emerging search for the alternative ways and means of the ISDL was quietly replaced by more fundamental disagreements about the basic goals of SEI. In that light, the Basic Principles present a classic example of how a commonly endorsed declaration on principles can exaggerate the purposefulness and ostensible policy coherence even of "friendly nations."

Whether or not the shortcomings mentioned above resulted from intentional neglect of the political leadership will not be investigated here. The point is that although important, if vaguely formulated, goals were laid down in an accepted program of common action, nothing much was undertaken by the CPEs to promote regional specialization according to common advantages, however these should or could be defined. Research on the basic elements of cooperation was initiated, but frequently wrapped with the convenient cloak of national political options. Political deliberations on the most important points of the program were pursued as well, but apparently no consensus could be hammered out. Instead of pursuing work on the basis of the program's provisions, a vituperative discussion erupted that concentrated officially on the inviolability of national sovereignty and the inalienable right of each CPE to select its own development path according to national advantage, or at least according to what was perceived as the country's long-term interest. This unfavorable climate was sparked off by the resolute opposition of certain CPEs, notably Rumania, to the gradual elaboration of a "superplan" and the particular interpretation of the objectives and instruments of SEI as subsumed in the Basic Principles.

Instead of taking the Basic Principles as the basic cue for concrete policy actions in national and regional affairs, three main trends emerged shortly after the document was endorsed. First, a wave of economic reforms started in several CPEs and eventually encompassed the entire area, albeit in varying intensity and scope. These reforms were of such a nature that the institutionalization of regional central planning according to the traditional criteria of physical detail, as in the central planning of each CPE, became more and more unlikely and, at least to some, extremely undesirable. In Tibor Kiss's words:

The joint planning concept proved to be unrealistic, not only because it was cumbersome technically and methodologically, but also in terms of its economic and, last but not least, political implications. It did not reckon, namely, with the fact that an improvement in the multilateral system of harmonization . . . did not depend simply on improving methodology but hinges primarily on questions of self-interest. [It] disregarded actual production conditions [of the CPEs] and the objective necessity of maintaining economic independence. [Kiss 1975, p. 747]

Second, the mid-1960s provided a more reliable political and economic climate for an upswing, especially of East–West cooperation. Under these new conditions, each CPE sought to press the issue of specialization according to more precisely defined criteria of economic choice and efficiency before entering into definite regional commitments. Third, although it is true that the expansion of the CPEs' economies and of regional trade slowed down, yet with hindsight it was a fruitful period devoted to a concentrated effort to come to grips with the more fundamental theoretical and practical problems of intrasocialist cooperation (price formation, labor and capital mobility, multilateralism, joint investments, and so on) and its role in the intensification strategy on the drawing boards in nearly all CPEs. Despite the fact that joint planning proved abortive at that stage, CMEA cooperation nevertheless advanced indirectly, chiefly under impact of efforts aimed at implementing very specific cooperation projects of a relatively modest, but not negligible, scale or at least ventures of a relatively uncomplicated nature. Most of these achievements resulted, however, not from Council actions but came into existence under pressure of the real needs of some of the CPEs.

The fundamental necessity of supranational planning as a prerequisite for SEI was suddenly revived in late 1968 (see especially Sorokin 1968, 1969), shortly after the traumatic events of the Czechoslovak crisis and its aftermath; but the "scientific" suggestion resurrecting Chruščëv's ghost was shortly thereafter quietly disowned by those who had apparently been behind the reopening of this rather sensitive topic. Indeed, economic reforms in most CPEs had progressed too far and too many policy makers had already become convinced of the drawbacks of traditional central planning to adopt detailed regional planning in order to streamline the economic structures in accordance with the precepts that the individual CPEs were attempting to implant in their own countries. The matter of common planning as

3. Official principles and methods of SEI

such was implicitly discredited during the twenty-third Council Session (Moscow, April 1969), which concluded that integration – a concept formerly reserved for the regionalization attempts of MTEs – should be pursued also in the CMEA framework. This meeting endorsed the strategic precepts of SEI instead of further refining the Basic Principles, and these recommendations became the overall guidelines of a two years' search for a formal integration program.

The objectives and instruments of SEI

Proposals on the goals and methods of SEI are numerous and of widely differing portent. One end of this spectrum is represented by the Hungarian proposals advocating market-based integration through a customs union, the coordination of macroeconomic policies, and the introduction of indirect instruments of economic control and guidance. At the other end of the range there is the emphasis on regional central planning. The disadvantages of instituting traditional central planning now at the regional level would admittedly be avoided, or at least mitigated, by supplementing central planning with a substantial degree of flexibility that is expected from the more appropriate utilization of instruments of coordinating economic decisions indirectly. Furthermore, regional central planning should be focused primarily at the basic tasks of long-term development and structural change, as distinct from the details of day-to-day cooperation and trade preoccupations.

Discussions about the introduction of multilateralism, scarcity prices, efficient international credits, and the like have been very intensive and far reaching. Yet it has also become apparent that the diversity of opinions is still too deep-rooted and fundamentally too irreconcilable, and hence precludes unanimous agreement on these focal issues of economic policy, except perhaps in an uncommittedly vague phrasing of principles. It is in this climate of disunity about steering the economies and the role of political priorities in regional cooperation, now reexamined under the impact of the Czechoslovak crisis and its implications,[23] that the Complex Program was drafted in the late 1960s and approved in July 1971.

Whereas previous policy statements referred vaguely to international specialization and economic cooperation as the goals of SEI, the new program calls for full integration as defined here (see Introduction), though the exact meaning of SEI is not fully spelled out in the program. Positive integration as an aim is the leading motive behind the Complex Program inasmuch as the CPEs appear to have agreed to gradually eliminate the man-made obstacles to the free flow of goods, services, and, to some extent, production factors too, and to reduce the impediments stemming from "natural" conditions by coordinating all relevant aspects of economic policy.[24] The law of the equalization of levels of economic development must be fully understood and implemented. Logically this would imply that the basic goal of SEI, as hesitantly suggested by some East European economists, is the full equalization of relative scarcities throughout the region. Specialization should therefore be intensified to exploit comparative advantages without underrating or disregarding the legitimate needs of each CPE, especially the less developed participants, to elaborate its own economic complex as an integral part of a streamlined regional economy. Each CPE is entitled to decide freely whether or not and when to participate in a particular project, but this "lack of interest" should not prevent other parties from carrying out their intentions.

The Complex Program is an exceedingly long and carefully worded document dealing with many aspects of SEI. Yet it is not fully consistent and it does not chart programmatically the policy goals and instruments of SEI. It reaffirms in detail the familiar principles and procedures of international socialist cooperation, and provides a complex compendium of the spheres and topics at which common efforts are to be directed. But the program amounts to little more than seventeen interim reports of Council organs, who in fact drafted them, and no attempt is made to harmonize the various propositions into anything resembling a coherent comprehensive concept of integration and how it should be enhanced. The backdrop to the integration debates sketchily painted above explains why the Complex Program was inevitably a compromise, preferring to put off major problems to the future in the interest of securing a satisfactory program of minimum integrative measures acceptable to all members.

In spite of its fuzziness with regard to the goals of SEI, the program contains a number of noteworthy passages that can be divided into two broad sections. First, it discloses a lengthy catalogue of separate areas in which agreement has been reached in principle on the elaboration of common forecasting, the construction of concrete projects, and the working out of a number of agreements furthering cooperation especially in mining, engineering, agriculture, and transportation. Second, it contains a number of broad suggestions regarding the future work of the CPEs and the Council on creating a meaningful mechanism of SEI. This comprises three principal axles, namely, legal, economic, and institutional-organizational facets of SEI, which will have to be overhauled and, where necessary, partly or wholly replaced in order to facilitate production specialization, plan coordination, and scientific-technical cooperation. Though very detailed and highly relevant to practical integration work, the first set of measures will not be discussed here in detail. It is judged more important to focus the discussion instead on the program's specifications regarding the mechanism, or parts of it, by which the CPEs hope to foster the integration processes because on it depends the intensification of cooperation in general as well as the implementation of the concrete steps already agreed upon in the program.

The economic mechanism of SEI can be defined parallel to the economic model of CPEs as the set of interrelated measures comprising policy instruments, institutions, and behavioral rules mobilized to attain some regional goals in harmony with the policies and institutions of the participating countries. Although the Complex Program does not embody a rounded integration mechanism, it does set forth a number of interesting views on essential components of such an ideal model of integration that will have to be elaborated and agreed upon in the near future.

The economic aspects of the integration mechanism are naturally most important for the purposes of this study. The program sets forth three principal types of instruments to be perfected in the process of SEI: policy consultations, the dovetailing of economic plans, and indirect coordination instruments.

The CPEs agreed that the harmonization of national economic plans should serve as the chief subset of instruments directed at promoting coordination because SEI is inherently a process "regulated in a deliberate and planned way." The national central planning boards bear the responsibility for all plan coordination activities in "broad cooperation" with the official and other Council organs. The coordination of plans will involve deepening common efforts in several directions simultaneously.

First, the CPEs agree to embrace forecasting future demand and supply policies in a coordinated fashion as the basic source of information for drawing up concrete plans. Second, long-term perspective planning, with a horizon of ten to twenty years, will be undertaken to determine main developments of key economic activities. It also includes reaching compromise on the basic aims of economic policies, broadly defined, of each CPE. Third, the traditional methods of coordinating medium-term plans need to be improved in the sense that the compass of coordination will be shifted more and more from the sphere of trade to that of production and investment strategies (including scientific-technical cooperation, production specialization in accordance with regional market forces, the joint construction of specific investment projects, and the scope and timing of reciprocal commodity exchanges). Finally, plan coordination will also be sought in the form of joint planning of selected economic branches or specific production types (Wasilkowski 1971, pp. 46–47). However vaguely defined in the Complex Program, joint planning is a distinct category inasmuch as it could become an embryonic form of international planning with the special feature at this juncture, however, of being facultative. On the other hand, the obligation to participate in annual and medium-term plan coordination follows from the CMEA charter and a number of resolutions adopted by the Council Session.

Treating these highly involved issues of plan coordination and joint planning on a rather general level, the Complex Program mentions that the members will work out an operational program for closer planning cooperation in the course of 1971. With the exception of the coordination of medium- and long-term plans, which should be routinized as a matter of principle, the subject matter of forecasting, joint planning, and the exchange of experiences is left up to "interested members." The synchronization of medium- and long-term plans will however gain in stature because the various governments are expected to submit draft plans to the other CPEs and the Council organs.

These preliminary plans on investment and distribution strategies will serve as a starting point for detailed discussions on the most advantageous prospects of each CPE and the community as a whole, but no one can be compelled to scratch a particular project if it is deemed "untouchable," even if its realization may endanger the regional cooperation objectives and interfere with the interests of other Council members.

A particularly conspicuous place in plan coordination is reserved for the promotion of scientific-technological cooperation, comprising research, development, and production specialization, with the assistance of planning and indirect coordination instruments. The elaboration of a "mechanism of scientific-technological" cooperation is held to be essential to the fostering of technical progress and the intensification of production in the CPEs and the region as a whole.

Second, plan coordination will not be pursued in a vacuum, but will be concerned primarily with shaping the outcome of high-level policy consultations into operational plan tasks with the assistance of other policy instruments. An important role in SEI will be played by frequent bilateral and multilateral consultations on a vast array of national and international economic policies, not only on the government and planning levels, but in fact by all those responsible for drafting and implementing plans. Although this would normally entail some important organizational consequences, as outlined below, none are really specified. The levels, forms, and procedures of these consultations as well as the topics to be tabled are indeed to be decided upon by interested members, who will commit themselves in principle to certain common targets, but at the same time preserve the right in each case to determine what will have to be done concretely, including the prerogative of opting out.

Third, the Complex Program devotes a good deal of attention to the means of coordinating economic decisions indirectly. These instruments are expected to underpin economic integration in the draft phase of the plans and to assist in the implementation of coordinated plans. Such monetary and financial market-type instruments (for example, prices, exchange rates, wage rates, interest rates, and credits) will not, however, be allotted a key role in the stage of plan formulation or in the process of setting up common projects, for this domain is preempted for planning and plan coordination. Though the crucial role of instruments of indirect coordination is acknowledged, these instruments will not become the overriding criteria in selecting common tasks, but they may help in the concrete formulation and implementation of SEI. Comparative advantage indicators will be utilized, but in the framework of common and coordinated planning.

The sections of the program dealing with these monetary and financial instruments and institutions are not particularly noteworthy for their programmatic detail or for spelling out in operational terms how, in the context of plan coordination, they are expected to function. The matters elaborated are of interest because of the deadlines specified for studying the possible role of these instruments in SEI following which concrete actions are anticipated. Price formation in regional trade will in the near future remain as before. At the same time, a comprehensive study of the issue was to be launched and possible improvements were to be discussed in 1971–1972. Price formation, multilateralism of nonquota trade, and related matters were to be subjected to more precise procedures in 1973. The role of the transferable ruble was to be enhanced by creating the real conditions to ensure its stability and by adopting measures to facilitate transferability and multilateralism. Before 1973 the CPEs were to study the nature of the transferable ruble's exchange rate. Measures of how to improve multilateral transactions, to ensure regional balancing, and to extend the sphere of application of the transferable ruble in CMEA relations as well as in other foreign areas were also to be embraced by 1973. Exchange rates between the transferable ruble and the national currencies, especially for noncommercial transactions, were to be updated before 1974. It was also resolved to establish in the second half of the 1970s the preconditions for the emergence of a single exchange rate of each CPE's currency by harmonizing consumer and producer goods' prices. It was projected that sometime around 1980 the CPEs were to decide whether and when these uniform rates would become applicable. The question of making the transferable ruble convertible, particularly in noncommercial transactions and in the capitalization and operations of the IEOs, was to be studied in 1971–1972 and joint measures were to be introduced in 1973. Monetary and financial issues would of course require certain adjustments in the organization of the two common banks, but no fundamental ones are mentioned in the Complex Program.

An increasingly important role in harmonizing the activities of sovereign states and avoiding or arbitrating conflicts is the creation of a legal framework capable of accommodating international law in support of diverse integration processes. As legal provisions in the CPEs differ substantially, one of the important tasks of SEI is to make uniform the existing legal frameworks and to draft new legislation through international agreements and treaties in order to cope with the expected sharp increase in economic, commercial, and scientific-technical cooperation. It is judged especially important to devise general legal norms and conditions governing the status and operations of IEOs and, more generally, the mobility of capital and labor across the region. In addition to working out normative rules and procedures, it is helpful to be able to arbitrate disputes about the interpretation of agreements or contracts and to provide for effective sanctions consonant with the damage incurred by nonfulfillment of or improper adherence to obligations assumed under them. It was also resolved to protect inventions, trade marks, and samples. Once again, a schedule for further discussions and the selection of the levels at which these legal deliberations are to be conducted is left for subsequent consultations.[25]

Finally, much more intensive cooperation among CPEs depends in an important way on an appropriate organizational and institutional infrastructure. Regarding contacts among CPEs, the program mentions briefly that direct regional economic relations between enterprises, as distinct from more informal contacts at the lower rungs of the planning hierarchies, are not expected to play a central role in plan coordination or in the formulation and implementation of concrete aspects of SEI. In fact, as far as the internal organization of the CPEs is concerned, the program remains notably silent or is noncommittal. The program simply reaffirms that each country organizes its planned economy according to its own conditions by taking "steps to create within the framework of national economic planning and management systems the requisite economic, organizational, and legal conditions for successful realization of the [program]." The members envisage some changes in the trade sector, especially the transition toward multilateralism, among others, by seeking greater flexibility in BTPAs through making due allowance for nonquota trade, less rigorous annual balancing, greater capital mobility, and so on. With regard to the Council and its organs, the program records (as reported in section 2 above under "The future role of the Council") that the members agree to seek a sharp improvement of traditional principles, methods, and tasks of economic cooperation and to study a few new possibilities within the existing CMEA framework. But no new forms or institutions of regional cooperation are slated for introduction before 1990 (the program is expected to remain the chief guideline for SEI for a period of fifteen to twenty years). SEI will therefore have to be fostered within the existing institutions of the CPEs and with the methods presently available in the CMEA organization.

In sum, the program specifies integration merely as a long-term aim, and presumably for that reason it is vaguely phrased. This aim is to be promoted by instruments and institutions whose precise type and role will have to be more closely studied in the near future. Methods of plan coordination and joint planning, procedures for policy consultations, and the nature and scope of coordination instruments are vaguely described and will presumably require further intensive consultations and detailed negotiations among the members before they will be able to support the integration strategy. In spite of this vagueness, the members have at least set themselves a number of deadlines for the study and solution of crucial topical questions, especially those relating to plan coordination, convertibility, transferability, multilateralism, and regional pricing. Neither the emergence of a market mechanism nor the institutionalization of central planning at the regional level, even if only for selected tasks, is to be envisioned for a long time to come. Certainly, the program calls for improvements of the existing framework of the Council and of the separate planning centers, but the implementation of the program itself is not intended as a means of inducing drastic departures from the existing divergent economic mechanisms of the individual CPEs. Whatever the merits of the general goals of SEI, the restriction on the methods of future cooperation is by far the most significant as well as the most disappointing feature of the program. From the earlier discussions, it seems almost self-evident that unless each CPE is willing to pursue greater flexibility in internal planning in combination with delegating some decision-making authority to the Council organs, SEI cannot proceed very far.

4. The methods of cooperation in the 1970s

When reading the official CMEA documents, it is disquieting that one searches in vain for a reference to the precise principles that are to guide SEI. It would seem that most outstanding questions of intra-CMEA cooperation have been acknowledged as problematical in the official blueprints, especially in the Complex Program, which is considerable progress indeed. Providing answers that will enable the actors in CPEs to work more systematically toward SEI evidently remains contingent on the elaboration of principles to be drafted, discussed, and, if possible, approved in the future. In this respect it would seem fair to conclude that the integration program has not changed the fundamental aims of the CMEA; it has merely expanded and codified more precisely the system of rules regarding specialization, cooperation, joint ventures, and trade that the CPEs have been cultivating for at least the past ten to fifteen years, if not overtly from the outset in 1949.

Admittedly, the above skeptical remarks should not be overemphasized. But it is striking nevertheless that the CPEs' official horizon of SEI reaches very far into the unknown future and, yet, the members have not been able to reach consensus on more concrete means whereby this program can be clarified and carried out. Plan coordination is much too vague a policy instrument to answer all outstanding questions of SEI. The situation is not unlike the second and third phases of West European integration, but at least its first stage was charted relatively clearly when the Rome treaties were signed in the mid-1950s. An interesting three-stage periodization of CMEA integration, offering some clues of the magnitude of the obstacles ahead, has been suggested by three eminent Soviet specialists in matters of East European cooperation (Alampiev 1971, pp. 85–88). The first phase of SEI, extending over some fifteen to twenty years, will in their view involve "solving the integration tasks for which the prerequisites are already available." The second, undated, phase will be characterized by "the formation of a uniform system of domestic reproduction processes on the basis of the results of the first phase," and is expected to give rise to a fully integrated "international economic complex" in Eastern Europe. Finally, the third phase will involve the dissolution of all CPEs into a "uniform international [*sic!*] economy" guided by one common plan. However, the authors carefully observe that a more precise definition of this third phase "transcends the framework of the visible future, and it would be a gross mistake to take the strategic goal [of SEI] as the objective towards which further steps should be taken in the immediate future; [one should first] work out the preconditions for the unfolding of the integration processes" (Alampiev 1971, pp. 87–88). This suggests that the Complex Program embodies an attempt to strengthen regional cooperation by the means presently at the disposal of the CPEs.

Although none of the basic components of an integration mechanism could be unambiguously specified in the program, the ensuing process of giving operational meaning to the numerous tasks slated for further study and negotiation has been characterized very clearly by two features. First, the debate on the principles and methodology of plan coordination and joint planning on the one hand, and harmonizing monetary and financial coordination instruments with planning activities on the other, ran a stimulating course for a few years, roughly until 1974, without however resulting in generally acceptable solutions for any of the fundamental issues (Pecsi 1977, pp. 30–39). To be sure, the deadlines incorporated into the program have so far been respected, at least from a purely formal point of view because the solutions or revisions in the monetary and financial cooperation mechanisms adopted so far would appear to have fallen far short of what could reasonably have been anticipated in the light of the expectations of the policy makers and commentators revealed at the time the Complex Program was endorsed and in the ensuing debates. Second, parallel with the more detailed examination of principles and methods of SEI, practical matters have tended to be tackled more and more within the traditional framework of plan coordination, especially after the world price inflation, the raw material shortage, and the recession in the developed MTEs that have drastically curtailed the list of options available to most market-minded CPEs.

More recently, integration discussions have been focused nearly exclusively on improving plan coordination, especially for fairly detailed projects about which specific specialization or coordination agreements have been concluded. In this connection, two types of documents are of singular consequence for the evolving process of SEI. First, in 1975 the CPEs endorsed the "Concerted Plan of Multilateral Integration Measures," which is currently in the process of implementation. Second, since 1976 the CPEs have been formulating "Long-term Target Programs of Cooperation," the first three of which were adopted in mid-1978 and the other two in mid-1979, to mold the course of SEI for the next decade or so.[26]

The Concerted Plan worked out jointly in 1974–1975 is the first concrete, common integration plan of the CPEs and aims at very specific targets in a number of important economic activities, which broadly speaking can be divided into five different classes. First, it contains details regarding the material, financial, and, in some instances, labor transfers for the joint projects started in the mid-1970s (the most important of which are the cellulose manufacturing complex Ust'-Ilimsk, the asbestos enrichment plant in Kiembaev, the gas-condensate facility in Orenburg and the 2,750-kilometer gas pipeline Sojuz to the Soviet–Czechoslovak border, the high-voltage power line from Vinnica to Albertirsa, part of the metallurgical complex in Kursk, and the nickel complex in Cuba). This part of the Concerted Plan amounts to some 9,000 million transferable rubles, about 7,000 of which will be disbursed in 1976–1980 (Karpic 1976, pp. 10–11), mostly in the USSR. Second, a large number of multilateral specialization and cooperation agreements, especially in the engineering and chemical sectors (such as computer technology, herbicides, synthetic dyes, container transport, atomic power stations, private cars, and so on), are stipulated, although no concrete details have been disclosed. Third, several scientific and technological cooperation projects are included, especially to improve and expand new sources of energy, fuels, and essential raw materials, including a common expedition to Mongolia to ascertain new deposits of valuable raw materials.

Fourth, a special section is devoted to measures to enhance the development of Mongolia. Finally, consequences of the common actions vis-à-vis third countries following from the Concerted Plan are drawn (Vorkauf 1977, p. 12). Also new in this respect is that the relevant parts of the Concerted Plan provisions for the individual participants have become an integral component of the current medium-term plans (1976–1980) and have the force of law in the participating countries through the annual implementation plans, which include a section on integration measures.

The Concerted Plan is certainly an important innovation in East European cooperation in that it is explicitly directed at the piecemeal improvement of SEI, but its significance should not be overrated. Because there is still no adequately formulated long-term development strategy or even a commonly accepted set of sound ideas about the SEI path, the gestation of the Concerted Plan was difficult and its formulation as such, as R. Nyers observed, "can be counted as a success" (Nyers 1977, p. 423) in many ways because it will greatly alleviate the shortage of some goods on the CMEA market and improve production specialization in a few well-defined fields. However, the Concerted Plan is only an interim solution, pending the approval of dovetailed long-term programs of common action in which the coordination of jointly funded or realized investments will presumably be aimed at framing complementary structures rather than isolated ventures (Biskup 1978, p. 10).

The elaboration of Long-term Target Programs of Cooperation, in which the desirable and binding joint development path in selected fields to be traveled by the CPEs will be outlined, was first suggested in 1975, and the concrete formulation of such strategies has been in preparation ever since. Focused on selected activities and with a time horizon set at about ten years, although more recently this has been extended up to twenty years, these programs are designed to cope with a number of important aspects of plan coordination that the CPEs find difficult to accommodate within the framework designed for the dovetailing of annual and medium-term national economic plans, which by necessity are all-encompassing. Initially, five areas of special significance for long-term growth and the maturing of SEI were identified and agreed upon by the highest decision-making echelons. Actual formulation of the programs was entrusted to the CMEA organs and numerous research institutes of the CPEs, and comprehensive drafts should have been available in mid-1977. The goals of the target programs and the fields selected for intensive cooperation are the following: (1) to solve the problems encountered in maintaining balance in energy, fuels, and raw materials; (2) to enhance specialization and to eliminate duplication in the engineering branches; (3) to improve the balance in basic food supplies and increase the effectiveness of agricultural output; (4) to improve the supply and quality of a wide range of industrial consumer goods; and (5) to establish a fully integrated transportation system for the region. In these programs, demand and supply developments will be forecast, and investment intentions as well as anticipated trade flows will be coordinated in an effort to attain greater efficiency in the regionwide allocation of resources (Kormnov 1977).

Since the endorsement of these programs by the thirtieth Council Session (Berlin, July 1976), intensive preparatory work has been accomplished, but it has also become evident that specifying concrete integration tasks of such wide range and assuring their operationality has been a much more arduous task than originally anticipated. Consequently, the thirty-first Council Session (Warsaw, June 1977) recommended that attention should be directed in the first instance at the programs dealing with energy, fuels, and raw materials, foodstuffs and agriculture, and machine building in support of the other two programs mentioned. Furthermore, the projects presented at the Council Session in Bucharest (June 1978) and at the latest one in Moscow (June 1979) are probably far less comprehensive than what was originally envisaged. Though the blueprints are not yet available, scattered evidence suggests that they are focused especially on essential investment projects that will help to ensure the partial autarky of the region (Chodow 1976, p. 23). In the meantime, the CPEs have already concluded a number of important multilateral specialization agreements, including one on electrical energy and the engineering required to link up the various energy systems of the CPEs, in order eventually to attain a unified power grid for all CMEA members, except Albania, Cuba, and Vietnam, and on the construction of atomic power stations in the smaller CPEs as well as two units in the USSR that will be hooked into the Mir power grid. Most of the agreements disclosed to date have 1990 as a time horizon, but the signatory countries expect to extend this time framework and to dovetail the agreements with new plans to be worked out up to the year 2000. Because these protocols will have to be specified in detail in the context of the traditional annual and medium-term plans of the CPEs, the Concerted Plan presently being implemented will become a recurrent planning instrument in the implementation of the Target Programs and associated bilateral and multilateral specialization agreements (Vorkauf 1977, p. 21).

Do these new developments suggest that for all practical purposes the integration program adopted in 1971 is or will no longer be the central guideline of common actions, especially once these target programs will be formulated in detail, probably in time for the next medium-term plans? Although the developments in SEI matters since 1974 justify an affirmative answer, there is unfortunately still too much of a gap in the information stream on what the intentions of the CPEs with respect to the future evolution of SEI may be. Once the broad outlines and specific objectives of the Target Programs become traceable, a less speculative answer can be given. Nonetheless, it bears stressing that the Complex Program offers a rather general, sometimes quite vague, framework. It may therefore be unequivocal that the Target Programs will amount to no more than a further concretization of the general tasks outlined in the Complex Program, as is currently claimed in the East European literature. Although it is undoubtedly true that policy instruments other than some type of plan coordination have been deliberately downplayed in the discussions about how to enhance SEI, it bears stressing that the enactment of Concerted Plans and Target Programs fits in rather well with the various types of "plan coordination" discussed in the Complex Program (see "The objectives and instruments of SEI" in section 3 above). Of far greater interest, however, is a clarification of how the CPEs expect these new Target Programs to contribute to the enhancement of SEI, a topic that will be considered in more detail in the next chapter.

5. Concluding remarks

Considering that the CPEs have worked out a number of formal policy documents and a large number of other statements pertaining to the goals and instruments of their integration strategy, broadly defined, how far along are they and what developments in the near future can be anticipated?

The CMEA documents published in the past two decades may be interpreted in two different ways. A positive appraisal would probably applaud the fact that policy statements regarding SEI have been expanded in breadth and in depth. At least, the existence of numerous obstacles hindering intra-CMEA economic cooperation has been acknowledged in official documents, and a number of suggestions have been made on how to eliminate these hindrances; but high-level deliberations would not seem to have yielded as yet generally acceptable solutions. Moreover, pronouncements related to the distant and perhaps elusive goals of the communist welfare state and the unanimous joining of all forces in the service of this objective have gradually been overshadowed by a much more pragmatic discussion of the more immediate and tangible problems that the CPEs must in fact face and come to master before even less tractable issues can be realistically tackled. A negative appraisal would be based mainly on the fact that the same questions are being reiterated in each new policy statement, albeit perhaps in another, lengthier form, and that many of the crucial topics stipulated for further deliberations do not really receive sufficient attention in subsequent policy discussions and fail to be the beacon of concrete cooperation activities.

Both interpretations can be justified. Without doubt, most CPEs (including the superpower) sincerely intend to move ahead with internationalizing the various CPEs and stimulating greater cohesion in an integrated Eastern Europe. Their reasons for doing so are several. But one important force, if not the most crucial one, of "historical necessity" is that doing nothing has proved too costly, also and not the least for the dominant power. But, and here comes the sting, neither the helmsman nor several of the officers of the CMEA boat have been eager to remove the barriers presented by the vagaries of ocean riding within their own field of competence (i.e., laying the foundations of regional integration by revising the organization of economic processes in each CPE in such a way that greater interdependence in decision making can be accommodated). Or to continue the metaphor, the officers are reluctant to coordinate fully the wide range of activities and obligations of the crew. Consequently, the boat moves back and forth and ahead, first, by the sheer force of the wind (especially the Soviet demand for manufactures and its readiness to supply primary material inputs to the CPE allies) and also as a result of the various forces exerted by one or more crew members (e.g., specialized bilateral cooperation agreements between smaller CPEs). Attempts to create the conditions for greater coherence from outside are introduced as contemplated in the official documents, but these efforts are fairly quickly frustrated by the panoply of fundamental impediments inherent in integrating economies governed by national central plans. The previous chapters attempted to clarify some of these problems in a broad analysis of different issues affecting the external sector of the typical CPE. In the next chapter, the trade and integration topics will be placed in a more coherent framework in order to assess the stage of integration reached and the potential future evolution of SEI.

5

Socialist economic integration in retrospect and issues for the future

Regarding the nature and the evolving processes of regional integration efforts in Eastern Europe during the past thirty years or so, the preceding chapters have highlighted in considerable detail four important angles of this endeavor: (1) the overall internal and external organizational features of the CPEs; (2) the internal and external economic policies pursued by these economies; (3) the institutional aspects and role of the CMEA as a common regional organization under whose auspices, officially at least, SEI is to be fostered; and (4) the most important policy statements that disclose some guidance as to the cooperation efforts intended in the past, the present stage of integration, and the gradual maturing of SEI.

To pull the various strands of thought outlined in the preceding chapters together, this chapter addresses several interrelated issues with the goal of forecasting one possible scenario of the likely scope and direction of SEI in the 1980s. Several related topics will be examined. How far along on the integration path are the CPEs? If they have not yet obtained the level of regional interdependence envisaged in the official policy documents, what have been the main obstacles encountered and how could these encumbrances be removed prospectively as a prerequisite for smoothing the cooperation path to be trodden in the near future? Finally, what has been the influence exerted by the outside world on integration activities of the CPEs? Though East–West trade and cooperation are not, of course, the subject proper of this study, the presence of alternative trade outlets and the comparatively lower state of economic development prevailing in the CMEA, as already indicated, warrant an evaluation of the actual or potential impact of trade and cooperation

245

with third markets on the pattern and evolution of SEI. In an endeavor to answer these questions, an attempt will be made to separate the essential determinants of SEI from what would seem to be removable at little or no cost in terms of the development objectives and associated sociopolitical goals coveted by the CMEA member countries.

The first section evaluates the overall features of the present stage of SEI in order to put into perspective some widespread contentions about the advanced or, alternatively, low degree of supranationalism, economic integration, and production specialization prevailing in Eastern Europe. This will prepare the ground for section 2, which briefly surveys the various measurements of the degree of integration achieved in the CMEA, an important but rather enigmatic topic. Section 3 addresses especially the role of interregional cooperation in the process of SEI. The exogenous conditions delineating the feasible integration space, and hence the field in which target manipulation of endogenous variables can be anticipated, are summarized in section 4. Finally, the more transient features of the CPEs are separated from their fundamental goals in order to develop a feasible integration scenario for the foreseeable future.

1. On the present state of CMEA integration

Rationalizations and interpretations of the institutions, behavioral rules, and processes of decision making in the CPEs on the one hand, and the known facts about intra-CMEA cooperation efforts on the other, suggest unambiguously that SEI to this day continues to be a rather vaguely defined goal instead of the focus of an evolving but comprehensive regional economic policy that inspires target policy actions of each member. Furthermore, the available evidence of cooperation achievements in the area tends to support the view that so far the CPEs have made but limited progress in internationalizing their economies and in molding the region into a coherent, interdependent market in which a variety of intersecting instruments, institutions, and behavioral rules are manipulated with the goal of mobilizing resources most effectively. If the past and present of SEI reveal anything at all about the most likely future evolution of regional cooperation, the analyses reported in this study demonstrate that SEI will by no means be the implicit outcome of traditional central planning under the direct supervision, if not the complete tutelage, of the dominant CMEA member. The narrative followed here so far has hopefully contributed to a better understanding of the economic realities of the CPEs and to a fairer assessment of the Council's role.

Although it is incontrovertible that the CMEA as a common economic institution plays an important role in the process of synchronizing the economic and trade plans of the CPEs, misrepresentations of the Council's real part in this are legion. It is, for instance, distressing to read in a scholarly study that the coordination of trade intentions of the CPEs vis-à-vis third countries is one of the CMEA's chief functions, in addition to dovetailing the members' national economic plans. The studiously sought conclusion drawn from this perceived view of the Council's role is that: "In carrying out these functions [the CMEA] has become, in effect, a supranational organization guided and controlled by the Soviet Union" (Smith 1973, p. 205). G. A. Smith bases this erroneous inference on the notion that the Council "has already established standardized planning methods, and it coordinates long-term economic plans and investments. It has also established joint planning offices for individual branches of industry and is developing a unified planning center that will have the power to issue instructions" (Smith 1973, pp. 205–206). Although such interpretations perhaps reflect the Soviet objectives of SEI's future coveted in the early 1960s, and, hence, may throw light on how the USSR would transform the Council had it a free hand to do so, the above view or variations on the same theme appear to be a serious misreading of both the theory and the practice of the past cooperation of the CPEs; at least, they do not accurately reflect the elements of comprehensive economic integration only now hesitantly emerging.

Irrespective of the precise direction of the long-term intentions of Soviet foreign policy with respect to SEI or the hoped-for evolution of a socialist "common market" since the war, there is very little concrete evidence to buttress the proposition that economic policies promoting or slowing down SEI originate exclusively in Moscow. In fact, recent independent analyses by Western researchers and some scholarly studies of East European economists tend to disprove the rather widespread notions that: (1) The USSR is relatively the largest and perhaps the only benefactor of intra-CMEA cooperation, (2) Soviet policy views alone are dominant[1] in molding the conception and implementation of SEI, and (3) the present framework of integration completely mirrors Soviet policy intentions and indeed solely reflects actions initiated by the USSR.

Similar views advocating the advanced degree of SEI or the thesis of one-sided, Moscow-based integration can be found in a number of other Western publications (e.g., Broner 1975; Pelzman 1976). However, by far the majority of observers remains skeptical and stresses the snail's pace at which the CPEs have been harmonizing their economies. This predominant view flatly rejects the thesis advanced in most Bulgarian, East German, and Soviet analyses that SEI is being systematically implemented in accordance with a commonly agreed and dovetailed integration plan, which itself reflects the "law of SEI." In fact, most Western observers (incidentally joined by a score of East European, especially Hungarian and Polish, scholars) rather suspect sweeping conclusions such as the following: "Neither from a theoretical point of view nor from empirical evidence are there sufficient reasons to hold that the CMEA countries are less integrated than Western economies" (Broner 1975, pp. 217–218). Contrary to such highly positive interpretations, most independent observers, including this one, argue that the progress of SEI, although on the whole positive, has been rather sluggish, owing largely to the fact that the CPEs harbor sincere intentions of narrowing their economic and other differences, but that they have no precisely defined and generally accepted principles for implementing such goals.

Although the confusion in some of the Western literature about the precise nature of SEI and the stage attained to date is rather disappointing, East European specialized studies are far from helpful inasmuch as the conclusions reached are, if possible, even less uniform, ranging from outright rejection of the thesis that progress has been steadily achieved to unbridled praise. However, quite a few of these scholarly views stand in sharp contrast to the relatively uniform laudatory position propounded by most East European political leaders. Since the inception of the Complex Program, one is almost daily confronted with numerous reports about the new achievements in the field of SEI, particularly in terms of fulfilling the tasks set by the program. The latter is sometimes viewed as a "plan" to be carried out or "a law" to be adhered to at all costs, something countries involved are said to have studiously obeyed. However, this claim should not detract from the reality that specification of integration targets continues to be rather vague and imprecise. Without underrating outrightly the credibility of these claims about the realization of various sections of the program since 1971, the following considerations may help to comprehend better the many integration events reported in the East European literature.

First, coordinated or joint planning along the lines charted in the Complex Program can only yield decisive results in the medium to long run. Although it is certainly true that some concrete integration measures were implemented as a result of their explicit inclusion in the annual economic plans for 1974–1975 of some CPEs,[2] regionwide dovetailed measures inspired by the program could be incorporated into a comprehensive setting only in the current medium-term economic plans (1976–1980), and concrete results therefore only became visible toward the end of the 1970s (as demonstrated, for example, by the recent completion of several construction projects of the Concerted Plan).

Second, it is useful to distinguish between actual reductions of the existing disparities in relative costs – the gauge of economic integration success adopted here – and preliminary steps that may eventually lead to this narrowing. As discussed below, most measures taken so far probably fall by and large in this second category precisely because, after several years of wrangling over the most important means by which the Complex Program should be implemented, it is only recently that effective integration measures have been introduced in the form of a realistically coordinated plan. As an East German planner has correctly noted, the Concerted Plan "can be characterized *in se* as the first document [of the CPEs] that expresses, by means of plan targets addressed to the countries, the shared interests in dovetailing the efforts directed at solving concrete economic problems" (Vorkauf 1977, p. 11).

Third, the general atmosphere engendered by the integration debate has led to many intensive mutual consultations on desirable economic cooperation involving a tremendous exchange of information and technical know-how, so much so that one may expect production specialization to be pursued much more intensively than was the case hitherto. This in itself may be rationalized as a successful implementation of the program, although tangible results in the production, consumption, and trade spheres will become apparent only in the future.

Finally, little attention seems to have been paid so far to the precisely defined deadlines for common action mentioned in the program, in spite of the initially highly positive expectations. But agreement on other, isolated questions in the microeconomic sphere has been attained in the meantime (see below). However, if these agreements had produced the impact forecast in the program and in accompanying statements, would the recent literature not have been replete with much more lively and intensive discussions of such achievements? Because this has not been the case, it appears plausible that the CPEs have already fallen substantially behind schedule in several key areas of integration.[3]

In any event, there is at the moment a considerable lack of uniformity in Eastern as well as Western assessments of integration achievements. Most of the divergent views would seem to stem either from conceptual problems of what integration is all about and of how its effects could be quantified in a synthetic indicator, or from substantive problems of interpreting what is claimed to have been measured. Though the CPEs established close reciprocal economic relations in the early postwar years and contend that they have been actively pursuing SEI for a number of years, the effect of this regionalization effort is by no means clear. Because SEI is by and large a vaguely defined policy objective and its precise implementation mechanism remains unclear, it is difficult to conceptualize this policy operationally, and, hence, to specify what should be quantified. Second, even if the first type of problem can be surmounted, the researcher faces the quite formidable task of resolving numerous methodological and pure data problems typical for such an exercise. Nevertheless, it will be of interest to obtain some broad idea and a quantitative gauge of the possible effects of SEI.

2. Measuring integration effects for Eastern Europe

According to one astute observer, "full integration between two or more countries . . . is not reached as long as they still show the volume of trade between them" (Machlup 1977, p. 24). By that standard, no association of independent economies, except perhaps the BLEU, can be termed "fully integrated." Given the definition of economic integration of this study, the stage reached is essentially a relative concept whose measurement involves a ratio of actually realized to potentially attainable opportunities for a regional division of labor. The crucial problem in pursuing such an endeavor, as F. Machlup points out, is now precisely that "we may have learned how to measure actual trade, actual migration, actual capital movements, but we have not yet learned how to measure the unused potential" (Machlup 1977, p. 27). Furthermore, integration policies affect to a varying extent the entire "environment" of the participants, and measurements of the degree of integration attained will hence get bogged down in intractable conceptual problems of "welfare." Before discussing the various types of empirical exercises found in the literature, it will be worthwhile to digress briefly and take up the issue of what integration is likely to produce.

On the effects of integration

If integration means the gradual narrowing of differences in relative economic scarcities between two or more economies, clearly, quantification of results involves the assessment of real relative scarcities at various points in time, something that economists do not really know how to pin down exactly. Direct measurement is therefore not feasible. But an indirect measure is possible on the assumption that integration decisions impact on trade, for trade normally helps to bridge differences in relative scarcities. Though foreign trade is not necessarily the direct goal of integration policies, it is frequently its most visible result and, in most experiments, the most conspicuous medium through which the participants hope to narrow their disparities and, incidentally, also to further their more general sociopolitical objectives. In other words, trade is the quintessence of economic integration, the central filter for promoting the regional division of labor.

In spite of the fact that union formation does not only affect trade, most empirical inquiries of integration achievements have been cast around the price effect of tariff changes. Prices and tariffs provide a useful starting point because they are measurable in money, whereas other trade restrictions lifted as a result of integration cannot be analyzed as subtly and rigorously; and because tariffs are more susceptible than other restrictions to concerted international action, the most interesting integration element from the analytical and policy point of view is the revision of custom duties. These and other shifts in trade controls entail a restructuring of prices and, hence, of demand and supply schedules. To estimate the trade effects of such adaptations, several studies have focused on a comparison of overall or compositional trade shares or trade levels before and after the implementation of revised tariffs. Provided one adopts a strong assumption on how trade would have developed without the tariff changes, the estimation of the size and sign of trade effects stemming from integration is, conceptually at least, quite straightforward.

CPEs cannot anchor a similar phasing of their integration process to gradual tariff harmonization simply because they do not seek to regulate foreign trade, especially in the CMEA, by means of conventional trade instruments such as tariff walls.[4] Analytically speaking, the actual differences between internal and trade prices of CPEs can be treated as implicit tariffs and subsidies designed to promote some socioeconomic objectives of the planner and to discriminate de facto between CMEA and other regions (Broner 1975, p. 30; Pelzman 1977, p. 713). But substantive differences between such tariffs in MTEs and in CPEs should be noted: In the latter, implicit tariffs are not ad valorem because they are defined as the difference between internal and external prices, they are known only ex post, and the size of the tariff varies also with shifts in domestic prices, which are enacted administratively, not necessarily in response to real economic forces. In an operational sense, then, such tariffs cannot be utilized to study integration effects for CPEs nor for that matter do differences between internal and external prices yield reliable yardsticks about the level of protection maintained in the CPEs as long as these economies insist on pursuing autonomous domestic price policies and the MFT precludes effective competition from abroad.

Even if one were to embark on estimating the customs union effects in CPEs by utilizing implicit duties, severe conceptual problems are necessarily encountered. For example, trade of the CPEs prior to the "integration decision" is probably suboptimal, owing to the fact that the CPEs are generally in persistent disequilibrium, including in trade. The suboptimal trade position not only implies less trade than would be desirable on the basis of comparative cost considerations. The CPEs also trade goods that under competitive conditions would not have materialized. Furthermore, SEI only marginally resembles market integration, where prices are a key allocation criterion and price movements are instrumental in gradually narrowing differences in relative scarcities. For these and other reasons, SEI may or may not change the members' static trade conditions, as distinct from the future implications of production specialization – the main vehicle to enhance greater regional interdependence in Eastern Europe. In particular, changes in the level, composition, or distribution of trade cannot be imputed to changes in relative prices. In view of intra-CMEA price-setting techniques, it is in any case unclear whether SEI entails shifts in trade prices and that they are reduced relative to prices faced in trade with nonmembers. Furthermore, given that domestic prices in CPEs do not clear markets and trade decisions are not solely based on comparative advantage indicators, the decision to integrate may or may not stimulate regional trade, perhaps through trade diversion. On the strength of the above arguments, it is difficult to specify a priori how SEI will transform trade of the CPEs.

The CPEs endeavor to strengthen their regional dependence especially through the extensive use of "agreed specialization" in preference to more customary market instruments. In some essential aspects this policy resembles the advice frequently given to developing countries (Harrod 1962; Kojima 1970; Myrdal 1956), but there are also palpable differences, especially those arising from the peculiar planning and other institutions of the CPEs. In both cases, however, the essence of integration consists of securing the scale economies of belonging to a larger market, not ex post chiefly by tariff manipulations, but ex ante by some previous agreement about the future profile of economic activities in these countries, and the members may have to resist pressure from more competitive producers outside the integrating markets. In other words, participants in agreed specialization are primarily interested in dynamic effects that, given the diversity of resource endowments and potential for development, may in any case be larger than the static gains from trade, especially in countries such as the CPEs whose economies are protection-ridden and who are similar in the structure of industrial production.

To the extent that precise information is available on the implementation of specialization agreements, it should be a rather simple exercise to quantify the resulting trade effects, if not the precise welfare gains. However, specialization enacted in the CMEA region so far does not seem to have greatly influenced domestic and trade prices, which in any case continue to be governed by nonscarcity considerations, for the effects of scale economies on real costs are largely ignored in the formation of CMEA trade prices. Furthermore, getting pertinent information on specialization protocols in order to obtain an estimate of trade effects is virtually impossible. Even less is known about the implementation of these agreements and their influence on production and trade profiles. The concrete circumstances and special features of CMEA specialization therefore appreciably complicate a reasonable assessment of the trade effects of SEI.

Methods of measuring integration effects

Most quantification efforts use one or another conventional approach anchored to observable trade events. Trade effects of integration can be estimated either ex ante or ex post (Verdoorn 1972). In both cases a comparison is made between actual events and a hypothetical *anti-monde* – in the ex ante case, that integration policies themselves will not modify demand and supply, and, in the ex post case, that without integration policies the observable preintegration world would have prevailed indefinitely.

In the ex ante measurement technique as applied in most studies, prices and their expected changes before and after integration appear explicitly in the model as exogenous variables. To apply this technique in the case of CPEs, one would have to build a model of their trade behavior in conjunction with a realistic strategy linking real costs rather than prices with trade decision making, owing to the special formation of domestic and trade prices in these countries. Although such a model could undoubtedly be constructed, obtaining meaningful empirical evidence to test integration effects is virtually precluded for want of pertinent information and also because of data paucity.

Ex post measurements are usually based on some kind of residual imputation technique, which inevitably lumps together a number of distinctly different effects (e.g., tariff effects on trade flows, exchange rate corrections to maintain balance of payments equilibrium, tariff and exchange rate effects on production patterns, cost effect of larger markets, and so on). In addition, these techniques cannot separate the enumerated effects from such immeasurables as increased promotional efforts, increased factor migration, and so on following from integration. In spite of these drawbacks, most estimates of the trade effects of SEI rely on one variant or another of residual imputation of shifts in trade levels, the geographical distribution of trade, or in the observed expenditure shares of apparent consumption between any year and one or more hypothetical trade predictions derived from the counterfactual world specified. Such shifts are examined and interpreted in the light of known integration decisions or other special measures that bear on trade participation and the distribution of trade. The advantage of the share approach, for example, is that it requires a fairly simple technique for which data can be constructed and that it shows directly and separately trade creation and trade diversion. The disadvantages are, however, considerable. As in most ex post studies, the supply side of trade is neglected and so is the evolution of price ratios between competing imports, which impairs the conclusions with regard to trade diversion. Furthermore, systematic shifts in the home share arising, for instance, from growth policies, home pressure of demand, structural changes outside the framework of integration policies, and other such factors, are neglected; this may throw some doubt on the conclusions derived from the trade creation estimates. Similar problems arise with forecasting trade levels under an hypothesized structure. Some of these drawbacks could be eliminated by choosing an alternative estimation technique (Verdoorn 1972) that takes into account supply as well as demand. However, such refinements cannot be applied to the CPEs until a larger volume of consistent data becomes available.

Depending upon the impact of integration on domestic production and consumption, trade effects of integration will be felt by the region or other partners or both. With reference to the expenditure share approach, the concept "trade creation" is reserved for instances of a reduction in the domestic share, which can be absorbed by partners or nonmembers or both. The term "trade diversion" denotes a decrease in the trade share of members (nonmembers) absorbed by the nonmembers (members) or by domestic production or both. It is also possible, though perhaps rather implausible, that the domestic share increases at the expense of trade with both members and nonmembers. That case is referred to as negative trade creation or trade erosion. The possible pattern of decomposed shifts in apparent consumption shares is outlined in Table 2, but usually some combination of the events listed occurs. The normal trade effects of integration are expected to be trade creation at least with the region and trade diversion at most external to the region. These are the familiar Vinerian effects of customs union formation.

Trade effects and CMEA integration

The concepts trade creation, diversion, and erosion are typically defined as shifts induced by price changes. Thus, a reduction in the domestic price is a necessary condition for Vinerian trade creation for which the level of consumption is held constant, but can of course also result from an increase in consumption. Without a decline in domestic prices, there may be no trade creation but there can be external trade diversion. Now, because domestic prices in the CPEs do not perform the allocatory role attributed to prices in MTEs and are not synchronized with actual trade prices, how can trade creation, diversion, or erosion occur when trade decisions are not chiefly based on prices?

As discussed, the prime instrument for enhancing SEI is the dovetailing of production intentions, especially through detailed

Table 2. *Possible pattern of shifts in apparent consumption shares*

	Domestic	Partners	Nonmembers
Trade creation			
External	−	0	+
Internal	−	+	0
Trade diversion			
External	0	+	−
Internal	0	−	+
Trade erosion			
External	+	0	−
Internal	+	−	0

specialization agreements that in time will directly affect the structure of production and, presumably, real costs of the signatory countries. Provided these decisions can be identified, one could still interpret the ensuing trade shifts in terms of trade creation, diversion, or erosion by attributing these events to changes in *real* costs of which the planners may or may not be explicitly aware. The real problem of justifying the use of Western terminology in the context of SEI stems not so much from the difficulties engendered by different price policies and institutions, but from a combination of the following factors.[5]

The concepts trade creation, diversion, and erosion are typically defined for economies that are in equilibrium: A change in static efficiency conditions, for instance, resulting from relative price changes through tariff revisions, will require a different allocation of domestic resources and trade. Similarly for agreed specialization, which will affect the dynamic conditions for efficient resource allocation. Shifts in production and trade away from what would have prevailed without integration measures will be interpreted in terms of trade creation and diversion.

If such specialization measures are now adopted by economies that are not in equilibrium, the observed shifts in production and trade are likely to be a combination of the effects of agreed specialization and adjustment measures that move the economic structure of the members toward greater equilibirum. Given that the CPEs tolerate persistent disequilibria in internal and external resource allocation, when these economies specialize it is conceivable, and in some instances highly probable, that shifts will be induced in resource allocation that are not all related to these agreements. Thus, the share of imports in apparent consumption, for instance, may or may not increase, and it is by no means assured that the share of members in apparent consumption will rise. In other words, the formulation of the probable counterfactual world, quite formidable in the case of MTEs, is further compounded by features inherent in the actual institutions and policies of the CPEs. The problem is even more complex because CPEs choose trade partners on the basis of criteria in which relative prices are not necessarily the main consideration. For instance, the high level of regional trade concentration of the CPEs is probably not mainly because of economic factors. Any policy designed to improve efficiency would have called for greater attention to relative prices and, hence, might have induced shifts in the participation in trade as well as in its distribution, regardless of regional integration policies. Similarly, a relaxation of tensions separating CPEs from other countries may induce shifts in the distribution of trade and, possibly, in the trade level as well.

Because the CPEs have recently shown great concern for promoting "intensive growth" by reallocating resources and better planning, it would seem unrealistic to expect, for example, consumption shares calculated for any representative past period to persist for any length of time even in the absence of specialization agreements. Regardless of SEI efforts, the CPEs could have been expected to seek greater reliance on trade in general. To what extent this may yield a bias in estimated trade effects depends, of course, on the strategy associated with domestic growth priorities of the CPEs. On the strength of these arguments, it would seem advisable to construct several alternative counterfactual scenarios at least to test the sensitivity of results derived from constant share hypotheses.[6]

Estimated trade effects

Partial or overall effects of SEI for one or more CPEs have been estimated by a number of scholars in East and West. Most West-

ern empirical analyses have focused on the overall trade participation of the CPEs and have emphasized that the CPEs' trade
level is generally substantially below that which would be anticipated for MTEs of similar size and level of development.
Whether this trade aversion stems from SEI or not is a moot
point, though some researchers have attributed the CPEs' "low
level" of trade to their participation in the CMEA. Others have
projected the CPEs' trade on the basis of some past or "typical"
performance, and compared actual and hypothetical levels of
trade specifically in the light of SEI decisions. East European
scholars have rarely attempted to quantify in a synthetic measure the trade effects of SEI; at least, few such investigations
have been published. Most of the available empirical studies
have been constructed around the following: (1) savings in outlays resulting from a single cooperation venture; (2) analyses of
the level, commodity composition, and geographical distribution
of trade; or (3) one measure or another of production specialization. The more interesting quantification endeavors will be
briefly reviewed below.

East European measurements
The demonstration of unity in sociopolitical and economic affairs in conjunction with some observations about regional trade
dependences are usually taken as sufficient evidence for the success of SEI, though not all East European economists content
themselves so easily. Indeed, a score of these scholars has leveled
harsh criticism against the sluggish pace of SEI and the lack of
enthusiasm or political will to modernize the "integration mechanism" and its supporting institutions. Regardless of the writer's
bent, however, the paucity of published empirical inquiries into
the matter at hand is quite remarkable; even rarer are studies
that disclose comprehensive details about data sources and
methodology.

If they buttress at all their assessment of SEI by empirical
measures, most East European investigators take trade data in
evidence. Inevitably, reference is to the high level of growth of
intraregional trade, the large share of regional to total trade,
and the "progressive" structure of trade in that a large share of
trade is in finished manufactures. This usually leads to optimistic conclusions as, from the early postwar years, the CPEs have

transacted the bulk of their overall trade among themselves. Though there have been some slight variations in time and across countries, it is still true that the CPEs clear roughly 40 percent (in the case of Rumania) to 80 percent (in the case of Bulgaria) of total trade with the CMEA, by far the largest part with the USSR. Consequently, the trade dependence of any CPE is largely also a function of the economic conditions and institutional arrangements characteristic of the CMEA region. From an economic point of view, however, this high degree of regional trade dependence in itself cannot be taken as a pointer of the advanced stage of SEI, though it does, of course, support the thesis of the advanced stage of regional trade dependence (possibly with political and other ramifications implied by this trade dependence). If one were to accept the proposition that integration leads to a higher concentration of trade with the preferred area, one would as a matter of fact have to conclude to an apparent disintegration of the CMEA, as trade with other countries from about 1965 to 1975 expanded very rapidly in volume and quantum and, with few exceptions, exceeded the growth of regional trade.

The degree of regional specialization in production is potentially a more useful concept in that it directly bears on the definition of integration adopted here. To the extent that members decide to concentrate production, at least to some degree, according to regional comparative advantages, promoting specialization agreements will presumably narrow differences in relative scarcities and will, hence, signal a more advanced stage of regional integration. East European reports usually measure the degree of regional specialization as the share of export or import products about which the members have signed specialization protocols relative to total regional trade. Owing to the special definition embraced, these indices are not very illuminating because they fail to express the degree to which the agreements have been implemented, if at all, and, hence, to what extent they have impacted on actual production and consumption behavior in the region (see Brabant 1974, pp. 270–275). To take one example, East Germany reportedly increased its export specialization index from 1 percent in 1970–1971 to 17 percent in 1974–1975 (*Die Wirtschaft*, 1976:5, p. 25; Haupt 1978, p. 31), and is currently aiming at raising it to 25 to 30 percent by 1980. Similar figures can be cited for many other members. Clearly, because the composition of East Germany's CMEA exports in 1970–1975 did not change drastically and no determined, indepth transformation of the export profile under impact of specialization agreements can be identified, the measure does not appear to be very useful. Sometimes such indices are supplemented with indicators of the number of bilateral and multilateral specialization agreements, the participation of various CPEs in them, or the share of production affected by such protocols. Needless to say, such supplementary information, though not completely devoid of interest, is not very helpful in assessing empirically the trade effects of SEI measures.

Partial indicators of SEI effects abound, but they are difficult to evaluate, and aggregating them into a synthetic measure is contingent on a very complex procedure that is likely to yield questionable results, expecially because a number of components can only be roughly guessed. To give two examples, it is said that the cost of the Družba pipeline – about 400 million rubles – was recovered after two to three years of substituting pipeline shipment for more conventional carriers (Kohlmey 1974, p. 138); or by the end of 1977 the CPEs had saved more than twice the cost they would have incurred had they not had access to electrical energy through the Mir power grid (Bauman 1978, p. 25). Sometimes savings in hard currency imports as a result of specialization measures (e.g., special types of ball bearings) are given in volume substituted for. Because these East European measures do not yield a synthetic indicator of what the trade effects of SEI may have amounted to, they will be discussed no further here.

Some Western analyses
Generally speaking, three different but related types of measurement of the trade effects of SEI can be identified: (1) a comparison of actual with "normal" trade levels, (2) a comparison based on actual and hypothetical trade levels, and (3) an examination of production specialization.

Many scholars, including some East Europeans, have made comparisons between actual and "normal" trade levels of CPEs. Normal in this context is defined as the trade that the CPE could have attained had it traded as an "average economy" of approximately equal size and economic wealth as the sample countries deemed to be normal traders. Usually, simple export or import

functions for MTEs are estimated, and the parameter values are
then utilized to derive hypothetical levels of total trade or trade
by commodity groups for CPEs (Brabant 1973, pp. 194–201).
Comparing these hypothetical trade levels with trade attained,
these studies purport to show that the CPEs generally trade substantially below their "potential" and that their commodity composition of trade differs markedly from what would have been
attained had the CPEs behaved like comparable MTEs. This
approach is not capable of disclosing anything about the geographical distribution of trade, though some researchers have
speculated about the reasons for the "low" trade level and the
differences in commodity composition, in that in addition to the
trade-inhibiting features of central planning endemic to each
CPE separately, they also regard their belonging to the CMEA
region as trade-reducing.

   In order to assess geographical trade preferences, several investigators have estimated "normal" bilateral trade flows by dis-
aggregating import demand and export supply functions of
"typical" countries into bilateral trade flows. These equations are
usually specified as one variant or another of the gravity equation of international trade flows, whose general form is as follows:

$$X_{ij} = f(Y_i, Y_j, N_i, N_j, D_{ij}, P_{ij}, O_{ij}) \qquad (11)$$

where X_{ij} is exports (or imports) of country i to (from) country j;
Y is a macroeconomic aggregate such as GNP; N is population; D
is the distance separating the markets of i and j; P is a preference
variable for relations between i and j; and O stands here for
other variables that may be specified (e.g., level of development,
shifts in economic structure). Depending upon the particular
objective of the study, estimated parameters of equation 11 in
cross-section analyses are used to obtain hypothetical trade levels
of CPEs, and these magnitudes are then compared with actual
trade levels. Alternatively, equation 11 is estimated for one
period on the basis of data for CPEs or MTEs or both. Projections into the future of trade levels for CPEs are then used to obtain an inference about integration effects.

   On the basis of the first approach – the estimation of
"normal trade levels" in cross-section analysis – researchers
have generally confirmed speculation that CPEs trade substantially below normal levels and that they have a strong pref-

erence for trade with the CMEA. This approach was pioneered by Pryor 1963, pp. 27–28, and many others have followed up with refinements. Whether or not the difference between actual and hypothetical or potential trade levels is attributable to SEI is usually left unanswered. A. Broner, however, has explicitly used the model to infer about the effects of SEI on the level and geographical direction of trade of the seven CPEs included in this study (Broner 1975, 1976) and claims to have found evidence that the CPEs, excepting the USSR, trade substantially above typical levels of MTEs and that their above-"normal" interaction with their preferred region is in large measure attributable to SEI policies. Because most writers do not explicitly link their findings to SEI, further discussion of this type of analysis will be confined to an examination of Broner's investigation (for details about other studies, see Brabant 1978; Brada 1978; Hewett 1976a). Some researchers have used the gravity equation to project the CPEs' counterfactual world on the basis of their trade behavior before the "decision" to adhere to SEI policies, and these findings have been linked directly with conclusions about the trade effects of SEI. The latter are estimated as the difference between projected trade (i.e., the aggregate of X_{ij} for some sets of js) and actually observed trade volume on the assumption that the trade structure estimated for some set of countries in a period preceding SEI decisions would have remained unchanged if the CPEs had not adopted an integration strategy.

Using 1960 and 1970 observations on trade flows for fourteen non-CPE exporting countries with eighty-three importing countries, including CPEs, Broner recently estimated the trade effect of SEI for each of the seven CPEs. The interpretation of the results differs slightly in terms of terminology from that underlying the definitions introduced here. Broner and Pelzman, whose findings are discussed below, denote the sum of differences between projected and actual trade with the region "gross trade creation" (GTC), whereas a similar sum for non-CMEA partners is called "trade diversion" (TD), which, if positive, is actually external trade creation (as defined in Table 2) when GTC is positive and internal trade diversion when GTC is negative. Though the writers cannot distinguish rigorously between trade creation and trade diversion, their net result – called "net trade creation" (NTC) – is a concept that will be

Table 3. *Estimates of trade creation and trade diversion in the CMEA for 1970* (in millions of current U.S. dollars)

	Broner[a]	Pelzman[b]
Bulgaria		
GTC[c]	1,332	1,308
TD[d]	−107	−60
NTC[e]	1,439	1,368
Czechoslovakia		
GTC	1,730	1,623
TD	771	552
NTC	959	1,071
East Germany		
GTC	2,250	2,351
TD	1,432	818
NTC	818	1,533
Hungary		
GTC	1,129	1,090
TD	−155	−39
NTC	1,284	1,129
Poland		
GTC	1,434	957
TD	509	−316
NTC	925	1,274
Rumania		
GTC	623	642
TD	−196	−314
NTC	819	956
Soviet Union		
GTC	4,330	5,249
TD	11,527	−518
NTC	−7,197	5,767
Total		
GTC	12,828	13,222
TD	13,780	122
NTC	−952	13,099

[a] Calculated from Broner's normal estimates and his data for actual trade in 1970 (Broner 1976, pp. 488–490).
[b] Pelzman 1976a, pp. 10–11. These data are pre-

utilized below because it is comparable to the concepts introduced above in the section "Methods of measuring integration effects."

For the CMEA area as a whole, NTC in 1970 in Broner's findings was negative (see Table 3), owing to the very strong TD effect allegedly experienced by the USSR. Although all CPEs attained a respectable level of GTC amounting in the aggregate to roughly $13,000 million, TD was even larger (some $14,000 million). For all countries but the USSR, the extent of TD was substantially less – in some cases of negative sign, signaling external trade creation – than the amount of internal trade creation. A ratio of GTC to actual regional trade yields a range of 62 to 68 percent (the lower level is for the USSR and the higher applies to Bulgaria); these shares are attributed to SEI or "explained" in the wake of SEI decisions.

A slightly different, but potentially more interesting, approach was chosen by J. Pelzman (Pelzman 1976, 1976a, 1977). Using the gravity equation estimated for a combined period 1960–1964 for all CPEs, he projected "normal" trade in subsequent years, including 1970, the results of which are reproduced in Table 3. With a somewhat higher GTC effect than that reported by Broner, Pelzman found TD only on the order of $122 million, yielding an overall NTC effect of about $13,000 million. The results for individual CPEs, except Poland and the USSR, reported in the two investigations are roughly identical. However, results for the two other CPEs differ substantially and

---

Notes to Table 3 (*cont.*)

sumably revisions of the estimates published in Pelzman 1976, p. 47, especially for Poland and Rumania, and agree with the totals reported in Pelzman 1977, p. 718.

[c] "Gross trade creation," in Pelzman's definition, is equivalent to "net internal trade creation" as defined in the text.

[d] "Trade diversion" is the sum of trade replaced by trade with the region and trade from the region. A negative sign signals, in the terminology used here, "external trade creation" *on balance.*

[e] The algebraic sum of GTC and TD as defined by Pelzman.

for the USSR the reverse sign of NTC is obtained. With regard to the share of trade attributed to SEI, Pelzman obtains a range of 67 percent for Czechoslovakia and 87 percent for Bulgaria. Judged on the basis of these findings, SEI is purported to have very strongly impacted on the trade of all CPEs, and the magnitudes reported border at the fantastic. It would indeed be hard to imagine even the most avid CMEA proselytizer suggesting in earnest that such high shares of regional trade of the CPEs in 1970 as obtained by Broner and Pelzman should be imputed to SEI.

The two experiments briefly reviewed here are unsatisfactory inasmuch as the investigations suffer from a number of conceptual, data, and methodological shortcomings that cloud the results (see Brabant 1977b, 1978; Brada 1978). Fundamental problems arise from one or more of the following: (1) The question of "normality" is not adequately addressed; (2) differences in price regimes in intra- and extra-CMEA trade are not taken into account; (3) the models cannot differentiate between trade creation attributable to SEI and that resulting from the substantial trade-promoting policies pursued by the CPEs in recent years; (4) in some cases, the specification retained for projection exercises is inadequate; and (5) no attempt is made to take into account the appreciable differences in trade behavior of the various CPEs and MTEs.

It is admittedly very difficult to quantify the trade effects of SEI, if only because such a policy has never been spelled out in detail so that it could be handled operationally in analogy to tariff reductions in MTEs. Yet, some further empirical evidence can be constructed on the basis of various alternative assumptions. For this reason, a more narrowly focused study was undertaken with reference to Hungary's regional trade dependence, which yields as a by-product alternative estimates of trade effects on the assumption, in one version, that all shifts in trade shares between some base period and prospective actual shares resulted from integration measures.[7] Some of the results are summarized in Table 4. Admittedly, the findings should be interpreted with caution for reasons explained below.

Alternative estimates yield uniformly a net internal trade creation effect for Hungary of about $178 million to $267 million in 1970, which is substantially less than the roughly $1,100 million obtained by both Broner and Pelzman. Furthermore, these results show that there has been apparently a considerable volume of TD and some trade erosion as well, especially affecting the non-CMEA partners. Most of the NTC occurred between 1965–1970, a period of rapid expansion in Hungary's trade resulting to a large extent from the very drastic shifts in economic policies then consistently implemented. Finally, in recent years the TD effect on balance tends to outweigh the trade creation realized with all partners taken together. It bears stressing, however, that these results are tentative and cannot solely be attributed to SEI. To the extent that they shed light on SEI, they show that, with few exceptions, trade effects have been rather small if not adverse altogether. Moreover, in none of the alternative scenarios about how shares in apparent consumption would have fluctuated without SEI (Brabant 1979a) was it found that the timing of major SEI decisions – such as the documents endorsed in 1962 and 1971 – had any significant impact on Hungary's changing import dependence, at least in a short- to medium-term perspective. But this may indicate also that one should not restrict the investigated horizon too much, as argued in more detail below.

A third and final set of empirical investigations has attempted to detect the effect, if any, of CMEA specialization in industrial finished manufactures on various sources of supply of the apparent domestic consumption of such investment goods. J. M. Montias pioneered this type of inquiry for Rumania (Montias 1968, pp. 135–140) and found that, generally speaking, the CMEA supply of investment goods is much more embedded in the domestic consumption of such goods than procurements from outside the region, but still considerably less than the role of domestic supply. This would tend to indicate that the CMEA supply of engineering goods is better integrated in Rumania's demand than what is procured from the world market. However, on the basis of results obtained by applying a similar technique to data for Bulgaria, Hungary, Poland, and Rumania over a longer time span than could be used by Montias, it was found difficult to generalize Montias's hypothesis for all CPEs investigated and indeed to sustain it over time (Brabant 1974, pp. 281–293). Furthermore, it was unclear whether such security of supply from the region increased over time or not, and whether

Table 4. *Summary of trade effects for Hungary (millions of constant U.S. dollars[a])*

	Base 1960[b]			Base 1965		Base 1970	
	1965	1970	1976	1970	1976	1975	1976
Gross trade creation[c]	154.2	605.5	808.3	471.9	632.6	488.3	187.8
Internal	132.9	289.7	622.6	229.7	544.8	468.9	176.2
External	21.3	315.8	185.7	242.2	87.8	19.4	11.6
Trade erosion[d]	70.3	8.1	73.9	90.2	80.4	142.6	119.0
Internal	39.1	−80.7	−187.1	6.2	−100.9	−103.0	−222.6
External	31.2	88.8	261.0	84.0	181.3	245.6	341.6
Trade diversion[e]	55.3	200.5	309.6	45.1	186.2	272.4	88.9
Internal	46.6	103.0	113.4	45.1	43.7	—	
External	8.7	97.5	196.2	—	142.5	272.4	88.9
Net trade creation[f]	28.6	396.9	424.8	336.6	366.0	73.3	−20.1
Internal	47.2	267.4	696.3	178.4	602.0	571.9	398.8
External	−18.6	129.5	−271.5	158.2	−236.0	−498.6	−418.9

The data are the sum of trade effects for the five commodity groups of the Hungarian trade classification, as discussed in detail in Brabant 1978b, 1979a.

[a] *Deviza* forint values in comparable CMEA unit values of 1972 are converted into predevaluation U.S. dollars at the official exchange rate.

[b] The commodity group machinery is evaluated against the 1962 base-year for reasons explained in Brabant 1978b, 1979a.

[c] The sum of gross internal and external trade creation. "Internal trade creation" is the value of the increase in regional

trade when actual domestic supply is lower than the value of the hypothetical supply. Likewise for "external trade creation," which refers to the increase in nonmember trade.

[d] The sum of internal and external trade erosion. "Internal trade erosion" is the value of regional trade replaced by the increase in domestic supply, relative to the hypothetical level; likewise for "external trade erosion." A negative sign indicates that the value of domestic supply increased but so did trade with the region or, as the case may be, with other partners.

[e] The sum of internal and external trade diversion. "Internal trade diversion" is the value of trade with the region that is apparently being replaced by an increase in trade with other partners; "external trade diversion" is the reverse.

[f] The sum of net internal and external trade creation. "Internal trade creation" is the algebraic sum of gross trade creation, trade diversion, and trade erosion with the region; likewise for "net external trade creation."

the CMEA actually acts as a more stable supplier than the rest of the world, at least for the type of traded goods dealt with in the study. Generally speaking, it was found that for most countries and for most time periods investigated, the level of purported specialization in the apparent domestic consumption of machinery and equipment did not increase sharply and, on the aggregate level studied, in several instances it declined.

Summary and pointers for SEI effects

Without embarking on an in-depth investigation of the comparative merits of the various quantification efforts briefly summarized here, one must recall that the issue of assessing trade effects stemming from integration policies is very complex and that the available results are far from conclusive – indeed, sometimes they conflict. Nonetheless the reported magnitudes tend to indicate that, when noticeable at all at the aggregate level of these studies, the trade effects of SEI appear to have been rather small and, in any case, substantially less than what would seem to be subsumed or claimed by many East European assessments of SEI's positive contribution to the economic development of the CPEs. This does not, of course, unambiguously prove that without SEI the CPEs could have reproduced the levels of trade or the rate of national income growth actually attained in the past decades. Although this point might, admittedly, seem to contradict what was said earlier, upon reflection it will be found not to be so.

First, owing to the disequilibrium state of the CPEs, SEI efforts have probably induced a more rational allocation of resources, especially on the microeconomic level, which in turn has given rise to a substitution of traded products. In other words, without SEI the CPEs might have found it very difficult to sustain the level and composition of traditional trade activities or the trade that would have come on stream as a result of completely uncoordinated domestic industrialization policies – a possibility that cannot be tested by the techniques applied in the empirical investigations.[8]

Second, a familiar phenomenon accompanying rapid economic change is that import substitution occurs and caters to additional demand requirements but is not necessarily embraced to replace all basic imports. This will necessarily compress the import share in domestic consumption.

Third, most integration measures agreed upon by the CPEs are designed to lead to adjustments in the production structure. The implementation process is likely to be prolonged because it is spread over several plan periods and ratification of specialization protocols does not necessarily imply that effective measures will be embraced to transform the affected production units accordingly.

Finally, SEI is also concerned with issues that transcend trade or that affect trade activities only indirectly. In some cases the trade effects may even be negative. For example, the free exchange of technical and scientific information agreed upon already in 1949 – whatever its inherent merits – probably compressed imports of some products and, hence, reduced the "integration index." Whether this is good economic policy from the point of view of SEI really depends on comparative cost considerations, which cannot be assessed on the basis of the available evidence.

The relatively discouraging empirical evidence reported above, however, should not be taken as the last word in evaluating SEI effects. Especially in the context of "agreed specialization," to which some CPEs have been avidly dedicated since the mid-1950s, it is recommendable to combine quantitative evidence with supporting qualitative information, even though the latter is much more intractable and may entail considerable misunderstanding. Nonetheless, in that light agreed specialization has been doubtlessly bearing fruit, especially since the late 1960s, but this may well fail to show up in trade statistics. To illustrate this proposition, it is useful to separate the evidence on agreed specialization into several classes.

Perhaps the greatest progress in SEI has been attained in a number of fields that contribute only indirectly as supportive branches to regional trade expansion and, partly for that reason, the evidence found on the basis of trade data is so meager and inconclusive. By coordinating joint efforts, the CPEs have succeeded in making substantial advance in elaborating a common infrastructure that facilitates the movement of goods and services. As mentioned in Chapter 4, achievements have been most

conspicuous in rationalizing general-purpose transportation facilities (such as the common wagon and container pool, freight
and railroad shipping, and so on) and in the construction of
special-purpose facilities (such as the common power grid, gas
and oil pipelines, and the generation of nuclear energy). SEI's
infrastructure has also been appreciably enhanced as a result of
joint efforts targeted at increasing the regional supply of basic
raw materials and fuels through capital and labor movements
across the region. These projects remain, of course, the property of the host country, which also plans and controls the construction projects and dovetails production with its overall economic and trade plans by means of fixed contracts for deliveries
in repayment of principal and interest to the participating CPEs.
The effect of these measures on trade has been nearly exclusively trade creating, albeit in some cases at the expense of interregional trade, in the sense that without such undertakings a
steady expansion of regular commercial relations would have
been much more difficult, if not precluded altogether.

Substantial efforts have been channeled into coordinating
economic activities through detailed bilateral and multilateral
specialization agreements, sometimes negotiated with the assistance of one or more Council organs including in some cases
IEOs, especially in the chemical and engineering branches. In
most instances, however, these specialization agreements, as
noted for the infrastructural agreements, have been contracted
in those fields for which the present and future advantages are
"indisputable" (Rutkowski 1977, p. 9), whereas a determined
search for streamlining the various production structures particularly to encourage intraproduct specialization has not so far
materialized in concrete agreements. Even in the case of finished products, for which most specialization protocols have
been signed, implementation remains uncertain. It has been estimated, for example, that only about half the signed agreements are actually put on stream in the participating CPEs, and
even for those that do get translated into concrete production
and trade targets, there are substantial deviations, ranging from
15 to 50 percent, from the volumes originally agreed upon
(Budnikowski 1977, p. 16).

Regardless of how these agreements are actually dovetailed
with current production, if at all, it is quite difficult to assess

their effect on trade of the signatory countries. The reason for this is that, although many contracts are clearly signed with a view toward creating trade, others are also inspired by concerns about saving on traditional hard currency outlays through regional import substitution or they are aimed at transforming the export or import profiles of the CPEs involved by weeding out "unwanted" products. Evaluation of the benefits of these agreements is even more difficult, for in many instances these agreements simply sanction the existing production structure in one branch or another (Rutkowski 1977, p. 10). Although some specialization agreements have certainly succeeded in curbing the magnitude of parallelism in some products with many variants that require essentially the same resource commitment, thereby enabling the CPEs to take advantage of scale economies (e.g., in ball bearings, rolled steel products), by their very nature most can succeed in fusing the relevant capacities only in a longer time frame. The majority of agreements implemented with a view toward creating trade can be grouped under two headings.

First, a significant number of agreements actually in force do not envisage the elimination of the existing degree of unwanted parallelism in the products under consideration by reallocating committed resources, but rather aim at the regulation and control of future resource allocations in combination with attrition of existing facilities. The immediate effect of these contracts is therefore small, if tangible at all, and in most cases amounts to stabilizing present trade patterns for the products under consideration. With regard to the medium and long run, however, the operative instrument of these agreements is how the present production and trade configuration will be transformed in future plan periods. Additions to capacity are expected to be planned only after compulsory dovetailing future needs and availabilities of the signatory countries (e.g., basic iron and steel capacities of most CPEs will henceforth be patterned according to CMEA-wide demand and supply) by means of specific trade contracts sought later in the context of medium- and long-term plan synchronization. As a result of these agreements, the so-called specialization index increases instantaneously, but most benefits of such SEI attempts for trade, production, and consumption will only materialize in the future. It should be noted also that most of these agreements have as their object the division of labor in finished products rather than a patient search for the least costly production assembly on the basis of parts and components procured from different partners. Examples here are ships (Poland), buses (Hungary), fork lifts (Bulgaria), and trucks (USSR).

Second, most successful agreements have been concluded for new products or potential additions to the product range offered on the CMEA market that generally require sophisticated, capital-intensive technologies well beyond what CPEs in isolation can afford. Perceptible results have been registered or are expected from jointly meeting present and future needs (e.g., microelectronics, computers, electronically controlled tooling equipment). In such cases, research, development, and production efforts are to be pooled with the explicit aim of stimulating technical progress from within the area.

In addition to infrastructural projects and agreements that are explicitly directed at specific production techniques, it should be acknowledged that cooperation in basic research has picked up momentum. Whether and to what extent these efforts will enhance specialization and SEI cannot be assessed with the information on hand, though scientific-technical cooperation is potentially perhaps the most crucial domain from which the CPEs will be able to extract measurable integration advantages in the long run, especially if these countries remain reluctant to enact internal and external economic reforms on a much more intensive scale than appears possible through the present administrative mechanisms of SEI.

3. East–West cooperation and SEI

The considerable relaxation of political and strategic tensions between East and West, especially on the European continent since the mid-1960s, has been accompanied by a very sharp upward drift in interregional trade, industrial cooperation, and capital movements (the latter mostly from West to East). Whereas until about the early 1960s, trade with MTEs was often resorted to as a temporary stop-gap covering for shortcomings or failures in CMEA planning and trade arrangements (Brown

1968a), as described in Chapter 3, more recently the CPEs have been activating the channels of reciprocal exchange offered by the advanced MTEs on a more extensive, perhaps permanent, basis. East–West trade has indeed become an increasingly important funnel for propping up and stimulating the intensification strategy of the CPEs and, more generally, for implementing desirable structural adaptations that otherwise would not have materialized at this stage, owing largely to the technological inferiority of most CPEs and also the innovation inhibitions embedded in their centralized planning system.

In the light of the by now vast literature on East–West trade and cooperation, to write something new or original on the topic is a difficult task. The arguments about the causes, content, and probable consequences of this burgeoning interregional interaction tend to be generally well known, and little if anything can be added without repeating worn-out clichés and restating some conventional wisdom about the advantages and possible drawbacks of this exchange. The fundamental premise subsumed in nearly all discourses on the reasons behind the surge in interregional relations amounts to the following: The CPEs badly needed technology to reinvigorate their economies, to attain once again high rates of growth, and to raise the levels of living of the population.[9] To reach these objectives, the CPEs are said to have been willing to relax international tensions. On the other hand, faced with growing unemployment, a shortage of raw materials, chronic inflation, and baffling balance of payments problems, the West allegedly saw in the CMEA markets a target or opportunity that would help to alleviate these various crises. In a political perspective, it is usually assumed that the CPEs were willing to grant political concessions in order to gain access to Western markets, particularly capital and advanced technology; and, conversely, the West was disposed toward accommodating such economic intercourse as a means of promoting political gains. Whatever the merits of this simplified thesis, the interested reader is probably sufficiently familiar with the full-scale argument or otherwise has ready access to the voluminous literature on East–West trade and cooperation. The causes, impacts, and drive of the markedly buoyant interaction are not the subject proper of this study and will only be referred to insofar as they intersect with SEI endeavors.

Although concerns about West European integration have been allotted some prominent role in explaining the importance of East–West trade, most studies have neglected to look into the possible impact of this interdependence on SEI. Though there are some valid reasons for eschewing the issue of SEI, inter-regional economic interaction has nonetheless potentially a non-trivial bearing on SEI, and the purpose of this section is to look at this hitherto largely neglected aspect of economic relations between the two powerful blocs. Although these topics have not been completely left untouched in the specialized literature, it is felt that many of the commonly embraced notions tend to be in-complete, if not altogether shortsighted.

There seems to be a consensus in the West about one or more of the following propositions: (1) East–West trade has been ex-ploited by the CPEs as a substitute for the prematurely aban-doned socioeconomic reforms; (2) this exchange offers more dy-namic possibilities than SEI for modernizing the economic profile of a majority of CPEs and, hence, leads to a better satis-faction of consumers in these countries; (3) the CPEs are not re-ally interested in pursuing SEI, and East–West trade has there-fore opened up promising vistas that should have been accessed decades ago; and (4) East–West trade has noneconomic over-tones that fit into the external policy concepts held overtly or covertly by one or another of the inherently antagonistic part-ners. Can one really make a genuine case for the proposition that buoyant East–West cooperation retards SEI? Does inter-regional trade intensification really affect SEI and, if so, to what extent? What are its implications for present and future region-alization efforts? Should one not also look into the reverse rela-tion and ask what might be the consequence of SEI for East–West trade?

Under the slogan "The economic recession in the West has done more to bind East Europe to the Soviet Union than all the plans dreamt up by bureaucrats in Moscow," N. Beloff recently stated (Beloff 1978, p. 38) in no uncertain terms a view widely shared by a number of Western observers: SEI is not coveted by a majority of the CPEs and will only be sought either if domestic production cannot cater to local demand or if alternative mar-kets cannot be tapped without incurring serious balance of pay-ments deficits or alienating the dominant partner in Eastern

Europe. This appears to be an oversimplified assessment of the very complex network of economic and other forces motivating the CPEs and MTEs into enlarging reciprocal contacts.

The linchpin of CMEA trade relations and supporting common activities has thus far been largely the USSR's willingness and ability to absorb increasing amounts of finished manufactures from the CMEA in exchange for fuels and industrial raw materials. On the basis of this empirical evidence, J. M. Montias has made a case for the following proposition (Montias 1974, p. 676): The smaller CPEs will be found reluctantly willing to endorse SEI or at least to cement their joint cooperation in some fields only for as long as the CMEA market is capable of satisfying basic import needs for raw materials and fuels at reasonable prices in exchange mainly for manufactures that cannot be sold in Western markets at prices comparable to those prevailing in the CMEA. This assertion implies that once the CMEA market – basically the USSR – is no longer in a position for economic or other reasons to support this exchange at favorable terms, the raison d'être "of CMEA would largely be gone as its members would be forced to seek other suppliers" (Korbonski 1976, p. 586). Korbonski has extended this proposition in advancing the thesis that "the continued growth of East–West trade is at the present time incompatible with an increase in the level of [SEI]" (Korbonski 1976, p. 570).

The crucial assumption implicit in most of the purported negative effects of East–West cooperation for SEI appears to be that the CPEs are either not genuinely interested in strengthening SEI or that efforts in that direction have been persistently frustrated under the impact, for instance, of the obstructions arising from the special type of organization and planning typical of these economies. Seeking intensive cooperation with non-CMEA partners would henceforth amount to a fundamental restructuring of the CPEs' international economic relations, not as a tactical device to shift the foundations of structural growth anchored to SEI without unduly burdening the domestic economies, but as a strategic choice with long-term implications for each CPE in particular and the region as a whole. Because it is already presumed that SEI will not be endorsed, there is little or no point in examining its possible impacts on East–West trade. By abstracting from the admittedly rather weak SEI results to date, one must inevitably arrive at the conclusion that there exists a substitution relationship, possibly irreversible, between the two alternative world markets.

Without denying that this proposition holds, of course, some measure of plausibility, especially in the short run, it is deemed instructive to look into the merits also of allowing for a degree of complementarity between the two separate channels for trade and cooperation. In contradistinction to the rather sweeping conclusions referred to above, it can be argued *a contrario* that, without doggedly pursuing SEI options, the CPEs will not be in a position to sustain intensive interchange with MTEs. This proposition's logic is essentially embedded in the cited negative appraisals. The smaller CPEs export to the CMEA basically manufactures in exchange for raw materials. Most of these products cannot be earmarked on satisfactory terms in the developed MTEs because they are substandard in one way or another (Holzman 1979, pp. 77–78). If now the USSR were to become unable to maintain this exchange because of: (1) its own interest in acquiring advanced technology in exchange for fuels and raw materials, which are assumed to be readily marketable in the West, (2) the soaring cost of producing raw materials, or (3) its ability to supply most manufactures presently acquired from the CMEA partners from home production, then the CPEs would have eventually to incur a devastating loss in terms of trade, thereby severely inhibiting further growth for as long as it would take to restructure their economic profile. To avert such an outcome, the CPEs are forced under the circumstances to seek measurable progress in SEI, especially by modernizing their industrial structure on the basis of complementarity without necessarily foregoing financial or other supports that will enable them to secure a basic supply of primary goods from within the region. Accordingly, the further maturing of SEI would take firm hold on the basis of production specialization, which is not inevitably anchored to the interbranch exchange of raw materials for below-standard manufactures. East–West trade may play a pivotal role in paving the road for or in bridging the difficulties associated with unavoidable structural adjustments, but it cannot substitute completely for SEI. Clearly, this proposition rests to a considerable extent on the assumption that the East European region will be able and permitted to explore alternative supply sources for fuels and raw materials when the region is no longer capable of propping up virtual autarky in those commodities. This scenario should not be dismissed prematurely, especially if the trading world will be spared a resurgence of a convoluted situation beset by disruptive political and strategic tensions entailing prohibitive protectionism. Without drawing the parallel too far, why would the CPEs not be able to pattern their economies on the basis of specialization in manufacturing branches, as has occurred in Western Europe?

By now it has become commonplace to emphasize the crucial role played by East–West cooperation in rapidly promoting technological transfer to the CMEA and, hence, significantly enhancing the CPEs' productivity levels. Similarly, the limits envisaged are seen largely in the CPEs' ability to modernize themselves while avoiding balance of payments deficits that would be difficult to sustain, owing to Western financial prudence or, alternatively, because persistent financing might entail a considerable political cost stemming from economic and financial dependence that the CPEs under the given constraints cannot tolerate except at great risk for the delicate balance in the region. Although the influence of East–West trade on recent growth of the CPEs has been investigated from various angles, few explicit statements are available with respect to its role in fostering SEI and even fewer on the role of SEI for East–West trade.

Z. Fallenbuchl has recently made a case for viewing the basic determinants of SEI in the light of three sets of developments: (1) East–West détente, (2) the implications of stagflation in nonsocialist markets for the CPEs, and (3) the existence of the SEI program (Fallenbuchl 1977, p. 7). The third factor will be taken up in a subsequent section. The first two are, of course, of direct relevance in the present discussion. The influence of détente and the concurrent surge in East–West economic cooperation has certainly been crucial, especially in the context of the intensive growth strategy pursued by all CPEs and the ensuing repercussions for regional specialization. However, the impact has perhaps not been as immense as is frequently suggested. It would appear that the case for dependence has been overstated for a number of reasons.

First, within the overall investment and modernization drive activated by the CPEs, dependence on Western technological superiority has not been as substantial or fundamental as is frequently argued, except in isolated production lines.[10] Second, rather than interpreting the CPEs' policy shifts as solely deriving from their clamoring for access to advanced technology, the redirection of trade can also be viewed as partly inspired by considerations about taking advantage of oversupply in MTEs; additional production factors, especially financial resources, could be absorbed at little or no cost in terms of domestic constraints, at least in the short run. This strategy was certainly selected quite deliberately by Poland in the early 1970s in support of the crash modernization efforts adopted by the Gierek team.[11] Third, many observers have emphasized that brisk interregional interaction is preferred by most CPEs to domestic economic reforms (Fallenbuchl 1977, pp. 8–10). The argument rests on the assumption that the contested reform concepts of the 1960s might have unleashed forces other than those envisaged in the blueprints because, it is argued, decentralization stimulates rapid productivity gains only if the reform is coupled with wide-ranging "liberalization" in the CPEs. Once again, the Hungarian experience would seem to conflict with this line of thinking. Certainly, imported technology has enabled the CPEs to enhance productivity levels by other means than those that could have been mustered if essential components of the domestic reforms had not been prematurely abrogated. But the relatively modest increase – in some cases, a decrease – in real import dependence of Western markets can hardly support the thesis that East–West trade was deliberately substituted for domestic reforms. Furthermore, whatever its merits, East–West trade intensification has not obviated the need of reforming basic parts of the traditional CPE and indeed of intra-CMEA relations, as witnessed by recent organizational changes in Eastern Europe.

In sum, although East–West trade may play a substantial role in the formulation of a regional development and cooperation strategy in Eastern Europe and in its implementation as well, the causal relationship is far from unidirectional. A direct inverse relationship trading off SEI against East–West trade can be upheld only inasmuch as the CPEs, as other economies, are working within given constraints on resources: Stimulating East–West trade will of necessity entail, if not a cut, at least a temporary slackening of CMEA trade activities. However, trade shifts as such are not the only manifestation of SEI, nor can stronger ties between East and West be rationalized as directed uniquely at the local economy of the CPE concerned. For example, in a number of recent cooperation agreements on technological transfer the possibility of directing productive exploitation at the entire CMEA market is heavily stressed. In that vein, East–West cooperation may galvanize the disparate interests of the CPEs to a greater extent than is commonly taken for granted.

It follows from the above that progress with SEI does not necessarily produce a cutback in East–West trade, except perhaps in the short run, or for that matter, entail strained ties between the two regions. If SEI is actively sought in branches that offer a viable solution to the CPEs' trading needs in the long run (the indepth specialization in manufactures coupled with the USSR's willingness and ability to assure a basic supply of fuels and raw materials), then one can expect the emergence of more competitive CPEs also in Western markets. To reach this goal, the CPEs need not attain the highest technological levels of economic activity *in abstracto*. They should simply exploit their comparative advantage primarily in relatively uncomplicated manufactures and primary goods (in comparison with developed MTE output, of course). To the extent that the CPEs will be allowed to compete in MTE markets without being unduly discriminated against or hindered by trade obstacles that protect inefficiencies in MTEs, one can predict some impact on the West of SEI in the coming years. In fact, it does not seem far fetched to anticipate that the emergence of the CPEs on Western markets will necessitate greater structural adjustments in the advanced MTEs than have already been required to accommodate the increased export supply of manufactures coming on stream in a number of developing countries.[12] But the influence of SEI need not be confined to traditional trade competition. To the extent that the CPEs continue to inch forward in coordinating their economies and the political climate remains favorable, one can envisage East–West cooperation directly or indirectly stimulating greater regional cohesion in Eastern Europe. It would perhaps be stretching the imagination too far to predict a duplication of the integration in Western Europe under the combined impact of capital imports and labor mobility from outside the integrating region. But some feeble trends warranting the guarded entertainment of such a policy option are already emerging, among other reasons, under the impact of the activity of a number of transnational companies active in Eastern Europe.

Clearly, the above scenario depends crucially on the assumption that the CPEs are indeed willing, if only reluctantly by force of circumstance, to move ahead with SEI as a result of taking positive actions to eliminate a number of factors that have thus far obstructed the maturing of integration efforts. If true, the examination of key exogenous and endogenous conditions of SEI is crucial in preparing a plausible scenario of policy actions in the foreseeable future.

4. On the conditions of SEI

Integration is a most complex endeavor that may ultimately affect the entire socioeconomic fabric of the participants. Yet its extension is necessarily bounded by and its manifestations are to be molded within the concrete conditions under which the process is conceived and carried out. Some of these crucial determinants are exogenous, embedded as they are in concrete geopolitical characteristics of the environment in which integration is pursued. Others are set deliberately by the participants. The key positive and negative conditions of SEI will be briefly explored here with the aim of separating areas in which the CPEs can hope to achieve improvement or even replacement through target reforms from others that would appear to be rather immutable.

The exogenous conditions

From the analyses presented in the preceding chapters, four principal factors appear to set the environment for the maturing of SEI: (1) the geopolitical situation, (2) the socialist growth strategy, (3) the economic model, and (4) the CMEA's organization.

The geopolitical environment of integration

The new economic policy inaugurated after the war aimed at the fast restructuring of the traditional economies of Eastern Europe. From the common ideology embraced by the CPEs and the postwar distribution of political forces in the area, a determined effort directed at dovetailing the CPEs into a closely knit economic bloc would have been logical in order to exploit the potential of the region as a whole. Instead of drawing the CPEs into a common polity and a uniform economic framework, the USSR for a long time consistently favored the gradual extension of a diversified economic structure in each CPE, as this was deemed ideologically correct and politically expedient. Although preferring autonomous development, the CPEs needed some measure of economic interaction to overcome underdevelopment and, to provide for this, the USSR drew them into its orbit by tying the CPEs to strict BTPAs, in each of which the USSR had a stake, so that the CPEs would have to be concerned primarily with domestic economic issues.

The most significant overall factor in intra-CMEA relations is the great disparity in population, territory, resource endowment, and military power between the USSR and the other members, individually and collectively. Intra-CMEA relations are therefore inevitably asymmetrical. Because the superpower might be tempted to usurp its strong position, there is a serious risk of the CMEA being molded according to the USSR's predilections, whereas the relatively small CPEs will gradually become indentured to this power. Any such relationship of asymmetrical interdependence offers opportunities for the strong to take advantage of the weak. In a historical perspective, the CPEs have certainly become subordinated to the USSR's preeminent domination, especially owing to the latter's political and military supremacy in the area; favoring this development were also the fact that at least four of the small CPEs (Bulgaria, East Germany, Hungary, and Rumania) had been on the wrong side during the Second World War and that the other partners had to rely upon the Soviet market as a substitute for the postwar economic power vacuum. An interesting question is therefore whether the USSR's political and military supremacy has also been asserted to dominate the CPEs economically, a circumstance that might preclude genuine integration.

The logic of the situation in Eastern Europe and some of the known facts about CMEA developments would at first sight seem to support an unhesitating affirmative. Whereas the USSR may have taken some advantage of postwar developments (politically, economically, and ideologically), some indications, especially in recent developments, warrant a far more cautious answer. Apart from whether and to what extent the USSR may have been tempted to mold the CMEA to its own exclusive advantage and predilections,[13] it is not contested that this superpower imposes de facto formidable restrictions on the latitude enjoyed by the other partners to experiment and implement alternatives to the past and present forms of SEI. The simple fact that the small CPEs depend for a very large share of their national product on the Soviet market underscores this proposition, and its implications should be clear too: Foreign trade and other reforms initiated by the CPEs can only produce tangible long-term benefits if they are not out of tune with developments in the USSR. Even if the latter does not seek to exert its supremacy directly by proscribing or aborting reforms, organizational and other transformations contemplated in the small CPEs should not clash with the precepts of the *primus inter pares,* for that invites retaliation in one form or another. This is the first and most general limitation on SEI. As long as the USSR denies, for example, a role to market-based instruments in clearing regional trade, the smaller CPEs can hardly expect to attain encouraging results on a broad enough scale by introducing such instruments in their own mutual relations, even if that were unconditionally favored by all other CPEs.

These considerations also apply in reverse. Whereas national sovereignty, equal partnership, mutual advantage, and the like are ritually stressed as the leading motives of cooperation, these admirable principles have not always inspired actual political and economic behavior, even though their powerful implications should not be completely rejected out of hand. In maintaining a steady supply of fuels and raw materials to Eastern Europe, for instance, the USSR has not attempted to exploit its quasi monopoly to the full by exacting permanently exorbitant prices. At least in some domains, the ideological convictions of Soviet leaders have had a formative impact on SEI.

These two sides of the position of the dominant partner in SEI are likely to confine further integration experiments to forms of cooperation that can be accommodated within the present framework of the separate CPEs or are already there but not yet fully explored. This means, for example, that plan coordination is not just an empty slogan or that it has become a palatable substitute for supranational planning, as some Western observers contend. It also implies that an attempt to further improve the scope and techniques of planning and plan coordination will be sought, perhaps in conjunction with a more adroit utilization of monetary and financial instruments, inasmuch as they facilitate economizing. This first exogenous constraint seems to exclude the introduction of full convertibility, free multilateral exchange, or a completely free choice in allocating trade, to name but a few implications, for a long time to come.

The socialist growth strategy

Rapid industrial transformation of traditional economies depends primarily on the redeployment of domestic resources on the basis of strictly binding central plans focused on the construction and elaboration of key sectors that are expected to generate rapid growth also in other economic activities; at the same time, current consumption is compressed to the bare minimum in order to mobilize as many resources as possible for growth. Preconceived notions about desirable structural change tend to preclude the setting of growth objectives and their implementation on the basis of real internal and external scarcities. The strategy is embedded in a framework of centralized planning, in which internal activities are almost completely insulated from external influences, because trade poses intricate problems for national central planning and the CPEs seek to avoid too large a dependence on uncertain foreign markets, which might disrupt internal planning or indeed might prematurely outcompete nascent industries.

These crucial features of extensive development have traditionally been interpreted as immutable and, as a result, planners did not persevere in finding economic justification and evaluation for their at times arbitrary choices. Regarding the strategy for prospective growth, policy makers now devote serious attention to the conditions under which economic efficiency can be raised and the cost of further indiscriminate industrialization can be contained, in particular with reference to foreign markets. But the situation in the various CPEs is far from similar: Those with a relatively ample domestic supply of labor (Bulgaria and Rumania) will probably persist in delaying meaningful reforms in policies and institutions until their preferred economic complex, characterized by a diversity of manufacturing sectors and a modern agriculture, has taken firm root.

The basic thrust of the socialist development strategy is there to stay. All CPEs continue to emphasize the need for priority development in industrial sectors, though not necessarily by spreading incompletely used resources to more and more industrial activities or by overconcentrating resources in selected endeavors so as to attain a high demonstration effect from an upgraded, but lopsided, industrial profile. Such shifts in emphasis do not affect the essential ingredient of the strategy, which is the continuous extension of the material-technical basis of communism through planned proportional development driven by high investment rates in conformity with the predilections of central authorities. Changes, if any, will mainly occur in reaction to the wasteful implications of extensive accumulation policies, including the high burden on the distribution of income. Especially, the perceived need to raise measurably levels of living will compel policy makers to shift toward more efficient allocation policies within the general growth framework. Nonetheless, the gradual creation of a relatively balanced economic complex in each CPE and the harmonization of these units into an interdependent ISDL along the strategic lines charted is the second basic determinant of SEI.

The economic model

It is perhaps trivial or banal to stress that the most essential ingredient of the CPE has been central planning and control of all economic activities in the service of attaining the economic, social, and other objectives sacrosanct to socialist leaders. The mechanics of central planning have never been formulated with an eye toward ensuring efficiency, in the sense that with given means the highest return in terms of material and other goods for present and future consumption could reasonably be expected. Planning by means of material balances may help the planner to reach consistent decisions, but does not ensure efficiency and optimality. In recent years, this planning instrument has been supplemented with a host of other techniques aimed in particular at guiding the selection among predetermined alternatives in rather narrowly defined areas (e.g., project selection in investments). Similarly, in matters of foreign trade and cooperation, partial attempts have been made to displace material balances as the preeminent instrument for selecting the level and composition of trade.

To widen the means and scope of rational selection among alternatives, the CPEs have come to recognize the acute drawbacks of past price policies. Although they will almost certainly seek further improvements in price formation and its role in decision making, the CPEs will also cling to some other aspects of past price policies. In particular, prices will not be used as the exclusive yardstick of rational economic allocation, especially in the distribution of disposable income; relatively constant prices will be sought, particularly for consumer goods, whose prices will be set with a view toward equating demand and supply, and to carry out important social objectives. But for producer prices, the CPEs have been abandoning Marxist price rules in favor of mirroring more closely real relative scarcities, and there is little doubt that strenuous efforts will be made to improve the realism and role of producer goods prices. Other essential instruments of the traditional model are likely to be maintained as well. For instance, fiscal, credit, and monetary policies, whose traditional task has been to facilitate plan implementation, will not be assigned more ambitious tasks in the foreseeable future. However, the particular purposes and mode in which these instruments are applied will undergo substantial changes in order better to serve as aids in resource allocation.

In addition to supporting traditional planning methods with partial or general optimization techniques, the CPEs are bound to rely more than hitherto on direct relations between microeconomic units, without, however, dispensing altogether with central directives. This will also remain the overriding concern in foreign trade regulation, without weakening the MFT. In its role as an intrinsic expression of the collective ownership of the means of production and as a powerful instrument of control, the MFT's prerogatives will be strengthened. But in asserting its role in the planning process, numerous details are bound to be transformed or adapted to the exigencies of intensive growth.

To reduce the uncertainty from trade and, hence, to enhance the realization of domestic plans, the CPEs will continue to seek firm ex ante knowledge about the trade intentions and projections of possible partners, among others, by concluding formal trade agreements as a complement to national plans. The economies willing and able to enter into such firm commercial commitments are naturally those with a similar need to forecast and control trade, whence the heavy reliance on intra-CMEA commercial traffic by means of formal and comprehensive BTPAs.

Although the imposition of bilateralism may have been more a result of the political environment in the postwar period than an express desire of the CPE planner, its endurance as the chief component of the CPEs' foreign trade system cannot be explained by political motives only. The CPEs have had some opportunities to whittle the stifling constraints on trade and cooperation after the emergence of polycentrism in Eastern Europe. The reason for perpetuating this anachronistic policy and model is far more complex than simply the fact that for a long time trade considerations did not play an overriding role in the formulation of development plans.

It appears realistic to predict that the CPEs will maintain some type of separation between internal and external economic relations with non-CPE partners, especially in price formation. As in the past, administrative means will be the key instrument here, though the role and scope of parametric instruments of economic control (e.g., duties, subsidies, and taxes) will become more explicit in insulating internal from external prices. Regarding CMEA trade, BTPAs too are likely to remain central, if only because it is very difficult to ensure a regional equilibrium in trade through the conclusion of comprehensive multilateral agreements. Trade decisions, although contingent on more intricate economic arrangements than in the past, will be chaperoned by overall economic policy concerns and, therefore, by administrative regulation, if not direct intervention on the part of the MFT. However, BTPAs do not invariably require the imposition of prohibitive balancing constraints on trade and specialization, and here some marked changes may be forecast, especially in the direction of gradually multilateralizing regional trade and payments within the planning framework typical of a majority of the member countries.

Stability in CMEA trade and payments will be preferred as an integral component of the premium put on stability in domestic planning. This implies, for instance, that the CPEs will continue to pursue their policy objectives relatively independently of WMPs, though this does not forcibly preclude the eventuality that future prices be calculated in order to reflect better the basic supply and demand conditions on the CMEA market. For such prices to stimulate a relatively preferential treatment of CMEA partners, all countries involved must deem stability to be a desirable policy objective. This implies, for instance, that trade or specialization agreements must be supplemented with ample economic and legal instruments to enforce adherence to the agreements, to sanction violation in a way acceptable to all partners, and to encourage specialization.

The CPEs are likely to seek more stability in other relations as well, and comprehensive planning cum detailed agreements will become increasingly important. They will certainly attempt to emulate the well-tried methods of CMEA cooperation also in dealing with other countries. As recent trends in trade with both the advanced and the developing MTEs demonstrate, the CPEs are bent on securing access to markets by concluding far-reaching package agreements. Whether these must necessarily take the shape of the now current buyback or countertrade type is immaterial as long as reciprocal trade is explicitly provided for, thereby enabling the CPE to avoid the recurrent balance of payments trap stemming largely from internal conditions (Holzman 1979), but also from obstacles to market access.

In the CMEA area, the role of plan coordination as the chief instrument for enhancing SEI will perceptibly increase. Whereas many past efforts have been frustrated, owing to fears that plan coordination might lead to supranational planning or because of severe shortcomings in linking coordinated agreements to domestic plans (Kiss 1975), improved methods of plan harmonization have in the 1970s enabled the CPEs to make progress in reconciling better their production and trade intentions. But plan coordination has never encompassed all aspects of the national plans, and indeed the objective of plan coordination concerns especially the dovetailing of main sectors and selected types of commodities. As outlined in Chapter 4, the CPEs have now committed themselves to the comprehensive coordination of plans in the hope of achieving a more efficient allocation of resources in the region as a whole. As a basic input to concrete bilateral and multilateral agreements on current and prospective regional trade, a regional collation and reconciliation of national plans has been effected. Although improvements in the mechanism of regionwide plan coordination will be encouraged, the prospective course of SEI will probably be strongly charted by the CPEs' ability to reconcile flexible BTPAs with coordinated plans in the service of all partners involved.

The organization and functioning of the Council

Because the Council is no more than an interstate organization without executive power, its policies and activities have been exclusively charted by the compromise decisions reached in the process of top-level discussions among the CPEs and the particular interests of the least integration-minded member(s). These will most likely remain the chief determinants of the Council's future activities.

Referring to the discussions of Chapter 4, it appears fair to assert that the Council's institutions are not effectively geared toward promoting SEI and its policy documents cannot be considered adequate guidelines for fostering this process, even in the limited sphere in which the Council is called upon to act. Both features are likely to undergo but modest changes in detail, and none in substance. It may be anticipated that the Council will concentrate on working out standardized procedures for plan coordination, specialization, and joint integration projects, including improvements in key economic parameters that are of considerable concern in selecting among alternatives. A larger degree of legal clarity and uniformity will also be pursued. More initiative than in the past is bound to be cultivated by the CMEA organs because it is well-nigh impossible to implement plans without a prior selection of common points of reference or standard criteria for reaching satisfactory "recommendations." All this is unlikely to go far beyond the well-tried methods of the past, as the national governments continue to safeguard their own interests.

Provided the leaders of the CPEs harbor sincere intentions about intensifying regional interdependence, the institutional framework of the CMEA will have to be stabilized and improved in depth, not in breadth. In particular, careful attention should be paid to combating the inertia of the Council's official organs that has been so typical over the past decades especially in initiating and supervising, if not controlling, the implementation of SEI measures. The Standing Commissions and Council Committees must be permitted to assume a more permanent role in working out and policing SEI efforts. At present they appear to be too dependent on the whims of the national governments or political bodies, which have charge of and in fact dictate in detail the scope and actual form of the CMEA's activities. This also applies to such matters as the transition to multilateralism, where either the IBEC or the Commission for currency and finance will have to be invested with more comprehensive powers, without necessarily yielding to supranationalism. In this connection, a more realistic interpretation and a less strident expression of national sovereignty, safeguarding equality, and so on should be made compatible with more ambitious forms of SEI than those that have so far emerged on the initiative of the Council and its organs (Vogt 1977).

These are considered the main pillars supporting the principal economic environment for further SEI and, at the same time, the most important exogenous conditions imposed on the possible forms that SEI can assume, at least far into the 1980s.

The endogenous conditions

Conditioned largely by the USSR's preeminence, the particular implementation of the growth strategy, the creation of a centralized planning model, and the adherence to a bilateral system of trade and cooperation, postwar policies in Eastern Europe have produced a number of consequences, not all of which were intended. Most of these by-products of East European planning or attendant policies have probably not been essential components of the ideal CPE, although in some cases they may have been instrumental in carrying out cherished priorities. But as the perceptions of the CPE leaders change, these elements will have to be excised, mitigated, or appropriately adjusted. During the past

decade, the planners have launched several attempts to eliminate or to alleviate these features without, however, touching too
much on their formative causes. The topics that have been at the
forefront of recent discussions and that are of particular importance in implementing genuine integration may be grouped
under three headings: (1) trade and cooperation, (2) internal
economic reforms, and (3) revisions in the institutions and tasks
of the Council.

Trade conditions for integration

In evaluating the possibilities of enhancing SEI through trade,
as discussed, it is enlightening to recall that the CPEs have no
single policy instrument (comparable, for instance, to that used
during the first phase of West European integration), whose correct application and timely adjustment according to circumstance may be a necessity for fostering more comprehensive
measures that will help to reduce regional disparities through
the mobility of goods and services. Instead, trade and cooperation tasks must be tackled in their entirety, including their interdependence with the internal relations of the integrating members. The following is an attempt to pinpoint areas where more
or less significant changes may be in the offing.

Socialist price policies and specialization. Because CPE planning
relies primarily on material balances and on quantitative success
indicators, prices are not good indicators of real scarcity and opportunities, and their allocative function is severely conscripted.
This choice may have been wise to facilitate drastic structural
changes, but nonscarcity pricing considerably hampers effective
participation in trade and the implementation of regional cooperation. Even if the CPE confines its external transactions largely
to countries with similar planning and strategy options, but for
which the entire region is not the actual planning horizon for
want of a unified plan, this commerce cannot be cleared at internal prices. Because the CPEs also wish to realize some specific
common CMEA principles, they have gradually built up a system of socialist WMPs linked, but not necessarily equal, to some
average WMPs computed over a medium-term period and held
constant over time (although since 1975 this period has been
compressed to one year). Although in principle such prices

could be very useful, in practice they may be and have been counterproductive in implementing SEI for reasons examined in detail in Chapter 3.

The CPEs have felt for a long time that this price system is obstructing cooperation, and three possible alternatives have been extensively debated and examined from various angles. In the early and mid-1960s, attention focused on the construction of an independent system of trade prices, possibly anchored to an average of domestic wholesale prices in the producing CPEs. Another option envisaged maintaining the basic tenets of the Bucharest stipulations on price formation, but to let prices better reflect actual WMP trends. Finally, the gradual elaboration of an independent price system based on real scarcities within the CMEA region, and each CPE in particular, was suggested, especially by the advocates of linking up internal and external markets. The latter is clearly the better alternative from an allocative point of view, but for it to meet with success, the CPEs will have to institute far-reaching internal economic reforms, which so far they have been unwilling or unable to enact (possibly excepting Hungary). Despite numerous protracted debates, high-level conferences, and explicit documents on the desirable changes in price policies, the paramount question concerning the formation of CMEA trade prices remains as unsettled as before.

Recent policy documents emphasize that WMPs will remain the basic criterion for evaluating intra-CMEA trade transactions. This may in fact mean no more than paying lip service to the particular interest of one or more CPEs and to the necessity of allowing but a narrow margin of divergence between socialist WMPs and actual or potential alternatives in other markets. SEI must be enhanced by exploiting differences in relative real costs, which in the process will gradually be equalized on the margin. The transition period will probably be marked by three trends: (1) the gradually increasing influence of domestic costs on the process of CMEA price formation; (2) the closing of the gap between CMEA trade prices and actual WMPs without, however, any continuous attempt to imitate price fluctuations in world markets; and (3) greater uniformity of actual price policies in the CMEA members and in regional trade as a precondition for multilateralism and regional specialization.

For a number of years, the possibility of establishing a mixed three-tier price system for the CMEA according to the relative importance of the supplying region, including the possibility of using domestic prices in trade, has been extensively discussed (Bozyk 1977, pp. 172–184). In view of the USSR's preponderance in the CMEA, the adoption of that country's wholesale prices has also been suggested by a number of writers (e.g., Savov 1975, pp. 209–211; Velickov 1976, pp. 140–153). Especially in connection with specialization agreements and the operation of IEOs, a new price-formation formula tied to domestic price gestation has been contemplated as an incentive for both the specializing CPE and potential importers (Kormnov 1973a); this variant would be utilized particularly to enhance specialization in components and subassemblies for which imitating WMPs is most troublesome. As reported in Chapter 3, until now ad hoc pricing has been resorted to, even though this is not a fully satisfactory solution for encouraging SEI through production specialization. In other words, practice does not quite conform to theory, and no generally accepted principles (except the now out-of-date Bucharest principles) have been endorsed – precisely because practice diverges so much from theory and the CPEs have not yet firmly settled the directions of their own future policies at home.

Though the Complex Program targeted a comprehensive review of CMEA price formation from which practical consequences were to be drawn before 1975, so far there have been but marginal changes: The adoption of sliding prices in 1975 is, by and large, simply a confirmation of past practices. Further study of ways to improve the situation in line with the requirements of SEI are said to be pursued vigorously and simultaneously in several CMEA organs (Janota 1977, pp. 19–21), but no tentative scenario of desirable or likely changes has so far emerged. However, within the constraints of planned prices and moderate price stability under central planning, further target action may be expected in the future, perhaps at the time of the new five-year plans in 1980–1981.[14]

Product preferences. For a variety of reasons studied in Chapter 4, since the mid-1950s the CMEA market has been segmented more and more into "soft" and "hard" goods, where the latter are those products that can be easily earmarked in non-CPE markets at the current prices prevailing there and that, partially for that reason but also for a host of other circumstances, tend to be in short supply in Eastern Europe. In any event, chronic shortages of some basic materials have occasionally jeopardized steady planning for growth, especially for CPEs that rely on imports of industrial inputs and foodstuffs. During the 1960s, the CPEs attempted to cure part of the market imbalance by, among other methods, extending target loans for the specific development of selected primary goods, a policy that has recently been revived on a much larger scale. However, the financial mechanism of the CMEA is still too incomplete to reward the various actors adequately, and it may be conjectured that these capital movements did not result from a realistic assessment of CMEA-wide or, better still, worldwide investment opportunities and the most effective redistribution of CMEA investment funds.

Structural bilateralism is a highly anachronistic and detrimental trade policy, but in the context of the present features of the CMEA, it has not been completely illogical for some CPEs. To eliminate it, the CPEs will have to find ways to reestablish balance between demand and supply either by adapting prices to real costs or by diverting trade to outside markets. The reversal in the mid-1970s of the earlier unfavorable terms of trade trend, especially for the USSR, has certainly tempered the strongly pronounced preference for exporting manufactures rather than agricultural or mineral products. However, natural endowments predicate that future growth of most CPEs be sought inevitably in exporting manufactures, though this need not be carried forward indiscriminately, for then the regionwide disequilibria cannot be attenuated, not even by trade diversion: Production specialization will have to be fostered much more intensively than hitherto.

Trade diversion. The balancing problems of the CMEA market should logically have entailed a strong trade diversion effect so that exportable manufactures could be exchanged for primary goods in third markets. Provided the terms of trade prevailing in such markets were acceptable, this could indeed have alleviated the chronic imbalance of the CMEA. Paradoxically, trade diversion occurred in reverse, with the exporters of primary goods exploring world markets in search of modern equipment. The USSR has not fully taken advantage of this situation and, in fact, has consistently covered for falling export markets of the developed CPEs. Indeed, the USSR has so far avoided a strong disengagement from political, moral, and other obligations with respect to the other CPEs, and is unlikely to do otherwise merely because intra-CMEA prices might be relatively unfavorable for the producers of primary goods.[15] Of much greater importance will be the gradual exhaustion of relatively cheap sources of supply in the western parts of the USSR and the country's penchant for showing a more developed profile also in trade.

Trade diversion on the scale apparently needed to reestablish equilibrium in the CMEA can only be envisaged through broad interaction with outside partners. Most of these potential markets cannot be tapped in the short run precisely because the CPEs' export supply is not really geared to the import demand of non-CMEA markets, including a number of developing countries. Modernization in conjunction with intensive production specialization offers the only long-range solution, but this transformation cannot be carried forward without extensive departures from traditional development policies. Nevertheless, corrective action in the short run will probably be confined to the exploration of stable, planned trade relations especially with some developing countries, a strategy that has been termed "very promising" (Alampiev 1971, p. 57), though it has not yet induced significant reciprocal exchange. Whereas the opportunities for creating significant amounts of trade with the developing countries should not be underrated, it appears almost certain that most developing countries will no longer be satisfied with simply exhanging their primary goods for manufactures. The CPEs will therefore have to redouble their efforts to modernize their manufacturing branches, which would enable them to exploit their comparative advantage and to compete effectively with the developing as well as developed MTEs.

Specialization. A complementary way out of mounting incompatibilities in CMEA trade, and a most promising source of future growth, is the gradual elimination of imbalances directly by sponsoring specialization on a wide scale, especially in manufactures. Whereas the specialization drive has picked up some momentum in the 1970s, achievements continue to lag far behind expectations, owing to the problems of assessing real benefits and costs, coordinating specialized procurements, the desire for relative self-sufficiency in many endeavors, and, mainly, the fact that the CPEs have not so far recast their domestic organization and institutions with a view toward integration requirements.

Short of having unambiguous criteria with which to compute static and dynamic comparative advantages, and in the absence of alternative reliable criteria for regional choice by way of central planning, the CPEs have settled some agreements that have declared the current structure of production immutable, redistributed some of the available capacities for products with many variants, forestalled further duplication, or pooled resources for developing advanced technologies. Of course, specialization has been all but completed in some branches of primary goods, but the almost exclusive reliance on the USSR for vitally needed inputs can hardly be considered an integration achievement, except perhaps if regional self-sufficiency were one of the main goals of the CMEA. As may be deduced from numerous policy statements, regional specialization still has a long way to go, though some important common projects have undoubtedly been realized and significant inroads are being accomplished. This is particularly the case of collaboration in the field of scientific-technical cooperation, the development of sophisticated technologies, and the like.

Provided the CPEs can be found willing to seek it, a region-wide division of labor in manufacturing will be the most promising avenue for vigorously pushing SEI, though this cannot be forged on the basis of the well-tried methods of the past. Instead, bold action is needed in the monetary and financial field to assess real scarcities, and in the organizational and planning domain to dovetail rationality criteria with central planning and control. Concrete action targeted at enabling producing firms to seek specialization directly under central guidance will have to be inaugurated soon too, though the CPEs do not yet seem to be ready for it (Bogacka 1978, p. 22). The adjustment process may be painful, but is unlikely to destabilize the main pillars of a socialist society.

Instead of seeking production specialization by fiat, the CPEs must eliminate the market inconsistencies by allowing the lower

levels of the plan hierarchy to act. It is frequently more un-
manageable to solve a particular problem through general
agreement than to focus on one or a few topical questions, which
may act as catalysts for more comprehensive changes. Although
some CPEs have allowed enterprises to participate directly in
joint ventures, none has relaxed national controls to such an extent that broad international cooperation could be stimulated
from below. Many problems of a legal nature, commodity and
currency inconvertibility, ownership rights, planning authority,
and so on are still unsolved. That such questions are important,
but a solution still pending, is heavily stressed in policy documents, and it seems reasonable to expect in the near future a
more pragmatic approach in joining forces.

Trade policies. Intra-CMEA relations have so far relied on bilateralism, which needlessly restricts trade and unnecessarily
limits international specialization. Though well aware of the antitrade and antispecialization effects of bilateralism (and some
timely conclusions must already have been drawn from these incompatibilities), the CPEs have done next to nothing to let more
suitable policies and institutions supersede bilateralism. Instead,
members have tried to widen the scope for trade and specialization within the bilateral mold by introducing trade-stimulating
techniques or structural bilateralism, but such policies are not
very conducive to long-range specialization.

The CPEs have tried to mitigate some of the drawbacks of
bilateralism also by institutionalizing a particular type of payments multilateralism without, however, implementing measures to eliminate trade bilateralism. Multilateralism has not
been very important because the CPEs have not been able or
willing to adapt production and consumption decisions according to the implications of multilateral exchange. In particular,
they have been reluctant to introduce commodity convertibility,
not to speak of currency convertibility, precisely because this
kind of arrangement might jeopardize the delicate separation of
internal and external markets; and as long as this rigid separation cannot be moderated through market-based foreign relations or CMEA-wide planning, there will be no solid basis for
deepening and widening SEI to the lowest levels of the plan
hierarchies in the various countries.

The overriding concern in pursuing specialization should be the gradual development of economic criteria of choice. This implies, for instance, scarcity prices, transferability (if not necessarily full convertibility) of currencies, multilateral settlement of accounts, and so on. These should be the principal topics in a discussion of the present and future role of indirect coordination in the process of harmonizing draft plans. But such changes can hardly be attained without the enactment of incisive organizational reforms, for it is primarily in the domain of the final producer and user that the success of SEI will be brought to the test. Administrative measures taken on the governmental level or apparent political consensus there are likely to be without practical implications, as the past amply testifies, if the ultimate producer and user are kept in the dark about the economic criteria upon which their decisions should be synchronized with overall policy objectives (Bogacka 1978, p. 22).

Plan coordination. Whereas the overall framework of SEI through the coordination of national plans is an exogenous condition, its concrete application can be improved in several respects without invalidating the power of central planning or disavowing the great value placed on central planning in formulating and implementing socialist policies. Two parallel lines for further improvement can be traced. On the one hand, the planned control of economic processes, especially investment intentions, must be further perfected. Apart from ameliorating the organizational mechanics of plan coordination, the CPEs must also seek to dovetail in one way or another more suitable instruments of indirect coordination with central planning, possibly by accommodating greater decentralization. The argument propping up this proposition parallels that made for domestic planning: Material balances for the CMEA as a whole can reveal the shortages and surpluses of the products under consideration but cannot provide suitable orientation for regional efficiency and equilibrium. Moreover, detailed coordination of individual material balances obscures a comprehensive assessment of SEI opportunities and the identification of fields in which concrete specialization agreements should be negotiated (Kiss 1975, p. 752), possibly by enterprises themselves rather than by top levels of the planning hierarchies.

Plan coordination in the past has suffered from a number of encumbrances, the most important of which are the following. First, the methodology of reconciling plans is fluid and imprecise, and some CPEs are not inclined to relax their own national preferences, possibly in view of the danger of supranationalism. Second, the formulation of coordinated plans hinges crucially on properly harmonizing national draft plans and combining them with the recommendations hammered out in the coordination sessions. Third, short- and long-term plans are frequently revised, redrafted, or simply interrupted in the wake of sudden, unexpected changes in the national or international environment. Fourth, coordination has been aimed at too many details, thus often losing track of the essence and needlessly complicating deliberations; in many instances, the goal of plan coordination had to be scaled down to the harmonization of trade intentions only. Finally, a critical defect has been that ostensibly harmonized plans are not properly implemented in the CPEs for want of economic rationality and precision in the coordination process, not to mention the absence of tangible incentive criteria.

Most of the obstructions enumerated could be attenuated or eliminated altogether by seeking a greater role for monetary and financial coordination instruments, properly involving producers from different CPEs in the planning process, and focusing central planning and plan coordination especially on major economywide issues. It appears to follow therefore that alterations in the goals and mechanism of SEI are contingent on the introduction of domestic reforms as part and parcel of establishing greater regional interdependence.

Economic reforms

To counter the flagging growth that emerged or became a serious prospect in the early 1960s, all CPEs embarked to a varying extent on organizational changes with weighty implications for foreign trade and cooperation. But with the possible exception of Hungary and perhaps Poland, no CPE has so far created direct links between internal and external economic activities. Furthermore, no CPE has succeeded in establishing up-to-date market shadow indicators, which would help in the allocation of resources. Although some details of the planning process underwent significant streamlining, the primary role of central planning by physical yardsticks has largely remained intact. Above all, no CPE has shown a determined effort to mold its further development course in line with the results of a patient search for its proper place in the world economy, or even in the CMEA market. Independently conceived strategic aims continue to be drawn up chiefly on the basis of national interests. Even in the few instances where potentially significant alterations were contemplated, excepting Hungary, implementation was put off, the original intentions were diluted, or the reform faded away under the mounting pressure for more central control over goals and instruments. As may be deduced from recent CMEA policy documents, further reforms will have to be enacted at the discretion of each CPE separately, because supranationalism or the joint coordination of integration-related reforms is not contemplated. Yet, a promising SEI program cannot be activated with realistic hopes of success without first moderating the insulation of the internal markets.

Perhaps the most critical task to be tackled in designing reforms is how to provide for modernization, the absorption of technological knowledge, and the stimulation of technical progress from within, while avoiding political and economic consequences that will have to be aborted for one reason or another. This threefold goal is perforce a precondition for attaining a growth climate receptive to actual or potential foreign competition, endorsing regional specialization, and engaging in mutually beneficial East–West trade without incurring serious balance of payments problems. Whereas this agenda, naturally, cannot be pondered all at once in the hope of producing quick solutions, it is useful to spell out the obstacles to technical progress embedded in the traditional planning system. Innovation in the CPE is left somewhat wayside for the following reasons: (1) The predominant trade partner fails to encourage the CPEs to concentrate on technologically up-to-date products because it is willing to accept goods that could not normally be marketed elsewhere; (2) the planning framework is far too rigid to reward innovation appropriately because the material stimuli used have a short-term horizon; and (3) CMEA provisions for exchanging technical and scientific knowledge at a token cost discourage technical progress, especially in the developed CPEs (Bykov

1976, pp. 130–132). Although the third encumbrance has been officially attenuated since 1967, the CPEs find it difficult to evaluate properly the benefits of technological diffusion. Determined efforts to pool research resources bilaterally and multilaterally, although very intensively pursued in recent years, continue to be hampered because an agreement regarding the proper utilization of financial and monetary criteria of choice, evaluation, and reward has not yet been settled.

It is doubtless true that the CMEA framework has greatly aided regional industrialization by enabling some CPEs to avail themselves of absorptive, not very exacting, import markets. However, the developed CPEs, including the USSR, have in some sense actually done these less developed CPEs a considerable disservice, especially from the standpoint of the long-range competitiveness and hence viability of these relatively new export sectors. The true cost of acquiring advanced technology incurred recently in East–West trade or as a result of local efforts has hopefully swayed the CPEs into imposing more exacting quality and technical standards on regional trade. To make this an effective constraint, however, it is critically important to seek a higher degree of devolution and accountability.

The reward system of the CPEs has been dominated disproportionately by physical indicators and concerns about socialist egalitarianism. The reforms of the 1960s aimed to some extent at tying success indicators to internal and external market performance, but in several CPEs the attempt foundered precisely because central planning inhibited enterprise activity that could succeed only in a longer perspective than that of the operative plans. Instead of retrenching further, central planning should be rendered more flexible and enterprise interests need to be reconciled with macroeconomic policy objectives. Harmonization of central planning with possibly improved instruments of indirect economic coordination will have to be patiently pursued, in the first instance perhaps against the backdrop of the Hungarian reform experiences. Prices will inextricably be of critical concern in this search for improving the realization of the overall social and planning priorities of the CPEs. Needless to add, this cannot be a once-and-for-all reform attempt. To obtain the desirable results from the incentive system, micro- and macroeconomic policies should be properly streamlined with changes in the economic environment.

The future role of the Council
Without underrating the Council's potential role in formulating and implementing SEI, it is nevertheless true that comprehensive integration in the area will only take root properly if measures launched from within the economies make it attractive to embark upon suitable changes in the mechanism of SEI. Although these steps are a basic precondition, multilateral cooperation can only work smoothly and properly if there is a central agency furthering the true interests of the community as a whole and of the members individually. This will have to be the Council with its affiliated agencies, however large its past and present resistance to change or in spite of the immobility of a bureaucracy that was not set up to fulfill the tasks it is apparently called upon to face now.

The Council will not be transformed into a supranational planning agency in the foreseeable future because this has been proscribed explicitly in a vast number of policy statements. From the point of view of the planned organization of the CPEs, this may be a regrettable decision. Under the circumstances, the Council should at least mature into an imaginative organ devoted to East European regionalism and provided with the necessary instruments to carry out its detailed and complex tasks in support of efforts initiated by the CPEs. The Council should include in its activities a broad investigation of the economic arguments favoring specialization in one branch or another, leaving the details to those competent in such matters, that is, the lower echelons of the planning hierarchies. It will also be incumbent on the agency to prepare operational alternatives to the present type of economic organization and decision making, for example, to facilitate the implementation of well-founded specialization agreements, to reconcile the members' divergent interests rooted in the inevitable conflicts between national industrialization and regional complementarity, and to enhance consistency in fostering SEI.

For too long the institutions of the Council have been dominated de facto by concerns about national growth per se and an inward-looking supporting model. Furthermore, the recent official policy documents intended as guides for future action by the Council have next to nothing to say about necessary and desirable changes in the organization and functioning of the common organ, though it has been stressed in no uncertain terms in the discussions about SEI that rather incisive reforms will be an inescapable concomitant to internal reforms. Barring its transformation into a supranational planning agency with duties not unlike those of traditional Soviet-type planning, the Council will be enabled to execute its tasks much more readily and effectively if the CPEs gradually adopt more flexible criteria of choice, even if these will not be the exclusive yardstick in selecting and implementing the strategic elements of SEI.

5. An assessment and a scenario for the future

The official endorsement of SEI as the overriding policy goal of the CPEs has confronted these countries, both in theory and practice, with the task of innovating forms of cooperation that fully respond to the new stage of their mutual economic relations. As experience has amply demonstrated, the CPEs may be brought to the waters of concord but cannot be made to drink. As a result of their inability or reluctance to tackle the strategic ways and means of reconciling divergent interests in SEI, these countries individually and collectively still face the demanding task of charting a consistent course of action aimed at the tenacious improvement of SEI.

The fuel and raw material crisis and the attendant recession in the West on the one hand, and the initial resilience of the CPEs to these disturbances, in spite of a marked deceleration in growth during the past few years partly on account of the transmission of these world market disturbances also to the CMEA market, on the other, have hopefully substantiated the important advantages ensuing from planning secure markets for exports of manufactures from the smaller CPEs in exchange for primary industrial inputs. The predicament, especially of the CPEs without sufficient indigenous resources of fuels or raw materials, looks bleak if SEI continues to be deliberately stalled under impact of the reluctance of some partners to search patiently for the proper channels of harmonizing their interests with the concerns of other CPEs, who have a penchant for synchronizing themselves with conditions prevailing in the region. The future of SEI processes must therefore be cast against the backdrop of prospective growth conditions of the CMEA members and their interaction with the world economy.

Growth prospects for the 1980s

In the context of the global economic environment of the mid-1970s, the output performance of the CPEs has been substantial, but CMEA's initial insulation against adverse international events has slowly given way to serious impediments to steady expansion, especially since 1976. Economic conditions in many of the CPEs have proved to be considerably more complex than anticipated in the current medium-term plans (1976–1980) and also in the successive annual plans of this period, which already slated targets well below the course charted in the mid-1970s. In 1978, for example, the region recorded the lowest aggregate growth pace experienced in almost two decades; it was also the third consecutive year of growth deceleration, largely on account of a number of internal and external imbalances.

There are basically two different sources of these imbalances. Some stem from temporary below-plan output levels in fuel and raw material sectors, bottlenecks in construction and transportation, several successive crop setbacks, or tight restrictions on imports and below-plan export performance. Others are due essentially to constraints on the supply of primary factor inputs in the production process, as demographic characteristics are now curtailing the growth of the labor force, the expansion of new capital funds for investment purposes has to be slowed down in order to satisfy growing consumer needs and to avoid exacerbating the already strained external imbalance, and an increasing share of appropriated investment funds has to be preempted for sectors with long gestation lags (particularly fuels and raw materials) or lower productivity profiles (such as consumer services). Although some of these growth impediments are of a passing nature and will resolve themselves under impact of adjustments in the planning process during the current phase of reduced growth emphasis, others appear to have serious implications for long-term growth and hence will be important determinants of the future evolution of SEI.

On the basis of plausible forecasts of growth factors in the 1980s, it now appears likely that the CMEA region will have to come to grips with reduced output growth, roughly from a level of 7 percent in 1960–1975 to perhaps 5 percent in the coming decade.[16] Although the less developed CPEs will probably succeed in surpassing this benchmark, others, especially the USSR, will fall short of it. This deceleration appears to stem essentially from longer-term internal and external supply constraints, the most important of which will be briefly touched upon below.

The growth of the labor force in the CMEA region is expected to decline substantially from an average of about 2 percent in 1960–1975 to about 0.7 percent in the 1980s, owing especially to demographic trends of the past and longer formal education. The situation will be compounded by a rapid increase of the service sector, which is generally more labor-intensive than material production and has a lower level of productivity, and by more restrictive conditions than in the past for redeploying labor out of the agricultural sector, unless there will be a sharp acceleration in the injection of capital funds. In some developed countries, the growth of the labor force will become trivial or even negative.

Following the rapid surge in the cost of primary industrial inputs in world and CMEA markets, the CPEs will have to embrace stringent conservation measures or face a serious growth constraint. Future costs are likely to inch up further as supply from within the CMEA region will have to be secured from remote, harsh climatic regions or from world markets, where an abatement particularly of fuel prices is not in sight.

As a result of the fast expansion in consumption and incomes in the early 1970s and the maintenance of a relatively high pace of investment expenditures, partly through international borrowing, CMEA policy makers may find it difficult to curtail future consumption growth in favor of domestic accumulation. Although some net capital inflow from abroad can be expected to continue, its rate of expansion in the 1980s will probably not suffice to sustain the sharp acceleration of capital outlays experienced in the early 1970s. Domestic demand, however, will expand steadily, owing to the CPE policy makers' objective of increasing consumption and improving living conditions on the one hand, and the high demand for new capital funds, especially for energy, basic raw materials, infrastructure (particularly housing and transportation), and the protection of the environment, on the other. There will hence be serious competition for capital funds, and the material production sphere will have to reckon with slower expansion of new funds in the years ahead.

Up to about the beginning of the 1970s, the trade participation of the CPEs was based largely on the relatively unconstrained availability of cheap fuels and raw materials from within the CMEA, rapid industrialization in breadth anchored to steady increments in the supply of capital and labor, and the existence of a large-scale market receptive to practically any additional supplies. These conditions for mutually reinforcing growth from within the region are no longer valid now that the major WMP adjustments of the mid-1970s are being fed through in the CMEA market as well. This is reflected, for example, in the deterioration of the regional terms of trade for all CPEs, except the USSR and to a lesser extent Poland; the substantial investment requirements to secure steady increments in the regional output of fuels and raw materials, even at a lower rate than consumption, which will have to be met increasingly through joint efforts; and the rising quality standards imposed by potential importers, even within the CMEA region. Although these factors largely antedate in origin and extent recent world market developments, in combination with the latter they have changed substantially the conditions for future regional growth.

Nevertheless, the limits imposed on future growth that emanate from domestic supply constraints could be substantially alleviated if the CPEs succeed in: (1) steadily deepening and widening their participation in world trade, including strong regional integration; (2) emphasizing much more than before the crucial role of technology for efficient production and specialization; and (3) taking effective measures to increase efficiency in the use of primary factors of production and intermediate inputs also through shifts in output profile. In fact, the feasible output growth rates cited above already assume that the CPEs will pursue rapid trade expansion.

However, the balance of payments situation will affect to a significant extent the foreign trade and hence domestic growth prospects of all CPEs, even if means of financing deficits with the developed MTEs will be forthcoming and intra-CMEA imbalances can be smoothened as in the past. External finance will be needed in the early 1980s unless the CPEs were to consider constraining domestic demand below expected levels, which in turn would affect growth prospects later in the decade.

To reach the 5 percent average annual growth objective, the CPEs need to embrace a number of policy initiatives conducive to stimulating supply quantitatively as well as qualitatively. Perhaps the most important policy measures will be those that support "production intensification," that is, the enhancement of the role of science and technology in all kinds of productive activities with a view to raising efficiency. This will involve better training and education of the labor force, a reduction in specific material inputs through changes in technology or shifts in production patterns, more modern technology, mutations in the production profile, and, possibly, organizational transformations. A related matter of paramount importance is the more comprehensive coordination of economic activities within the CMEA by enhancing SEI, thereby taking advantage of larger markets and economies of scale.

Considering the magnitude of the supply constraints, steady growth at the level indicated appears feasible if medium-term plans for the 1980s will incorporate specific targets for the structure of future output to reflect better the real shifts in comparative advantage. The countries may find it also appropriate to seek implementation of these targets within an economic model that supports policy initiatives directed at alleviating the security of supply constraints and that enhances the quality of output according to shifts in domestic and foreign demand. Changes in the management systems of these countries may in the short run require a slowdown in economic activity, but this temporary loss can be offset later on by productivity gains, especially resulting from regional and international specialization.

The effects on external trade and cooperation

The gradual restructuring of the CPEs sought within the intensification strategy of the 1970s has on the whole exerted a very positive influence on the region's interaction with third markets, especially the developed MTEs. Could recent policy shifts, particularly the deceleration of import growth in response to external and internal constraints, eventually entail a more permanent retrenchment of trade as a result of a movement toward greater self-reliance of the CPEs individually or in concert? If this were to materialize, it would preceptibly affect the prospective involvement of the CMEA region with the world economy.

Concerns about restoring internal and external balance in 1976–1979 have already induced greater self-sufficiency, especially through common efforts within the CMEA, and have slowed down the implementation of the outward-oriented modernization drive. These would appear to be temporary responses, rather than signals of a major shift in development policies. In view of the growth factors reviewed above, especially the more modest expansion of factor availabilities and the growing imbalance between demand and supply of basic materials, the CPEs are unlikely to embark, as they did at other times in the postwar period, on a considerably more inward-turned type of economic development. To maintain stable and relatively rapid growth through factor productivity gains, the CPEs will have to foster structural adjustments in line with changes in their comparative advantage. Accordingly, the present short-term shifts in growth emphasis do not appear to have affected the basic trends underlying development strategies, which still point in the direction of finding the proper place of the CPE in the world economy. The trade-intensification strategy adopted about a decade ago will probably remain intact in the foreseeable future, but the CMEA countries are unlikely to resume the course that was monitored in the earlier half of the decade. Rapid import growth will be sought, but external constraints on trade with developed MTEs and internal balancing considerations within the CMEA region appear to enhance the prospects of trade with developing MTEs.

The CMEA will on balance become more dependent on imports of fuels, foodstuffs, and basic raw materials from outside the region. To support such increased imports, trade intensity and the pattern of regional specialization have thus become major determinants of regional cooperation. This interaction will depend to a large degree on the rate of growth of regional supplies of primary industrial inputs and the feasibility of trans-

forming present production profiles, especially in manufacturing, through intrasectoral and particularly intraproduct
specialization.

The growth of regional output of fuels and raw materials
depends largely on resource endowments and technologies enabling the economic exploitation of reserves and on the extent to
which the CMEA members collectively succeed in stepping up
output. Nevertheless, even under favorable internal and external conditions, it now appears difficult to expand regional output in line with demand and to maintain the present degree of
self-reliance. Under reasonable growth assumptions, an increasing regional deficit for fuels and a number of basic raw materials
will exert pressure for exploring alternative supply markets. In
combination with the relative decline of the role of some primary products in exports from the region, owing to rising internal demand, the CPEs will need to explore alternative trade
outlets to support stable growth.

The degree of regional specialization in manufactures depends largely on how successful the CMEA countries are in
coordinating development plans, elaborating concrete specialization agreements, and implementing these comprehensive protocols. Although production specialization, especially in chemical and engineering sectors, has accelerated markedly in the
1970s, the potential scope for further progress is still considerable. As noted, the CPEs have encountered severe hindrances in
promoting trade of parts and components – the crucial variable
in the postwar expansion of trade among advanced MTEs. The
reason for this is complex, but the major inhibition stems from
the practical obstacles being faced in dovetailing demand and
supply through the coordination of economywide plans, especially when the criteria of choice used by the various participants
are not completely synchronized or, in some cases, they are even
inconsistent (Szelecki 1978).

Regional integration is slated to be measurably enhanced in a
number of sectors as a result of the implementation of the
Target Programs. The growing role of coordinated development plans may entail an inward-turning in certain branches or
products, but the CPEs are not expected on the whole to seek
perceptible disengagement from interaction with non-CMEA
markets. However, the pace and extent of such interregional

trade depends to a large extent on the intensity of intra-CMEA cooperation and the apparently inevitable deficit in a number of basic products on the one hand, and the restructuring of production profiles according to comparative advantage on the other.

A reversal of the factors underlying the recent decelerating trends in trade with developed MTEs would appear possible, although the pace of future interaction is unlikely to approach once again the very fast acceleration recorded in the first half of the 1970s. Reciprocal trade can expand at a brisk pace if the CPEs succeed in improving their foreign supply through domestic investment or incentive systems or by establishing external linkages, such as countertrade, that in fact reserve foreign markets for future exports. Clearly, it will also be necessary to avoid obstructing market access, through tariff barriers or other, less subtle, means of market regulation, for products in which CPEs have a genuine comparative advantage. Because the growth of the exportable surplus of foodstuffs, fuels, and raw materials from the CMEA will decline, at least in relative terms, the region's import demand for advanced technology can be satisfied only if simultaneously it succeeds in accelerating exports of manufactures to MTEs. In light of their shifting comparative advantage and effective competition on the part of developing MTEs in Western markets, the CPEs will have to conquer new outlets for more complex manufactures. If they cannot attain this goal for internal or external reasons, balance of payments pressures will necessitate a compression of imports below levels desirable from the point of view of a more effective division of labor.

The level of trade with developing MTEs is still low and the bulk of trade consists of the exchange of primary goods for manufactures. The potential for trade expansion would therefore appear to be considerable. Rapid growth depends to a significant extent on structural adjustments in the CPEs to accommodate manufactures from the developing MTEs and the ability of the latter to increase simultaneously their exports of primary goods. Significant shifts could be forthcoming in the medium to long run because the CPEs can compete effectively in markets of developing MTEs for a number of technically involved manufactures and the developing MTEs have a comparative advantage in less complicated, labor-intensive manufactures; balance of payments considerations will therefore be less of a hindrance to trade expansion than in relations between the CPEs and the developed MTEs. Although such shifts are being contemplated, the CPEs have not yet finalized concrete plans for future adjustments. Closer coordination of economic policies of CPEs and developing MTEs in order to facilitate planned adjustments, could measurably improve the trade potential of the two regions.

An integration scenario

On the strength of the above, growth prospects of the CPEs hinge critically on how the CMEA members succeed in implementing structural adjustments at home in response to changes in their comparative advantage. From the long catalogue of outstanding issues discussed especially in section 4, the most likely integration scenario for the near future would appear to shape up as follows. There will probably be few changes in the basic features of the CPEs and their common organization. The current literature is replete with indications that, although they may entail an aversion to SEI, the strategy of socialist industrialization, the fundamental components of the economic model, the CMEA organization, and the preeminence of the USSR in common efforts are unlikely to undergo drastic restructuring, though here and there minor alterations may well germinate. It seems reasonable to anticipate a slow transition in favor of a more intensive type of economic growth, and the planners may choose to devolute economic authority further in less crucial fields of decision making with the express intention of strengthening central planning and the regional coordination of national plans, including perhaps also the more willing receptiveness toward joint planning of selected activities within the established interstate framework of CMEA cooperation. Within these more or less unalterable features of the superstructure, the actual organization of the CPEs and the CMEA institutions, several rather important mutations or shifts in emphasis are wholly plausible.

The evolution of SEI in the next decade or so will probably be shaped by a two-pronged tackle. First, the degree of production specialization will be reinforced and joint efforts directed at alleviating the short supply of critical materials will be stepped up, regardless of what may materialize on the monetary and financial front. This is all the more likely to come about if the preeminent partner shows itself committed to strengthening CMEA cohesion, a probable course given the present constellation of forces in the region. And central planning will be the chief instrument mobilized to accomplish the contemplated moves.

Specific decisions will be linked primarily to the tasks embedded in the Target Programs, which are expected to be forged into the mainstay of economic cooperation until the turn of the century. Primary attention will revolve around the exploitation of Soviet raw materials and related processing facilities, tasks that are in fact not dissimilar from those included for the first time in the Concerted Plan. Such activities have required on balance a transfer of substantial capital and labor resources from the smaller CPEs to the Soviet Union, in return for which the other CPEs are guaranteed security of supply over some predetermined period; they may also gain from a more "lenient attitude" in other matters on the part of the USSR (Brabant 1971, pp. 99–111). The most plausible candidate for such joint activities in the future will be the fuel and raw material sectors. In connection with these locomotive projects, there will also be an appreciable transfer of materials and equipment from the smaller CPEs to the USSR in order to effect the capital transactions. The USSR can be expected to seek more than hitherto steady improvements in quality and technical standards of the processes earmarked for common investments. Although it is too early to trace the pincer movements embedded in the Target Programs still under construction, it is clear that their adoption will necessitate an acceleration of joint investment efforts. According to one estimate, the total volume of productive investment expenditures presently earmarked to implement the Target Programs in the 1980s amounts to some 80,000 to 90,000 million rubles in constant prices (Semenov 1978, p. 104), which is far beyond the amount of coordinated investments undertaken ever before.[17]

As a crucial component part of regular bilateral or other trade agreements, all CPEs, especially the developed ones, will insist on much more effective specialization in manufactures. Fears that production specialization will stifle development and possibly lock some CPEs into an entrenched position of producer of agricultural and primary goods for the rest of the region need, hopefully, no longer be mollified, owing to past industrialization efforts and strident opposition to intersectoral specialization. Indeed, the sole country presently "forced" to behave in trade as a developing country is the USSR. Without completely foregoing the mobilization of its rich resources, this country apparently expects to widen its range of exportables also to the CMEA market, something that in the absence of a sharp acceleration in specialization will inevitably entail serious conflicts in trade intentions, and may therefore endanger growth prospects of the small CPEs. This outlook itself should allay the recalcitrant CPEs' insistence on the inviolability of national sovereignty, their fundamental prerogative to any type of industrialization at the expense of established markets, strictly bilateral cooperation, and so on – still very powerful obstacles to the deepening of SEI. Clearly, the course of future action will to a considerable extent be codetermined by the prospective East–West environment, and the CPEs' ability to restructure their own economic profiles, mainly on the basis of resources at their disposal.

Although one may expect the ISDL to be furthered also as a result of the Target Programs for consumer durables, foodstuffs, and transportation, the performance in these sectors (except perhaps transportation, which in recent years has become a critical bottleneck sector in a number of CPEs), will not dramatically alter the stage of trade and specialization opportunities, unless a number of other conditions of CMEA cooperation will be measurably improved. If the CPEs will seek a minimum degree of regional cooperation in order to support high levels of trade and industrial activity at home without focusing with determination on the continuous improvement in economic organization and policy instruments, SEI gains will materialize not as ends in themselves – the preferred structure of long-term regional interdependence – but as means to the end of maintaining rapid growth through relentless industrialization and regional cooperation on the basis of the well-tried methods of the past – on the whole a retrogression.

The second type of adjustment that might be envisaged consists of redesigning the present organizational and institutional provisions with a view toward relaxing the CPEs' built-in obstructions to the implementation of comprehensive specialization. Although such reforms or adaptations will also help to accommodate the foundations for the first type of actions, they will play an immensely greater role in nursing the creation of a fully interdependent regional economy charted along more rational economic lines. Such a dovetailed economy would furnish viable markets for the chief exportables of the CPEs in exchange for basic supplies of strategic primary goods, without necessarily being predicated on attaining regional autarky.

Reforms enabling the participants to carry out the salient features of the Target Programs, at least to the extent that these measures can be gauged at this time, center critically on ameliorating the methodology and mechanics of planning and plan coordination, something that is not perforce insurmountable. Much more significant, however, is fostering cooperation through the coordinated exploitation of current and prospective comparative advantages, for which the CPEs will have to add important components to the present SEI mechanism. In devising regional specialization, market-based criteria of choice and coordination instruments will of necessity have to be recognized for their technical allocatory function, without vitiating any of the basic tenets of socialism, challenging the preeminence of the USSR, or sacrificing the sacrosanct concept of national sovereignty far beyond the present degree of compromise. Of critical importance will also be the moderation of bilateralism and the elimination of structural bilateralism in the trade model and trade policies, and the effective relaxation of the almost complete disjunction between internal economic activity and external trade and cooperation. To carry this out, the CMEA price-formation mechanism will have to be reformulated, a revision that could usefully be coupled with transformations in internal price policies, though the one is not necessarily contingent on the other. To exploit the advantages of prices and other indirect instruments in resource allocation, producers should be enabled to establish direct contacts across national boundaries, clearly within the overall policy guidelines of the CPEs involved (though, incidentally, macroeconomic controls in the various countries need not be perfectly synchronized). Direct contacts and more flexible price formation on the basis of market forces will help to implement multilateralism in trade, payments, and cooperation. This in turn will facilitate the regional mobility of goods and services in search of equalizing relative scarcities throughout the region.

As noted, a critical component of the potential for sharply accelerating SEI is the diversification of markets, and hence the future role of developed and developing MTEs in propping up SEI indirectly. Whereas the unprecedented expansion in trade with the developed MTEs in the early 1970s was on the whole a welcome trend, inasmuch as it enabled the CPEs to gather valuable experience in marketing exportables in a more competitive environment and to realize a pronounced increase in the inflow of technology, this temporarily burgeoning interregional trade has also had pronounced negative implications. Perhaps the most severe constraint on the future continuation of this interaction is the emergence in the 1970s of persistent large deficits in the East–West balance of payments. Whereas these pressures could be alleviated temporarily by the high liquidity of Western financial markets, the strategy envisaging self-liquidating loans has on the whole miscarried. Part of the blame for the chronic deficits stems from successive adverse crops and consumer pressure that have been only to some extent of the CPEs' making. More to the point is the chronic issue of gaining greater access to Western markets. Although Western import demand in the mid-1970s continued to be sluggish for far longer than anticipated, the CPEs were unable in many instances to implement their envisaged export strategies, in part because their export profile was mismatched with Western demand and also because of the inward-turning of the MTEs as a group and competition in the advanced MTE markets from products coming on stream in the developing MTEs. Though intensive trade expansion will be sought in the 1980s, including appreciable transfers of capital funds to the CMEA to finance some portion of the expected increase in the import demand for technology, it is hardly likely that the growth path charted in the first half of the 1970s will be resumed soon.

Interaction with the developing MTEs will probably become a very dynamic component of the CPEs' trade. As noted, one source of this growth is likely to emerge as a result of the expected increase in the CPEs' demand for foodstuffs, basic materials, and fuels – sectors in which regional supply constraints in the 1980s will be much more stringent than before. In view of the developing MTEs' comparative advantage in labor-intensive processes, especially consumer durables, and the forecasted marked shift in the CPEs' comparative advantage further against labor-intensive production, owing to the growing scarcity and rising cost of labor, the CPEs will be compelled to seek structural shifts within the region that entail larger imports of manufactures. In view of their ability to compete effectively for outlets of a number of more complex manufactures, in relation with developing MTEs, balance of payments considerations will here perhaps be less severe than in relations with the developed MTEs.

On balance, these interregional trends may further decrease the regional concentration of the CPEs' trade, perhaps combined with a decline in the share of the developed MTEs, but will sharply augment the share of the developing MTEs. It would be a gross mistake, however, to interpret these eventualities as a disintegration of the CMEA or as one further instance spelling the bankruptcy of SEI. As argued in greater detail in section 3, such a trend would exert further pressure on pursuing without wavering more logical and more demanding integration policies than those practiced to date.

6. Concluding remarks

Clearly, a positive appraisal of the SEI's future hinges to a large extent on the CPEs' ability to enact innovative changes in the organized forms of planned integration as an alternative to some type of market mechanism. Although the obstacles ahead should not be taken too lightly, there is some ground for guarded optimism, in the sense that the CPEs can achieve a far larger degree of SEI through planning than attained so far, provided the will to do so is unambiguous and the environment, including East–West relations, remains receptive to the enactment of the required adaptations. Certainly, autonomy relinquished to the lowest level of the plan hierarchy may affect the power base of the ruling leaders of the CPEs, and regional integration may lock these countries into a position where decisions can be made effectively only by including in their scope possible impacts on other economies. These developments are doubtlessly real and should be carefully watched, but it is not clear why devolution within the CPE would inevitably destroy the fabric of the socialist society as perceived by the elite in charge or why a reinforcement of SEI would only "serve as a mechanism to fuse the national economies . . . into that of the Soviet Union" (Abonyi 1977, pp. 145–146). Abstaining from such adjustments will in the not too distant future strangle the small CPEs, if the earlier assessment of growth prospects is correct.

There are no cut and dried methods that will deterministically yield SEI, though some policy makers in Eastern Europe may cherish the illusion of charting everything beforehand in detailed central plans. Leaders doubtlessly conceive possible courses of action, and they should do so within the frame of events and in actual encounters. As M. Djilas has observed: "Every time leaders deduce courses of action out of their own heads and their own fond hopes, they are mercilessly punished by reality and taught a lesson – if indeed they are still in a position to learn" (Djilas 1977, p. 8). One may hope that the doctrinaire approach to SEI will be realistically attenuated in the near future, and that the CPEs will demonstrate sufficient flexibility to correct their preconceived plans to the benefit of the region as a whole.

Notes

Introduction

1 The full title reads: *The Comprehensive Program for the Further Extension and Improvement of Cooperation and the Development of Socialist Economic Integration by the CMEA Member Countries*. The official version of the program was first made available in all main party newspapers of 7 August 1971, and has been reproduced in many books (e.g., Tokareva 1972, pp. 29–103), pamphlets (Complex 1972), and periodicals. The document will hereafter be referred to as "Complex Program" because the equivalent of the Russian *kompleksnyj* is either "complex" or "comprehensive," and both renderings have been used in the literature, and also because the program is far from comprehensive in the sense that it does not exhaustively and programmatically cover all main aspects of SEI.

2 "Commodity–money relations" is socialist jargon for most instruments of indirect economic coordination. For an East European definition, see Bozyk 1977, p. 146. A summary of Eastern and Western views is provided in Brabant 1977, pp. xv–xxv.

3 That is, pertaining to the objective sought. A specialization agreement phrased in general terms of socialist friendship, mutual advantage, respect for national interest and sovereignty, and the like will be considered "irrelevant," although this may well be a necessary diplomatic phase in the process of working out more concrete contracts.

4 This is a very brief sketch of the highly involved literature regarding the nonantagonistic nature of the various national interests and responsibilities of the members in the process of enhancing closer cooperation.

5 For more about the cognitive problems of studying CPEs, see Campbell 1966; 1974, pp. 174–177; Stehr 1978, pp. 525–537; and Treml 1974, pp. 72–74.

6 Several recent East European publications have stressed this without, however, offering convincing proof (see, for instance, Larionov 1973, p. 71; and Nazarkin 1973, p. 83).

319

Chapter 1. The initial framework of East European economic cooperation

1 For a more comprehensive political analysis covering in detail the complex background of the late 1940s, see Brzezinski 1961 and Yergin 1977. M. Kaser has drawn a stimulating economic, political, and ideological picture (Kaser 1967).

2 If such a blueprint of the purposefulness and policy coherence of the USSR in fact existed, it has never been revealed. Much of what is now considered as Stalin's policy for Eastern Europe amounts to an ex post rationalization of the big power conferences during and after the war, and of the events of postwar East European history, insofar as this has become known at all. For some inside glimpses, see Dedijer 1971; Djilas 1963; and Ionescu 1965.

3 The legacies of prewar developments were important in that they made some of the East European leaders agitate in favor of the creation of a regional institution with sufficient power to initiate an embryonic form of economic integration. Unfortunately, this interesting period cannot be explored here in any detail. For an initiation to the many vexing problems, the reader is referred to, among others, Basch 1943a; Hertz 1947; Marczewski 1956; and Rothschild 1974.

4 The USSR's allergic reaction to the Marshall Plan, as briefly summarized here, continues to be reflected in the current literature (e.g., Faddeev 1974b, pp. 30–32; 1974c, pp. 19–20; Lukin 1974, pp. 43–45).

5 Wandycz 1970 is a very useful historical source for these projects. For other details, see Basch 1943a, pp. 51–69; Kuhl 1958, pp. 31–38; and Marczewski 1956, pp. 96–98.

6 For a firsthand account, see Djilas 1963, pp. 94–98. Also Berend 1971, pp. 10–16, offers useful details. See also the next section for Stalin's meddling in schemes to promote regionalism without the USSR's aid.

7 It seems that such a proposal was made by the Polish representative E. Szyr during one of the first deliberations leading up to the creation of the CMEA.

8 A high-level official of the CMEA, Igor Žuzavlev, argued this point in a personal interview with G. Amundsen (Amundsen 1971, p. 80), but did not disclose further details (private correspondence with the interviewer).

9 For some details, see the interesting series of articles in various issues of *Közgazdasági Szemle* of 1966 and 1968.

10 Although the Cominform must have devoted some of its debates and activities to economic matters, they certainly were not its leading preoccupation. The opposite is argued, for instance, in Kis 1964, pp. 122–124. Similar views are propounded in Ferrell 1966, p. 122, who terms the Cominform a "bogus economic plan."

11 This terminology, which is by no means standard, will be avoided

here. There are at least three series of hastily improvised attempts to bolster cooperation, including the CMEA's foundation, that have been labeled the "Molotov Plan" in the West.

12 It seems hardly likely that Yugoslavia's condemnation and isolation were the principal goals behind the CMEA's creation. There is just too little evidence to support the views adopted, for instance, by Agoston 1965, p. 26. But it is generally agreed that the CMEA contributed to Yugoslavia's isolation (Cizkovsky 1971, pp. 59–60).

13 N. V. Faddeev has published numerous articles about the CMEA's evolution and three editions of the CMEA's history, none of which yields solid information on the matter.

14 Even Kaser confuses the issue by suggesting 22 January (Kaser 1967, p. 11). He may have mixed up 22 February, when Albania joined the CMEA (which it did not, for example, in January 1949 [Rutkowski 1964, pp. 238–239], April 1949 [Kohler 1965, p. 81], or in 1950 [UN 1966, p. 8]).

15 As an illustration of how odd sources can be, T. I. Kis indicates that the Council was set up during a meeting in Warsaw (Kis 1964, p. 130), though there is no evidence to support this. Kis probably confounded the Cominform's creation at a secret meeting in Poland in September 1947 with the one that apparently inaugurated CMEA.

16 The Rumanian version of the document contains some ambiguities that appear to be inconsistent, for example, with contemporary socialist treaty language. Officers of the U.S. Legation held the document to be genuine. It was perhaps a draft treaty in need of further political deliberations. The genesis and portent of the document are traced in Brabant 1979, which also contains a full English translation of the original Rumanian-language version.

17 The literature is not always consistent here. Albania became a member in February 1949, Cuba in 1972, and Vietnam in 1978. Albania ceased to participate in the CMEA's activities in late 1961, although formally remaining a full member. Yugoslavia apparently requested admission in 1949, which would tend to refute that it was the CMEA's explicit objective to boycott Yugoslavia, but was rebuffed because of the Stalin–Tito disagreement. It is therefore quite erroneous to include Yugoslavia, of all countries, among the founder members (Meyer 1966, p. 365). But it is equally misleading to include Albania (as in Richter 1968, p. 18), unless one dates the Council's foundation as April 1949.

18 Čížkovský quotes from *Osnovnye dokumenty vnešnej politiki SSSR, 1949*, p. 76 – a source that is not apparently available to Western researchers. Dedijer's story of the Stalin–Tito rift claims that Yugoslavia was in the picture of the conference's purposes (Dedijer 1971, p. 197), though Yugoslavia protested officially on 1 February 1949 that it had neither been invited nor informed about the CMEA's formation (Carlyle 1953, p. 443).

19 According to Foreign 1976, p. 4, Sulzberger's source was either the State Department or the U.S. Legation in Bucharest, which obtained

a copy of the treaty. In private correspondence, Sulzberger has informed this writer that he cannot recall whether he ever saw the document and, if so, under what circumstances.

20 In 1949 rubles, equivalent at that time to about 19 million dollars. At the exchange rate introduced as a result of the Soviet monetary reform of 1 March 1950, the fund would have equaled 25 million dollars. However, according to the document, the pledged shares could be contributed also in rubles (Brabant 1979), which, depending upon the exchange rate one might choose to apply, would have reduced the dollar value of the contemplated fund.

21 To avoid needless confusion, it bears remarking that a permanent Secretariat with such a name was established during the fourth CMEA Session in 1954. The body called into existence during the first CMEA Session in April 1949 is usually referred to as the Bureau of the Council, which was endowed with a supporting secretariat in charge of technical matters (see below). The purported founding treaty, however, speaks of a Secretariat General – an unusual phrasing (Brabant 1979).

22 This was an important element of the Polono-Czechoslovak project of 1947 (Spulber 1957, p. 427).

23 There is no further indication of such a meeting. The reference to Czechoslovakia is unclear, except perhaps in view of that country's forced withdrawal from the Marshall Plan deliberations and late entry into the Soviet orbit.

24 Kaser suspects that a charter was under discussion during the second Session. Amundsen obtained similar information regarding the drafting of preliminary statutes in January 1949 (Amundsen 1971, p. 80), but J. Sandorski deems it "very unlikely" that there were statutes before 1959 (Sandorski 1968, p. 571).

25 I. Friss has provided this piece of information in a critique of Berend's skeptical remarks about East European integration intentions in the late 1940s. In a more recent contribution, Berend acknowledges that "some feeble hopes for integration may have existed" (Berend 1971, p. 14). See also Kiss 1973, pp. 109–114.

26 The exact date is not known. Some sources state 24–25 November, whereas others give 25–27 November 1950 or 24 November. The chronicle by the Council's secretary, or rather the latest version of his views of the CMEA's evolution, indicates the first date. This is apparently a revision, for the first edition stated October rather than November 1950. In Cizkovsky 1971, p. 171, 24 November is indicated, but other dates are available in the current literature, including the contributions commemorating the CMEA's thirtieth anniversary.

27 An almost identical text in Kis 1964, p. 132, is referenced as "quoted from official written declarations," without disclosing precise sources.

28 There is indeed not a single scrap of hard evidence to support this.

The statement should perhaps be interpreted in the light of Rumania's postwar role. This country had, of course, been included in some of the proposals dealing with the Balkan Federation, Confederation, or Union, though it has not been reported as a main participant in the debates. The context might also have been Rumania's reaction to the emasculation of Tito's influence in Eastern Europe. It would seem more plausible, though, that the initiatives, if any, were instigated by other communist organizations that happened to be headquartered in Rumania. After Yugoslavia's expulsion from the Cominform, its secretariat was relocated from Belgrade to Bucharest. The Danube Commission – the East European successor to the interwar European Danube Commission – was also headquartered in Bucharest (it was created no more than six months before the CMEA). As host to both organizations, Rumania may have played an active diplomatic role in the CMEA's gestation.

29 It is, however, unclear whether these issues were actually agreed upon in January 1949. But from the context it would seem to refer to resolutions adopted during the January meeting (see also Mirosnicenko 1968, p. 91). Other sources appear to take the April Session as point of reference (Kaser 1967, p. 48; Ribi 1970, p. 93).

30 Naturally, the USSR has been powerful enough to impose on its allies whatever was deemed to be in its interest. SEI could have been pushed through had there not been other short- and long-term interests in the region that contravened the realization of what appeared to be a limited objective.

31 According to well-placed CMEA officials, the Secretariat's library contains a full set of the archival materials, sometimes (as in Faddeev 1974b, p. 50; and Lukin 1974, p. 45) obliquely referred to as "founding documents," but access is absolutely restricted to a handful of CMEA officials and high-level CPE policy makers.

32 Whether or not the communiqué amounts to a legally binding treaty and the Council as such was thereby legally established, can be nicely debated. In most of the Western literature about the Council, East European references to the "founding document(s)" are interpreted to mean the founding communiqué and the documents of the first Council Session (as for instance in Szawlowski 1963, p. 670), which is apparently erroneous if the information adduced here is reliable.

33 As A. Nove has argued (Nove 1970, p. 295), the reason for Voznesenskij's dismissal and elimination is probably far more complex. In recent articles discussing Voznesenskij's contribution to Soviet planning (see Sorokin 1973), one searches in vain for his opinions on "integration." Contemporary foreign assessments of the "Voznesenskij affair" suggest that the brilliant planner vacated Gosplan possibly to head the CMEA organization (Foreign 1976, p. 595).

34 Too little is known about these earlier plans to conclude unequivocally that from their very inception they were as rigid as the Soviet plans of the 1930s.

Chapter 2. Salient features of domestic economic developments

1 However, when socialist ideologists write that the laws are objective in that they express "essential, internal, and necessary economic relationships independent of human consciousness and preferences" (Rumjancev 1973, p. 17), they mean something quite different from, say, the objective validity of the law of gravity. There are many works dealing with the laws of socialist development, but the intellectual and theoretical heritage is well explained in Sweezy 1968, especially pp. 75–130.

2 If it were a natural development recently identified by "leading economic thought" (Dudinskij 1970, p. 3), it should logically follow that, until recently, this law was wrongly interpreted, for in the past "integration" was typically taken to be a truly capitalist activity and hence a concept alien to socialist international relations. In fact, until the late 1960s, it was considered tantamount to exploitation and domination, and therefore inapplicable to socialist cooperation.

3 Kornai, for example, has not made it clear whether a disharmonious economic policy directed at redressing a disharmonious economy is "harmonious" or "disharmonious."

4 This was initially understood as an economy producing nearly everything, but not necessarily as an economy capable of producing everything efficiently. For a short but useful discussion, see Dodge 1970, especially pp. 338–346.

5 For a summary of East European views, see the proceedings of a conference on intensive and extensive development in *Vestnik moskovskogo universiteta*, 1972:1. A useful distinction is also drawn in Kohlmey 1966.

6 Although general-equilibrium theories may well not be directly applicable to policies of the CPEs, nor can they be translated into action-oriented policies for MTEs without substantial modifications and extensions, components of this compact theory will be borrowed because economic rationality *in se* is independent of social systems; no normative conclusions will be drawn from the theoretical arguments.

7 Further details of the traditional model are available in, among other sources, Bergson 1964; Wellisz 1964; and Wiles 1962. A synoptic survey of old and new in the CPE model is given in Campbell 1974; Marczewski 1973; and Wilczynski 1972.

8 Details about these norms are, for example, in Feiwel 1965; Granick 1954; and Kornai 1959.

9 For an analytical treatment of such phenomena encountered in the Czechoslovak reform of the late 1950s, see Wedel 1971, 1974, and 1976.

10 Rational, correct target, optimal, efficient, and other such notions

are normally used here as defined in general-equilibrium analysis without suggesting that central planners can draw scholastic inferences, as in neoclassical theory, from a set of production possibility functions and community or state welfare functions. J. Kornai (Kornai 1971, pp. 100–113; 1972, pp. 52–60) emphasizes that planners are actually guided more by empiricism, or by what is considered "normal" elsewhere, than by abstract formulations for optimal decisions.

11 Market-type relations denote here the type of demand and supply forces typical of stylized MTEs, but also the simulation on a central level of what the rational alternatives are from which the best solution can be selected for implementation.

12 Putting it in Kornai's terms, a drastic change in the average price of foodstuffs relative to that of other consumer goods, for example, may induce consumers to spend 28 rather than 30 percent of their income on foodstuffs, but certainly not 10 or 50 percent (Kornai 1972, p. 33).

13 The evils of the "law of value" in MTEs are usually invoked to justify the marginal role of prices in guiding economic activities in CPEs. But there seems to be quite a difference between "spontaneity," or the law of value as interpreted and rejected by some socialist writers, and the implementation of indirect policy regulators to assure greater rationality in the planning process.

14 Of course, physical targets can also be manipulated. For classical examples of faulty execution in terms of central expectations and of open-ended physical plan specifications, see Granick 1954 and Kornai 1959.

15 Important exceptions are the peasant market, the handicraft sector, private services, and the black or gray markets in many spheres of production and consumption where prices are to a large extent influenced by demand and supply. Also, as in the USSR, there may be a number of "republican" price levels for segmented markets (e.g., foodstuffs) calculated on the basis of average costs in a region (Bornstein 1978).

16 M. Ellman argues that the direct financing of industry during the Soviet first five-year plan and later on in China did not originate in agriculture (Ellman 1975, 1978). Empirical evidence for the USSR suggests that agriculture was actually receiving more in terms of goods and services than it paid in "tribute" through forced procurements, low prices, and so on. It is not known whether this proposition can be corroborated for Eastern Europe. Note, however, that the findings are preliminary and do not necessarily contradict that a substantial portion of accumulation earmarked for industry actually originated in the state's expropriation of part of the agricultural surplus. Further refinements of the measurement (e.g., the influence of inventories on the balance sheet) would also be commendable.

17 For a brief but lucid description, see Marczewski 1973, pp. 32–38. A perceptive analysis of the various agricultural policies until the mid-1950s is still Sanders 1958.
18 Full employment has been a key social and economic objective of the CPEs. But the absence of unemployment does not necessarily indicate optimal employment. Within certain limits, labor could be withdrawn from agriculture in favor of industry without depressing output. Similarly, up to a point capital can be substituted for labor without affecting productivity or output. Once the upper limit of this factor substitution is reached, however, one of the essential sources of extensive growth will be exhausted.
19 For a much more elaborate discussion of the overall features of the reforms, see, for instance, Bornstein 1973, 1975; Hohmann 1972; JEC 1974, 1977; Marczewski 1973; Selucky 1972; and Wilczynski 1972. For detailed discussions of individual reforms, the reader is referred to the special literature on the various CPEs.
20 For a useful discussion of the place of this concept in current ideological and political debates, see Evans 1977; Haffner 1978; and Lavigne 1978.

Chapter 3. The role and organization of trade

1 It is implicitly assumed that the matrixes are well-behaved (joint products are not permitted, negative output is ruled out, and the coefficients are fixed at some level of the plan hierarchy).
2 Imports are noncompeting in the sense that the choice of alternative techniques is presumably completed beforehand by the selection of processes included in the planner's purview. Planners may, of course, try out several combinations of alternative processes, but this possibility is obviously limited in the short run for which this model is designed. Essential elements of export and import selection will be ignored here for "we know little about the basis upon which such foreign trade decisions are made" (Holzman 1966, p. 262) in the traditional CPE. However, the issue will be revisited later in this chapter.
3 According to the assumptions stated in "A simple model of the CPE's trade behavior," any feasible solution satisfying equation 3 will be adopted. A more realistic formulation would also include an upper limit on R.
4 The definition of foreign price equivalents in the models above ignored that WMPs are not unique even if reduced to a common currency denominator. This is unrealistic, for price differentiation is of enormous importance in understanding the CPE's trade behavior as examined below.
5 There are, of course, many other problems related to the exchange rate in CPEs. For more details on each type of exchange rate, see Brabant 1977, pp. 245–299.

6 In the case of East Germany, the accounting of trade is in a special commercial exchange rate paralleling the function of the official exchange rate in other CPEs.

7 Usually, machinery; primary and semifinished goods for industrial purposes; foodstuffs; and durable consumer goods. These are the broad groups of the Brussels' trade nomenclature, as modified in the uniform CMEA nomenclature, which are frequently referred to in CPE trade negotiations and discussions. These groups will, of course, be further disaggregated for important transactions as, for instance, in negotiations with the USSR on plans for the second group (see Brabant 1975).

8 For a more detailed argument along the line suggested here, see, among others, Boltho 1971, pp. 37–48; Kalecki 1969, pp. 61–62; and Levine 1968, pp. 259–260.

9 It seems best not to confuse the theory of the CPE's trade with rationalizations, descriptions, and guesses about actual trade behavior. Bearing this in mind, the above proposition in no way contradicts what is sometimes called "the theory of trade in CPEs" (see Holzman 1972).

10 This method is still very important (Grote 1973, pp. 95–98). For an acknowledgment of the persistent drawbacks of this planning tool, see Kormnov 1973, pp. 104–105.

11 For a typology of direct interventions in the exchange market and the place of bilateralism, see Ellis 1941, pp. 1–13.

12 Any good survey of German external economic policies in the 1930s (such as Child 1958) provides a comprehensive analysis of this variety of methods.

13 Under complete specialization and free trade there is no need for a break-even solution. Also, in some types of bilateralism it may be necessary to separate internal and external markets through explicit or implicit taxes and subsidies to support a competitive equilibrium in the internal economy and, separately, in the foreign markets of the home country.

14 Other important factors in selecting bilateralism over alternative policies and instruments are examined in greater detail elsewhere (e.g., Brabant 1973, pp. 70–74).

15 These include all kinds of services not directly related to trade in physical goods (e.g., transport services for merchandise trade are "commercial" but for tourism they are "noncommercial").

16 However, the small country assumption should be used with circumspection. In particular it does not imply in the case of the CPE facing infinitely elastic demand and supply schedules that the MFT would be so much easier to operate, as Dobrin contends for Bulgaria. The same obstacles would occur provided the MFT had to perform the functions it has had in fact. In seems incorrect too to support the proposition (as in Dobrin 1973, p. 102) that CPEs could divert any product at short notice to the Soviet market at given fixed prices.

17 This is apparently the way in which should be understood such statements as "at any world price, the Soviets may, if they choose, export or import additional large quantities without affecting prices" (Holzman 1968, p. 300). Not only is the market for Soviet demand and supply affected, sudden changes can indeed have large repercussions on individual WMPs (e.g., the WMP of grain in 1972–1973).

18 These rules were formally accepted during the ninth CMEA Session in 1958. The most complete and systematic East European source on this – the official document has not been released – is probably Tarnovskij 1968. An excellent summary is in Hewett 1974, pp. 31–37, and revealing analyses of the price practice are provided in Ausch 1969; Basiuk 1975; Mitrofanova 1978; Velickov 1976; and Zukov 1969.

19 In early 1975 it was suddenly decided to discontinue the former practice of keeping starting prices unchanged for several years. As an interim solution, 1975 prices were computed as averages of WMPs prevailing in 1972–1974.

20 For some empirical details, see Ausch 1969, pp. 115–126; and 1972, pp. 72–120. For further evidence of the theoretical debate and references, see Brabant 1970; 1978, pp. 88–90; and Hewett 1974, pp. 60–110.

21 The complexities of East–West trade cannot be dealt with here. For a historical perspective, see Campbell 1974a; and Wilczynski 1969.

22 Statistical reports do not distinguish between trade proper and reexports (defined in the wider sense of flows between two countries that will be deflected to other partners without any further processing by the first importer). Hard evidence on recent reexports can be established on the basis of Hungarian foreign trade statistics (see Brabant 1978a).

23 These limits were neither constant nor well defined until 1964. Since 1972 all swing credits are subject to a modest interest rate, and the overall volume cannot surpass 2 percent of planned regional trade (Brabant 1977, pp. 66–102).

24 Price adjustments for balancing reasons are documented, for example, in Bodnar 1969, pp. 47–48; and Csikos 1969, pp. 55–56. There are, however, other reasons for price adjustments, which are examined below.

25 Trade in specialized products is also frequently regulated by way of supplementary agreements and at different prices. This will be examined in detail in Chapter 5.

26 Principles and practice of labor migration are documented in Vajs 1973, 1974, and 1976.

27 Details on capital mobility are provided with references in Brabant 1977, pp. 103–244.

28 Exceptions are the joint ventures such as Haldex and Przyjaźń (see Chapter 4).

29 The relative degree of hardness will exert pressure on the real terms of trade in bilateral exchange, though this may not be apparent from

aggregate statistics. This is possibly also reflected in negotiated bilateral prices, though the evidence for this until the late 1960s was scant. For the relationship of the relative degree of hardness of goods to the exchange rate, see section 5.

30 This was one of the peculiar characteristics of intra-CMEA cooperation prior to the approval of the integration program in 1971 (see, for example, Ptic+ 1974, pp. 6–8).

31 This does not mean that the doctrine of comparative advantage is universally endorsed. In some cases, as in a recent East German source (Bleßing 1977, pp. 147–148), it appears that the principle is not even properly understood.

32 A more or less comprehensive sample of such indicators is provided in Bleßing 1977, pp. 58–120; Boltho 1971, pp. 62–94; ESE 1965, pp. 43–55; Marczewski 1973, pp. 160–179; and Rybakov 1975.

33 This part of the Rumanian financial and economic reform measures, which were to be introduced in January 1979, appears to have been postponed, possibly until the start of the next medium-term plan.

34 A useful survey of limits on price flexibility in the Hungarian reform is available in Vincze 1972 and elsewhere in Gado 1972. For a summary of theory and practice, see Brabant 1974, pp. 242–269.

35 The exact contours and portent of the announced reforms cannot yet be assessed with full clarity. For a highly instructive, yet broad, outline, see Csikos 1978.

36 Earlier efforts to establish common enterprises, disregarding the notorious joint-stock companies of the immediate postwar period, did not lead to the results hoped for (see Chapter 4).

Chapter 4. The evolution of the Council

1 Whenever the agenda includes key cooperation issues, the Session tends to be merged with the Conference of Communist Parties, even though formally speaking it is still a proper CMEA Session because each CPE nominates its delegates ad hoc.

2 The inclusion of some of the organs (especially some of the IEOs) here is admittedly debatable. However, a pragmatic approach is preferred to a purely legalistic one.

3 The frequency of the meetings has been quite irregular. Initially the Council should have been in session four times a year, but this frequency was never attained. The original version (1959) of the charter stipulated that regular sessions would be convened at least twice a year. This reduced tempo was attained in 1949, 1954, 1958, 1959, 1961, and 1962. But at the sixteenth Session (June 1962), now referred to as "extraordinary," the frequency requirement was reduced to once a year. Since then, the Council has been convened annually, except in 1964 and 1968 (probably in view of the open disagreement with Rumania and the aftermath of the Czechoslovak crisis). Two sessions were held in 1969, the second of which is con-

sidered "special." The geographical rotation seems to apply only to the regular meetings and apparently only to the European capitals.

4 This is sometimes reported as "special," in contradistinction to the 1962 meeting, which is labeled "extraordinary" (Schlicker 1974, p. 12). Other authors call both "extraordinary" (e.g., Cizkovsky 1971, p. 172; Huber 1974, p. 20).

5 Officially, the Bureau of the Executive Committee for Integrated Planning Problems, set up in 1962. It became important in late 1963 (Kaser 1967, pp. 111–112).

6 For further official details, see the bylaws of these commissions in Tokareva 1976, pp. 31–38, 41–44.

7 There has been speculation that there is at least one more Commission on armaments. In view of the "unintegrated" nature of armaments in the CPEs and the existence of the Warsaw joint command, this would seem implausible, though. In the latest collection of official documents published by the Secretariat (CMEA 1976), the Commissions for foreign trade and standardization are omitted, though recent meetings of these organs have been reported elsewhere.

8 Thus the occasional meetings of banking and financial experts in the late 1950s apparently "recommended" the establishment of a permanent commission on currency and finance and the creation of the IBEC. It was apparently the Conference on Health that led to the Permanent Commission for Health Care.

9 It was reported recently that Rumania does not participate in the Commission on public health, although it endorsed its establishment (CMEA 1976b, p. 12), and the Institute on economic problems (CMEA 1978, pp. 29–30). The reason for this absence is not clear. Rumania perhaps wanted to set a precedent in abstaining from the work of the health Commission or it simply saw this action as one more way of venting its displeasure with current integration developments (Semradova 1975, p. 16).

10 A survey of the IEOs with membership and main tasks is provided, among others, in Apro 1969; Caillot 1971; Konstantinov 1977; Lavigne 1973; Menzinskij 1971; Szawlowski 1976; Tokareva 1976a; Trend 1975; Valek 1979; and Veljaminov 1977. But none is really complete.

11 The third criterion will not be discussed here. Note that not all members take part in all IEOs. In some IEOs the members are governmental institutions, whereas in others they are individual enterprises of the participating CPEs.

12 The financial institutions are examined in detail in Brabant 1977, pp. 103–244.

13 Another joint German–Polish venture on the construction of a common barrel bearings factory in East Germany was agreed upon in 1973 (Rolow 1974, p. 13), and formal protocols were signed in September 1974 (Bien 1975, p. 473). Its present status is, however, uncertain. East Germany also agreed to construct a plant for technolog-

ical equipment for the electronics industry in Novovolynsk together with Poland and the USSR. Though it started operations in 1976 (Karpic 1976, p. 11), it is unclear whether the venture functions as a joint enterprise (*Ėkonomičeskaja gazeta*, 1978:33, p. 20). Intransmaš, the Bulgarian–Hungarian venture dealing with the design of intrafirm transportation systems, is also reported as a joint enterprise. However, it does not appear to function as such and will therefore be included here with the branch-technical IEOs. Similarly for Interlichter, created in 1978 by Bulgaria, Czechoslovakia, Hungary, and the Soviet Union to facilitate the transshipment from ocean liners to river transportation; the organization is concerned with the design and development coordination of "mother" ships that can take on standardized barges.

14 For a more rounded view of the economics of IEOs, see Brabant 1977, pp. 279–293.

15 Even knowledgeable East European specialists do not share the rather optimistic interpretations entertained, for instance, in Hewett 1974, pp. 10–13.

16 Such exchanges are sought primarily outside regular BTPAs and, at least on some occasions, the members have made objections to the bilateral balancing requirements of these supplementary agreements (*Horizont*, 1973:11, p. 23).

17 The combination of iron ore from the Kursk Magnetic Anomaly with Polish coke in a joint metallurgical plant currently under construction in the USSR is one of the large projects included in the current, coordinated medium-term plans.

18 Stoian's rather impetuous outburst signals by no means a basic shift in Rumania's attitude toward SEI. It probably reflects the reportedly vituperative intramural exchange of views that preceded the thirty-second Council Session.

19 There is some reason to believe that previously some statutes may have guided the Council's work, but they were never disclosed and possibly not endorsed by all members (see Chapter 1).

20 But Rumania is adamant on the sacrosanct nature of these principles and their implications (Stoian 1978), and other members occasionally embrace them in defense of actions that do not quite conform with a regional integration movement.

21 It is also to be noted that neither the Basic Principles nor the Complex Program are legal documents because they were not ratified by the national parliaments. Strictly speaking, these declarations of intentions are therefore not binding on the signatories.

22 At the time the Basic Principles were in the making, the members apparently envisaged the construction of a significant number of IEOs; hence the call in IBEC's agreement to further such endeavors, to be instituted in due course in support of the ISDL through joint planning. The Executive Committee apparently adopted in February 1963 a list of projects in metallurgy, smelting, machine tools and tooling industries, transportation equipment, and ball bearings, and

these projects were on its plan agenda through 1965. Only some came into existence as interstate economic organizations (Janik 1975, p. 101).

23 The socioeconomic environment in which the Complex Program was negotiated in 1969–1971 was clearly overshadowed by the 1968 events in Czechoslovakia, the so-called Brežnev doctrine of limited sovereignty, and generally by the perception that serious centrifugal forces tended to hollow out the cohesion of the region. Such political and strategic considerations are set forth chronologically in Schaefer 1972.

24 The document ritually repeats a number of other, largely noneconomic, goals of socialist internationalism (Brabant 1974, p. 107).

25 There has been a very intensive debate on the question of a "mechanism of legal integration," but only some of these interesting topics can be touched upon here. For further details, the reader is referred to the specialized literature (e.g., Kampa 1976; Seiffert 1972, 1972a, 1972b).

26 None of these plans and programs has so far been published in detail. The components mentioned here are a summary of statements in the press and specialized literature. For a more comprehensive analysis of the target-programming approach, see Brabant 1979b.

Chapter 5. East European economic cooperation in retrospect and issues for the future

1 The USSR is, of course, dominant in the sense that without its overt or tacit approval, SEI cannot be carried out; but this does not forcibly imply that all positive progress is exclusively in line with Soviet policy objectives.

2 As noted, the twenty-seventh Council Session recommended that the national plans should devote a special section to integration measures. For details concerning the Soviet and East German plans, see Huber 1974a, pp. 569–571. On related methodological questions, see Rybakov 1974, pp. 40–48.

3 Recall, however, that the program contains two different types of deadlines: (1) measures affecting the present planning and management of concrete industrial projects, and (2) deadlines related to monetary and financial instruments. Although the latter are deemed more important in this study, it may well be true that the literature is referring only or mainly to the first type, but this is not unambiguous.

4 One school of thought on SEI argued a few years ago that the prerequisites for the emergence of such a policy should be enacted (Csikos 1971, pp. 110–112; Kiss 1971, pp. 125–142; and Brabant 1974, pp. 113–117, for a summary). Certainly, some CPEs have promulgated detailed tariff schedules, but these have not yet been implemented or where they are used effectively, as in Hungary, trade decisions continue to be predominantly based on criteria other than

relative prices; in any case, tariff barriers do not apply to trade with other CPEs.

5 Pelzman argues that the annual trade negotiations actually imply a proxy for a real tariff (Pelzman 1977, p. 713). However, current trade does not matter much in formulating and implementing agreed specialization. It would therefore appear proper to utilize a less contrived justification for introducing MTE terminology.

6 A more detailed discussion of the need for sensitivity analyses to obtain plausible ranges of integration effects is in Brabant 1979a.

7 Complete details regarding data construction, methodology, and interpretation of results are in Brabant 1978b and 1979a.

8 In the case of Hungary, for instance, it was found (Brabant 1979a) that the internal trade creation effect was attained especially from industrial raw materials and manufactures, though this was partly offset (especially for manufactures) by external trade diversion. This result would seem to conflict with the frequently aired thesis that Hungary, among other CPEs, has become increasingly more dependent on imports of investment goods as a whole from the developed MTEs.

9 This has become a major objective not only because it is *in se* a crucial concern of the policy makers of the CPEs, but also because the markedly risen expectations of the East European consumer, after years of austerity, have forced the leadership to seek economic policies that may help to bridge insufficiencies in national and regional arrangements.

10 The results for Hungary reported in the preceding section and elsewhere (Brabant 1978b, 1979a) would seem to buttress this.

11 That this "maneuver" has actually backfired with dire consequences for developments in the late 1970s and beyond cannot be blamed solely on Gierek or his advisers.

12 In CPE exports to developed MTEs in the 1970s, the most dynamic component has been manufactures (especially textiles, clothing, footwear) that directly compete with exports of the developing MTEs. Further expansion of such products may entail serious conflicts. Given the current "north–south" dialogue and the protectionist bent of the developed MTEs, the latter may wish to attenuate these trade conflicts by acting in favor of the developing MTEs. In any case, the CPEs do not appear to have a long-term comparative advantage in such labor-intensive goods and need therefore explore more sophisticated exportables.

13 Without elaborating at length on this question, it is useful to draw attention to the following. It is frequently argued (e.g., Marer 1974) that the USSR has exploited its allies by means of unrequited transfers through such devices as reparation payments, joint-stock companies, compensations for the stationing of Soviet troops, discriminatory prices, and so forth. Whether these postwar transactions can in fact be identified as benefits of SEI enjoyed by the USSR at the expense of other CPEs is doubtful. Most of these purported benefits resulted from settlements directly related to the defeat of Germany

and its allies as hammered out in Potsdam, well before the Sovietization of Eastern Europe. Even if this region had not been drawn into the Soviet orbit, the USSR would probably not have renounced its claims (which were perhaps the thorniest issue in postwar negotiations), and the USSR's wartime allies in turn would probably not have denied reparations. In that light, it would appear proper to scale down estimates of the CPEs' tribute imposed by their integration in the CMEA. In any case, it seems rather inappropriate to interpret these transfers one-sidedly as the "benefits of SEI" enjoyed by the USSR.

14 The revised price formula adopted in early 1975 is said to be valid for the current medium-term planning period. Although no concrete guidelines for revision in the years ahead have thus far been announced, it would appear logical to seek such changes especially in connection with facilitating the implementation of the Target Programs. There are a few indications (Brabant 1979b) that important changes are in the offing.

15 This has been contended by some Western writers (e.g., Hewett 1974, pp. 108–114; Marer 1974, pp. 160–161). In view of the other objectives of the USSR and the means at its disposal to attenuate the purported burden of associating with CPEs, this proposition is rather naive. The suggestion that the USSR has not taken positive steps to alleviate presumed losses from CMEA trade, partly because it has been relatively unconcerned about costs, is too simple to make the above proposition regarding future allegiances palatable.

16 Projections are inevitably contingent on a number of assumptions. The present section is based on different projections, but especially UN 1978.

17 Coordinated investments for 1976–1980, as forecast in the Concerted Plan, amount to some 7,000 million transferable rubles, although some additional sum should be allowed for on account of the unvalued specialization and scientific-technical cooperation measures included in the plan and additional expenses associated with other SEI endeavors. Nevertheless, the total sum in question cannot have been more than 10,000 million rubles, which is substantially less than what would seem to be in the offing for the next two medium-term planning periods. However, the estimates cited are still preliminary, pending detailed agreements on how the Target Programs will be disaggregated into successive Concerted Plans. In a recent interview, Ju. S. Sirjaev, presently director of the CMEA economic research institute, estimated that common projects in the 1980s would call for from 66,000 to 86,000 million transferable rubles (*Die Presse*, 10 March 1979). It is unfortunately not known what portion of these estimated totals will involve regional capital and labor transfers. For a more detailed examination of the East European growth strategy apparently embedded in the Target Programs, see Brabant 1979b.

Bibliography

Abonyi, A. (1977), and I. J. Sylvain. "CMEA Integration and Policy Options for Eastern Europe." *Journal of Common Market Studies* 2:132–154.

Ágoston, I. (1965). *Le marché commun communiste – principes et pratique du COMECON*, 2d ed. Geneva: Droz.

Alampiev, P. M. (1971), O. T. Bogomolov, and Ju. S. Širjaev. *Ėkonomičeskaja integracija – ob"ektivnaja potrebnost' razvitija mirovogo socializma.* Moscow: Mysl'.

Alekseev, A. (1974). "V rusle socialističeskoj integracii." *Mirovaja ėkonomika i meždunarodnye otnošenija* 3:13–25.

Alexandrowicz, C. (1950). "Comecon: The Soviet Retort to the Marshall Plan." *World Affairs* 1:35–47.

Altman, O. L. (1960). "Russian Gold and the Ruble." *Staff Papers* 3:416–438.

Amundsen, G. L. (1971). *Le conseil d'entraide économique – structure, réalisations, perspectives.* Strasbourg: Institut des Hautes Etudes Européennes.

Apró, A. (1969). *Sotrudničestvo stran-členov SĖV v ėkonomičeskich organizacijach socialističeskich stran.* Moscow: Ėkonomika.

Ausch, S. (1969), and F. Bartha. "Theoretical Problems of CMEA Intertrade Prices." In Foldi 1969, pp. 101–126.

——— (1972). *Theory and Practice of CMEA Cooperation.* Budapest: Akadémiai Kiadó.

Bajbakov, N. (1976). "Novoe v koordinacii narodnochozjajstvennych planov stran-členov SĖV." *Ėkonomičeskoe sotrudničestvo stran-členov SĖV* 3:8–12.

Barčák, A. (1974). "Die Bedeutung der wirtschaftlichen Zusammenarbeit der ČSSR im Bereich des Aussenhandels mit den RGW-Mitgliedsländern." *Aussenhandel der Tschechoslowakei* 9:3–6.

Basch, A. (1943). "European Economic Integration." *American Economic Review* 1/2:408–419.

——— (1943a). *The Danube Basin and the German Economic Sphere.* New York: Columbia University Press.

Basiuk, J. (1975), M. Jaroszyńska, and B. Krawczyk. *Ceny handlu zagranicznego na rynku krajów RWPG.* Warsaw: PWE.

Batizi, Gy. (1978). 'A szocialista külkereskedelmi árrendszer tovább-fejlesztése." *Külgazdaság* 10:38–47.

Bauman, L. (1978), and B. Grebennikov. "Gorizonty socialističeskoj integracii." *Meždunarodnaja žizn'* 9:16–28.

Bautina, N. V. (1973), Ju. F. Kormnov, and M. A. Borisovskaja. *Osobennosti meždunarodnogo socialističeskaja proizvodstva.* Moscow: Ekonomika.

Beloff, N. (1978). "The Comecon Bumble-bee." *Banker* 5:38–42.

Berend, I. T. (1968). "A közép- és kelet-európai integráció kérdéséhez." *Közgazdasági Szemle* 5:547–567.

———(1971). "The Problem of Eastern European Integration in a Historical Perspective." In Vajda 1971, pp. 1–28.

Bergson, A. (1964). *The Economics of Soviet Planning.* New Haven, Conn.: Yale University Press.

Bień, E. (1975), J. Biskup, and G. Nosiadek. "Międzynarodowe organizacji ekonomiczne krajów socjalistycznych." *Gospodarka Planowa* 7/8:466–475.

Biskup, J. (1978), and G. Nosiadek. "Formy współpracy krajów RWPG w ramach międzynarodowych organizacji ekonomicznych." *Handel Zagraniczny* 1:10–11.

Bleßing, H., ed. (1977). *Effektivität der Außenwirtschaftsbeziehungen der sozialistischen Wirtschaft.* Berlin: Die Wirtschaft.

Bodnar, A. (1969). "Price Problems in the Trade between CMEA Countries." In Foldi 1969, pp. 47–53.

Bogacka, M. (1978). "Specjalizacja i kooperacja produkcji między krajami RWPG." *Handel Zagraniczny* 10:21–23.

Boltho, A. (1971). *Foreign Trade Criteria in Socialist Economies.* Cambridge: Cambridge University Press.

Bornstein, M., ed. (1973). *Plan and Market – Economic Reforms in Eastern Europe.* New Haven: Yale University Press.

———ed. (1975). *Economic Planning, East and West.* Cambridge, Mass.: Ballinger.

———(1978). "The Administration of the Soviet Price System." *Soviet Studies* 4:466–490.

Bożyk, P. (1977), and M. Guzek. *Teoria integracji socjalistycznej.* Warsaw: PWE.

Brabant, J. M. van (1970). "Socialist World Market Prices: Content and Controversy." *Osteuropa Wirtschaft* 3:168–189.

———(1971). "Long-term Development Credits and Socialist Trade." *Weltwirtschaftliches Archiv* 107/1:92–122.

———(1973). *Bilateralism and Structural Bilateralism in Intra-CMEA Trade.* Rotterdam: Rotterdam University Press.

———(1974). *Essays on Planning, Trade and Integration in Eastern Europe.* Rotterdam: Rotterdam University Press.

———(1975). *A Reconstruction of the Composition of Intra-CMEA Trade.* Berlin: Berichte des Osteuropa-Instituts Berlin.

———(1976). "Zur Rolle 'Ostmitteleuropas' im Rahmen des RGW." *Osteuropa Wirtschaft* 1:1–20.

(1977). *East European Cooperation – The Role of Money and Finance.* New York: Praeger.

(1977a). "The Relationship between Domestic and Foreign Trade Prices in Centrally Planned Economies – The Case of Hungary." *Osteuropa Wirtschaft* 4:235–258.

(1977b). "Trade Creation and Trade Diversion in Eastern Europe: A Comment." *ACES Bulletin* 1:79–97.

(1978). "Autarky in Centrally Planned Economies: A Comment." *Kyklos* 1:86–92.

(1978a). "Le rouble transférable et son rôle dans le commerce est-ouest." In *Unités et monnaies de compte,* edited by J.-L. Guglielmi and M. Lavigne. Paris: Economica, pp. 77–106.

(1978b). "Specialization and Trade-Dependence in Eastern Europe – The Case of Hungary." *Jahrbuch der Wirtschaft Osteuropas – Yearbook of East European Economics* 8:213–247.

(1979). "Another Look at the Origins of East European Economic Cooperation." *Osteuropa Wirtschaft* 4:243–266.

(1979a). "Trade Creation and Trade Diversion in Eastern Europe – The Case of Hungary." *Jahrbuch der Wirtschaft Osteuropas – Yearbook of East European Economics* 9:forthcoming.

(1979b). "Target Programming – A New Instrument of Socialist Economic Integration?" New York, manuscript.

Brada, J. C. (1978), and E. A. Hewett. "Autarky in Centrally Planned Economies: A Comment." *Kyklos* 1:93–96.

Brauer, W. (1974), and H. Busch. "Die sozialistische ökonomische Integration – Ausdruck der Einheit von Politik und Oekonomie bei der Entwicklung des Sozialismus." *Deutsche Aussenpolitik* 2:293–304, 3:569–580.

Brezinski, H. (1978). *Internationale Wirtschaftsplanung im RGW.* Paderborn: Schöningh.

Broner, A. (1975). "Economic Integration in Eastern Europe." Princeton University, unpublished Ph.D. dissertation.

(1976). "The Degree of Autarky in Centrally Planned Economies." *Kyklos* 3:478–494.

Brown, A. A. (1968), and E. Neuberger, eds. *International Trade and Central Planning – An Analysis of Economic Interactions.* Berkeley: University of California Press.

(1968a). "Towards a Theory of Centrally Planned Foreign Trade." In Brown 1968, pp. 57–93.

Brunner, G. (1976). "Etwas korrekter, bitte!" *Die Wirtschaft* 26:22.

Brzezinski, Z. K. (1961). *The Soviet Bloc – Unity and Conflict.* New York: Praeger.

Budnikowski, A. (1977), and M. Kulczycki. "Wspólpraca produkcyjna krajów RWPG a system kierowania gospodarką." *Handel Zagraniczny* 9:13–17.

Bykov, A. N. (1976). *Sozialistische ökonomische Integration – Wissenschaft und Technik.* Berlin: Staatsverlag.

Caillot, J. (1971). *Le C.A.E.M. – aspects juridiques et formes de coopération économique entre les pays socialistes.* Paris: Pichon & Durand-Auzias.

Campbell, R. W. (1966). "On the Theory of Economic Administration." In Rosovsky 1966, pp. 186–203.

(1974). *Soviet-type Economies – Performance and Evolution.* London: Macmillan.

(1974a), and P. Marer, eds. *East–West Trade and Technology Transfer – An Agenda of Research Needs.* Bloomington, Ind.: International Development Research Center.

Carlyle, M., ed. (1953). *Documents on International Affairs, 1949–1950.* London: Oxford University Press.

Caves, R. E. (1974). "The Economics of Reciprocity: Theory and Evidence on Bilateral Trading Arrangements." In *Essays in Honour of Jan Tinbergen – International Trade and Finance,* ed. by W. Sellekaerts. London: Macmillan, pp. 17–54.

Child, F. C. (1958). *The Theory and Practice of Exchange Control in Germany.* The Hague: Nijhoff.

Chodow, L. (1976). "Auf dem Wege zu gemeinsamen Strategien." *Die Wirtschaft* 19:23.

Chruščёv, N. S. (1962). "Nasuščnye voprosy razvitija mirovoj socialističeskoj sistemy." *Kommunist* 12:3–26.

Čížkovský, M. (1968). "Les entreprises communes dans la sphère du conseil d'aide économique mutuelle." *Cahiers de Droit Européen* 3:289–296.

(1970). "Internationale Koordinierung der Volkswirtschaftspläne im Comecon." In *Planung IV,* ed. by J. H. Kaiser. Baden-Baden: Nomos, pp. 243–264.

(1971). *Mezinárodní plánování – zkušenost a možnosti RVHP.* Prague: Academia.

CMEA (1975). *Primernye položenija o finansirovanii i osuščestvleniі rasčёtov meždunarodnych organizacij zainteresovannych stran-členov SĔV.* Moscow: SĔV sekretariat.

(1976). *Osnovnye dokumenty soveta ėkonomičeskoj vzaimopomošči.* Moscow: SĔV sekretariat.

(1976a). "Kommjunike o XXX zasedanii sessii soveta ėkonomičeskoj vzaimopomošči." *Ėkonomičeskoe sotrudničestvo stran-členov SĔV* 4:48–52.

(1976b). *Collected Reports on Various Activities of Bodies of the CMEA.* Moscow: SĔV sekretariat.

(1978). *Information on Activities of the CMEA in 1977.* Moscow: SĔV sekretariat.

Complex (1972). *Comprehensive Program for the Further Extension and Improvement of Cooperation and the Development of Socialist Economic Integration by the CMEA Member Countries.* Moscow: SĔV sekretariat.

Condliffe, J. B. (1940). *The Reconstruction of World Trade – A Survey of International Economic Relations.* New York: Norton.

Constantinescu, R. (1973). "Sur les organisations internationales économiques et technico-scientifiques des pays socialistes." *Revue Roumaine d'Etudes Internationales* 1:63–88.

Cristea, G. (1978), and I. Niţă. "Cadru favorabil pentru ridicarea pe o treaptă superioară a activităţii de comerţ exterior." *Revista Economică* 29:13–14.

Csikós-Nagy, B. (1969). "Some Theoretical Problems of the Price System in CMEA Intertrade." In Foldi 1969, pp. 55–67.

(1971). "Some Theoretical Problems of the Price System in the Trade between CMEA Countries." In Vajda 1971, pp. 101–112.

(1975). *Socialist Price Theory and Price Policy.* Budapest: Akadémiai Kiadó.

(1978). "Adalék az ármechanizmus elméletéhez." *Pénzügyi Szemle* 8/9:570–580.

Dedijer, V. (1971). *The Battle Stalin Lost – Memoirs of Yugoslavia, 1948–1953.* New York: Viking Press.

Dewar,·M. (1951). *Soviet Trade with Eastern Europe, 1945–1949.* London: Institute of International Affairs.

Djilas, M. (1963). *Conversations with Stalin.* Harmondsworth, Eng.: Penguin Books.

(1977). *Wartime.* New York: Harcourt Brace Jovanovich.

Dobrin, B. (1973). *Bulgarian Economic Development Since World War II.* New York: Praeger.

Dodge, N. T. (1970), and C. K. Wilber. "The Relevance of Soviet Industrial Experience for Less Developed Economies." *Soviet Studies* 3:330–349.

Dudinskij, I. V. (1970). "Ėkonomičeskaja integracija – zakonomernost' razvitija socialističeskogo sodružestva." *Meždunarodnaja žizn'* 10:3–12.

Dymšic, V. E. (1975). "Sotrudničestvo stran-členov SĖV v oblasti material'no-techničeskogo snabženija." *Ėkonomičeskoe sotrudničestvo stran-členov SĖV* 4:30–33.

Ellis, H. S. (1941). *Exchange Control in Central Europe.* Cambridge, Mass.: Harvard University Press.

Ellman, M. (1975). "Did the Agricultural Surplus Provide the Resources for the Increase in Investment in the USSR During the First Five-Year Plan?" *Economic Journal* 4:844–864.

(1978). "On a Mistake of Preobrazhensky and Stalin." *Journal of Development Studies* 3:353–356.

ESE (1965). *Economic Survey for Europe in 1962, part II.* Geneva: United Nations.

Evans, A. B. (1977). "Developed Socialism in Soviet Ideology." *Soviet Studies* 3:409–428.

Faddeev N. V. (1966). "Die Entwicklung der wirtschaftlichen Beziehungen im Rahmen des RGW." *Probleme des Friedens und des Sozialismus* 1:30–36.

(1967). "Mnogostoronnee ėkonomičeskoe sotrudničestvo – važnyj faktor razvitija socialističeskich stran." In Tokareva 1967, pp. 3–12.

(1974). "Dwiedzieśćia pięć lat RWPG." *Życie Gospodarcze* 2:13.

(1974a). "25 Jahre RGW – Internationale Wirtschaftorganisation sozialistischer Länder, 1949–1974." *Einheit* 1:10–23.

(1974b). *Sovet ėkonomičeskoj vzaimopomošči – XXV*. 3rd ed. Moscow: Ėkonomika.

(1974c). "25 let dejatel'nosti SĖV." In *XXV let SĖV –itogi, zadăci, perspektivy*, ed. by M. V. Senin. Moscow: Sekretariat SĖV, pp. 17–45.

Fallenbuchl, Z. M. (1977). "L'intégration économique en Europe de l'est." *Revue d'Etudes Comparatives Est-Quest* 2:7–20.

Feiwel, G. R. (1965). *The Economics of the Socialist Enterprise*. New York: Praeger.

Ferrell, R. H. (1966). *George C. Marshall*. New York: Cooper Square.

Ficzere, L. (1978), and J. Nyers. "Nemzetközi gazdálkodó szervezetek a KGST-országok együtmüködési rendszerében." *Külgazdaság* 1:10–20.

Fischer, M. (1978). "Wirtschaftliche Rechnungsführung in internationalen ökonomischen Organisationen der RGW-Mitgliedsländer." *Sozialistische Finanzwirtschaft* 10:29–30.

Fiumel, H. de (1967). *Rada wzajemnej pomocy gospodarczej – studium prawnomiędzynarodowe*. Warsaw: PWN.

(1975). *Les aspects institutionnels de l'intégration économique socialiste*. Mimeographed. Louvain: Centre d'Etudes Européennes.

Földi, T. (1969), and T. Kiss, eds. *Socialist World Market Prices*. Leyden: Sijthoff; Budapest: Akadémiai Kiadó.

Foreign (1975). *Foreign Relations of the United States – Diplomatic Papers, 1948, vol. IV*. Washington, D.C.: Government Printing Office.

(1976). *Foreign Relations of the United States – Diplomatic Papers, 1949, vol. V*. Washington, D.C.: Government Printing Office.

Franzmeyer, F. (1973), and H. Machowski. "Willensbildung und Entscheidungsprozesse in der Europäischen Gemeinschaft und im Rat für gegenseitige Wirtschaftshilfe." *Europa-Archiv* 2:47–60.

Frisch, R. (1948). "The Problem of Multicompensatory Trade." *Review of Economics and Statistics* 4:265–271.

Friss, I. (1966). "Berend T. Ivan könyvéröl." *Közgazdasági Szemle* 1:98–105.

(1971). *Economic Laws, Policy, Planning*. Budapest: Akadémiai Kiadó.

(1974). "Socialistićeskaja ėkonomićeskaja integracija i postroenie socializma v Vengrii." *Acta Oeconomica* 12/1:1–29.

(1977). "A KGST-országok együttmüködésének törvényszerüségeiröl." *Közgazdasági Szemle* 5:506–523.

Gadó, O., ed. (1972). *Reform of the Economic Mechanism in Hungary – Development 1968–71*. Budapest: Akadémiai Kiadó.

Gajzágó, O. von. (1966). *Preisentwicklung und Preispolitik im sowjetischen Außenhandel, 1955–1963*. Cologne: Wissenschaft und Politik.

Gamarnikow, M. (1971). "Wirtschaftsreform und Comecon." In *Reformen und Dogmen in Osteuropa*, ed. by A. Domes. Cologne: Wissenschaft und Politik, pp. 215–227.

Garland, J. S. (1977). *Financing Foreign Trade in Eastern Europe.* New York: Praeger.

Góra, S. (1974), and Z. Knyziak. *Międzynarodowa specialiazacja produkcji krajów RWPG.* Warsaw: PWE.

Granick, D. (1954). *Management of the Industrial Firm in the USSR.* New York: Columbia University Press.

Grote, G., ed. (1973). *Planung der Außenwirtschaft in der DDR.* Berlin: Die Wirtschaft.

Guzek, M. (1972). *Międzynarodowa integracja gospodarcza w socjalizmie.* Warsaw: PWE.

Haffner, F. (1978). "Die ökonomischen Grundzüge der 'entwickelten sozialistischen Gesellschaft'." *Osteuropa* 7:586–603.

Halle, L. J. (1967). *The Cold War as History.* New York: Harper & Row.

Harrod, R. (1962). "Economic Development and Asian Regional Co-operation." *Pakistan Development Review* 1:1–22.

Haupt, H.-G. (1978), and D. Schubert. "Der Einfluß der sozialistischen ökonomischen Integration auf die Vervollkommnung der materiell-technischen Basis in den RGW-Ländern." *Deutsche Aussenpolitik* 1:26–35.

Hertz, F. (1947). *The Economic Problems of the Danubian States – A Study in Economic Nationalism.* London: Gollancz.

Hewett, E. A. (1974). *Foreign Trade Prices in the Council for Mutual Economic Assistance.* Cambridge: Cambridge University Press.

——— (1976). "A Model of Foreign Trade Planning in an East European-type Economy." In *Economic Analysis of the Soviet-type System,* ed. by J. Thornton. Cambridge: Cambridge University Press, pp. 156–175.

——— (1976a). "A Gravity Model of CMEA Trade." In *Quantitative and Analytical Studies in East–West Economic Relations,* ed. by J. C. Brada. Bloomington, Ind.: International Development Research Center, pp. 1–16.

Hirschman, A. O. (1958). *The Strategy for Economic Development.* New Haven, Conn.: Yale University Press.

Höhmann, H.-H. (1972), M. C. Kaser, and K. C. Thalheim, eds. *Die Wirtschaftsreformen Osteuropas im Wandel.* Freiburg i.B.: Rombach.

Holzman, F. D. (1966). "Foreign Trade Behavior of Centrally Planned Economies." In Rosovsky 1966, pp. 237–265.

——— (1968). "Soviet Central Planning and Its Impacts on Foreign Trade Behavior and Adjustment Mechanisms." In Brown 1968, pp. 280–305.

——— (1968a). "The Operation of Some Traditional Adjustment Mechanisms in the Foreign Trade of Centrally Planned Economies." *Economies et Sociétés* 2:407–444.

——— (1972). "La théorie du commerce extérieur des économies centralement planifiées." *Revue de l'Est* 3:5–36.

——— (1976). *International Trade under Communism – Politics and Economics.* New York: Basic Books.

——— (1979). "Some Systemic Factors Contributing to the Convertible Cur-

342   Bibliography

rency Shortages of Centrally Planned Economies." *American Economic Review* 2:76–80.

Huber, G., ed. (1974). "25 Jahre zielstrebige internationale sozialistische Arbeitsteilung, die unsere sozialistische Staatengemeinschaft zur dynamischsten Wirtschaftsregion der Welt werden ließ." *Die Wirtschaft* 2A: supplement.

(1974a), and P. Sydow. "Sozialistische Produktionsverhältnisse und ökonomische Integration der RGW-Länder." *Einheit* 5:562–571.

Ikonnikov, I. (1969). "Rol' SĖV v sotrudničestve stran socializma." *Meždunarodnaja žizn'* 4:89–96.

Ionescu, G. (1965). *The Break-up of the Soviet Empire in Eastern Europe.* Harmondsworth, Eng.: Penguin Books.

Janik, A. (1975). "Problematyka prawna wspólnych przedsiębiorstw RWPG" *Sprawy Międzynarodowe* 7/8:101–111.

Janota, O. (1977), L. Rusmich, and J. Větrovský. "Kolektivní měna jako základ devizově finanční soustavy členských státu RVHP." *Finance a Úvěr – Ctvrtletní Příloha* 3:9–27.

JEC (1974). *Reorientation and Commercial Relations of the Economies of Eastern Europe,* ed. by Joint Economic Committee of U.S. Congress. Washington, D.C.: Government Printing Office.

(1977). *East European Economies Post-Helsinki,* ed. by Joint Economic Committee of U.S. Congress. Washington, D.C.: Government Printing Office.

Kalecki, M. (1969). *Introduction to the Theory of Growth in a Socialist Economy.* Oxford: Blackwell.

Kampa, O. (1976), and W. Seiffert. "Staatliche Leitung und Rechtsmechanismus der sozialistischen ökonomischen Integration." *Staat und Recht* 11:1146–1153.

Karpič, V. (1976). "Proizvodstvenoto sŭtrudničestvo meždu stranite ot SIV – osnova za progresivnoto razvitie na technija stokoobmen." *Vŭnšna tŭrgovija* 9:9–12.

Kaser, M. C. (1966). "Les préoccupations actuelles du Comécon." *Projet* 7:815–826.

(1967). *Comecon – Integration Problems of the Planned Economies.* 2d ed. London: Oxford University Press.

Kiesewetter, B. (1960). *Der Ostblock – Außenhandel des östlichen Wirtschaftsblockes einschließlich China.* Berlin: Safari-Verlag.

Kirillin, V. I. (1977). "Aktual'nye problemy povyšenija ėffektivnosti naučno-techničeskogo sotrudničestva stran-členov SĖV." *Ėkonomičeskoe sotrudničestvo stran-členov SĖV* 5:32–35.

Kis, T. I. (1964). *Les pays de l'Europe de l'est – leurs rapports mutuels et le problème de leur intégration dans l'orbite de l'URSS.* Louvain: Nauwelaerts.

Kiss, T. (1971). *International Division of Labour in Open Economies – With Special Regard to the CMEA.* Budapest: Akadémiai Kiadó.

(1972). *Hol tart a KGST-integráció?* Budapest: Kossuth Könyvkiadó.

(1973). "The Development of the Forms of Economic Relations in the

CMEA Integration." In *The Market of Socialist Economic Integration*, ed. by T. Kiss et al. Budapest: Akadémiai Kiadó, pp. 109–126.

(1975). "Nemzetközi tervezési együttműködés a KGST-ben." *Közgazdasági Szemle* 6:736–753.

Klepacki, Z. M. (1975). "Membership and Other Forms of Participation of States in the Activities of the Socialist Economic, Scientific and Technical Inter-Governmental Organizations." *Polish Yearbook of International Law* 7:45–64.

Knížek, V. (1973). "Hospodářství ve světě: integrace a ceny." *Rudé Právo* 3/4 December.

Knorre, W. von (1961). *Zehn Jahre Rat für gegenseitige Wirtschaftshilfe (Comecon) – Entwicklung und Ergebnisse, 1949–1959.* Würzburg: Holzner.

Köhler, H. (1965). *Economic Integration in the Soviet Bloc – With an East German Case Study.* New York: Praeger.

Kohlmey, G. (1966). "From Extensive to Intensive Economic Growth." *Czechoslovak Economic Papers* 6:23–30.

(1974), et al., eds. *RGW-DDR: 25 Jahre Zusammenarbeit.* Berlin: Akademie-Verlag.

Kojima, K. (1970). "Towards a Theory of Agreed Specialization." In *Induction, Growth and Trade – Essays in Honour of Sir Roy Harrod*, ed. by W. A. Ellis et al. Oxford: Clarendon Press, pp. 305–324.

Konstantinov, Ju. A. (1977). "Finansi na meždunarodnite specializirani ikonomičeski organizacii." *Finansi i kredit* 2:3–14, 3:3–14, 4:3–12.

Korbonski, A. (1964). "Comecon." *International Conciliation*, September.

(1970). "Theory and Practice of Regional Integration: The Case of Comecon." *International Organization* 4:942–977.

(1975). "Political Aspects of Economic Reforms in Eastern Europe." In *Economic Development in the Soviet Union and Eastern Europe*, vol. 1, ed. by Z. M. Fallenbuchl. New York: Praeger, pp. 8–41.

(1976). "Détente, East–West Trade, and the Future of Economic Integration in Eastern Europe." *World Politics* 4:568–589.

Kormnov, J. F. (1972). *Specializacija i kooperacija proizvodstva stran SĖV v uslovijach socialističeskoj ėkonomičeskoj integracii.* Moscow: Ėkonomika.

(1973), and M. Čeburakov. "Soveršenstvovanie upravlenija otraslevoj integraciej stran-členov SĖV." *Voprosy ėkonomiki* 7:103–112.

(1973a), and A. D. Leznik. *Soglašenija o specializacii i kooperacii v proizvodstva meždu stranami-členami SĖV (osnovnye ėlementy).* Moscow: Meždunarodnyj centr naučnoj i techničeskoj informacii.

(1977). "Dolgosročnye celevye programmy sotrudničestva stran SĖV." *Voprosy ėkonomiki* 1:86–94.

Kornai, J. (1959). *Overcentralization of Economic Administration.* London: Oxford University Press.

(1971). *Anti-equilibrium.* Amsterdam: North-Holland.

(1972). *Rush versus Harmonic Growth.* Amsterdam: North-Holland.

Kostecki, M. M. (1978). "State Trading in Industrialized and Developing Countries." *Journal of World Trade Law* 3:187–207.

344   Bibliography

Kühl, J. (1958). Föderationspläne im Donauraum und in Ostmitteleuropa. Munich: Oldenbourg.

Ladygin, B. (1973). "O planomernosti razvitija mirovogo socialisticeskogo chozjajstva." Voprosy ekonomiki 12:92–101.

(1974). "Dvizuscie sily socialisticeskoj integracii (k itogam XXVIII sessii SEV)." Mezdunarodnaja zizn' 9:24–31.

Larionov, K. (1973). "Valjutno-finansovaja sistema na sluzbe socialisticeskoj ekonomiceskoj integracii." In Mezdunarodnaja socialisticeskaja valjuta stran-clenov SEV. Moscow: Finansy, pp. 59–75.

Lavigne, M. (1973). Le comecon – le programme du comecon et l'intégration socialiste. Paris: Cujas.

(1978). "La société socialiste avancée." In Economie politique de la planification en système socialiste, ed. by M. Lavigne. Paris: Economica, pp. 301–327.

Lehmann, G. (1973). "Zu einigen theoretischen und praktischen Fragen der Bildung und der Leitung gemeinsamer Betriebe von Mitgliedsländern des RGW." Wirtschaftswissenschaft 9:1312–1330.

(1977). "Planungszusammenarbeit in internationalen ökonomischen Organisationen der RGW-Länder." Volkswirtschaftsplanung – Beiträge zur Theorie und Praxis 10.

Levine, H. S. (1968). "The Effects of Foreign Trade on Soviet Planning Practices." In Brown 1968, pp. 255–276.

Lipgens, W. (1978). "Marshall-Plan und Anfangsphase der westeuropäischen Integration." In Marshall-Plan und Europäische Linke, ed. by O. N. Haberl and L. Niethammer. Essen: forthcoming.

Liska, T. (1954), and A. Máriás. "A gazdaságosság és a nemzetközi munkamegosztás." Közgazdasági Szemle 1:75–94. Translated in East European Economics, 1963:4, 3–15.

Lukin, L. I. (1974). "Pervoe desjatiletie soveta ekonomiceskoj vzaimopomosci." Voprosy istorii 4:39–57.

ed. (1974a). Dvadsat' pjat' let dejatel'nosti organov soveta ekonomiceskoj vzaimopomosci (chronologija zasedanij organov SEV). Moscow: SEV sekretariat.

Machlup, F. (1977). A History of Thought on Economic Integration. New York: Columbia University Press.

Machowski, H. (1970). "Organisatorische Probleme der wirtschaftlichen Zusammenarbeit im Rat für gegenseitige Wirtschaftshilfe." Vierteljahrhefte zur Wirtschaftsforschung 4:279–289.

Marczewski, J. (1956). Planification et croissance économique des démocraties populaires. Paris: Presses Universitaires de France.

(1973). Crise de la planification socialiste? Paris: Presses Universitaires de France.

Marer, P. (1969). "Foreign Trade Prices in the Soviet Bloc – A Theoretical and Empirical Study." University of Pennsylvania, unpublished Ph.D. dissertation.

(1972). Postwar Pricing and Price Patterns in Socialist Foreign Trade

(*1946–1971*). Bloomington, Ind.: International Development Research Center.

(1974). "Soviet Economic Policy in Eastern Europe." In JEC 1974, pp. 135–163.

Matevosjan, P. (1975). "Intermetall' za rabotoj." *Ėkonomičeskoe sotrudničestvo stran-členov SĖV* 3:71–73.

Mazanov, G. (1970). *Meždunarodnye rasčëty stran-členov SEV.* Moscow: Finansy.

McMillan, C. H. (1975). "The Bilateral Character of Soviet and Eastern European Foreign Trade." *Journal of Common Market Studies* 1/2:1–20.

Medvedev, R. A. (1972). *Let History Judge – The Origins and Consequences of Stalinism.* New York: Knopf.

Menžinskij, V. I., ed. (1971). *Meždunarodnye organizacii socialističeskich stran.* Moscow: Meždunarodnye otnošenija.

Meyer, M. (1966). "Le comécon: son organisation, son fonctionnement." *Annuaire de l'URSS:* 367–390.

Mezi (1975). "Rozvoj RVHP jako mezinárodní organizace." *Mezinárodní Vztahy* 6:60–64.

Meznerics, I. (1968) *Banking Business in Socialist Economy – With Special Regard to East–West Trade.* Leyden: Sijthoff.

Mikesell R. F. (1954). *Foreign Exchange in the Postwar Period.* New York: Twentieth Century Fund.

Mirošničenko, B. P., ed. (1968). *Problemy koordinacija narodnochozjajstvennych planov stran SĖV.* Moscow: Meždunarodnye otnošenija.

Mitrofanova, N. M. (1973). "O vzaimosvjazi vnutrennich i vnešnetorgovych cen v evropejskich socialističeskich stranach." *Planovoe chozjajstvo* 9:90–97.

(1978). *Ceny v mechanizme ėkonomičeskogo sotrudničestva stran-členov SĖV.* Moscow: Nauka.

Molotov, V. M. (1949). *Problems of Foreign Policy – Speeches and Statements.* Moscow: Foreign Languages Publishing House.

Montias, J. M. (1959). "Planning with Material Balances in Soviet-type Economies." *American Economic Review* 5. Reprinted in *Socialist Economies,* ed. by A. Nove and D. M. Nuti. Harmondsworth, Eng.: Penguin Books, pp. 223–251.

(1966). "Economic Nationalism in Eastern Europe: Forty Years of Continuity and Change." *Journal of International Affairs* 1:45–71.

(1967). *Economic Development in Communist Rumania.* Cambridge, Mass.: MIT Press.

(1968). "Socialist Industrialization and Trade in Machinery Products: An Analysis Based on the Experience of Bulgaria, Poland and Rumania." In Brown 1968, pp. 130–158.

(1969). "Obstacles to Economic Integration of Eastern Europe." *Studies in Comparative Communism* 1/2:38–60.

(1974). "The Structure of Comecon Trade and the Prospects for East–West Exchanges." In JEC 1974, pp. 662–681.

346   Bibliography

Morozov, V. (1974). "Perspektivnye formy sotrudničestva stran-členov SĚV." *Voprosy ėkonomiki* 6:95–103.

(1977). "Mnogostoronnie meždunarodnye ėkonomičeskie svjazi stran SEV." *Voprosy ėkonomiki* 9:108–115.

Myrdal, G. (1956). *An International Economy – Problems and Prospects.* New York: Harper.

Nazarkin, K. (1973). "Kompleksnaja programma integracii i zadači meždunarodnogo banka ėkonomičeskogo sotrudničestva." In *Meždunarodnaja socialističeskaja valjuta stran-členov SĚV.* Moscow: Finansy, pp. 76–87.

Nove, A. (1970). *An Economic History of the USSR.* London: Allan Lane The Penguin Press.

Nyers, R. (1977). "A KGST többoldalú integrációs intézkedéseinek hatása a magyar népgazdaságra az 1976–1980-as években." *Közgazdasági Szemle* 4:423–429.

Olejnik, I. P. (1969). *Mirovoe socialističeskoe chozjajstvo – kratkij očerk.* Moscow: Meždunarodnye otnošenija.

Organy (1978). "Orgány Rady Vzájemné Hospodářské Pomoci." *Zahraniční Obchod* 11/12: insert.

Pécsi, K. (1977). *A KGST termelési integráció közgazdasági kérdései.* Budapest: Közgazdasági és Jogi Könyvkiadó.

Pelzman, J. (1976). "Trade Integration in the Council for Mutual Economic Assistance: Creation and Diversion, 1954–1970." *ACES Bulletin* 3:39–59.

(1976a). *Economic Integration in C.M.E.A.* Mimeographed. Columbia: University of South Carolina School of Business Administration.

(1977). "Trade Creation and Trade Diversion in the Council for Mutual Economic Assistance: 1954–1970." *American Economic Review* 4:713–722.

Pisar, S. (1970). *Coexistence and Commerce.* New York: McGraw-Hill.

Polienko, A. M. (1960). *Dolgosročnye ėkonomičeskie soglašenija meždu evropejskimi socialističeskimi stranami.* Moscow: Vneštorgizdat.

Proft, G. (1973), H. Liebsch, and K. Werner. *Planung in der sozialistischen ökonomischen Integration.* Berlin: Staatsverlag.

Protocol (1949). *Protocol Prvind Crearea Unui Consiliu de Asistenta Mutuala Economica Intre Guvernale U.R.S.S., Rep. Polona, Rep. Cehoslovaca, Rep. Pop. Rom., Rep. Ungara si Rep. Bulgara Semnat la Moscova la 18 Ianuarie, 1949.*

Pryor, F. L. (1963). *The Communist Foreign Trade System – The Other Common Market.* London: Allen and Unwin.

(1970). "Barriers to Market Socialism in Eastern Europe in the Mid 1960's." *Studies in Comparative Communism* 2:31–64.

Ptaszek, J. (1972). "Postępy współpracy." *Życie Gospodarcze* 38:5.

Ptičkin, N. (1974). "Sovetu ėkonomičeskoj vzaimopomošči – 25 let." *Vnešnjaja torgovlja* 4:2–11.

Ribi, R. C. (1970). *Das Comecon – Eine Untersuchung über die Problematik der wirtschaftlichen Integration der sozialistischen Länder.* Zurich: Polygraphischer Verlag.

Bibliography 347

Richter, H., ed. (1968). *Freundschaft – Zusammenarbeit – Beistand: Grundsatzverträge zwischen den sozialistischen Staaten*. Berlin: Dietz.
Rolow, A. (1974). "Wspólne przedsiębiorstwa." *Życie Gospodarcze* 4:13.
Rosenstein-Rodan, P. N. (1943). "Problems of Industrialisation of Eastern and South-Eastern Europe." *Economic Journal* 2/3:202–211.
Rosovsky, H., ed. (1966). *Industrialization in Two Systems – Essays in Honor of Alexander Gerschenkron*. New York: Wiley.
Rothschild, J. (1974). *East Central Europe between the Two World Wars*. Seattle: University of Washington Press.
Rumjancev, A. F. (1973), et al., eds. *Politische Oekonomie des Sozialismus*. Berlin: Die Wirtschaft.
Rüster, L. (1977). "Zur Entwicklung der Rechtsformen der Tätigkeit des RGW." *Staat und Recht* 1:34—44.
Rutkowski, J. (1964). *Światowy rynek kredytowy*. Warsaw: PWE.
(1977). "Ekonomiczne problemy specjalizacji produkcji krajów RWPG." *Handel Zagraniczny* 10:8–10.
Rybakov, O. (1974), and N. Chmelevskij. "Nekotorye metodologičeskie aspekty planirovanija integracionnych meroprijatij." *Planovoe chozjajstvo* 1:39–48.
(1975). *Ekonomičeskaja effektivnost' sotrudničestva SSSR s socialističeskimi stranami*. Moscow: Mysl'.
Sanders, I. T., ed. (1958). *Collectivization of Agriculture in Eastern Europe*. Lexington: University of Kentucky Press.
Sandorski, J. (1968). "L'URSS et le conseil d'entraide économique." *Annuaire de l'URSS:* 569–580.
Savov, M. N. (1973). "Sovet ekonomičeskoj vzaimopomošči (osnovnye celi, principy, funcii i struktura)". *Izvestija akademii nauk SSSR – serija ekonomičeskaja* 4:49–62.
(1973a). "Razvitie na vŭnšnata tŭrgovija i stokova-paričnite otnošenija." In *SIV – dostiženija i perspektivi*, ed. by M. N. Savov et al. Varna: Dŭržavno izdatelstvo, pp. 112–132.
(1975). *Socialističeskata ikonomičeska integracija – vŭnšnotŭrgovski i cenovi problemi*. Varna: Bakalov.
Schaefer, H. W. (1972). *Comecon and the Politics of Integration*. New York: Praeger.
Scheller, J. (1978). "Internationale Wirtschaftsgemeinschaft – ein sich entwickelnder Typ internationaler Wirtschaftsorganisation." *DDR Aussenwirtschaft* 17, supplement: 5–10.
Schlicker, W., ed. (1974). "RGW – Gestern, Heute, Morgen." *Horizont* 5:3–12.
Seiffert, W. (1972). "Theoretische Probleme der Herausbildung des sozialistischen internationalen Wirtschaftsrechts." *Staat und Recht* 3:368–387.
(1972a), "Sozialistische Wirtschaftsintegration und rechtliche Regelung." *Staat und Recht* 4:581–589.
(1972b). "Der Prozeß der Herausbildung des Rechtssystems der sozialistischen Wirtschaftsintegration." *Staat und Recht* 8:1305–1322.

348   *Bibliography*

Selucký, R. (1972). *Economic Reforms in Eastern Europe – Political Background and Economic Significance.* New York: Praeger.

Semënov, A. (1978). "Novaja stupen' sotrudničestva." *Mirovaja ėkonomika i mezdunarodnye otnošenija* 9:100–109.

Semrádová, L. (1975). "Nový orgán RVHP: stálá komise RVHP pro spolupráci v oblasti zdravotnictví." *Zahranični Obchod* 12:16–17.

Širjaev, Ju. S. (1974). "K 25-letiju soveta ėkonomičeskoj vzaimopomošči." *Izvestija akademii nauk SSSR – serija ėkonomičeskaja* 5:5–6.

Skubiszewski, K. (1966). "Le conseil d'entraide économique et ses actes." *Annuaire français de droit international* 12:544–576.

Smith, A. J. (1977). "The Council of Mutual Economic Assistance in 1977: New Economic Power, New Political Perspectives and Some Old and New Problems." In JEC 1977, pp. 152–173.

Smith, G. A. (1973). *Soviet Foreign Trade – Organization, Operations, and Policy, 1918–1971.* New York: Praeger.

Sorokin, G. M. (1968). "Problemy ėkonomičeskoj integracii stran socializma." *Voprosy ėkonomiki* 12:77–86.

——— (1969). "Leninskie principy sotrudničestva socialističeskich stran." *Planovoe chozjajstvo* 3:3–11.

——— (1973). "Talantlivyj teoretik i organizator planirovanija (k 70-letiju so dnja roždenija N.A. Voznesenskogo)." *Voprosy ėkonomiki* 12:82–91.

Spiller, H. (1978). "Rechtsprobleme der Finanzierung internationaler Wirtschaftsorganisationen." *Staat und Recht* 5:431–441.

Spulber, N. (1957). *The Economics of Communist Eastern Europe.* New York: Wiley.

Stehr, U. (1978). "Stereotype Merkmale sowjetischer Politikanalysen dargestellt am Beispiel von RGW-Interpretationen." *Osteuropa* 6:524–537.

Stoian, I. (1978). "Relațiile economice de colaborare între țarile socialiste – Activitatea României în cadrul C.A.E.R. și principiile care călăuzesc această activitate." *Era Socialistă* 17:30–32.

Sulzberger, C. L. (1949). "Moscow Satellites Bound in 20-Year Economic Pact." *New York Times,* 4 June 1949, pp. 1, 4.

Sweezy, P. M. (1968). *The Theory of Capitalist Development.* New York: Modern Reader.

Szawlowski, R. (1963). "L'évolution du C.O.M.E.C.O.N. 1949–1963." *Annuaire français de droit international* 9:670–694.

——— (1976). *The System of the International Organizations of the Communist Countries.* Leyden: Sijthoff.

Szelecki, Gy. (1978). "A gépipari gyártásszakosítás tapasztalatai a szocialista országokkal." *Világgazdaság* 3 Nov. 1978, p. 3; 4 Nov. 1978, p. 3.

Szita, J. (1968). "Az Európai szocialista országok gazdasági integrációja kérdéséhez." *Közgazdasági Szemle* 6:739–752.

——— (1971). "A szocialista gazdasági integráció közgazdaságtudományi kérdéseihez." *Társadalmi Szemle* 11:29–42.

Tarnovskij, O. I. (1968), and N. M. Mitrofanova. *Stoimost' i cena na mirovom socialističeskom rynke.* Moscow: Nauka.

Tokareva, P. A. (1967), M. D. Kudrjašov, and V. I. Morozov, eds. *Mnogostoronnee ėkonomičeskoe sotrudničestvo socialističeskich gosudarstv – sbornik dokumentov.* Moscow: Juridičeskaja literatura.
ed. (1972). *Mnogostoronnee ėkonomičeskoe sotrudničestvo socialističeskich gosudarstv – sbornik dokumentov.* 2d ed. Moscow: Juridičeskaja literatura.
(1976) et al., eds. *Mnogostoronnee ėkonomičeskoe sotrudničestvo socialističeskich gosudarstv (dokumenty za 1972–1975 gg.).* Moscow. Juridičeskaja literatura.
(1976a). *Učreždenie mežgosudarstvennych ėkonomičeskich organizacii stran-členov SĖV.* Moscow: Nauka.
Treml, V. G. (1974). "Of Encyclopedias and Economists." *Problems of Communism* 2:71–74.
Trend, H. (1975). *Comecon's Organizational Structure.* Mimeographed. Munich: Radio Free Europe.
U.N. (1966). *Economic Integration and Industrial Specialization among the Member Countries of the Council for Mutual Economic Assistance.* Geneva: United Nations.
(1968). "Note on the Institutional Developments in the Foreign Trade of the Soviet Union and Eastern European Countries." *Economic Bulletin for Europe* 1:43–52.
(1973). "Recent Changes in the Organization of Foreign Trade in the Centrally Planned Economies." *Economic Bulletin for Europe* 1:36–49.
(1978). *Overall Economic Perspective for the ECE Region up to 1990.* Mimeographed. Geneva: United Nations.
Uschakow, A. (1962). *Der Rat für gegenseitige Wirtschaftshilfe (Comecon).* Cologne: Wissenschaft und Politik.
(1972). *Der Ostmarkt im Comecon.* Baden-Baden: Nomos.
Vajda, I. (1971), and M. Simai, eds. *Foreign Trade in a Planned Economy.* Cambridge: Cambridge University Press.
Vajs, T. A. (1973), and L. Degtjar'. "Sotrudničestvo stran SĖV v ispol'zovanii trudovych resursov." *Planovoe chozjajstvo* 12:95–100.
(1974). "Sotrudničestvo stran SĖV v ispol'zovanii rabočej sily." *Ėkonomičeskie nauki* 7:67–73.
(1976). *Problemy sotrudničestva stran SĖV v ispol'zovanii trudovych resursov.* Moscow: Nauka.
Válek, V. (1978). "Mezinárodní hospodářské organizace členskych států RVHP a problematika devizového plánovaní v ČSSR." *Plánováné Hospodářství* 2:36–45.
(1979). "Mezinárodní ekonomické organizace členských států RVHP." *Svět Hospodářství* 4: supplement.
Veličkov, N. (1976), O. Tarnovskij, and M. Savov. *Vŭnšnotŭrgovskoto cenoobrazuvane pri socialističeskata ikonomičeska integracija.* Varna: Bakalov.
Vel'jaminov, G. M. (1977). "Meždunarodnye ėkonomičeskie organizacii socialističeskich stran." *Bjulleten' inostrannoj kommerčeskoj informacii – priloženie* 1:3–37.

350 Bibliography

Verdoorn, P. J. (1972), and C. A. van Bockhove. "Measuring Integration Effects: A Survey." *European Economic Review:* 3:337–349.

Vincze, I. (1972). "World Market Prices and Domestic Prices." In Gado 1972, pp. 131–145.

Viner, J. (1944). "International Relations between State-controlled National Economies." *American Economic Review* 2:315–329.

Vogt, W. (1977). "Die Bereicherung des Inhalts der staatlichen Souveränität im Prozeß der sozialistischen ökonomischen Integration." *Deutsche Aussenpolitik* 11:61–75.

Vorkauf, H. (1977). "Studie zu Problemen der Entwicklung des abgestimmten Planes mehrseitiger Integrationsmaßnahmen zu einer qualitativ neuen Form der Planungszusammenarbeit der RGW Länder." *Volkswirtschaftsplanung – Beiträge zur Theorie und Praxis* 4.

Wandycz, P. S. (1970). "Recent Traditions of the Quest for Unity: Attempted Polish–Czechoslovak and Yugoslav–Bulgarian Confederations, 1940–1948." In *The People's Democracies after Prague.* ed. by J. Lukaszewski. Bruges: De Tempel, pp. 35–93.

Wasilkowski, A. (1971). "Coordination of National Economic Plans of the Member Countries of CMEA." *Polish Yearbook of International Law* 4:37–48.

Weber, A. (1975). "Razvitie sotrudničestva v oblasti malotonnažnoj chimii – naša zadača." *Ėkonomičeskoe sotrudničestvo stran-členov SĖV* 4:52–53.

Weber, E. (1971). *Stadien der Außenhandelsverflechtung Ostmittel – und Südosteuropa.* Stuttgart: Fischer.

Wedel-Parlow, W. von (1971). "Der Prozeß der Zielbestimmung im sozialistischen Industriebetriebe." *Osteuropa Wirtschaft* 4:263–278.

(1974). "Zielbildung und Zielkonflikte im sozialistischen Industriebetrieb." Mimeographed. Berlin.

(1976). *Betriebliche Zielausrichtung und die Eignung der Preise als Instrument der Plandurchsetzung.* Wuppertal: Gesamthochschule.

Wellisz, S. (1964). *The Economics of the Soviet Bloc.* New York: McGraw-Hill.

Wilczynski, J. (1969). *The Economics and Politics of East–West Trade.* London: Macmillan.

(1972). *Socialist Economic Development and Reforms.* London: Macmillan.

Wiles, P. J. D. (1962). *The Political Economy of Communism.* Oxford: Blackwell.

(1968). *Communist International Economics.* Oxford: Blackwell.

Yergin D. (1977). *Shattered Peace – The Origins of the Cold War and the National Security State.* Boston: Houghton Mifflin.

Zauberman, A. (1964). *Industrial Progress in Poland, Czechoslovakia and East Germany.* London: Oxford University Press.

(1975). *The Mathematical Revolution in Soviet Economics.* London: Oxford University Press.

Zschiedrich, H. (1975). "Internationale Wirschaftsvereinigungen der RGW Mitgliedsländer." *Deutsche Aussenpolitik* 11:1678–1687.

Žukov, V. N. (1969), and Ju. Ja. Ol'sevič. *Teoretičeskie i metodologičeskie problemi soveršenstvovanija cenoobrazovanija na rynke SĖV.* Moscow: Nauka.

Zwass, A. (1974). *Zur Problematik der Währungsbeziehungen zwischen Ost und West.* Vienna and New York: Springer-Verlag.

Index

development strategy (*cont.*)
  definition of, 59
  implications of, 65–7
  laws and, 63–5
  role of trade in, 68–9, 81, 134
Dewar, M., 28, 38
Djilas, M., 318
Dobrin, B., 327
Domochim, 205
Družba pipeline, 206, 263
Dubna institute, 193

East–West trade
  and bilateralism, 122–3, 148
  and capital mobility, 123, 137,
    169–70, 202–3, 281–2
  and clearing, 122–3, 169–70
  and intensive growth, 96, 158,
    169–70, 228, 278, 281–2, 289,
    333
  and postwar developments, 28–30,
    34–5, 42, 45, 46, 49, 51, 55,
    141–2, 328
  and structural bilateralism, 155
Economic Commission for Europe,
  180, 186
economic model, 9–10, 12, 57, 58,
  60, 69–82
  bureaucratization and, 71
  collectivization in, 71, 72, 80
  coordination instruments and, 66,
    71, 76–80
  definition of, 69
  efficiency in, 66, 75–8
  and nationalization, 71, 72
  and planning, 70–1, 73–5
  and trade, 72, 81–2
  see also economic reforms, indirect
    coordination instruments, inte-
    gration mechanism, plan coordi-
    nation, planning in CPEs, prices
    in CPEs, specialization, trade
    model, trade reforms
economic reforms, 68, 82–98, 308–9,
  312, 314–16, 317–18
  and coordination instruments,
    90–6
  and East–West trade, 96, 158,
    169–70, 333
  and effect on CMEA, 95–6, 174,
    216–18
  and model, 50, 81–5, 86–98, 235–6
  and strategy, 82–7, 226–9, 235–6

and trade, 86, 88–9, 92, 95–8,
  293–4
  see also economic model, economic
    strategy, indirect coordination
    instruments, integration
    mechanism, trade model, trade
    reforms
Ellman, M., 325
embargo, 29–30, 34, 35, 42, 49, 51,
  55
embassy system, 47, 53
Engels, F., 60
England, 68
Erdénét, 205
Ethiopia, 178
European Communities, 180
European Danube Commission, 323
European Payments Union, 201
European Recovery Program (ERP),
  20, 29
exchange rate, 43, 56, 117–19, 126,
  127, 204, 213, 255, 322, 326,
  327, 328
  in integration, 211–15, 233–4
  for internal exports, 118
  for merchandise trade, 118, 160–1
  in noncommercial transactions,
    118–19, 234
  for tourism, 118–19
  in trade reforms, 159–66
  see also bilateralism, economic
    model, indirect coordination in-
    struments, integration
    mechanism, trade model, trade
    reforms
extensive development, 65–70, 85,
  285–6, 324

Faddeev, N. V., 31, 35, 36, 39, 43,
  185, 321, 322
Fallenbuchl, Z. M., 279
federalism in Eastern Europe, 24–5,
  48, 320
financial bridges, 160–1, 164, 167
  see also indirect coordination in-
    struments, trade reforms
Finland, 169, 178
fiscal policies, 79, 116–17, 161–2,
  164, 166, 252–3, 288, 327
  see also economic model, indirect
    coordination instruments
Fiumel, H. de, 44

Molotov, V. M., 22
Molotov Plan, 29, 320–1
money and finance
  in economic model, 10–11, 78–80,
    286–90, 300–2, 315–17
  in integration debates, 7–9, 39–40,
    50–1, 56, 175, 201–3, 213, 284–5,
    286, 297, 300–2, 315–17
  in reforms, 90–6, 322
  see also CMEA documents, indirect
    coordination instruments, inte-
    gration mechanism, socialist
    economic integration (SEI)
Mongolia, 14–15, 177, 178, 205, 239,
  321
Mongolsovcvetmet, 205
monopoly of foreign trade and payments (MFT), 72, 81–2, 89–90,
    101–3, 117, 121, 141–2, 159, 165,
    168–9
  and bilateralism, 142
  definition of, 101–3
  in future of SEI, 287–9
  in reforms, 159, 165, 167, 168–9
  and small country, 327
  see also trade model
Montias, J. M., 267, 277
Morozov, V. I., 197
Moscow Conference, 32–9, 42–4, 51
multilateral clearing, 42–3, 45–6,
    50–1, 56, 124, 201–2, 225–9, 285,
    289, 298, 316
  see also capital mobility, IBEC, indi-
    rect coordination instruments, in-
    tegration mechanism

nationalism, 23, 66, 121
New Course, 108, 152, 174, 220–2
noncommercial transactions, 118, 136,
  234, 327
norms in planning, 73, 88
  see also planning in CPEs
North Korea, 178
North Vietnam, 178
  see also Vietnam
Nove, A., 323
Novovolynsk joint project, 331
Nyers, R., 240

Orenburg joint project, 204, 239
  see also Sojuz
Organisation for European Economic
  Co-operation (OEEC), 22, 48

Paris Conference, 22
Pécsi, K., 238
Pelzman, J., 263, 264, 265, 266, 267,
  333
Permanent Representative, 181, 183,
  185
Petrobaltik, 206
Pisar, S., 31
plan coordination
  and bilateralism, 128–9
  and CMEA documents, 223, 224–8,
    231–6, 237, 241–2
  and future of SEI, 284–5, 289–90,
    299–303, 310–11, 313–15
  in integration process, 11, 128,
    175–6, 195, 209–10, 231–4, 236,
    238–9
  and international economic organi-
    zations, 198–9, 201, 204, 206,
    211–16
  in postwar debates, 37–44, 46–8,
    50–3, 56, 176, 184–5, 187
  see also CMEA documents, indirect
    coordination instruments, inte-
    gration mechanism
planning in CPEs, 6–9, 50–2, 56, 60,
    70, 71, 72–80, 87–90, 124, 323
  see also economic model, integration
    mechanism, material balances
Poland, 20, 21, 22, 26, 28, 35, 37, 42,
    59, 174, 204–5, 264, 265, 267, 274,
    280, 300, 307, 321, 330–1
  economic reform in, 89, 92
  trade reform in, 158–60, 162–3, 166,
    168–9
  politics and trade, 101, 114, 121, 123,
    127–8, 141, 148
Preobraženskij, E. A., 80
price discrimination, 100, 125, 139,
    141, 143, 144–5, 149, 326
price-equalization mechanism,
    117–18, 165
  see also autarky, economic model,
    integration mechanism, trade
    model, trade reform
prices and bilateralism, 135–41, 145–6,
    149, 328
prices in CMEA trade, 43, 47, 57, 100,
    121, 136–41, 144–6, 148, 149,
    184, 226–8, 229, 233–4, 266, 285,
    288–9, 291–6, 315, 327, 328, 334
  see also Bucharest principles, indirect
    coordination instruments, inte-
    gration mechanism, socialist

For EU product safety concerns, contact us at Calle de José Abascal, 56–1°, 28003 Madrid, Spain or eugpsr@cambridge.org.

www.ingramcontent.com/pod-product-compliance
Ingram Content Group UK Ltd.
Pitfield, Milton Keynes, MK11 3LW, UK
UKHW042210180425
457623UK00011B/124